C PROJECTS

C PROJECTS

Reeta Sahoo

KHANNA BOOK PUBLISHING CO. (P) LTD. DELHI

C PROJECTS

Reeta Sahoo

ISBN: 978-81-875223-0-0

Published by:
Khanna Book Publishing Co. (P) Ltd.
4C/4344, Ansari Road, Darya Ganj, New Delhi-110 002
Phone: 011-23244448 Telefax: 011-23244447
E-mail: contact@khannabooks.com
Website: www.khannabooks.com

Regd. Off: 1694-95, 1st Floor, Nai Sarak, Delhi-110006 (India)
Phone: 011-23283211 Telefax: 011-23256658

Printed in India by:
S.P.S. Printers & Binders, Delhi

ACKNOWLEDGMENT

I would like to thank the reviewers, all the students in my school, and the people at SCOT Computer Education for the outstanding job, who provided valuable comments, many of which have been incorporated into the text of C++.

I am also very much thankful to my husband, Mr. Gagan B. Sahoo, for his valuable practical and theoretical guidance and constant encouragement that have been a source of inspiration to my entire project.

Finally, my thanks to reputed publisher **KHANNA BOOK PUBLISHING CO.(P) LTD.** for publishing this book errorlessly with good outlay and nicety.

Reeta Sahoo

Contents

Chapters

1. Introduction 1
2. Restaurant Billing System 8
3. Electronic Voting System 57
4. Banking System 143
5. Pay Manager 205
6. Library Management System 276
7. Music Shop Management 384
8. Year Calendar 449
9. Drawing Logo 463
10. Bricks Game 474
11. Charts & Graphs 498
12. Graphics Demo 535
13. Utility Services 588

Appendixes

A. Inbuild Functions 639

B. ASCII Character Set 548

How This Book Is Organized

This book has total 13 chapters on different projects and two appendices. In all the chapters the project development idea has been discussed with individual project concerned. Also almost in every chapter there are some functions of graphics commands and operational knowledge is emphasized to make good demonstration to the projects. Whereas the graphics section are implemented in different functions only.

Chapter 1 "Introduction" being demonstrates the graphics methods to implement in C language.

Chapter 2 "Restaurant Billing System" keeps all the details of the items (veg or non-veg) and maintains a price list for the customers. The items are only transacted when a customer orders a certain item at the bill counter.

Chapter 3 "Electronic Voting System " keeps the record of the list of candidates and voters information for voting purpose. Also, after voting to there respective candidates, it can display the result with proper format.

Chapter 4 "Banking System" is one of the projects which creates bank accounts and maintains customers console updations, daily transaction, monthly report, global report which can be accessed by management.

Chapter 5 "Pay Manager" concentrates on building applications in C. It provides a step-by-step process for developing records keeping, changing and deleting records. Individual employee detail reports and salary slip to each individual at the month end etc. Also this project maintains the record in an automatic generation manner.
Chapter 6 "Library System" project describes the library management system of books, and library members. In the library the books are stored by acquisition number wise, and the registered members are issued the books from library if their registration date not expired. Also, both library books and member databases are maintained as a console

operation mode to update daily transactions.

Chapter 7 "Music Shop Managemet" project keeps stock of different cassettes for sales, purchases, opeing and closing stocks, expenses of Cassettes & CDs on monghly basis.

Chapter 8 "Year Calendar" being designed to display the calendar of any year monthwise and we can find any date by just typing the month and year.
Chapter 9 "Drawing Logo" which you can draw different objects using keyboard. This program uses number of colour patterns and object movement at the time of drawing. This logo manages through a circle by which you can move into different directions.

Chapter 10 to 13 teaches you how to build graphics applications for DOS and how to tap into important library functions. Chapter 8 is a GUI demonstration of different visual graphs like color demo, palette demo, random bars, circles etc. using the graphic functions. Chapter 9 displays different types of charts from a temperature scale. Chapter 10 is a game where two players can play using a cross (X) and a circle (O) symbols with different names. Chapter 11 is a bricks game where the tracking bulb hits the bricks and scores a successful result till three bulbs are left. Chapter 12 is one of the interesting utility services which will help you to manage the directories and files either in your hard drive or floppy disk drive.

Prerequisites

The prerequisite is a working knowledge of small C or a C-like subset of C++, including basic data types, operators, control structures, functions, classes, and input and output.

In this book a 3-1/2-inch high-density floppy disk is available containing all the projects program listings. To use the disk, you need a computer having

- a PC or PC/XT or PC/AT or higher
- minimum 16 MB RAM
- Turbo C/C++ compiler
- MS-DOS version 3.2 or above.

Disk Index

Chapter	File No#	File Name
2	1	RES.C
3	1	VMENU.C
	2	VOTING.C
	3	VOTING1.C
	4	VOTING3.C
4	1	BANK.C
5	1	COMPRO.C
6	1	LIB.C
7	1	MUSIC.C
8	1	CALMENU.C
	2	GIC.C
	3	CAL.C
9	1	LOGO.C
10	1	BRICK.C
11	1	INTRO1.H
	2	TEST.C
12	1	INTRO1.H
	2	BAR1.C
13	1	INTRO.H
	2	UTIL.C

So, from the above disk index listing, the user or reader has to use both the header file and the program file (.cpp) to execute any project. While for graphics, you have to execute the program file from your graphics driver file (i.e., C:\TC or C:\TURBO or any C installation directory).

Introduction

ENIAC, built in the late 1940s, was one of the world's computers. It was a large, standalone machine that filled a room and used more electricity that all the houses on an average city block. ENIAC contained hundreds of miles of wire and thousands of head-producing vacuum tubes. The mean time between failures was less than an hour, yet because of its fantastic speed, when compared to hand-operated electromechanical calculators, it was immensely useful.

In the earlier 1950s, IBM sold its first business computer. At the time it was estimated that the world would never need more than ten such machines, yet its awesome computational power was a mere 1/200 of the typical 200-megahertz Pentium personal computer purchased for about $1000 in 1998. Today, there are hundreds of millions of computers in the world, most of which are PCs, unless one also counts the billions of computers embedded in such everyday products as handled calculators, cars, refrigerators and soon even clothing.

The first computers could perform only a single task at a time. Input and output were handled by such primitive means as punch cards and paper tape.

In the 1960s, time-sharing computers, costing hundreds of thousands and even millions of dollars, became popular at organizations large enough to afford them. Even back then, computers were so much faster that 30 people could work on such a computer simultaneously and each field as if he or she were the sole user. Each person sat at a teletype connected by wire to the computer. By making a connection through the telephone system, teletypes could even be placed at a great distance from the computer. The teletype was a primitive device by today's standards. It looked like an electronic typewriter with a large roll of paper attached. Keystrokes entered at the keyboard were transmitted to the computer, which then echoed them back on the roll of paper. In addition, output from the computer's programs was also printed on this roll.

In the 1970s, people began to see the advantage of connecting computers in networks and the wonders of e-mail and file transfers were born.

In 1980s, PCs appeared in great numbers and soon thereafter, local area networks of interconnected PCs become popular. These networks allowed a local group of PCs to communicate and share such resources as disk drives and printed with each and with large centralized multi-user computers.

As computers become faster and faster, the need for programs that can handle large amount of input becomes more acute. Paradoxically, this requires more careful attention to efficiency, since inefficiencies in programs become most obvious when input sizes are large. By analyzing a project before it is actually coded, student can decide if a particular solution will be feasible. For example, in this project, students look at specific problems and see how careful implementation can reduce the time constraint for large amount of data from 16 years to less than a second. Therefore, no project or program is present without an explanation of its running time. In some cases, minute details that affect the running time of the implementation are explored. The goal of all this projects are to teach students good programming and algorithm analysis skills simultaneously so that they can develop such programs with the maximum amount of efficiency. Students should have some knowledge of intermediate programming, including such topics: file handing, pointers, and data structures etc.

This book is written with two main goals, to help you become more familiar with C file handling, graphics programming and to help people with different programming backgrounds become more proficient in C.

These two major goals encompass a number of specific aims:

- This project book introduces you to the powerful programming tools provided in your Turbo C.
- Programmers need a thorough understanding of each programming language they intend to use. You will find that this book covers all the important programming concepts in C, handling and graphics programming like utility, games etc.
- If you are familiar with C program codes, then you can grasp easily all the concepts of the packages and graphic concepts.

I believe in teaching by example. I have made every efforts to make each project in this book simple, complete, and bug-free. You can study these projects, alter them, and expand them into programs tailored to fit your needs. Two major concepts files and graphics are discussed in almost all projects as command sequence with different algorithms.

Files and Streams

C views each file simply as a sequence of bytes (Figure A). Each file ends either with an end-of-file marker or at a specific byte number recorded in a system-maintained, administrative data structure. When a file is opened, an object is created and a stream is associated with the object. In the following projects we will see that different objects are created for us automatically-**printf, scanf** and **clog**. The streams associated with these objects provide communication channels between a program and a particular file or device. For example, the **scanf** object (standard input stream object) enables a program to input data from the keyboard, the **printf** object (standard output stream object) enables a program to output data to the screen, the **cerr** and **clog** objects (standard error stream objects) enable a program to output error messages to the screen.

Figure A. C's view of a file of n bytes.

To perform file processing in C, the header files **<stdio.h>** must be included.

Graphics

Displays can normally be used either in a text or a graphics mode. Programs which output to text displays are generally much faster than graphic displays because the characters displayed on a text display are preprogrammed into the hardware of the computer. Whereas, on graphics display the program must map each dot (pixel) onto the screen. A PC text show typically display characters in an array of 80 columns by 25 rows, whereas in graphics mode the screen is made up of individual pixels, such as 640 pixels in the x-direction and 480 in the y-direction. Many currently available software packages display information in graphical form. If the basic interface is displayed in graphical form it is known as a graphical user interface (or GUI). Popular GUIs include Microsoft Windows and X-Windows. Typically, graphics are used in applications which require high-resolution images. These include schematic diagrams, circuit simulation graphs, animation, and so on.

Graphics are not an intrinsic part of most programming languages. They are normally found in a graphics library. These certain functions that can range from the generation of simple line drawings to 3D bit-mapped graphics manipulation. Many different libraries can be purchased but this chapter discusses Turbo/Borland C graphics. Note that ANSI-C does not include graphics functions so that the code produced will only work on DOS-based PC using Turbo/Borland C.

To use the graphics routines the header file graphics.h should be included at the top of the file as shown below. This helps the compiler check for incorrect uses of the functions. It also includes definitions that relate to colours, line styles, fill styles, and so forth.

```
#include <graphics.h>
```

The Turbo C, Borland C libraries implement a complete library of more that 50 graphics routines. The main operations are as follows:

- Simple graphics operations, such as putpixel, line and rectangle;
- High-level calls, such as setviewport, circle, bar3d, and drawpoly;
- Several fill and line styles;
- Bit-oriented routines, like getimage and putimage;
- Several fonts that may be magnified, justified and oriented.

The basic graphics screen is made up of pixels, which are accessed using an x-y coordinate system. The x-direction is horizontally across the screen and the y-direction is vertically down the screen. The top left-hand corner is the (0,0) x-y point and the bottom of the screen is the (MaxX, MaxY) point. A diagram of this is shown in Figure B

A graphics display is interfaced to the PC system using a video driver card. The resolution and the number of displayable colours depend on the type of graphics driver and display being used. A program can automatically detect the graphics driver and load the required file that contains information on how the program interfaces to the driver. This file is called a driver file. Listing A. shows typical graphics drivers and their associated driver files.

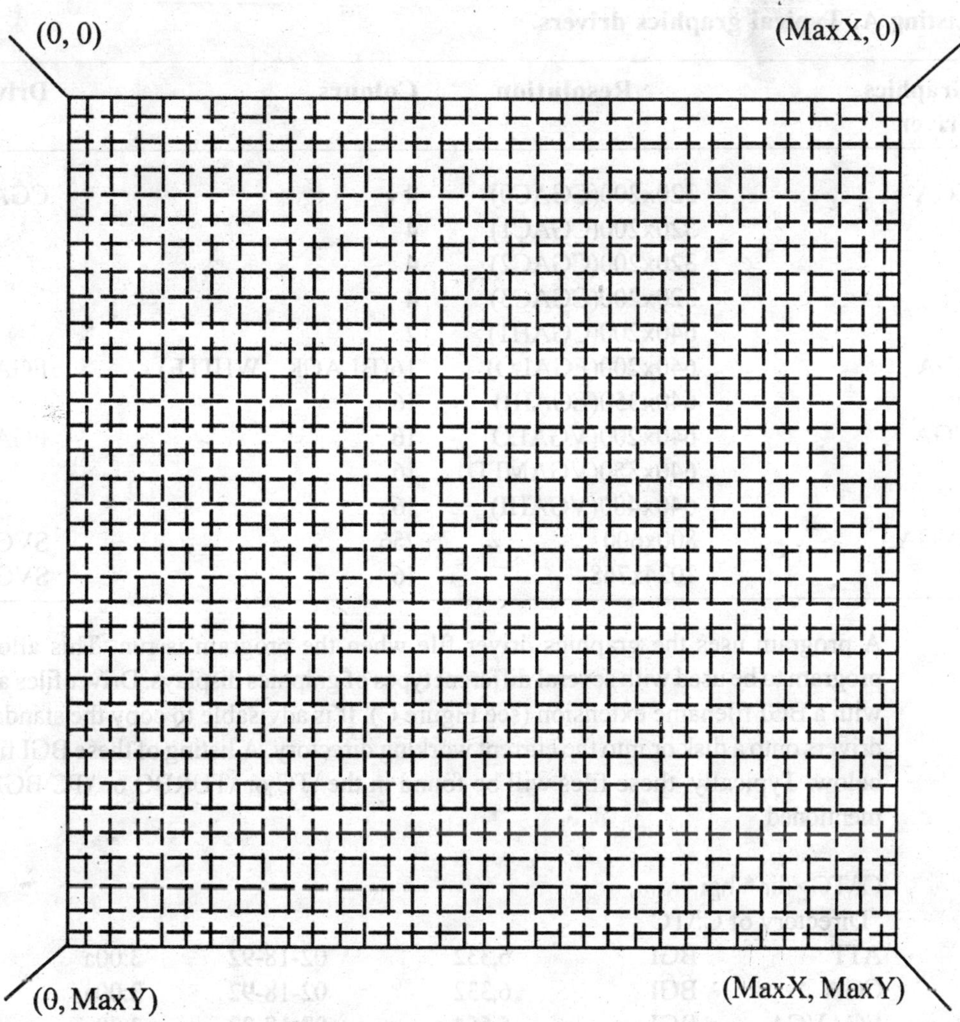

Figure B. Screen resolution

Listing A. Typical graphics drivers.

Graphics driver	Resolution	Colours	Driver file
CGA	320x200(CGAC0)	4	CGA.BGI
	320x200(CGAC1)	4	
	320x200(CGAC2)	4	
	320x200(CGAC3)	4	
	640x200(CGAH1)	2	
EGA	640x200(EGALO)	16(BLACK...WHITE)	EGAVGA.BGI
	640x350(EGAHI)	16	
VGA	640x200(VGALO)	16	EGAVGA.BGI
	640x350(VGAMED)	16	
	640x480(VGAHI)	16	
SVGA	800x600	256	SVGA256.BGI
	1024x768	16	SVGA16.BGI

A program uses the graphics driver file when the program is run. This allows a single program to be used with several different types of graphics displays. Driver files are identified with a BGI filename extension (see Figure C). It is advisable to copy the standard graphics drivers onto a disk or into the current working directory. A listing of these BGI files is shown below. Typically, these files will be found in the \TC or \TURBO or \TC\BGI or any you mentioned.

```
C:\TC> dir *.bgi
 Directory of C:\TC
ATT        BGI     6,332   02-18-92   3:00a
CGA        BGI     6,332   02-18-92   3:00a
EGAVGA     BGI     5,554   02-18-92   3:00a
HERC       BGI     6,204   02-18-92   3:00a
IBM8514    BGI     6,665   02-18-92   3:00a
PC3270     BGI     6,012   02-18-92   3:00a
```

Other drivers are available such as SVGA.BGI (16-colour SVGA) and SVGA256.BGI (256 colour SVGA). EGA and VGA monitors can display at least 16 colours. Within a program these are accessed either as a numerical value or by a symbolic name, as given in Listing B.

The setcolor() function sets the current drawing colour. For example, to set the drawing colour to white the setcolor(WHITE); or setcolor(15); statement is used. The former is preferable as it is self documenting.

Appendix A outlines graphics and other functions which is used in this project book.

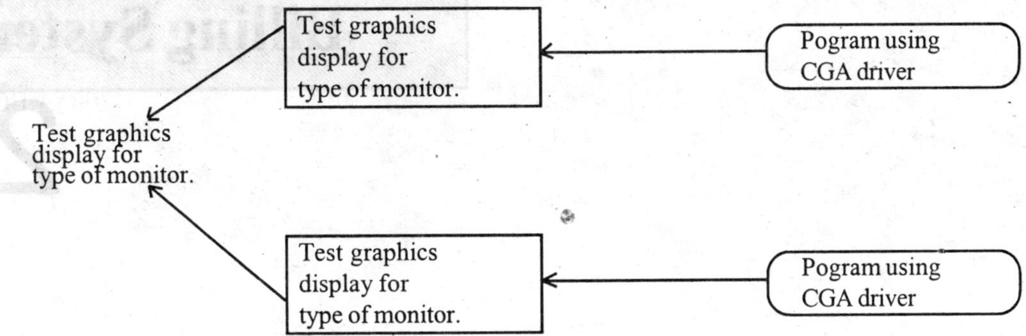

Figure C. BGI files required for CGA/EGA and VGA graphics drivers.

Listing B. Displayabls colours.

Numeric value	Symbolic name	Numeric value	Symbolic name
0	BLACK	8	DARKGRAY
1	BLUE	9	LIGHTBLUE
2	GREEN	10	LIGHTGREEN
3	CYAN	11	LIGHTCYAN
4	RED	12	LIGHTRED
5	MAGENTA	13	LIGHTMAGENTA
6	BROWN	14	YELLOW
7	LIGHTGRAY	15	WHITE

There are two main display modes: text and graphics. The initgraph() function changes the mode from text to graphics and the closegraph() function changes it back into text mode.

Restaurant Billing System

2

The McDonalds restaurant decides to computerise its restaurant on the consumable item and the billing system for daily transaction. The restaurant keeps all the details of the items (veg or non-veg) and maintains a price list for the customers. The items are only transacted when a customer orders a certain item at the bill counter.

According to the menu items the customer orders from the menu (veg or non-veg) and subsequent bill is promoted for the desired items. After the transaction is executed, the customer receives a bill with the table for final payment. The system is designed to operate with a menu driven program such as :

FILE   EDIT   PRINT   HELP   EXIT

and with the following sub menu(s).

(a) The FILE menu contains options which is displayed on the screen as :

New item	-	Add new items on category wise
Display Info	-	Display the items on VEG or NON-veg wise
Display List	-	Display all the available items
Bill	-	Display the bill according to order wise
Order	-	Enter the customer's order
Return	-	Return to main menu

(b) The EDIT menu contains the modification of items as :

Modify item	-	Modify your existing item
Delete item	-	Delete an existing item
Return	-	Return to main menu

(c) The PRINT menu contains all the options of the FILE menu and produce similar type of output as FILE menu. But the different is that the options outputs are directed to the printer. So, if you want any hard copy of the bills, items, orders etc. make active your printer and do the operations.

(d) The HELP menu display certain instruction for the users when the are in the program at runtime.

Program Source Codes RES.C

```
// Required Header files
#include <graphics.h>
#include <string.h>
#include <stdlib.h>
#include <stdio.h>
#include <ctype.h>
#include <conio.h>
#include <dos.h>

// Public Functions Required By Many Different Functions.
void statusbar(char[]);
void getlinedelchar(char *, int, int, int *);
void getline(char *, int);

// The Drawing Functions & The Main Screen.

void lineh(int, int, int, char);        // Drawing horizontal lines
void linev(int, int, int, char);        // Drawing vertical lines
void box(int, int, int, int, char);     // Drawing boxes

void mscreen(); // Main screen of the Restaurant program

// Functions For Drawing Main Menus
void main_menu();
int vertical_menu(char [] [20], int, int, int, int);
int horizontal_menu(char [] [20], int, int, int, int);
void help();    // Display some help messages

// All The Fields Related To available restaurant items
struct restaurant
{
        int  itemcode, dd, mm, yy ;
        char itemname[31], itemcat[31];
        float price;
};
```

```
// Fields related to order of a partcular bill no.
struct order
{
        int itemcode;
        int billno, dd, mm, yy ;
        char itemname[31];
        int itemqty;
        float price;
};


int fcode(int); // Function to know the code is present
int billcode(int); // Function to know the bill no. is exists or not.
int date(int, int, int);      // Check a valid date
void display1(char tcat[]);  // Displaying the categories
void display(int);

// All The Functions Related To restaurant

void Item_add(); // Adding new items in restaurant
void Order_add1();       // Adding the customers order
void Item_modify();      // Modifying any item in the restaurant
void Item_del();         // Deleting the item from the list
void displaycode();      // Displaying the items
void showlist(); // Showing the item list
void Bill_slip(); // Printing the bill(s)
void print(int, int, int, int);        // Activates the printer to print information

// FUNCTION : lineh
// DESCRIPTION : To Draw A Horizontal Line (x1, x2, y)
void lineh (int row1, int row2, int column, char c)
{
        for (row1; row1 <= row2; row1++)
        {
                gotoxy (row1, column) ;
                printf ("%c",c) ;
        }
}
```

```
// FUNCTION : linev
// DESCRIPTION : To Draw A Vertical Line (y1, y2, x)
void linev (int column1, int column2, int row, char c)
{
        for (column1; column1 <= column2; column1++ )
        {
                gotoxy (row, column1) ;
                printf ("%c",c) ;
        }
}

// FUNCTION : box
// DESCRIPTION : To Draw A Box  (x1, y1, x2, y2)
void box(int row1, int column1, int row2, int column2, char c)
{
        char ch=218 ;
        char c1, c2, c3, c4 ;
        char l1=196, l2=179 ;
        if (c == ch)
        {
                c1 = 218 ;
                c2 = 191 ;
                c3 = 192 ;
                c4 = 217 ;
                l1 = 196 ;
                l2 = 179 ;
        }
        else
        {
                c1 = c ;
                c2 = c ;
                c3 = c ;
                c4 = c ;
                l1 = c ;
                l2 = c ;
        }
        gotoxy(row1,column1) ;
        printf ("%c",c1) ;
        gotoxy(row2,column1) ;
        printf ("%c",c2) ;
```

```
        gotoxy(row1,column2);
        printf ("%c",c3);
        gotoxy(row2,column2);
        printf ("%c",c4);
        row1++;
        row2--;
        lineh(row1, row2, column1, l1);
        lineh(row1, row2, column2, l1);
        row1--;
        row2++;
        column1++;
        column2--;
        linev(column1,column2,row1,l2);
        linev(column1,column2,row2,l2);
}

// FUNCTION : mscreen
// DESCRIPTION : To Paint The Screen With the The Opening Screen.
void mscreen()
{
        int gd=DETECT, gm;
        int t,i;
        long int k,m,j;
        initgraph(&gd, &gm, "\\turboc3");

        setcolor(LIGHTGRAY);
        rectangle(0, 0, getmaxx(), getmaxy());
        setfillstyle(SOLID_FILL, LIGHTGRAY);
        floodfill(getmaxx()/2, getmaxy()/2, LIGHTGRAY);

        for( t = 1; t < 115; t++)
        {
                setcolor(DARKGRAY);
                for( m = 0; m < 103000.0; m++);
                        rectangle(getmaxx()/2-t-150, getmaxy()/2+t, getmaxx()/2+t+150,
                                getmaxy()/2-t);
                floodfill(getmaxx()/2, getmaxy()/2, DARKGRAY);
        }

        setcolor(WHITE);
```

```
settextstyle(GOTHIC_FONT, HORIZ_DIR, 7) ;
settextjustify(CENTER_TEXT, CENTER_TEXT) ;
outtextxy(getmaxx()/2, getmaxy()/2-60, "WELCOME" ) ;
outtextxy(getmaxx()/2, getmaxy()/2+60, "YOU" ) ;

for (j = 0; j < 500; j++)
        for( k = 0; k < 40000.0; k++) ;
                setcolor(BLACK) ;

rectangle(0, 0, getmaxx(), getmaxy()) ;
setfillstyle(SOLID_FILL, BLACK) ;
floodfill(getmaxx()/2, getmaxy()/2, BLACK) ;

for( i = 1; i < 150; i++)
{
        setcolor(RED) ;
        settextstyle(GOTHIC_FONT, HORIZ_DIR, 7) ;
        settextjustify(CENTER_TEXT, CENTER_TEXT) ;
        outtextxy(160+i, 40+i, "McDonalds - RES" ) ;

        for(j = 0 ;j < 100; j++) ;
                setcolor(BLACK) ;

        settextstyle(GOTHIC_FONT, HORIZ_DIR, 7) ;
        settextjustify(CENTER_TEXT, CENTER_TEXT) ;
        outtextxy(160+i, 40+i, "McDonalds - RES" ) ;
}

setcolor(RED) ;
settextstyle(GOTHIC_FONT, HORIZ_DIR, 7) ;
settextjustify(CENTER_TEXT, CENTER_TEXT) ;
outtextxy(160+i, 40+i, "McDonalds - RES" ) ;

for(j = 0; j < 250; j++)
        for(k = 0; k < 40000.0; k++) ;

for(k = i; k > 50; k—)
{
        setcolor(RED) ;
        settextstyle(GOTHIC_FONT, HORIZ_DIR, 7) ;
```

```
        settextjustify(CENTER_TEXT, CENTER_TEXT) ;
        outtextxy(160+i, 40.0+k, "McDonalds - RES" ) ;

        for( j = 0; j < 100; j++) ;

        setcolor(BLACK) ;
        settextstyle(GOTHIC_FONT, HORIZ_DIR, 7) ;
        settextjustify(CENTER_TEXT, CENTER_TEXT) ;
        outtextxy(160+i, 40.0+k, "McDonalds - RES" ) ;
}
setcolor(RED) ;
settextstyle(GOTHIC_FONT, HORIZ_DIR, 7) ;
settextjustify(CENTER_TEXT, CENTER_TEXT) ;
outtextxy(160+i, 40.0+k, "McDonalds - RES" ) ;

for(j = 0; j < 250; j++)
        for(k = 0; k < 40000.0; k++) ;

for(i = 1; i < 200; i++)
{
        setcolor(LIGHTRED) ;
        settextstyle(GOTHIC_FONT, HORIZ_DIR, 5) ;
        settextjustify(CENTER_TEXT, CENTER_TEXT) ;
        outtextxy(0+i, getmaxy()/2-10, "Programmed by : " ) ;

        for( j = 0; j < 100; j++) ;

        setcolor(BLACK) ;
        settextstyle(GOTHIC_FONT, HORIZ_DIR, 5) ;
        settextjustify(CENTER_TEXT, CENTER_TEXT) ;
        outtextxy(0+i, getmaxy()/2-10, "Programmed by : " ) ;
}

setcolor(LIGHTRED) ;
settextstyle(GOTHIC_FONT, HORIZ_DIR, 5) ;
settextjustify(CENTER_TEXT, CENTER_TEXT) ;
outtextxy(0+i, getmaxy()/2-10, "Programmed by : " ) ;

for(j = 0; j < 250; j++)
        for(k = 0; k < 40000.0; k++);
```

```
for(i = 1; i < 300; i++)
{
        setcolor(GREEN);
        settextstyle(GOTHIC_FONT, HORIZ_DIR, 5);
        settextjustify(CENTER_TEXT, CENTER_TEXT);
        outtextxy(0+i, getmaxy()/2+50, "Reeta Sahoo" );

        for( j = 0; j < 100; j++);
        setcolor(BLACK);
        settextstyle(GOTHIC_FONT, HORIZ_DIR, 5);
        settextjustify(CENTER_TEXT, CENTER_TEXT);
        outtextxy(0+i, getmaxy()/2+50, "Reeta Sahoo" );
}

setcolor(GREEN);
settextstyle(GOTHIC_FONT, HORIZ_DIR, 5);
settextjustify(CENTER_TEXT, CENTER_TEXT);
outtextxy(0+i, getmaxy()/2+50, "Reeta Sahoo" );

for(j = 0; j < 250; j++)
        for(k = 0; k < 40000.0; k++) ;

for(i = 1; i < 315; i++)
{
        setcolor(LIGHTRED) ;
        settextstyle(GOTHIC_FONT, HORIZ_DIR, 5) ;
        settextjustify(CENTER_TEXT, CENTER_TEXT) ;
        outtextxy(0+i, getmaxy()/2+95, "&" ) ;

        for( j = 0; j < 10000; j++) ;

        setcolor(BLACK) ;
        settextstyle(GOTHIC_FONT, HORIZ_DIR, 5) ;
        settextjustify(CENTER_TEXT, CENTER_TEXT) ;
        outtextxy(0+i, getmaxy()/2+95, "&" ) ;
}

setcolor(LIGHTRED) ;
settextstyle(GOTHIC_FONT, HORIZ_DIR, 5) ;
settextjustify(CENTER_TEXT, CENTER_TEXT) ;
```

```
    outtextxy(0+i, getmaxy()/2+95, "&" ) ;

    for(j = 0; j < 250; j++)
            for(k = 0; k < 40000.0; k++) ;

    for(i = 1; i < 450; i++)
    {
            setcolor(GREEN) ;
            settextstyle(GOTHIC_FONT, HORIZ_DIR, 5) ;
            settextjustify(CENTER_TEXT, CENTER_TEXT) ;
            outtextxy(0+i, getmaxy()/2+140, "Gagan Sahoo" ) ;

            for( j = 0; j < 100; j++) ;

            setcolor(BLACK) ;
            settextstyle(GOTHIC_FONT, HORIZ_DIR, 5) ;
            settextjustify(CENTER_TEXT, CENTER_TEXT) ;
            outtextxy(0+i, getmaxy()/2+140, "Gagan Sahoo" ) ;
    }

    setcolor(GREEN) ;
    settextstyle(GOTHIC_FONT, HORIZ_DIR, 5) ;
    settextjustify(CENTER_TEXT, CENTER_TEXT) ;
    outtextxy(0+i, getmaxy()/2+140, "Gagan Sahoo" ) ;

    for(j = 0; j < 500; j++)
            for(k = 0; k < 40000.0; k++) ;

    for(i = 0; i < 550; i++)
    {

            for( j = 0; j < 50000.0; j++) ;
            setcolor(BLACK) ;
            rectangle(0+i, 0, 100+i, getmaxy()) ;
    }

    closegraph() ;
}
```

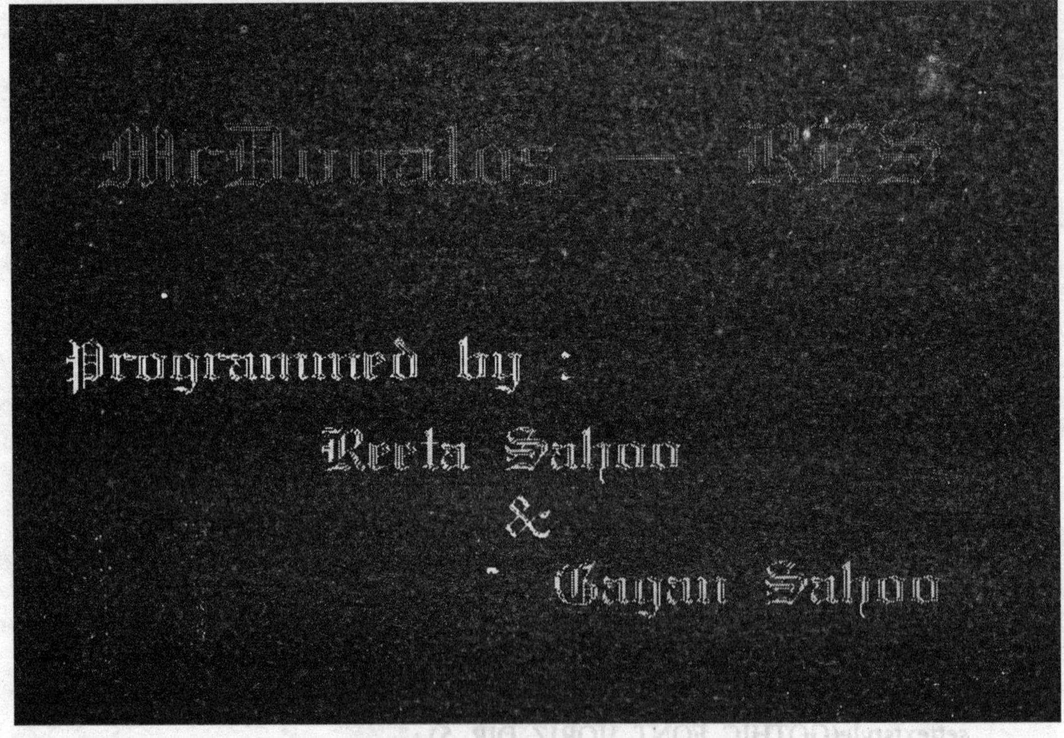

Figure 2.1 Main screen of restaurant program.

```
// FUNCTION : vertical_menu
// DESCRIPTION : To Make Vertical Menu.
int  vertical_menu(char menu[] [20], int present, int end, int x, int y)
{
        int ex=0 ;
        int i;
        char ch;
        box(x + 9, y, x + strlen(menu[0]) + 12, y + end + 1, 218) ;

        for ( i=0; i<end; i++)
        {
                gotoxy(x + 10, y + i + 1) ;
                printf ("%s",menu[i]) ;
        }
```

```
do
{
        int tpresent = present ;
        textcolor(BLACK) ;
        textbackground(WHITE) ;
        gotoxy(x + 10,y + present) ;
        cprintf(menu[present - 1]) ;
        textcolor(WHITE) ;
        textbackground(BLACK) ;
        ch = getch() ;

        switch (ch)
        {
                case 75 :
                        if (present == 1)
                                present = end ;
                        else
                                present— ;
                                break ;
                case 77 :
                        if (present == end)
                                present = 1 ;
                        else
                                present++ ;
                                break ;
                case 71 :
                        present = 1 ;
                        break ;
                case 79 :
                        present = end ;
                        break ;
                case 72 :
                        if (present == 1)
                                present = end ;
                        else
                                present— ;
                                break ;
                case 80 :
                        if (present == end)
                                present = 1 ;
```

```
                        else
                                present++ ;
                                break ;
                case 13 :
                        ex = 1 ;
                        break ;
                case 27 :
                        present = end ;
                        ex = 1 ;
            }

            gotoxy(x + 10,y + tpresent) ;
            cprintf(menu[tpresent - 1]) ;

        } while(!ex) ;
        return(present) ;
}

// CLASS : menu
// FUNCTION : horizontal_menu
// DESCRIPTION : To Make Horizontal Menu.
int horizontal_menu(char menu[] [20], int present, int end, int x, int y)
{
        int ex=0, i ;
        char ch;
        for (i = 0; i < end; i++)
        {
                gotoxy(x + (i + 2) * 10 - 5, y) ;
                printf ("%s",menu[i]);
        }

        lineh(1, 80, 2, 205) ;

        do
        {
                int tpresent = present ;
                textcolor(BLACK) ;
                textbackground(WHITE) ;
                gotoxy(x + (present + 1) * 10 - 5, y) ;
                cprintf(menu[present - 1]) ;
```

```
textcolor(WHITE) ;
textbackground(BLACK) ;
ch = getch() ;

switch (ch)
{
        case 71 :
                present = 1 ;
                break ;
        case 79 :
                present = end ;
                break ;
        case 75 :
                if (present == 1)
                        present = end ;
                else
                        present— ;
                break ;
        case 77 :
                if (present == end)
                        present = 1 ;
                else
                        present++ ;
                break ;
        case 72 :
                if (present == 1)
                        present = end ;
                clsc
                        present— ;
                break ;
        case 80 :
                if (present == end)
                        present = 1 ;
                else
                        present++ ;
                break ;
        case 13 :
                ex= 1 ;
                break ;
        case 27 :
```

```
                    present = end ;
                    ex = 1 ;
            }
            gotoxy(x + (tpresent + 1) * 10 - 5, y) ;
            cprintf(menu[tpresent - 1]) ;
        } while(!ex) ;
        return(present) ;
}

// FUNCTION : help
// DESCRIPTION : To Print The Help Screen For Various Important Operations.
void help()
{
        clrscr();
        printf ("\n\n\n\t\t\tAbout McDonald's Restaurant Management ");
        printf ("\n\nThis is a instruction set program for the user, who can");
        printf ("\n utilize it for better development purpose.");
        printf ("\n\n\n 1) Important instructions are displayed at the status bar at the  ");
        printf ("\n   bottom of the screen.");
        printf ("\n\n 2) Press escape key to exit the immediate screen at any time");
        printf ("\n   during the program.");
        printf ("\n\n\n\n");
        printf ("\t\t\t\t\t\tReeta Sahoo");
        printf ("\n\t\t\t\t\t\tGagan Sahoo");
        getch();
        clrscr() ;
        return ;
}

// FUNCTION : main
// DESCRIPTION : To Draw The Main Menu & Call Related Functions
/*      This menu displays its options on the top of the screen like

        FILE   EDIT   PRINTHELP EXIT

        and press enter to select any menu option with related menus

        Note : Select the PRINT menu when your printer is ON and the related items and bills are
        prepared.
*/
```

```
void main_menu()
{
	int end=5, present=1, upperlim1=6, currentpos1=1, upperlim2=3, currentpos2=1,
		upperlim3=4, currentpos3=1;
	char main[] [20] = { " FILE ", " EDIT ", " PRINT ", " HELP ", " EXIT " } ;
	char sub1[] [20] = { "New item    ", "Display Info ", "Display List ", "Bill  ",
			"Order","Return      " } ;
	char sub2[] [20] = { "Modify item    ", "Delete item ", "Return       " } ;
	char sub3[] [20] = { "Item Info  ", "Item List ", "Bill  ", "Return       " } ;

	// Display a colourful menu
	mscreen() ;
	do
	{
		_setcursortype(_NOCURSOR) ;
		present = horizontal_menu(main, present, end, 3, 1) ;
		switch (present)
		{
			case 1 :
				currentpos1 = vertical_menu(sub1, currentpos1, upperlim1, 3, 3) ;
				switch (currentpos1)
				{
					case 1 :
						_setcursortype(_SOLIDCURSOR) ;
						Item_add() ;
						_setcursortype(_NOCURSOR) ;
						break ;
					case 2 :
						_setcursortype(_SOLIDCURSOR) ;
						displaycode() ;
						break ;
					case 3 :
						showlist() ;
						break ;
					case 4 :
						_setcursortype(_SOLIDCURSOR) ;
						Bill_slip() ;
						_setcursortype(_NOCURSOR) ;
						break ;
					case 5 :
```

```
                        _setcursortype(_SOLIDCURSOR) ;
                        Order_add1() ;
                        _setcursortype(_NOCURSOR) ;
                        break;
            }
            clrscr() ;
            break ;
        case 2 :
            currentpos2 = vertical_menu(sub2, currentpos2, upperlim2, 13, 3) ;
            switch(currentpos2)
            {
                case 1 :
                        _setcursortype(_SOLIDCURSOR) ;
                        Item_modify() ;
                        _setcursortype(_NOCURSOR) ;
                        break ;
                case 2 :
                        _setcursortype(_NORMALCURSOR) ;
                        Item_del() ;
                        _setcursortype(_NOCURSOR) ;
                        break ;
            }
            clrscr() ;
            break ;
        case 3 :
            currentpos3 = vertical_menu(sub3, currentpos3, upperlim3, 27, 3) ;
            switch(currentpos3)
            {
                case 1 :
                        _setcursortype(_SOLIDCURSOR) ;
                        displaycode() ;
                        print(1,1,80,23) ;
                        _setcursortype(_NOCURSOR) ;
                        break ;
                case 2 :
                        _setcursortype(_NORMALCURSOR) ;
                        showlist() ;
                        print(1,1,80,23) ;
                        _setcursortype(_NOCURSOR) ;
                        break ;
```

```
                    case 3 :
                              _setcursortype(_NORMALCURSOR) ;
                              Bill_slip() ;
                              print(1,1,80,23) ;
                              _setcursortype(_NOCURSOR) ;
                              break ;
               }
               clrscr() ;
               break ;
          case 4 :
               help() ;
               clrscr() ;
               break ;
          }
     } while (present != end);
}
```

FILE EDIT PRINT HELP EXIT

New item
Display Info
Display List
Bill
Order
Return

Figure 2.2 Main Menu with FILE submenu's items.

```
// FUNCTION : fcode
// DESCRIPTION : To Return 0 If The Given Code Is Not Found
/*        This function is used to find the code of an item i.e.; the item is there in the database
restaur.dat or not. If the item is there, the fcode() function will return 1 otherwise it will return 0 to its
called program. */
```

```
int  fcode(int code)
{
        FILE *file ;
        int found = 0 ;
        struct restaurant temp;

        file = fopen("restaur.Dat", "rb+") ;
        while (fread(&temp, sizeof(struct restaurant),1,file))
        {
                printf("\n%d",found);
                getch();
                if (temp.itemcode == code)
                {

                        found = 1 ;
                        break ;
                }
        }

        fclose(file) ;
        return(found) ;
}
```

```
// FUNCTION : billcode()
// DESCRIPTION : To Return 0 If The Given billno is Is Not Found
/*      This function is used to find the billno of an order no i.e.; the bill no. is there in the database
order.dat or not. If the order no. is there, the billcode() function will return 1 otherwise it will return
0 to its called program. */

int  billcode(int code)
{
        FILE *file ;
        int found = 0 ;
        struct order temp;
        file = fopen("order.Dat", "rb+") ;
        while (fread(&temp, sizeof(struct order),1,file))
        {
                if (temp.billno == code)
                {
```

```
                    found = 1 ;
                    break ;
               }
          }
          fclose(file) ;
          return(found) ;
}

// FUNCTION : date
// DESCRIPTION : To Return '0' If The Date Received Is Invalid
int  date(int dd, int mm, int yy)
{
          int days=0, valid ;
          if ((yy>1980) && (yy<=1999))
                    valid = 1 ;
          else
          {
                    valid = 0 ;
                    return(0) ;
          }

          switch (mm)
          {
                    case 1 :
                              days = 31 ;
                              break ;
                    case 2 :
                              if (yy % 4 == 0)
                                        days = 29 ;                    // leap year
                              else
                                        days = 28 ;
                                        break ;
                    case 3 :
                              days = 31 ;
                              break ;
                    case 4 :
                              days = 30 ;
                              break ;
                    case 5 :
                              days = 30 ;
```

```
                    break ;
            case 6 :
                    days = 31 ;
                    break ;
            case 7 :
                    days = 31 ;
                    break ;
            case 8 :
                    days = 31 ;
                    break ;
            case 9 :
                    days = 30 ;
                    break ;
            case 10 :
                    days = 31 ;
                    break ;
            case 11 :
                    days = 30 ;
                    break ;
            case 12 :
                    days = 31 ;
                    break ;
            default :
                    valid = 0 ;
                    break ;
        }
        if ((dd > 0) && (dd <= days))
            valid = 1 ;
        else
            valid = 0 ;
        return (valid) ;
}
```

```
// FUNCTION : display
// DESCRIPTION : To Display A Record From "restaur.Dat"
/* This function is helpful to display the category wise items on the screen or printer according to main menu. When you will be enter VEG or NON-VEG or any, (according to your item entry) this menu will display category wise all the items with related option from the restaur.dat database. */
```

```
void display1(char tcat[31])
{
        FILE *file ;
        struct restaurant t ;
        char *initial ;
        file = fopen("restaur.Dat", "rb+") ;
        while (fread(&t, sizeof(struct restaurant),1,file))
        {
                if (strcmp(t.itemcat,tcat)==0)
                {
                        clrscr();
                        gotoxy(28,2) ;
                        printf ("CATEGORY WISE  INFORMATION");
                        gotoxy(30,3) ;
                        printf ("CATEGOEY   # %s",t.itemcat) ;
                        lineh(2,79,4,240) ;
                        gotoxy(20,6) ;
                        printf ("Name              :  %s",t.itemname) ;
                        gotoxy(20,8) ;
                        printf ("Code              :  %d" ,t.itemcode );
                        gotoxy(20,10) ;
                        printf ("Price          : Rs. %.2f",t.price) ;
                        lineh(2,79,22,240) ;
                        getch();
                }
        }
        fclose(file) ;
}
```

```
// Function display()
// This function is used to display the item code if exist in the restaur.dat data file
/*      This function is helpful to display the item information on the screen or printer according to
main menu. When you will press Display Item from the FILE or PRINT menu it will display all the
items with related option from the restaur.dat database. */

void display(int code)
{
        FILE *file ;
        struct restaurant t ;
        char *initial ;
```

```
	file = fopen("restaur.Dat", "rb+") ;
	while (fread(&t, sizeof(struct restaurant),1,file))
	{
		if (t.itemcode==code)
		{
			gotoxy(28,2) ;
			printf ("ITEM  INFORMATION");
			gotoxy(30,3) ;
			printf ("restaurant CODE #  %d",t.itemcode) ;
			lineh(2,79,4,240) ;
			gotoxy(20,6) ;
			printf ("Name             :   %s",t.itemname) ;
			gotoxy(20,8) ;
			printf ("Category         :   %s" ,t.itemcat );
			gotoxy(20,10) ;
			printf ("Price          : Rs. %.2f",t.price) ;
			lineh(2,79,22,240) ;
		}
	}
	fclose(file) ;
}

// FUNCTION : Item_add()
// DESCRIPTION : To Get Data About New restaurant
/* This function is used to input items and the related information with proper validation. Here the
itemcode will generate automatically when you will continue for next item at any time.	*/

void Item_add()
{
	struct restaurant t ;
	struct restaurant te ;
	FILE *file ;
	char ch, choice='Y';
	char d[3], m[3], y[5], price[10];
	int code=0, valid ;

	do
	{
		clrscr() ;
		_setcursortype(_SOLIDCURSOR) ;
```

```
gotoxy(28,2) ;
printf ("ADDITION OF NEW ITEM");
lineh(20,59,3,240) ;
gotoxy(31,4) ;
printf ("Item Code # ");
gotoxy(29,5) ;
printf ("~~~~~~~~~~~~~~~~~~~~~~~~~~~~~~");
gotoxy(5,8) ;
printf ("Name          : ............................");
gotoxy(5,10) ;
printf ("Catagory      : ............................");
gotoxy(5,12) ;
printf ("Price   (Rs) :  .........");

file = fopen("restaur.Dat", "rb+") ;

// Steps to generate automatic code after incrementing 1 with the
// reataur.dat file(s) itemcode

while (fread(&te, sizeof(struct restaurant),1,file)==1)
        code = te.itemcode ;

fclose(file) ;
code++ ;
t.itemcode = code ;
gotoxy(47,4) ;
printf ("%d",t.itemcode) ;
do
{
        valid = 1 ;
        statusbar(" ENTER THE NAME OF THE ITEM") ;
        _setcursortype(_SOLIDCURSOR) ;
        gotoxy(20,8) ;
        printf ("                    ");
        gotoxy(20,8) ;
        getline(t.itemname, 29) ;

        if (t.itemname[0] == '0')
                return ;
```

```
            if (strlen(t.itemname) < 1)
            {
                  valid = 0 ;
                  statusbar("\a ENTER CORRECTLY (LENGTH : 1..30)") ;
                  getch() ;
                  _setcursortype(_SOLIDCURSOR) ;

            }

      } while (!valid) ;

      do
      {
            valid = 1 ;
            statusbar(" ENTER CATEGORY OF THE ITEM") ;
            _setcursortype(_SOLIDCURSOR) ;
            gotoxy(20,10) ;
            printf ("                    ");
            gotoxy(20,10) ;
            getline(t.itemcat, 29) ;

            if (t.itemcat[0] == '0')
                  return ;

            if (strlen(t.itemcat) < 1)
            {
                  valid = 0 ;
                  statusbar("\a ENTER CORRECTLY (LENGTH : 1..30)") ;
                  getch() ;
                  _setcursortype(_SOLIDCURSOR) ;
            }
      } while (!valid) ;

      do
      {
            valid = 1 ;
            statusbar(" ENTER PRICE OF THE ITEM") ;
            _setcursortype(_SOLIDCURSOR) ;
            gotoxy(20,12) ;
```

```
            clreol() ;
            getline(price,9) ;
            t.price = atof(price) ;

            if (price[0] == 27)
                return ;

            if ((strlen(price) == 0) || (t.price>100000.0))
            {
                valid = 0;
                statusbar("\a SHOULD NOT BE GREATER THAN 100000") ;
                getch() ;
                _setcursortype(_SOLIDCURSOR) ;
            }

    } while (!valid) ;

    do
    {
            statusbar("\a Do you wish to save (y/n) : ") ;
            ch = getch() ;
            ch = toupper(ch) ;

            if (ch == '0'|| ch == 27)
                return ;

    } while (ch != 'Y' && ch != 'N') ;

    if (ch == 'N')
            return ;

    file = fopen("restaur.Dat", "ab+") ;
    fwrite(&t, sizeof(struct restaurant),1,file) ;
    fclose(file) ;

    statusbar("\a Add any more (y/n) : ") ;

    do
    {
            choice = getch() ;
```

```
                        choice = toupper(choice) ;
                        if (choice == 13)
                                choice = 'Y' ;
                        if (choice == 27)
                                choice = 'N' ;

                } while((choice != 'Y') && (choice !='N'));

        } while(choice == 'Y');
}
```

ADDITION OF NEW ITEM

```
==========================================================
                 Item Code #      6


     Name           : PALAK PANEER.........

     Category       : VEG......................

     Price   (Rs.)  :........................

Do you wish to save (y/n) :
```

Figure 2.3 Add item screen of FILE menu option.

```
// FUNCTION : Order_add1()
// DESCRIPTION : To Get Data About Order place
```

/* When any customer came into the restaurant, you have to take the order, and make a order list in your computer to produce a proper bill for record purposes. You can take any type of order and place to the customers accordingly. */

```
void Order_add1()
{
        struct order o ;
        struct restaurant te ;
```

```
FILE *file ;
char ch, choïce='Y';
char d[3], m[3], y[5], price[10];
int  code=0, valid = 0 ;

do
{
        clrscr() ;
        code = 0;
        valid = 0;
        _setcursortype(_SOLIDCURSOR) ;
        gotoxy (28,2) ;
        printf ("PLACING THE ORDER");
        lineh(20,59,3,240) ;
        gotoxy (31,4) ;
        printf ("Item Code # ");
        gotoxy (47,4) ;
        scanf ("%d",&o.itemcode) ;
        file = fopen("restaur.Dat", "rb+") ;

        while (fread(&te, sizeof(struct restaurant),1,file)==1)
        {
                if(o.itemcode==te.itemcode)
                {
                        strcpy(o.itemname,te.itemname);
                        o.price = te.price;
                        valid = 1;

                }
        }

        if (valid == 0)
        {
                printf (" Item not found");
                printf ("~~~~~~~~~~~~~~~~~~~~~~~~");
                break;
        }

        gotoxy(5,8) ;
        printf ("Name               : ............................");
        gotoxy(5,12) ;
```

```
printf ("Price    (Rs) :  .........");
gotoxy(22,8);
printf ("%s",o.itemname);
gotoxy (22,12);
printf ("%.2f",o.price);
gotoxy (60,3);
printf (" Bill Number :  ....");
gotoxy (76,3);
scanf (" %d",&o.billno);
gotoxy (5,14);
printf ("Quantity       :  ..........");
gotoxy (22,14);
scanf  ("%d",&o.itemqty);
fclose(file);

do
{
        statusbar("\a Do you wish to save (y/n) : ") ;
        ch = getch() ;
        ch = toupper(ch) ;

        if (ch == '0'|| ch == 27)
                return ;
} while (ch != 'Y' && ch != 'N') ;

if (ch == 'N')
        return ;

file = fopen("order.dat", "ab+") ;
fwrite(&o, sizeof(struct order),1,file) ;
fclose(file) ;

statusbar("\a Add any more (y/n) : ") ;
do
{
        choice = getch() ;
        choice = toupper(choice) ;

        if (choice == 13)
                choice = 'Y' ;
```

```
                if (choice == 27)
                        choice = 'N' ;
        } while((choice != 'Y') && (choice !='N'));
    } while(choice == 'Y');
}
```

```
            PLACING THE ORDER
=============================================== Bill Number : 90....
                    Item Code #      1

        Name            : DAL.................

        Price   (Rs.)   : 25.00 ................

        Quantity        : 3 .......
Add any more (y/n) :
```

Figure 2.4 Order of item menu.

```
// FUNCTION : Item_modify
// DESCRIPTION : To Provide With Necessary Data Required For Modification Of A Given Record
/* Modify your items information like, change the price, change the name of item etc. when necessary.
When the screen appears in front of you, you just enter the item code and then it will display the
information of the existing item and will speak for modification. If you won't modify any item the
previous information of that will remain in the item code in your restaur.dat database. */

void Item_modify()
{
        FILE *file ;
        struct restaurant t ;
        struct restaurant te ;
        FILE *file1 ;
        int  code, valid ;
```

```
char  ch, house='N', conv='N', choice='Y' ;
char  categ[31];
char  tprice[10] ;
float price=0 ;
clrscr() ;

do
{
        gotoxy(72,2) ;
        printf ("Esc=EXIT");
        gotoxy(5,5) ;
        printf ("Enter code of the item : ");
        scanf ("%d",&code) ;

        if (code == 0)
                return ;
        clrscr() ;

        // Steps to find either the billno is exist or not.
        if (!billcode(code))
        {
                gotoxy(30,24) ;
                printf ("\a Record not found");
                getch() ;
                return ;
        }

        display(code) ;
        gotoxy(72,2) ;
        printf("<0>=EXIT");
        gotoxy(24,2) ;
        printf ("MODIFICATION OF restaurant RECORD");

        do
        {
                statusbar("\a Do you wish to modify this record (y/n) ") ;
                ch = getch() ;
                ch = toupper(ch) ;
                if (ch == '0')
                        return ;
```

```
        if (ch == 13 )
                ch = 'Y' ;
        if (ch == 27 )
                ch = 'N' ;
} while (ch != 'Y' && ch != 'N') ;

if (ch == 'N')
        return ;
clrscr() ;

file = fopen("restaur.Dat", "rb+") ;

while (fread(&t, sizeof(struct restaurant),1,file)==1)
{
        if (t.itemcode == code)
                break ;
}

gotoxy(72,2) ;
printf ("Esc=EXIT");
gotoxy(26,2) ;
printf ("MODIFICATION OF ITEMS");
lineh(20,59,3,240) ;
gotoxy(31,4) ;
printf ("Item Code # %d ",code) ;
gotoxy(29,5) ;
printf ("~~~~~~~~~~~~~~~~~~~~~~~~~~");
gotoxy(5,8) ;
printf ("Name          : ");
gotoxy(5,10) ;
printf ("Catogray          : ...........................");
lineh(3,78,14,196);
gotoxy(5,12) ;
printf ("Price       (Rs) :  .........");
gotoxy(20,8) ;
printf ("%s",t.itemname) ;

do
{
        valid = 1 ;
```

```
            statusbar(" ENTER Category OF THE Item OR PRESS
                        <enter> FOR NO CHANGE") ;
            _setcursortype(_SOLIDCURSOR) ;
            gotoxy(21,9) ;
            printf ("                  ");
            gotoxy(21,10) ;
            getline(categ, 29) ;

            if (categ[0] == '0')
                return ;

            if (strlen(categ) > 30)
            {
                valid = 0 ;
                statusbar("\a Enter correctly (Range: 1..30)") ;
                getch() ;
                _setcursortype(_SOLIDCURSOR) ;
            }

        } while (!valid) ;

        if (strlen(categ) == 0)
        {
            strcpy(categ, t.itemcat) ;
            gotoxy(20,10) ;
            printf ("%s",categ) ;
        }

        do
        {
            valid = 1 ;
            statusbar(" ENTER PRICE OF THE ITEM");
            _setcursortype(_SOLIDCURSOR) ;
            gotoxy(25,12) ;
            clreol() ;
            getline(tprice,9) ;
            price = atof(tprice) ;

            if (price > 100000.0)
            {
```

```
                valid = 0 ;
                statusbar("\a SHOULD NOT BE GREATER THAN 100000") ;
                getch() ;
                _setcursortype(_SOLIDCURSOR) ;
        }

} while (!valid) ;

if (strlen(tprice) == 0)
{
        price = t.price ;
        gotoxy(32,12) ;
        printf ("%.2f",price) ;
}

strcpy(t.itemcat, categ) ;
t.itemcode = code ;
t.price = price ;

file = fopen("restaur.Dat", "rb+") ;
file1 = fopen("Tempmod.Dat", "wb+") ;
while (fread(&te, sizeof(struct restaurant),1,file)==1)
{
        if (t.itemcode != te.itemcode)
                fwrite(&te, sizeof(struct restaurant),1,file1) ;
        else
                break ;
}

fwrite(&t, sizeof(struct restaurant),1,file1) ;
while (fread(&te, sizeof(struct restaurant),1,file)==1)
        fwrite(&te, sizeof(struct restaurant),1,file1) ;
fclose(file) ;
fclose(file1) ;

file = fopen("restaur.Dat", "wb+") ;
file1 = fopen("Tempmod.Dat", "rb+") ;

while (fread(&t, sizeof(struct restaurant),1,file1)==1)
{
```

```
                fwrite(&t, sizeof(struct restaurant),1,file) ;
            }
            fclose(file) ;
            fclose(file1) ;

            gotoxy(5,25) ;
            clreol() ;

            do
            {
                statusbar("\a Do you wish to save (y/n) ") ;
                ch = getch() ;
                ch = toupper(ch) ;
                if (ch == '0')
                    return ;
            } while (ch != 'Y' && ch != 'N') ;

            if (ch == 'N')
                return ;

            statusbar(" Record Modified.") ;
            getch() ;
            statusbar("\a Modify any more (y/n) : ") ;

            do
            {
                choice = getch() ;
                choice = toupper(choice) ;

                if (choice == 13)
                    choice = 'Y' ;

                if (choice == 27)
                    choice = 'N' ;

            } while((choice != 'Y') && (choice !='N'));

        } while(choice == 'Y');
}
```

```
MODIFICATION OF restaurant RECORD        <0>=EXIT
            restaurant CODE #   1
==========================================================================

        Name            : DAL .........

        Category        : VEG ....................

        Price   (Rs.)   : 25.00 ......................

==========================================================================
Do you wish to modify this record (y/n) :
```

Figure 2.5 First screen modification of restaurant item.

```
    MODIFICATION OF ITEMS                 Esc=EXIT
=================================================

              Item Code #      1

    Name            : DAL .........

    Category        : VEG ......................

    Price   (Rs.)   : 22.00 ......................

Do you wish to save (y/n) :
```

Figure 2.6 Second screen modification of restaurant item.

```
// FUNCTION : del
// DESCRIPTION : To Delete A Record In "restaur.Dat"
/* You can delete an item when there is no required or not available in your restaurant */

void Item_del()
{
        struct restaurant t ;
        FILE *file ;
        FILE *file1 ;

        char ch ;
        int code ;
        clrscr() ;
        gotoxy(72,2) ;
        printf ("<0>=EXIT");
        gotoxy(5,5) ;
        printf ("Enter code of the ITEM : ");
        scanf ("%d",&code) ;

        if (code == 0)
                return ;
        clrscr() ;

        if (!fcode(code))
        {
                gotoxy(30,24) ;
                printf ("\a Record not found");
                getch() ;
                return ;
        }

        gotoxy(72,2) ;
        printf ("<0>=EXIT");
        gotoxy(23,1) ;
        printf ("DELETION OF THE restaurant RECORD");
        display(code) ;

        do
        {
                statusbar("\a Do you wish to remove this record (y/n) ") ;
```

```
        ch = getch() ;

        if (ch == 27)
                return ;

        if (ch == 13)
                ch = 'y' ;

        ch = toupper(ch) ;

        if (ch == '0')
                return ;

} while (ch != 'Y' && ch != 'N') ;

if (ch == 'N')
        return ;

file = fopen("restaur.Dat", "rb+") ;
file1 = fopen("Tempdel.Dat", "wb+") ;

while (fread(&t, sizeof(struct restaurant),1,file)==1)
{
        if (t.itemcode != code)
                fwrite(&t, sizeof(struct restaurant),1,file1) ;
}

fclose(file) ;
fclose(file1) ;

file = fopen("restaur.Dat", "wb+") ;
file1 = fopen("Tempdel.Dat", "rb+") ;

while (fread(&t, sizeof(struct restaurant),1,file1)==1)
{
        fwrite(&t, sizeof(struct restaurant),1,file) ;
}

fclose(file) ;
fclose(file1) ;
```

```
        clrscr() ;
        statusbar("\a Record Deleted") ;
        getch() ;
        statusbar("   Press any key to continue...") ;
        getch() ;
}
```

```
 DELETION OF THE restaurant RECORD       <0>=EXIT
                ITEM INFORMATION
                restaurant CODE #    5
==================================================

        Name           : TANDOORI..........

        Category       : NON.....................

        Price   (Rs.)  : 120.00.......................

==================================================
Do you wish to remove this record  (y/n) :
```

Figure 2.7 Deletion of an item in restaurant.

```
// FUNCTION : displaycode
// DESCRIPTION : To Obtain Code For Displaying A Record

void displaycode()
{
        char  tcat[31] ;
        clrscr() ;
        gotoxy(72,2) ;
        printf ("<0>=EXIT");
        gotoxy(5,5) ;
        _setcursortype(_SOLIDCURSOR) ;
        printf ("Enter Category of the items : ");
        scanf ("%s", tcat) ;
        clrscr() ;
```

```
        display1(tcat) ;
        statusbar("   Press any key to continue...") ;
        getch() ;
}

// FUNCTION : showlist
// DESCRIPTION : To Display The List Of restaurants

void showlist()
{
        struct restaurant t ;
        FILE *file ;
        int row = 6, found=0, flag=0 ;
        int d1, m1, y1 ;
        char ch ;
        struct date d;
        getdate(&d) ;
        d1 = d.da_day ;
        m1 = d.da_mon ;
        y1 = d.da_year ;
        clrscr() ;
        gotoxy(23,2) ;
        printf ("LIST OF ITEMS AS ON %d  . %d  .%d",d1,m1,y1) ;
        lineh(1,80,3,240) ;
        gotoxy(12,4) ;
        printf ("CODE #            NAME                PRICE");
        gotoxy(1,5) ;
        lineh(11,72,5,205) ;
        linev(4,22,10,186) ;
        linev(4,22,19,186) ;
        linev(4,22,51,186) ;
        linev(4,22,72,186) ;
        lineh(1,80,23,240) ;

        file = fopen("restaur.dat", "rb+") ;

        while (fread(&t, sizeof(struct restaurant),1,file)==1)
        {
                flag = 0 ;
                found = 1 ;
```

```
        gotoxy(12,row) ;
        printf ("%d",t.itemcode) ;
        gotoxy(21,row) ;
        printf ("%s",t.itemname) ;
        gotoxy(53,row) ;
        printf ("%.2f",t.price) ;

        if (row == 18)
        {
                flag = 1 ;
                row = 6 ;
                statusbar(" Press any key to continue or Press <ESC> to exit") ;
                ch = getch() ;

                if (ch == 27)
                        break ;
                clrscr() ;
                gotoxy(31,2) ;
                printf ("LIST OF ITEMS");
                lineh(1,90,3,240);
                gotoxy(2,4) ;
                printf ("CODE #            NAME                    PRICE");
                gotoxy(1,5) ;
                printf ("~~~~~~~~~~~~~~~~~~~~~~~~~~~~~~~~~~~~~~~~~~~~~~~~~~~~~~~~~~~~~~~~~~~~~~~~~~~~~~" );
        }
        else
                row++ ;
}

if (!found)
{
        gotoxy(26,14) ;
        printf ("\a Records not found");
}

if (!flag)
{
        statusbar("   Press any key to continue...") ;
        getch() ;
}
```

```
        fclose (file) ;
}
```

CODE #	NAME	PRICE
1	DAL	22.00
2	PANEER	40.00
3	CHICKEN	100.00
4	SALAD	10.00
5	TANDOORI	120.00
6	PALAK PANEER	45.00

LIST OF ITEMS AS ON 4 . 3 . 2000

Press any key to continue...

Figure 2.8 Existing items in the restaurant.

```
// FUNCTION : slip
// DESCRIPTION : To Print The Salary Slip Of An restaurant On The Screen
/* This function is used to display the bill of an order by enter the order no. When you enter the order no. or bill no. a proper bill format with the ordered items will display on the screen. You can also take its print out by selecting the this option in PRINT menu. */

void Bill_slip()
{
        FILE *file ;
        struct order t ;
        float total=0, nettotal=0 ;
        long float da = 0;
        int  code, valid=0, try;
        int  year ;
        int row;
        char  tdays[3], thours[4], tadvance[6], month[10] ;
```

```
int d1, m1, y1 ;
struct date d;
getdate(&d) ;
d1 = d.da_day ;
m1 = d.da_mon ;
y1 = d.da_year ;
clrscr() ;
gotoxy(5,5) ;
printf ("Enter Bill number  : ");
scanf ("%d",&code) ;

if (code == 0)
        return ;

if (!billcode(code))
{
        clrscr() ;
        gotoxy(30,25) ;
        printf ("\a Record not found");
        getch() ;
        return ;
}

lineh(1,80,1,223) ;
linev(1,23,1,222) ;
linev(1,23,79,222) ;
lineh(1,80,23,223) ;
// Printing the bill messages
gotoxy(32,2) ;
printf ("McDonalds Restaurant");
lineh(3,78,3,175) ;
gotoxy (4,4) ;
printf ("BILL NUMBER : %d",code) ;
gotoxy (50,4);
printf ("DATE : ");
printf ("%d - %d - %d",d1,m1,y1);
lineh(3,78,5,196) ;
linev(6,21,22,186) ;
linev(6,21,37,186) ;
linev(6,21,55,186) ;
```

```
gotoxy(5,6);
printf ("ITEM NAME");
gotoxy(30,6);
printf ("PRICE");
gotoxy(42,6);
printf ("QUANTITY");
gotoxy(65,6);
printf ("TOTAL");
lineh(3,78,7,196);

// Opens the order.dat file to read the records for a particular bill no.
file = fopen("order.Dat", "rb+");
row = 8;

while (fread(&t, sizeof(struct order),1,file)==1)
{
        if (t.billno == code)
        {
                gotoxy(5,row);
                printf ("%s",t.itemname);
                gotoxy(30,row);
                printf ("%.2f",t.price);
                gotoxy(42,row);
                printf ("%d",t.itemqty);
                total = t.itemqty * t.price;
                nettotal = nettotal + total;
                gotoxy(65,row);
                printf ("%.2f",total);
                row++;
        }
}
fclose(file);

gotoxy(54,22);
printf (" NET  :  ");
printf ("%.2f",nettotal);
lineh(3,77,21,196);
gotoxy(2,1);
getch();
}
```

McDonalds Restaurant			
BILL NUMBER : 90			DATE : 4 - 3 - 2000
ITEM NAME	PRICE	QUANTITY	TOTAL
PALAK PANEER	45.00	2	45.00
SALAD	10.00	2	20.00
DAL	25.00	3	75.00

NET : 185.00

Figure 2.9 Final bill of an ordered item.

```
// FUNCTION : print
// DESCRIPTION : To Read The Characters On The Screen & Save It
// To A Temp Variable And Then Send It To The Printer.

void print(int x1, int y1, int x2, int y2)
{
        const SEGMENT = 0xB800 ;
        unsigned norow = y2 - y1 + 1, nocol = x2 - x1 + 1 ;
        unsigned i = 0, noele = norow * nocol, *ptr ;
        unsigned row,col,offset;
        unsigned char ch;
        int count = 0 ;
        FILE *prn;
        prn = fopen ("PRN","w");
        ptr = ((unsigned *)malloc(noele) ) ;
        statusbar(" PRINTING PRINTING PRINTING PRINTING
                    PRINTING PRINTING PRINTING PRINTING PRINTI") ;

        for ( row=y1; row<=y2; row++)
```

```
	{
		for( col=x1; col<=x2; col++)
		{
			offset = 2*col + 160*row - 162 ;
			ptr[i++] = peek(SEGMENT,offset) ;
		}
	}

	for(i=0; i<noele; i++, count++)
	{
		ch = ptr[i] % 256 ;
		putc (ch,prn) ;
		if (count == 80)
		{
			fputs("\n",prn);
			count = 0 ;
		}
	}
	fclose(prn);
}

// The Main Menu, where the restaurant program starts
void main(void)
{
	main_menu() ;
}


// FUNCTION : statusbar
// DESCRIPTION : To make the status bar at prefixed coordinates at the bottom of the screen.

void statusbar(char m[])
{
	_setcursortype(_NOCURSOR) ;
	window(1,24,80,25) ;
	textcolor(BLACK) ;
	textbackground(WHITE) ;
	cprintf(m) ;
	clreol() ;
	window(1,1,80,24) ;
```

```
        textcolor(WHITE) ;
        textbackground(BLACK) ;
}

// FUNCTION : getlinedelchar
// DESCRIPTION : To Delete A Character For Getline

void getlinedelchar(char *s, int col, int p, int *len)
{
        int i ;
        for (i=p; i<len; i++)
                s[i - 1] = s[i] ;
        gotoxy(col + p - 1,wherey()) ;
        len— ;
        for (i=p - 1; i<len; i++)
                printf ( "%s",s[i]) ;
        printf ( "." );
}

// FUNCTION : getline
// DESCRIPTION : To Add Online Editing For Inputing A Line.
void getline(char *s , int limit)
{
        int i, curx, done, col ;
        col = wherex() ;
        for (i = 0; i<limit; i++)
                printf (".") ;
        gotoxy(col,wherey()) ;
        done = 0 ;
        curx = 0 ;
        i = 0 ;
        do
        {
                char ch = getch() ;
                ch = toupper(ch) ;
                switch (ch)
                {
                        case 0 :
                                ch = getch();
                                switch (ch)
```

```
		{
			case 75 : if (curx>0)
				{
					curx-- ;
					gotoxy(wherex()-1,wherey()) ;
				}
				break ;
			case 77 : if (curx<i)
				{
					curx++ ;
					gotoxy(wherex()+1,wherey()) ;
				}
				break ;
			case 83 : if (i>0)
				{
					if (curx<i)
					{
						getlinedelchar(s,col,curx + 1,&i) ;
						gotoxy(col + curx,wherey()) ;
						if (i == 0)
							s[i] = 0 ;
					}
				}
		}
		break ;
	case 8  :
		if (curx>0)
		{
			getlinedelchar(s,col,curx,&i) ;
			gotoxy(col + curx - 1,wherey()) ;
			curx-- ;
			if (i == 0)
				s[i] = 0 ;
		}
		break ;
	case 13 :
		done = 1 ;
		s[i] = 0 ;
		break ;
```

```
                case 27 :
                        done = 1 ;
                        s[0] = '0' ;
                        break ;
                default :
                        if (i < limit)
                        {
                                if (curx < i)
                                {
                                        s[curx] = ch ;
                                        printf ("%c",ch) ;
                                        curx++ ;
                                }
                                else
                                {
                                        s[i] = ch ;
                                        printf ("%c",ch) ;
                                        i++ ;
                                        curx = i ;
                                }
                        }
                        else
                                s[i] = 0 ;

        }
    } while (!done) ;
    printf ("\n");
}
```

Electronic Voting System

3

The electronic voting system is developed to manage the voter, candidate and voting on electronically. This system keeps the record of the list of candidates and voters information for voting purpose. The maintainance of the system is considered by a main menu of 4 options as :

1 For Voters
2 For Candidates
3 For start voting
4 Exit

and uses 4 different files to manage the complete system. All the files are included in this program and are called automatically when it is required.

voting1.c	- Program related to voters
voting1c.c	- Program related to candidates
voting3.c	- Abouting voting

The voting1.c manages the voters information with a proper menu system as:

FILE EDIT PRINT HELP EXIT

Here, the FILE menu manages the information of new voter, display information and display the existing voters list. The EDIT menu manages modification of voters information and make provision for deleting the voter information. Similarly the PRINT menu takes printout of the as usual copies of voter information. In this contexts, the voter.dat database keeps the record of the following information when a voter in added.

v_code	- Voter no.
v_name	- Voter name
v_address	- Voter address
v_city	- Voter city
v_pin	- Voter pincode no.
v_phone	- Voter phone no.
v_sex	- Voter sex
v_done	- Vote casted or not
v_age	- Voters age (greater than 18)

The voting1c.c manages the candidates information like voters. In this contexts, the candidate.dat database keeps the record of the following information when a voter in added.

c_code	- Candidate no.
c_name	- Candidate name
c_address	- Candidate address
c_city	- Candidate city
c_pin	- Candidate pincode no.
c_phone	- Candidate phone no.
c_sex	- Candidate sex
c_age	- Candidate age
total	- Total vote gained

The votint3.c, which is actually used to manage the electrinic voting maintainance for the candidates with voters.

Source Listing of VMENU.C

```
#include <conio.h>
#include <string.h>
#include <stdio.h>
#include <dos.h>
#include <dir.h>
#include <stdlib.h>
```

```
#include <graphics.h>

void statusbar(char[]) ;  // Prompt for status bar
void getlinedelchar(char *, int, int, int *) ; // Delete char
void getline(char *, int) ;
void vmain(void);          // Voter menu
void cmain(void);          // Candidate menu
void fmain(void);          // Voting menu

//*********************************************************************
// The Drawing Functions & The Main Screen.
//*********************************************************************

void lineh (int, int, int, char) ;
void linev (int, int, int, char) ;

void graphics();

//*********************************************************************
// FUNCTION : lineh
// DESCRIPTION : To Draw A Horizontal Line   (x1, x2, y)
//*********************************************************************

void  lineh (int row1, int row2, int column, char c)
{
        for (row1; row1 <= row2; row1++)
        {
                gotoxy (row1, column) ;
                printf ("%c",c) ;
        }
}

//*********************************************************************
// FUNCTION : linev
// DESCRIPTION : To Draw A Vertical Line (y1, y2, x)
//*********************************************************************

void linev (int column1, int column2, int row, char c)
{
        for (column1; column1 <= column2; column1++ )
```

```
        {
                gotoxy (row, column1) ;
                printf ("%c",c) ;
        }
}

//**********************************************************
// FUNCTION : box
// DESCRIPTION : To Draw A Box  (x1, y1, x2, y2)
//**********************************************************

void box(int row1, int column1, int row2, int column2, char c)
{
        char ch=218 ;
        char c1, c2, c3, c4 ;
        char l1=196, l2=179 ;
        if (c == ch)
        {
                c1 = 218 ;
                c2 = 191 ;
                c3 = 192 ;
                c4 = 217 ;
                l1 = 196 ;
                l2 = 179 ;
        }
        else
        {
                c1 = c ;
                c2 = c ;
                c3 = c ;
                c4 = c ;
                l1 = c ;
                l2 = c ;
        }
        gotoxy(row1,column1) ;
        printf ("%c",c1) ;
        gotoxy(row2,column1) ;
        printf ("%c",c2) ;
        gotoxy(row1,column2) ;
        printf ("%c",c3) ;
```

```
        gotoxy(row2,column2) ;
        printf ("%c",c4) ;
        row1++ ;
        row2— ;
        lineh(row1, row2, column1, l1) ;
        lineh(row1, row2, column2, l1) ;
        row1— ;
        row2++ ;
        column1++ ;
        column2— ;
        linev(column1,column2,row1,l2) ;
        linev(column1,column2,row2,l2) ;
}

//**********************************************************************
// FUNCTION : vertical_menu
// DESCRIPTION : To Make Vertical Menu.
//**********************************************************************

int vertical_menu(char menu[] [20], int present, int end, int x, int y)
{
        int ex=0 ;
        int i;
        char ch;
        box(x + 9, y, x + strlen(menu[0]) + 12, y + end + 1, 218) ;

        for ( i=0; i<end; i++)
        {
                gotoxy(x + 10, y + i + 1) ;
                printf ("%s",menu[i]) ;
        }

        do
        {
                int tpresent = present ;
                textcolor(BLACK) ;
                textbackground(WHITE) ;
                gotoxy(x + 10,y + present) ;
                cprintf(menu[present - 1]) ;
                textcolor(WHITE) ;
```

```
        textbackground(BLACK) ;
        ch = getch() ;

        switch (ch)
        {
                case 75 : if (present == 1)
                          present = end ;
                          else
                                present— ;
                          break ;
                case 77 : if (present == end)
                          present = 1 ;
                          else
                                present++ ;
                          break ;
                case 71 : present = 1 ;
                          break ;
                case 79 : present = end ;
                          break ;
                case 72 : if (present == 1)
                          present = end ;
                          else
                                present— ;
                          break ;
                case 80 : if (present == end)
                          present = 1 ;
                          else
                                present++ ;
                          break ;
                case 13 : ex = 1 ;
                          break ;
                case 27 : present = end ;
                          ex = 1 ;
        }
        gotoxy(x + 10,y + tpresent) ;
        cprintf(menu[tpresent - 1]) ;
    } while(!ex) ;
    return(present) ;
}
```

```
//*************************************************************
// CLASS : menu
// FUNCTION : horizontal_menu
// DESCRIPTION : To Make Horizontal Menu.
//*************************************************************

int horizontal_menu(char menu[] [20], int present, int end, int x, int y)
{
        int ex=0, i ;
        char ch;

        for (i = 0; i < end; i++)
        {
                gotoxy(x + (i + 2) * 10 - 5, y) ;
                printf ("%s",menu[i]);
        }
        lineh(1, 80, 2, 205) ;

        do
        {
                int tpresent = present ;
                textcolor(BLACK) ;
                textbackground(WHITE) ;
                gotoxy(x + (present + 1) * 10 - 5, y) ;
                cprintf(menu[present - 1]) ;
                textcolor(WHITE) ;
                textbackground(BLACK) ;
                ch = getch() ;
                switch (ch)
                {
                        case 71 : present = 1 ;
                                break ;
                        case 79 : present = end ;
                                break ;
                        case 75 : if (present == 1)
                                present = end ;
                                else
                                        present— ;
                                break ;
```

```
                    case 77 : if (present == end)
                                present = 1 ;
                              else
                                        present++ ;
                              break ;
                    case 72 : if (present == 1)
                                present = end ;
                              else
                                        present-- ;
                              break ;
                    case 80 : if (present == end)
                                present = 1 ;
                              else
                                        present++ ;
                              break ;
                    case 13 : ex = 1 ;
                              break ;
                    case 27 : present = end ;
                              ex = 1 ;
               }
               gotoxy(x + (tpresent + 1) * 10 - 5, y) ;
               cprintf(menu[tpresent - 1]) ;
          } while(!ex) ;
          return(present) ;
}

//**********************************************************************
// FUNCTION : help
// DESCRIPTION : To Print The Help Screen For Various Important Operations.
//**********************************************************************

void help()
{
          clrscr();
          printf ("\n\n\n\t\t\tAbout Electronic Voting System");
          printf ("\n\nThis is a menu driven voting system for candidates and voters ");
          printf ("\n\n\n 1) Important instructions are displayed at the status bar at the   ");
          printf ("\n    bottom of the screen.");
          printf ("\n\n 2) Press escape key to exit the immediate screen at any time");
          printf ("\n    during the program.");
```

```
        printf ("\n\n\n\n");
        printf ("\t\t\t\t\t\tReeta Sahoo");
        getch();
        clrscr() ;
        return ;
}

//**********************************************************************
// FUNCTION : print
// DESCRIPTION : To Read The Characters On The Screen & Save It
//          To A Temp Variable And Then Send It To The Printer.
//**********************************************************************

void print(int x1, int y1, int x2, int y2)
{
        const SEGMENT = 0xB800 ;
        unsigned norow = y2 - y1 + 1, nocol = x2 - x1 + 1 ;
        unsigned i = 0, noele = norow * nocol, *ptr ;
        unsigned row,col,offset;
        unsigned char ch;
        int count = 0 ;
        FILE *prn;
        prn = fopen ("PRN","w");
        ptr = ((unsigned *)malloc(noele) ) ;
        statusbar(" PRINTING PRINTING PRINTING PRINTING PRINTING
                        PRINTING PRINTING PRINTING PRINTI") ;

        for ( row=y1; row<=y2; row++)
        {
                for( col=x1; col<=x2; col++)
                {
                        offset = 2*col + 160*row - 162 ;
                        ptr[i++] = peek(SEGMENT,offset) ;
                }
        }

        for(i=0; i<noele; i++, count++)
        {
                ch = ptr[i] % 256 ;
                putc (ch,prn) ;
```

```
            if (count == 80)
            {
                fputs("\n",prn);
                count = 0 ;
            }
        }
        fclose(prn);
}

//**********************************************************************
// FUNCTION : statusbar
// DESCRIPTION : To make the status bar at prefixed coordinates at the bottom of the screen.
//**********************************************************************

void statusbar(char m[])
{
        _setcursortype(_NOCURSOR) ;
        window(1,24,80,25) ;
        textcolor(BLACK) ;
        textbackground(WHITE) ;
        cprintf(m) ;
        clreol() ;
        window(1,1,80,24) ;
        textcolor(WHITE) ;
        textbackground(BLACK) ;
}

//**********************************************************************
// FUNCTION : getlinedelchar
// DESCRIPTION : To Delete A Character For Getline
//**********************************************************************

void getlinedelchar(char *s, int col, int p, int *len)
{
        int i ;
        for (i=p; i<len; i++)
                s[i - 1] = s[i] ;
        gotoxy(col + p - 1,wherey()) ;
        len— ;
```

```
        for (i=p - 1; i<len; i++)
                printf ( "%s",s[i]) ;
        printf ( "." );
}

//**********************************************************
// FUNCTION : getline
// DESCRIPTION : To Add Online Editing For Inputing A Line.
//**********************************************************

void getline(char *s , int limit)
{
        int i, curx, done, col ;
        col = wherex() ;
        for (i = 0; i<limit; i++)
                printf (".") ;
        gotoxy(col,wherey()) ;
        done = 0 ;
        curx = 0 ;
        i = 0 ;

        do
        {
                char ch = getch() ;
                ch = toupper(ch) ;

                switch (ch)
                {
                        case 0 :
                                ch = getch();
                                switch(ch)
                                {
                                        case 75 : if (curx>0)
                                                  {
                                                        curx— ;
                                                        gotoxy(wherex()-1,wherey()) ;
                                                  }
                                                  break ;
                                        case 77 : if (curx<i)
```

```
                                {
                                        curx++ ;
                                        gotoxy(wherex()+1,wherey()) ;
                                }
                                break ;
                        case 83 : if (i>0)
                                {
                                        if (curx<i)
                                        {
                                                getlinedelchar(s,col,curx + 1,&i) ;
                                                gotoxy(col + curx,wherey()) ;
                                                if (i == 0)
                                                        s[i] = 0 ;
                                        }
                                }
                }
                break ;
        case 8  : if (curx>0)
                {
                        getlinedelchar(s,col,curx,&i) ;
                        gotoxy(col + curx - 1,wherey()) ;
                        curx— ;
                        if (i == 0)
                                s[i] = 0 ;
                }
                break ;
        case 13 : done = 1 ;
                s[i] = 0 ;
                break ;
        case 27 : done = 1 ;
                s[0] = '0' ;
                break ;
        default : if (i < limit)
                {
                        if (curx < i)
                        {
                                s[curx] = ch ;
                                printf ("%c",ch) ;
                                curx++ ;
                        }
```

```
                    else
                    {
                              s[i] = ch ;
                              printf ("%c",ch) ;
                              i++ ;
                              curx = i ;
                    }
          }
          else
                    s[i] = 0 ;
     }
   } while (!done) ;
   printf ("\n");
}

//*****************************************************************
// FUNCTION : mscreen
// DESCRIPTION : To Paint The Screen With the The Opening Screen.
//*****************************************************************

void mscreen()
{
   int i=1;
   int ea=0,eb=0,c,ec=0;
   char ch2;
   /* request auto detection */
   int gdriver = DETECT, gmode, errorcode;

   /* initialize graphics and local variables */
   initgraph(&gdriver, &gmode, "\\tcc\\bgi");

   clrscr();
   /* read result of initialization */
   errorcode = graphresult();

   if (errorcode != grOk)  /* an error occurred */
   {
        printf("Graphics error: %s\n", grapherrormsg(errorcode));
        printf("Press any key to halt:");
        getch();
```

```
            exit(1); /* terminate with an error code */
        }

        _setcursortype(_NOCURSOR);
        clrscr();
        cleardevice();

        while(!kbhit()&&i<17)
        {
            setbkcolor(BLACK);
            settextstyle(TRIPLEX_FONT,HORIZ_DIR,3);
            setcolor(YELLOW);
            moveto(0,0);
            setcolor(i);
            settextstyle(GOTHIC_FONT,HORIZ_DIR,10);
            moveto(5,5);
            outtext("E");
            delay(80);
            outtext("l");
            delay(80);
            outtext("e");
            delay(80);
            outtext("c");
            delay(80);
            outtext("t");
            delay(80);
            outtext("r");
            delay(80);
            outtext("o");
            delay(80);
            outtext("n");
            delay(80);
            outtext("i");
            delay(80);
            outtext("c");
            delay(80);
            moveto(125,125);
            outtext("V");
            delay(80);
            outtext("o");
```

```
		delay(80);
		outtext("t");
		delay(80);
		outtext("i");
		delay(80);
		outtext("n");
		delay(80);
		outtext("g");
		delay(80);
		moveto(245,245);
		outtext("S");
		delay(80);
		outtext("y");
		delay(80);
		outtext("s");
		delay(80);
		outtext("t");
		delay(80);
		outtext("e");
		delay(80);
		outtext("m");
		delay(80);
		settextstyle(TRIPLEX_FONT,HORIZ_DIR,2);
		setcolor(YELLOW);
		outtextxy(400,450,"Version 2.02");
		delay(80);
		i++;
	}

	if(i<17)
		getch();

	clrscr();
	cleardevice();
	setbkcolor(BLACK);
	setcolor(CYAN);
	ellipse(300,230,0,360,200,100);
	ellipse(300,230,0,360,210,105);
	ellipse(300,230,0,360,220,110);
	ellipse(300,230,0,360,230,115);
```

```
ellipse(300,230,0,360,240,120);
settextstyle(DEFAULT_FONT,HORIZ_DIR,1);
setcolor(LIGHTGRAY);
outtextxy(205,200,"Copyright (C) 1999-2000 ");
setcolor(LIGHTGREEN);
outtextxy(205,210,"Reeta Sahoo.");
setcolor(LIGHTGRAY);
outtextxy(205,220,"All rights reserved.");
setcolor(GREEN);
outtextxy(205,230," By : ");
setcolor(LIGHTMAGENTA);
moveto(235,240);
sound(800);
outtext("R");
delay(300);
nosound();
delay(100);
sound(800);
outtext("e");
delay(100);
nosound();
delay(100);
sound(800);
outtext("e");
delay(100);
nosound();
delay(100);
sound(800);
outtext("t");
delay(100);
nosound();
delay(100);
sound(800);
outtext("a");
delay(100);
nosound();
delay(100);
sound(800);
outtext(" ");
delay(100);
```

```
        nosound();
        delay(100);
        sound(800);
        outtext("S");
        delay(100);
        nosound();
        delay(100);
        sound(800);
        outtext("a");
        delay(100);
        nosound();
        delay(100);
        sound(800);
        outtext("h");
        delay(100);
        nosound();
        delay(100);
        sound(800);
        outtext("o");
        delay(100);
        nosound();
        delay(100);
        sound(800);
        outtext("o");
        delay(100);
        nosound();
        getch();
        closegraph();
        _setcursortype(_SOLIDCURSOR);
}

//**********************************************************************
// CLASS : menu
// FUNCTION : main
// DESCRIPTION : To Draw The Main Menu & Call Related Functions
//**********************************************************************
void menu()
{
        int ch1;
        char ch='Y';
```

```
int gdriver = DETECT, gmode, errorcode;
int userpat=1;
mscreen();
initgraph(&gdriver, &gmode, " ");
setbkcolor(BLACK);

do
{
        setcolor(15);
        setlinestyle(0, userpat, 3);
        rectangle(0,0,getmaxx(),getmaxy());
        line(0,0,25,25);
        line(638,0,613,25);
        line(0,475,25,450);
        line(638,475,613,450);
        rectangle(25,25,613,450);
        settextstyle(5,HORIZ_DIR,4);
        setlinestyle(0,userpat,1);
        outtextxy(105,50,"Electronic Voting Machine");
        setcolor(5);
        line(105,100,510,100);
        setcolor(8);
        settextstyle(2,HORIZ_DIR,7);
        outtextxy(250,135,"MAIN MENU");
        setcolor(14);
        line(250,160,355,160);

        setcolor(14);
        outtextxy(40,170,"1) Press 1 For Voters.");
        outtextxy(40,205,"2) Press 2 For Candidates.");
        outtextxy(40,240,"3) Press 3 For start voting.");
        outtextxy(40,275,"4) Press 4 To exit");
        outtextxy(60,305,"Enter Your Choice :- ");
        gotoxy(39,21);
        scanf ("%d",&ch1);
        closegraph();

        switch(ch1)
        {
                case 1:
```

```
                    clrscr();
                    vmain();          // see Voting1.C for voter
                    break;
               case 2:
                    clrscr();
                    cmain();          // see Voting1C.C for candidate
                    break;
               case 3:
                    fmain();// see Voting3.C for casting/checking vote
               case 4:
                    exit(0);
          }

          gotoxy(30,25);
          textcolor(BLINK+LIGHTGREEN);
          cprintf("Do You Want To Continue.......");
          textcolor(15);
          scanf ("%c",&ch);
     } while(ch=='Y'||ch=='y');
}

// Files related with voter, candidate and voting
#include "d:\turboc3\projectc\voting1.c"  // Voter
#include "d:\turboc3\projectc\voting1c.c"// Candidate
#include "d:\turboc3\projectc\voting3.c"  // Voting

void main()
{
     closegraph();
     menu();
}
```

ELECTRONIC

VOTING

SYSTEM

Figure 3.1 First output screen of main program.

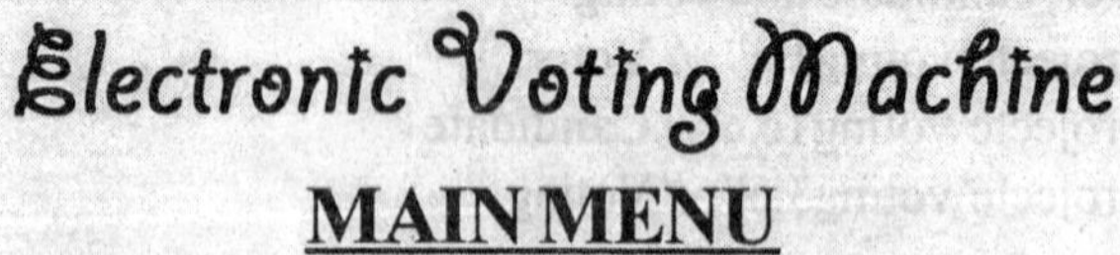

MAIN MENU

1) Press 1 For Voters.
2) Press 2 For Candidates.
3) Press 3 For start voting.
4) Press 4 To exit

Enter Your Choice : _

Figure 3.2 Output screen of main menu program.

Source Listing of VOTING1.C

```
//**********************************************************************
// All The Fields Related To Voter
//**********************************************************************

struct voter
{
        int  v_code ;
        char v_name[31], v_address[31], v_city[21], v_pin[7] ;
        char v_phone[10];
        char v_sex, v_done ;
        int  v_age;
};

int  fcode (int) ;// Finding the voter code
void display_voter (int) ;          // Displaying a voter's information

//**********************************************************************
// All The Functions Related To voter
//**********************************************************************

void add_voter () ;        // Adding new voter in the database
void modify_voter () ;  // Modifying the voter information
void del_voter () ;        // Deleting the voter from list
void displaycode_voter () ; // Checking the voter is exists or not
void showlist_voter () ; // Showing the voter's list

// Voter Menu to handle voter's information
void main_menu()
{
        int end=5, present=1, upperlim1=4, currentpos1=1, upperlim2=3, currentpos2=1,
                upperlim3=3, currentpos3=1;
        char main[] [20] = { " FILE ", " EDIT ", " PRINT ", " HELP ", " EXIT " } ;
        char sub1[] [20] = { "New voter    ", "Display Info ", "Display List ", "Return       " } ;
        char sub2[] [20] = { "Modify voter ", "Delete voter ", "Return       " } ;
        char sub3[] [20] = { "voter Info   ", "voter List ", "Return       " } ;
```

```
do
{
        _setcursortype(_NOCURSOR) ;
        present = horizontal_menu(main, present, end, 3, 1) ;

        switch (present)
        {
                case 1 :
                        currentpos1 = vertical_menu(sub1, currentpos1, upperlim1, 3, 3) ;

                        switch (currentpos1)
                        {
                                case 1 :

                                        _setcursortype(_SOLIDCURSOR) ;
                                        add_voter() ;
                                        _setcursortype(_NOCURSOR) ;
                                        break ;
                                case 2 :
                                        _setcursortype(_SOLIDCURSOR) ;
                                        displaycode_voter() ;
                                        break ;
                                case 3 :
                                        showlist_voter() ;
                                        break ;
                                case 4 :
                                        _setcursortype(_SOLIDCURSOR) ;
                                        _setcursortype(_NOCURSOR) ;
                                        break ;

                        }

                        clrscr() ;
                        break ;

                case 2 :
                        currentpos2 = vertical_menu(sub2, currentpos2, upperlim2, 13, 3);

                        switch (currentpos2)
                        {
                                case 1 :
```

```
                    _setcursortype(_SOLIDCURSOR) ;
                    modify_voter();

                    _setcursortype(_NOCURSOR) ;
                    break ;

                case 2 :

                    _setcursortype(_NORMALCURSOR) ;
                    del_voter() ;
                    _setcursortype(_NOCURSOR) ;
                    break ;
            }
            clrscr() ;
            break ;

        case 3 :
            currentpos3 = vertical_menu(sub3, currentpos3, upperlim3, 27, 3);
            switch (currentpos3)
            {
                case 1 :

                    _setcursortype(_SOLIDCURSOR) ;
                    displaycode_voter() ;
                    print(1,1,80,23) ;
                    _setcursortype(_NOCURSOR) ;
                    break ;
                case 2 :
                    _setcursortype(_NORMALCURSOR) ;

                    showlist_voter() ;
                    print(1,1,80,23) ;
                    _setcursortype(_NOCURSOR) ;
                    break ;
            }
            clrscr() ;
            break ;

        case 4 : help() ;
```

```
                    clrscr() ;
                    break ;
            }
    } while (present != end);
}
```

FILE EDIT PRINT HELP EXIT

New voter
Display Info
Display List
Return

Figure 3.3 Operational menu of voter.

```
//**************************************************************
// FUNCTION : fcode
// DESCRIPTION : To Return 0 If The Given Code Is Not Found
//**************************************************************

int  fcode(int code)
{
        FILE *file ;
        int found = 0 ;
        struct voter temp;
        file = fopen("voter.Dat", "rb+") ;

        while (fread(&temp, sizeof(struct voter),1,file))
        {
                if (temp.v_code == code)
                {
                        found = 1 ;
                        break ;
                }
        }
        fclose(file) ;
        return(found) ;
}
```

```
// FUNCTION : display_voter
// DESCRIPTION : To Display A Record From "voter.Dat"
//*****************************************************************

void display_voter(int code)
{
        FILE *file ;
        struct voter t ;
        char *initial ;
        file = fopen("voter.Dat", "rb+") ;
        while (fread(&t, sizeof(struct voter),1,file))
        {
                if (t.v_code == code)
                {
                        gotoxy(28,2) ;
                        printf ("VOTER INFORMATION");

                        if (t.v_sex == 'F')
                                initial = "Ms. ";
                        else
                                initial = "Mr. ";
                        gotoxy(30,3) ;
                        printf ("VOTER CODE # %d",t.v_code) ;
                        lineh(2,79,4,240) ;
                        gotoxy(20,6) ;
                        printf ("Name           : %s    %s",initial,t.v_name) ;
                        gotoxy(20,8) ;
                        printf ("Address        : %s" ,t.v_address );
                        gotoxy(40,10);
                        printf ("%s - %s",t.v_city,t.v_pin );
                        gotoxy(20,12) ;
                        printf ("Contact No.    : %s" ,t.v_phone );
                        gotoxy(20,14) ;
                        printf ("AGE            : %d",t.v_age) ;
                        gotoxy (20,16);
                        printf ("Vote Done      : %c ",t.v_done);
                }
        }
        fclose(file) ;
}
```

```
                    VOTER INFORMATION
                    VOTER CODE #     10
        ====================================================

            Name            : Mr. MASTER SANGRAM

            Address         : F-20/120, SEC-3, ROHINI

                              DELHI  -  110085

            Contact No.     : 7023422
            Age             : 20
            Vote Done       : N

Press any key to continue....
```

Figure 3.4 Displaying the individual voter information.

```
//**********************************************************************
// FUNCTION : add_voter
// DESCRIPTION : To Get Data About New voter
//**********************************************************************

void add_voter()
{
        struct voter t ;
        struct voter te ;
        FILE *file ;
        char ch, choice='Y';
        char d[3], m[3], y[5], basic[10], pf[6], da[6], ca[6], hra[6];
        int code=0, valid ;
        t.v_done = 'N';
        do
        {
                clrscr() ;
                _setcursortype(_SOLIDCURSOR) ;
                gotoxy(28,2) ;
```

```
printf ("ADDITION OF NEW VOTER");
lineh(20,59,3,240);
gotoxy(31,4);
printf ("VOTER Code # ");
gotoxy(29,5);
printf ("~~~~~~~~~~~~~~~~~~~~~~");
gotoxy(5,8);
printf ("Name        : ............................");
gotoxy(50,8);
printf ("Sex (M/F) : .");
gotoxy(5,10);
printf ("Address     : ............................");
gotoxy(50,10);
printf ("City      : ................");
gotoxy(5,12);
printf ("Pin Code    : ......");
gotoxy(50,12);
printf ("Phone No. : .........");
lineh(3,78,16,196);
gotoxy(5,14);
printf ("Age         : .........");

file = fopen("voter.Dat", "rb+");

while (fread(&te, sizeof(struct voter),1,file)==1)
{
        code = te.v_code ;
}
fclose(file);
code++ ;
t.v_code = code ;
gotoxy(47,4);
printf ("%d",t.v_code) ;

do
{
        valid = 1 ;
        statusbar(" ENTER THE NAME OF THE voter") ;
        _setcursortype(_SOLIDCURSOR) ;
        gotoxy(20,8);
```

```
        printf ("                    ");
        gotoxy(20,8) ;
        gets(t.v_name) ;

        if (t.v_name[0] == '0')
                return ;

        if (strlen(t.v_name) < 1)
        {
                valid = 0 ;
                statusbar("\a ENTER CORRECTLY (LENGTH : 1..30)") ;
                getch() ;
                _setcursortype(_SOLIDCURSOR) ;
        }
} while (!valid) ;

do
{
        statusbar(" ENTER IF voter IS MALE(M) OR FEMALE(F)") ;
        _setcursortype(_SOLIDCURSOR) ;
        gotoxy(62,8) ;
        clreol() ;
        t.v_sex = getch() ;

        if (t.v_sex == 27)
                return ;
        t.v_sex = toupper(t.v_sex) ;

        if ((t.v_sex == 27) || (t.v_sex == '0'))
                return ;
} while ((t.v_sex != 'M') && (t.v_sex != 'F')) ;

printf ("%c",t.v_sex) ;

do
{
        valid = 1 ;
        statusbar(" ENTER ADDRESS OF THE voter") ;
        _setcursortype(_SOLIDCURSOR) ;
        gotoxy(20,10) ;
```

```
        printf ("                    ");
        gotoxy(20,10) ;
        gets(t.v_address) ;

        if (t.v_address[0] == '0')
                return ;

        if (strlen(t.v_address) < 1)
        {
                valid = 0 ;
                statusbar("\a ENTER CORRECTLY (LENGTH : 1..30)") ;
                getch() ;
                _setcursortype(_SOLIDCURSOR) ;
        }
} while (!valid) ;

do
{
        valid = 1 ;
        statusbar(" ENTER CITY OF THE voter") ;
        _setcursortype(_SOLIDCURSOR) ;
        gotoxy(62,10) ;
        clreol() ;
        gets(t.v_city) ;

        if (t.v_city[0] == '0')
                return ;
        if (strlen(t.v_city) < 1)
        {
                valid = 0 ;
                statusbar("\a ENTER CORRECLTY (LENGTH : 1..20)") ;
                getch() ;
                _setcursortype(_SOLIDCURSOR) ;
        }
} while (!valid) ;

do
{
        valid = 1 ;
        statusbar(" ENTER PIN CODE OF THE voter") ;
```

```
            _setcursortype(_SOLIDCURSOR) ;
            gotoxy(20,12) ;
            printf ("                    ");
            gotoxy(20,12) ;
            gets(t.v_pin) ;

            if (t.v_pin[0] == '0')
                    return ;

            if (strlen(t.v_pin) != 6)
            {
                    valid = 0 ;
                    statusbar("\a ENTER CORRECTLY (LENGTH : 6)") ;
                    getch() ;
                    _setcursortype(_SOLIDCURSOR) ;
            }
    } while (!valid) ;

    do
    {
            valid = 1 ;
            statusbar(" ENTER PHONE NO. OF THE voter OR PRESS <enter>
                    FOR NONE") ;
            _setcursortype(_SOLIDCURSOR) ;
            gotoxy(62,12) ;
            clreol() ;
            gets(t.v_phone) ;

            if (t.v_phone[0] == '0')
                    return ;
            if ((strlen(t.v_phone) < 6 && strlen(t.v_phone) > 0) ||
                    (strlen(t.v_phone) > 7))
            {
                    valid = 0 ;
                    statusbar("\a ENTER CORRECTLY") ;
                    getch() ;
                    _setcursortype(_SOLIDCURSOR) ;
            }
    } while (!valid) ;
```

```
if (strlen(t.v_phone) == 0)
        strcpy(t.v_phone,"—") ;

do
{
        valid = 1 ;
        statusbar(" ENTER AGE OF THE VOTER") ;
        _setcursortype(_SOLIDCURSOR) ;
        gotoxy(20,14) ;
        clreol() ;
        scanf ("%d",&t.v_age);

        if (t.v_age == 0)
                return ;
        if (t.v_age < 18)
        {
                valid = 0 ;
                statusbar("\a ENTER CORRECLTY (AGE >= 18)") ;
                getch() ;
                _setcursortype(_SOLIDCURSOR) ;
        }
} while (!valid) ;

do
{
        statusbar("\a Do you wish to save (y/n) : ") ;
        ch = getch() ;
        ch = toupper(ch) ;

        if (ch == '0'|| ch == 27)
                return ;

} while (ch != 'Y' && ch != 'N') ;

if (ch == 'N')
        return ;

file = fopen("voter.Dat", "ab+") ;

fwrite(&t, sizeof(struct voter),1,file) ;
```

```
            fclose(file) ;
            statusbar("\a Add any more (y/n) : ") ;
            do
            {
                    choice = getch() ;
                    choice = toupper(choice) ;

                    if (choice == 13)
                            choice = 'Y' ;

                    if (choice == 27)
                            choice = 'N' ;

            } while((choice != 'Y') && (choice !='N'));

    } while(choice == 'Y');
}
```

```
                         ADDITION OF NEW VOTER
                ==================================================
                          VOTER Code #      10

Name          : MASTER SANGRAM                   Sex (F/M)     : M
Address       : F-20/120, SEC-3, ROHINI          City          : DELHI
Pin code      : 110085........                   Phone No.     : 7023422

Age           : 20

Do you wish to save (y/n) :
```

Figure 3.5 Adding new voter into database.

```
//*****************************************************************
// FUNCTION : modify_voter
// DESCRIPTION : To Provide With Necessary Data Required For
//              Modification Of A Given Record
//*****************************************************************

void modify_voter()
{
        FILE *file ;
        struct voter t ;
        struct voter te ;
        FILE *file1 ;
        int  code, valid ;
        char  ch, house='N', conv='N', choice='Y' ;
        char  address[31], city[21], pin[7], phone[10], desig[21] ;
        char  tbasic[10], tpf[6], tda[6], tca[6], thra[6] ;
        float basic=0, pf=0, da=0, ca=0, hra=0 ;
        int age;
        clrscr() ;

        do
        {
                gotoxy(72,2) ;
                printf ("Esc=EXIT");
                gotoxy(5,5) ;
                printf ("Enter code of the voter : ");
                scanf ("%d",&code) ;

                if (code == 0)
                        return ;
                clrscr() ;

                if (!fcode(code))
                {
                        gotoxy(30,24) ;
                        printf ("\a Record not found");
                        getch() ;
                        return ;
                }
```

```
display_voter(code) ;
gotoxy(72,2) ;
printf ("<0>=EXIT");
gotoxy(24,2) ;
printf ("MODIFICATION OF VOTER RECORD");

do
{
        statusbar("\a Do you wish to modify this record (y/n) ") ;
        ch = getch() ;
        ch = toupper(ch) ;

        if (ch == '0')
                return ;

        if (ch == 13 )
                ch = 'Y' ;

        if (ch == 27 )
                ch = 'N' ;

} while (ch != 'Y' && ch != 'N') ;

if (ch == 'N')
        return ;
clrscr() ;

file = fopen("voter.Dat", "rb+") ;
while (fread(&t, sizeof(struct voter),1,file)==1)
{
        if (t.v_code == code)
                break ;
}

gotoxy(72,2) ;
printf ("Esc=EXIT");
gotoxy(26,2) ;
printf ("MODIFICATION OF NEW VOTER");
lineh(20,59,3,240) ;
gotoxy(31,4) ;
```

```
printf ("Voter Code # %d ",code) ;
gotoxy(29,5) ;
printf ("~~~~~~~~~~~~~~~~~~~~~~~~~~");
lineh(3,78,7,196);
gotoxy(5,9) ;
printf ("Name          : ");
gotoxy(50,9);
printf ("Sex (M/F) : ");
gotoxy(5,11) ;
printf ("Address       : ............................");
gotoxy(50,11) ;
printf ("City      : ................");
gotoxy(5,13) ;
printf ("Pin Number   : ......");
gotoxy(50,13) ;
printf ("Phone No. : .........");
gotoxy(5,15);
printf ("Age           : .........");
lineh(3,78,17,196);
gotoxy(20,9) ;
printf ("%s",t.v_name) ;

gotoxy(62,9) ;
printf ("%c",t.v_sex) ;
fflush(stdin);

do
{
        valid = 1 ;
        statusbar(" ENTER ADDRESS OF THE voter OR PRESS <enter>
                FOR NO CHANGE") ;
        _setcursortype(_SOLIDCURSOR) ;
        gotoxy(20,11) ;
        printf ("                              ");
        gotoxy(20,11) ;
        gets(address) ;

        if (address[0] == '0')
                return ;
```

```
        if (strlen(address) > 30)
        {
            valid = 0 ;
            statusbar("\a Enter correctly (Range: 1..30)") ;
            getch() ;
            _setcursortype(_SOLIDCURSOR) ;
        }
    } while (!valid) ;

    if (strlen(address) == 0)
    {
        strcpy(address, t.v_address) ;
        gotoxy(20,11) ;
        printf ("%s",address) ;
    }

    do
    {
        valid = 1 ;
        statusbar(" ENTER CITY OF THE voter OR PRESS <enter>
            FOR NO CHANGE") ;
        _setcursortype(_SOLIDCURSOR) ;
        gotoxy(62,11) ;
        clreol() ;
        gets(city) ;

        if (city[0] == '0')
            return ;
        if (strlen(city) > 18)
        {
            valid = 0 ;
            statusbar("\a Enter correctly (Length : 1..18)") ;
            getch() ;
            _setcursortype(_SOLIDCURSOR) ;
        }
    } while (!valid) ;

    if (strlen(city) == 0)
    {
        strcpy(city, t.v_city) ;
```

```
        gotoxy(62,11);
        printf ("%s",city);
    }

    do
    {
        valid = 1 ;
        statusbar(" ENTER PIN CODE OR PRESS <enter> FOR NO
                CHANGE") ;
        _setcursortype(_SOLIDCURSOR) ;
        gotoxy(20,13);
        printf ("            ");
        gotoxy(20,13);
        gets(pin);

        if (pin[0] == '0')
                return ;

        if (strlen(pin) != 6 && strlen(pin) > 1)
        {
                valid = 0 ;
                statusbar("\a Enter correctly (Length : 6)") ;
                getch() ;
                _setcursortype(_SOLIDCURSOR) ;
        }
    } while (!valid);

    if (strlen(pin) == 0)
    {
        strcpy(pin, t.v_pin);
        gotoxy(20,13);
        printf ("%s",pin);
    }

    do
    {
        valid = 1 ;
        statusbar(" ENTER PHONE NO. OF THE voter OR PRESS
                <enter> FOR NO CHANGE") ;
        _setcursortype(_SOLIDCURSOR) ;
```

```
            gotoxy(62,13) ;
            clreol() ;
            gets(phone) ;

            if (phone[0] == '0')
                    return ;
            if ((strlen(phone) < 6 && strlen(phone) > 0) || (strlen(phone) > 7))
            {
                    valid = 0 ;
                    statusbar("\a Enter correctly") ;
                    getch() ;
                    _setcursortype(_SOLIDCURSOR) ;
            }
    } while (!valid) ;

    if (strlen(phone) == 0)
    {
            strcpy(phone, t.v_phone) ;
            gotoxy(62,13) ;
            printf ("%s",phone) ;
    }

    do
    {
            valid = 1 ;
            statusbar(" ENTER AGE  OF THE VOTER OR PRESS <enter>
                    FOR NO CHANGE") ;
            _setcursortype(_SOLIDCURSOR) ;
            gotoxy(20,15) ;
            clreol() ;
            scanf ("%d",&age);

            if (age  == 0)
                    return ;

            if (age < 18)
            {
                    valid = 0 ;
                    statusbar("\a Enter correctly (Range: >= 18)") ;
                    getch() ;
```

```
                _setcursortype(_SOLIDCURSOR) ;
        }
} while (!valid) ;

strcpy(t.v_address, address) ;
strcpy(t.v_city, city) ;
strcpy(t.v_pin, pin) ;
strcpy(t.v_phone, phone) ;
t.v_code = code ;
t.v_age = age ;

file = fopen("voter.Dat", "rb+") ;
file1 = fopen("Tempmod.Dat", "wb+") ;

while (fread(&te, sizeof(struct voter),1,file)==1)
{
        if (t.v_code != te.v_code)
                fwrite(&te, sizeof(struct voter),1,file1) ;
        else
                break ;
}

fwrite(&t, sizeof(struct voter),1,file1) ;

while (fread(&te, sizeof(struct voter),1,file)==1)
        fwrite(&te, sizeof(struct voter),1,file1) ;

fclose(file) ;
fclose(file1) ;

file = fopen("voter.Dat", "wb+") ;
file1 = fopen("Tempmod.Dat", "rb+") ;

while (fread(&t, sizeof(struct voter),1,file1)==1)
{
        fwrite(&t, sizeof(struct voter),1,file) ;
}

fclose(file) ;
fclose(file1) ;
```

```
        gotoxy(5,25) ;
        clreol() ;
        do
        {
                statusbar("\a Do you wish to save (y/n) ") ;
                ch = getch() ;
                ch = toupper(ch) ;
                if (ch == '0')
                        return ;
        } while (ch != 'Y' && ch != 'N') ;

        if (ch == 'N')
                return ;

        statusbar(" Record Modified.") ;
        getch() ;

        statusbar("\a Modify any more (y/n) : ") ;
        do
        {
                choice = getch() ;
                choice = toupper(choice) ;

                if (choice == 13)
                        choice = 'Y' ;

                if (choice == 27)
                        choice = 'N' ;
        } while((choice != 'Y') && (choice !='N'));
    } while(choice == 'Y');
}
```

```
MODIFICATION OF VOTER RECORD                    <0>=EXIT
        VOTER CODE #      10
=================================================

Name            : Mr. MASTER SANGRAM

Address         : F-20/120, SEC-3, ROHINI

                  DELHI - 110085

Contact No.     : 7023422
Age             : 20
Vote Done       : N
```

Do you wish to modify this record (y/n)

Figure 3.6 New voter modification first screen.

```
MODIFICATION OF NEW VOTER
=================================================
          Voter Code #      10
          ~~~~~~~~~~~~~~~~~~~~~~~~~~~

Name        : MASTER SANGRAM                Sex (F/M)     : M

Address     : F-20/120, SEC-3, ROHINI       City          : NEW DELHI

Pin code    : 110085........                Phone No.     : 7023422

Age         : 21
```

Do you wish to save (y/n) :

Figure 3.7 New voter modification second screen.

```
//**************************************************************
// FUNCTION : del_voter
// DESCRIPTION : To Delete A Record In "voter.Dat"
//**************************************************************

void del_voter()
{
        struct voter t ;
        FILE *file ;
        FILE *file1 ;
        char ch ;
        int code ;
        clrscr() ;
        gotoxy(72,2) ;
        printf ("<0>=EXIT");
        gotoxy(5,5) ;
        printf ("Enter code of the voter : ");
        scanf ("%d",&code) ;
        if (code == 0)
                return ;
        clrscr() ;

        if (!fcode(code))
        {
                gotoxy(30,24) ;
                printf ("\a Record not found");
                getch() ;
                return ;
        }

        gotoxy(72,2) ;
        printf ("<0>=EXIT");
        gotoxy(23,1) ;
        printf ("DELETION OF THE VOTER RECORD");
        display_voter(code) ;
        do
        {
                statusbar("\a Do you wish to remove this record (y/n) ") ;
                ch = getch() ;
```

```
        if (ch == 27)
            return ;

        if (ch == 13)
            ch = 'y' ;

        ch = toupper(ch) ;

        if (ch == '0')
            return ;
} while (ch != 'Y' && ch != 'N') ;

if (ch == 'N')
        return ;

file = fopen("voter.Dat", "rb+") ;
file1 = fopen("Tempdel.Dat", "wb+") ;

while (fread(&t, sizeof(struct voter),1,file)==1)
{
        if (t.v_code != code)
            fwrite(&t, sizeof(struct voter),1,file1) ;
}

fclose(file) ;
fclose(file1) ;

file = fopen("voter.Dat", "wb+") ;
file1 = fopen("Tempdel.Dat", "rb+") ;

while (fread(&t, sizeof(struct voter),1,file1)==1)
{
        fwrite(&t, sizeof(struct voter),1,file) ;
}

fclose(file) ;
fclose(file1) ;

clrscr() ;
statusbar("\a Record Deleted") ;
```

```
        getch() ;
        statusbar("   Press any key to continue...") ;
        getch() ;
}
```

```
                 DELETION OF THE VOTER RECORD              <0>=EXIT
                         VOTER INFORMATION
                         VOTER CODE #      10
         ==========================================================
            Name              : Mr. MASTER SANGRAM

            Address           : F-20/120, SEC-3, ROHINI

                                DELHI  -  110085

            Contact No.       : 7023422
            Age               : 20
            Vote Done         : N
Do you wish to remove this record (y/n)
```

Figure 3.8 Removing an existing voter from list.

```
//**********************************************************
// FUNCTION : displaycode_voter
// DESCRIPTION : To Obtain Code For Displaying A Record
//**********************************************************

void displaycode_voter()
{
        int code ;
        clrscr() ;
        gotoxy(72,2) ;
        printf("<0>=EXIT");
        gotoxy(5,5) ;
        _setcursortype(_SOLIDCURSOR) ;
        printf ("Enter code of the voter : ");
        scanf ("%d", &code) ;
```

```
        if (code == 0)
                return ;
        clrscr() ;
        if (!fcode(code))
        {
                _setcursortype(_NOCURSOR) ;
                gotoxy(30,25) ;
                printf ("\a Record not found");
                getch() ;
                return ;
        }

        display_voter(code) ;
        statusbar("   Press any key to continue...") ;
        getch() ;
}

//**********************************************************************
// FUNCTION : showlist_voter
// DESCRIPTION : To Display The List Of voters
//**********************************************************************

void showlist_voter()
{
        struct voter t ;
        FILE *file ;
        int row = 6, found=0, flag=0 ;
        int d1, m1, y1 ;
        char ch ;
        struct date d;
        getdate(&d) ;
        d1 = d.da_day ;
        m1 = d.da_mon ;
        y1 = d.da_year ;
        clrscr() ;
        gotoxy(23,2) ;
        printf ("LIST OF VOTERS AS ON %d  . %d  .%d",d1,m1,y1) ;
        lineh(1,80,3,240) ;
        gotoxy(12,4) ;
        printf ("CODE #              NAME                AGE");
```

```
gotoxy(1,5);
lineh(11,72,5,205);
linev(4,22,10,186);
linev(4,22,19,186);
linev(4,22,51,186);
linev(4,22,72,186);
lineh(1,80,23,240);

file = fopen("voter.dat", "rb+");

while (fread(&t, sizeof(struct voter),1,file)==1)
{
        flag = 0;
        found = 1;
        gotoxy(12,row);
        printf ("%d",t.v_code);
        gotoxy(21,row);
        printf ("%s",t.v_name);
        gotoxy(53,row);
        printf ("%d",t.v_age);

        if (row == 18)
        {
                flag = 1;
                row = 6;
                statusbar(" Press any key to continue or Press <ESC> to exit");
                ch = getch();

                if (ch == 27)
                        break;

                clrscr();
                gotoxy(31,2);
                printf ("LIST OF voterS");
                lineh(1,90,3,240);
                gotoxy(2,4);
                printf ("CODE #          NAME                AGE");
                gotoxy(1,5);
                printf ("~~~~~~~~~~~~~~~~~~~~~~~~~~~~~~~~~~~~~~~~~~~~~~~~~~~~~~~~~~~~~~~~~");
        }
```

```
        else
                row++ ;
    }
    if(!found)
    {
        gotoxy(26,14) ;
        printf ("\a Records not found");
    }
    if(!flag)
    {
        statusbar("   Press any key to continue...") ;
        getch() ;
    }

    fclose (file) ;
}
```

LIST OF VOTER AS ON 4 . 7 . 2000

Code #	Name	Age
1	VIMAL JAIN	20
2	MS. PRADEEP RANA	24
3	MS. PRIYA SINGH	23
4	MR. GOVIND RAO	26
5	SATPAL VERMA	22
6	RAMITA GHAI	21
7	VIPUL JAIN	24
8	NIRMAL BAL	25
9	MS. RITU VIS	24
10	MASTER SANGRAM	20

Press any key to continue....

Figure 3.9 Listing all the voters to vote.

```
//************************************************************************
// Main Menu
//************************************************************************

void vmain(void)
{
        main_menu() ;
}
```

Source Listing of VOTING1C.C

```
//************************************************************************
//  All The Fields Related To Candidate
//************************************************************************

struct candidate
{
        int  c_code ;
        char  c_name[31], c_address[31], c_city[21], c_pin[7] ;
        char  c_phone[10];
        char  c_sex;
        int  c_age;
        int  total;
};


int  fcode (int) ;// Finding a candidate code
void display (int) ;         // Display the candidate information
void add1 () ;  // Adding new candidate
void modify1 () ;            // Modifying candidates information
void del1 () ;   // Deleting candidate from list
void displaycode1 () ;   // Displaying the candidate information
void showlist1 () ;          // Showing the candidates list
void print (int, int, int, int) ;         // Activate the printer
```

```
//**************************************************************
// FUNCTION : main
// DESCRIPTION : To Draw The Main Menu & Call Related Functions
//**************************************************************/

void main_menu1()
{
        int end=5, present=1, upperlim1=4, currentpos1=1, upperlim2=3, currentpos2=1,
                upperlim3=3, currentpos3=1;
        char main[] [20] = { " FILE ", " EDIT ", " PRINT ", " HELP ", " EXIT " } ;
        char sub1[] [20] = { "New candidate     ", "Display Info ", "Display List ",
                        "Return      " } ;
        char sub2[] [20] = { "Modify candidate  ", "Delete candidate ", "Return          " } ;
        char sub3[] [20] = { "Candidate Info  ", "Candidate List ",  "Return       " } ;

        do
        {
                _setcursortype(_NOCURSOR) ;
                present = horizontal_menu(main, present, end, 3, 1) ;

                switch (present)
                {
                        case 1 :
                                currentpos1 = vertical_menu(sub1, currentpos1, upperlim1, 3, 3) ;
                                switch (currentpos1)
                                {
                                        case 1 :
                                                _setcursortype(_SOLIDCURSOR) ;
                                                add1() ;
                                                _setcursortype(_NOCURSOR) ;
                                                break ;
                                        case 2 :
                                                _setcursortype(_SOLIDCURSOR) ;
                                                displaycode1() ;
                                                break ;
                                        case 3 :
                                                showlist1() ;
                                                break ;
                                        case 4 :
                                                _setcursortype(_SOLIDCURSOR) ;
```

```
                                _setcursortype(_NOCURSOR) ;
                                break ;
                        }
                        clrscr() ;
                        break ;
                case 2 :
                        currentpos2 = vertical_menu(sub2, currentpos2, upperlim2, 13, 3);
                        switch (currentpos2)
                        {
                            case 1 :
                                _setcursortype(_SOLIDCURSOR) ;
                                modify1() ;
                                _setcursortype(_NOCURSOR) ;
                                break ;
                            case 2 :
                                _setcursortype(_NORMALCURSOR) ;
                                del1() ;
                                _setcursortype(_NOCURSOR) ;
                                break ;
                        }
                        clrscr() ;
                        break ;
                case 3 :
                        currentpos3 = vertical_menu(sub3, currentpos3, upperlim3, 27, 3);
                        switch (currentpos3)
                        {
                            case 1 :
                                _setcursortype(_SOLIDCURSOR) ;
                                displaycode1() ;
                                print(1,1,80,23) ;
                                _setcursortype(_NOCURSOR) ;
                                break ;
                            case 2 :
                                _setcursortype(_NORMALCURSOR) ;
                                showlist1() ;
                                print(1,1,80,23) ;
                                _setcursortype(_NOCURSOR) ;
                                break ;

                        }
                        clrscr() ;
```

```
                        break ;
                case 4 : help() ;
                        clrscr() ;
                        break ;
            }
        } while (present != end);
}
```

FILE **EDIT** **PRINT** **HELP** **EXIT**

New candidate
Display Info
Display List
Return

Figure 3.10 Operational menu of candidate.

```
//************************************************************
// FUNCTION : fcode
// DESCRIPTION : To Return 0 If The Given Code Is Not Found
//************************************************************

int fcode1(int code)
{
        FILE *file ;
        int found = 0 ;
        struct candidate temp;
        file = fopen("candidate.Dat", "rb+") ;

        while (fread(&temp, sizeof(struct candidate),1,file))
        {
                if (temp.c_code == code)
                {
                        found = 1 ;
                        break ;
                }
        }
        fclose(file) ;
```

```
        return(found) ;
}

//******************************************************************
// FUNCTION : display
// DESCRIPTION : To Display A Record From "candidate.Dat"
//******************************************************************

void display1(int code)
{
        FILE *file ;
        struct candidate t ;
        char *initial ;
        file = fopen("candidate.Dat", "rb+") ;

        while (fread(&t, sizeof(struct candidate),1,file))
        {
                if (t.c_code == code)
                {
                        gotoxy(28,2) ;
                        printf ("CANDIDATE INFORMATION");

                        if (t.c_sex == 'F')
                                initial = "Ms. ";
                        else
                                initial = "Mr. ";

                        gotoxy(30,3) ;
                        printf ("CANDIDATE CODE # %d",t.c_code) ;
                        lineh(2,79,4,240) ;
                        gotoxy(20,6) ;
                        printf ("Name           : %s    %s",initial,t.c_name) ;
                        gotoxy(20,8) ;
                        printf ("Address        : %s" ,t.c_address );
                        gotoxy(40,10);
                        printf ("%s - %s",t.c_city,t.c_pin );
                        gotoxy(20,12) ;
                        printf ("Contact No.    : %s" ,t.c_phone );
                        gotoxy(20,14) ;
                        printf ("AGE            : %d",t.c_age) ;
```

```
            gotoxy (20,16);
            printf ("Total Vote Gain  : %d ",t.total);
        }
    }
    fclose(file) ;
}
```

```
                    CANDIDATE INFORMATION
                    CANDIDATE CODE #    2
        =====================================================

        Name                    : Ms. SUSMA SWARAJ

        Address                 : 10TH JANPATH

                                  NEW DELHI  -  110001

        Contact No.             : 6432001

        Age                     : 40

        Total Vote Gain         : 0

Press any key to continue....
```

Figure 3.11 Displaying the individual candidate information.

```
//**********************************************************************
// FUNCTION : add
// DESCRIPTION : To Get Data About New candidate
//**********************************************************************

void add1()
{
    struct candidate t ;
    struct candidate te ;
    FILE *file ;
    char ch, choice='Y';
    char d[3], m[3], y[5], basic[10], pf[6], da[6], ca[6], hra[6];
```

```
int code=0, valid ;
t.total = 0;

do
{
        clrscr() ;
        _setcursortype(_SOLIDCURSOR) ;
        gotoxy(28,2) ;
        printf ("ADDITION OF NEW CANDIDATE");
        lineh(20,59,3,240) ;
        gotoxy(31,4) ;
        printf ("Candidate Code # ");
        gotoxy(29,5) ;
        printf ("~~~~~~~~~~~~~~~~~~~~~~");
        gotoxy(5,8) ;
        printf ("Name          : ..........................");
        gotoxy(50,8);
        printf ("Sex (M/F) : .");
        gotoxy(5,10) ;
        printf ("Address       : ............................");
        gotoxy(50,10) ;
        printf ("City       : ................");
        gotoxy(5,12) ;
        printf ("Pin Code      : ......");
        gotoxy(50,12) ;
        printf ("Phone No. : .........");
        lineh(3,78,16,196);
        gotoxy(5,14) ;
        printf ("Age           :.........");

        file = fopen("candidate.Dat", "rb+") ;

        while (fread(&te, sizeof(struct candidate),1,file)==1)
        {
                code = te.c_code ;
        }
        fclose(file) ;
        code++ ;
        t.c_code = code ;
        gotoxy(47,4) ;
```

```
printf ("%d",t.c_code) ;

do
{
        valid = 1 ;
        statusbar(" ENTER THE NAME OF THE CANDIDATE") ;
        _setcursortype(_SOLIDCURSOR) ;
        gotoxy(20,8) ;
        printf ("                    ");
        gotoxy(20,8) ;
        gets(t.c_name) ;

        if (t.c_name[0] == '0')
                return ;

        if (strlen(t.c_name) < 1)
        {
                valid = 0 ;
                statusbar("\a ENTER CORRECTLY (LENGTH : 1..30)") ;
                getch() ;
                _setcursortype(_SOLIDCURSOR) ;
        }

} while (!valid) ;

do
{
        statusbar(" ENTER IF CANDIDATE IS MALE(M) OR FEMALE(F)");
        _setcursortype(_SOLIDCURSOR) ;
        gotoxy(62,8) ;
        clreol() ;
        t.c_sex = getch() ;

        if (t.c_sex == 27)
                return ;

        t.c_sex = toupper(t.c_sex) ;

        if ((t.c_sex == 27) || (t.c_sex == '0'))
                return ;
```

```
} while ((t.c_sex != 'M') && (t.c_sex != 'F')) ;
printf ("%c",t.c_sex) ;

do
{
        valid = 1 ;
        statusbar(" ENTER ADDRESS OF THE candidate") ;
        _setcursortype(_SOLIDCURSOR) ;
        gotoxy(20,10) ;
        printf ("                    ");
        gotoxy(20,10) ;
        gets(t.c_address) ;

        if (t.c_address[0] == '0')
                return ;

        if (strlen(t.c_address) < 1)
        {
                valid = 0 ;
                statusbar("\a ENTER CORRECTLY (LENGTH : 1..30)") ;
                getch() ;
                _setcursortype(_SOLIDCURSOR) ;
        }
} while (!valid) ;

do
{
        valid = 1 ;
        statusbar(" ENTER CITY OF THE candidate") ;
        _setcursortype(_SOLIDCURSOR) ;
        gotoxy(62,10) ;
        clreol() ;
        gets(t.c_city) ;

        if (t.c_city[0] == '0')
                return ;

        if (strlen(t.c_city) < 1)
        {
                valid = 0 ;
```

```
                statusbar("\a ENTER CORRECLTY (LENGTH : 1..20)") ;
                getch() ;
                _setcursortype(_SOLIDCURSOR) ;
        }
} while (!valid) ;

do
{
        valid = 1 ;
        statusbar(" ENTER PIN CODE OF THE CANDIDATE") ;
        _setcursortype(_SOLIDCURSOR) ;
        gotoxy(20,12) ;
        printf ("                  ");
        gotoxy(20,12) ;
        gets(t.c_pin) ;

        if (t.c_pin[0] == '0')
                return ;

        if (strlen(t.c_pin) != 6)
        {
                valid = 0 ;
                statusbar("\a ENTER CORRECTLY (LENGTH : 6)") ;
                getch() ;
                _setcursortype(_SOLIDCURSOR) ;
        }
} while (!valid) ;

do
{
        valid = 1 ;
        statusbar(" ENTER PHONE NO. OF THE CANDIDATE OR
                PRESS <enter> FOR NONE") ;
        _setcursortype(_SOLIDCURSOR) ;
        gotoxy(62,12) ;
        clreol() ;
        gets(t.c_phone) ;

        if (t.c_phone[0] == '0')
                return ;
```

```
                if ((strlen(t.c_phone) < 6 && strlen(t.c_phone) > 0) ||
                            (strlen(t.c_phone) > 7))
                {
                        valid = 0 ;
                        statusbar("\a ENTER CORRECTLY") ;
                        getch() ;
                        _setcursortype(_SOLIDCURSOR) ;
                }
        } while (!valid) ;
        if (strlen(t.c_phone) == 0)
                strcpy(t.c_phone,"—") ;

        do
        {
                valid = 1 ;
                statusbar(" ENTER AGE OF THE CANDIDATE") ;
                _setcursortype(_SOLIDCURSOR) ;
                gotoxy(20,14) ;
                clreol() ;
                scanf ("%d",&t.c_age);

                if (t.c_age == 0)
                        return ;
                if (t.c_age < 18)
                {
                        valid = 0 ;
                        statusbar("\a ENTER CORRECLTY (AGE >= 18)") ;
                        getch() ;
                        _setcursortype(_SOLIDCURSOR) ;
                }
        } while (!valid) ;
        do
        {
                statusbar("\a Do you wish to save (y/n) : ") ;
                ch = getch() ;
                ch = toupper(ch) ;

        if (ch == '0'|| ch == 27)
                        return ;
```

```
        } while (ch != 'Y' && ch != 'N') ;

        if (ch == 'N')
                return ;
        file = fopen("candidate.Dat", "ab+") ;
        fwrite(&t, sizeof(struct candidate),1,file) ;
        fclose(file) ;

        statusbar("\a Add any more (y/n) : ") ;
        do
        {
                choice = getch() ;
                choice = toupper(choice) ;

                if (choice == 13)
                        choice = 'Y' ;
                if (choice == 27)
                        choice = 'N' ;
        } while((choice != 'Y') && (choice !='N'));

    } while(choice == 'Y');
}
```

```
ADDITION OF NEW CANDIDATE
==========================================================
                Candidate Code #    2

Name        : SUSMA SWARAJ             Sex (F/M)   : F
Address     : 10TH JANPATH             City        : NEW DELHI
Pin code    : 110001........           Phone No.   : 6432001

Age         : 40

Do you wish to save (y/n) :
```

Figure 3.12 Adding new candidate into database.

```
//**********************************************************************
// FUNCTION : modify
// DESCRIPTION : To Provide With Necessary Data Required For
//          Modification Of A Given Record
//**********************************************************************

void modify1()
{
        FILE *file ;
        struct candidate t ;
        struct candidate te ;
        FILE *file1 ;
        int  code, valid ;
        char  ch, house='N', conv='N', choice='Y' ;
        char  address[31], city[21], pin[7], phone[10], desig[21] ;
        char  tbasic[10], tpf[6], tda[6], tca[6], thra[6] ;
        float basic=0, pf=0, da=0, ca=0, hra=0 ;
        int age;
        clrscr() ;

        do
        {
                gotoxy(72,2) ;
                printf ("Esc=EXIT");
                gotoxy(5,5) ;
                printf ("Enter code of the candidate : ");
                scanf ("%d",&code) ;

                if (code == 0)
                        return ;
                clrscr() ;
                if (!fcode1(code))
                {
                        gotoxy(30,24) ;
                        printf ("\a Record not found");
                        getch() ;
                        return ;
                }
```

```
display1(code) ;
gotoxy(72,2) ;
printf ("<0>=EXIT");
gotoxy(24,2) ;
printf ("MODIFICATION OF CANDIDATE RECORD");

do
{
        statusbar("\a Do you wish to modify this record (y/n) ") ;
        ch = getch() ;
        ch = toupper(ch) ;

        if (ch == '0')
                return ;

        if (ch == 13 )
                ch = 'Y' ;

        if (ch == 27 )
                ch = 'N' ;
} while (ch != 'Y' && ch != 'N') ;

if (ch == 'N')
        return ;
clrscr() ;

file = fopen("candidate.Dat", "rb+") ;
while (fread(&t, sizeof(struct candidate),1,file)==1)
{
        if (t.c_code == code)
                break ;
}

gotoxy(72,2) ;
printf ("Esc=EXIT");
gotoxy(26,2) ;
printf ("MODIFICATION OF NEW CANDIDATE");
lineh(20,59,3,240) ;
gotoxy(31,4) ;
printf ("Candidate Code # %d ",code) ;
```

```
gotoxy(29,5) ;
printf ("~~~~~~~~~~~~~~~~~~~~~~~~~~~~");
lineh(3,78,7,196);
gotoxy(5,9) ;
printf ("Name        : ");
gotoxy(50,9);
printf ("Sex (M/F) : ");
gotoxy(5,11) ;
printf ("Address     :............................");
gotoxy(50,11) ;
printf ("City       : ................");
gotoxy(5,13) ;
printf ("Pin Number   : ......");
gotoxy(50,13) ;
printf ("Phone No. : .........");
gotoxy(5,15);
printf ("Age          : .........");
lineh(3,78,17,196);
gotoxy(20,9) ;
printf ("%s",t.c_name) ;

gotoxy(62,9) ;
printf ("%c",t.c_sex) ;

do
{
        valid = 1 ;
        statusbar(" ENTER ADDRESS OF THE CANDIDATE OR
                PRESS <enter> FOR NO CHANGE") ;
        _setcursortype(_SOLIDCURSOR) ;
        gotoxy(20,11) ;
        printf ("                   ");
        gotoxy(20,11) ;
        gets(address) ;

        if (address[0] == '0')
                return ;

        if (strlen(address) > 30)
        {
```

```
            valid = 0 ;
            statusbar("\a Enter correctly (Range: 1..30)") ;
            getch() ;
            _setcursortype(_SOLIDCURSOR) ;
        }

} while (!valid) ;

if (strlen(address) == 0)
{
        strcpy(address, t.c_address) ;
        gotoxy(20,11) ;
        printf ("%s",address) ;
}

do
{
        valid = 1 ;
        statusbar(" ENTER CITY OF THE CANDIDATE OR
                        PRESS <enter> FOR NO CHANGE") ;
        _setcursortype(_SOLIDCURSOR) ;
        gotoxy(62,11) ;
        clreol() ;
        gets(city) ;

        if (city[0] == '0')
                return ;

        if (strlen(city) > 18)
        {
                valid = 0 ;
                statusbar("\a Enter correctly (Length : 1..18)") ;
                getch() ;
                _setcursortype(_SOLIDCURSOR) ;
        }
} while (!valid) ;

if (strlen(city) == 0)
{
        strcpy(city, t.c_city) ;
```

```
        gotoxy(62,11);
        printf("%s",city);
}
do
{
        valid = 1 ;
        statusbar(" ENTER PIN CODE OR PRESS <enter> FOR
                        NO CHANGE") ;
        _setcursortype(_SOLIDCURSOR) ;
        gotoxy(20,13);
        printf ("             ");
        gotoxy(20,13);
        gets(pin);

        if (pin[0] == '0')
                return ;

        if (strlen(pin) != 6 && strlen(pin) > 1)
        {
                valid = 0 ;
                statusbar("\a Enter correctly (Length : 6)") ;
                getch() ;
                _setcursortype(_SOLIDCURSOR) ;
        }
} while (!valid);
if (strlen(pin) == 0)
{
        strcpy(pin, t.c_pin);
        gotoxy(20,13);
        printf ("%s",pin);
}

do
{
        valid = 1 ;
        statusbar(" ENTER PHONE NO. OF THE CANDIDATE OR
                        PRESS <enter> FOR NO CHANGE") ;
        _setcursortype(_SOLIDCURSOR) ;
        gotoxy(62,13);
        clreol();
```

```
        gets(phone) ;
        if (phone[0] == '0')
                return ;

        if ((strlen(phone) < 6 && strlen(phone) > 0) || (strlen(phone) > 7))
        {
                valid = 0 ;
                statusbar("\a Enter correctly") ;
                getch() ;
                _setcursortype(_SOLIDCURSOR) ;
        }
} while (!valid) ;

if (strlen(phone) == 0)
{
        strcpy(phone, t.c_phone) ;
        gotoxy(62,13) ;
        printf ("%s",phone);
}

do
{
        valid = 1 ;
        statusbar(" ENTER AGE  OF THE CANDIDATE OR PRESS
                                   <enter> FOR NO CHANGE") ;
        _setcursortype(_SOLIDCURSOR) ;
        gotoxy(20,15) ;
        clreol() ;
        scanf ("%d",&age);
        if (age == 0)
                return ;

        if (age < 18)
        {
                valid = 0 ;
                statusbar("\a Enter correctly (Range: >= 18)") ;
                getch() ;
                _setcursortype(_SOLIDCURSOR) ;
        }
} while (!valid) ;
```

```
strcpy(t.c_address, address) ;
strcpy(t.c_city, city) ;
strcpy(t.c_pin, pin) ;
strcpy(t.c_phone, phone) ;
t.c_code = code ;
t.c_age = age ;
file = fopen("candidate.Dat", "rb+") ;
file1 = fopen("Tempmod.Dat", "wb+") ;

while (fread(&te, sizeof(struct candidate),1,file)==1)
{
        if (t.c_code != te.c_code)
                fwrite(&te, sizeof(struct candidate),1,file1) ;
        else
                break ;
}
fwrite(&t, sizeof(struct candidate),1,file1) ;
while (fread(&te, sizeof(struct candidate),1,file)==1)
        fwrite(&te, sizeof(struct candidate),1,file1) ;
fclose(file) ;
fclose(file1) ;

file = fopen("candidate.Dat", "wb+") ;
file1 = fopen("Tempmod.Dat", "rb+") ;
while (fread(&t, sizeof(struct candidate),1,file1)==1)
{
        fwrite(&t, sizeof(struct candidate),1,file) ;
}
fclose(file) ;
fclose(file1) ;

gotoxy(5,25) ;
clreol() ;
do
{
        statusbar("\a Do you wish to save (y/n) ") ;
        ch = getch() ;
        ch = toupper(ch) ;
        if (ch == '0')
                return ;
```

```
        } while (ch != 'Y' && ch != 'N') ;

        if (ch == 'N')
                return ;
        statusbar(" Record Modified.") ;
        getch() ;
        statusbar("\a Modify any more (y/n) : ") ;

        do
        {
                choice = getch() ;
                choice = toupper(choice) ;
                if (choice == 13)
                        choice = 'Y' ;
                if (choice == 27)
                        choice = 'N' ;
        } while((choice != 'Y') && (choice !='N'));
    } while(choice == 'Y');
}
```

```
MODIFICATION OF CANDIDATE RECORD            <ESC>=EXIT
              CANDIDATE CODE.#     2
--------------------------------------------------------------
     Name                    : Ms. SUSMA SWARAJ
     Address                 : 10TH JANPATH

                               NEW DELHI - 110001

     Contact No.             : 6432001

     Age                     : 40

     Total Vote Gain         : 0
```

Do you wish to modify this record (y/n)

Figure 3.13 New candidate modification first screen.

MODIFICATION OF NEW CANDIDATE			Esc=EXIT
Candidate Code # 2			
Name	: SUSMA SWARAJ	Sex (F/M)	: F
Address	: 10TH JANPATH	City	: NEW DELHI
Pin code	: 110001........	Phone No.	: 6432001
Age	: 42		

Do you wish to save (y/n)

Figure 3.14 New candidate modification second screen.

```
//*****************************************************************
// FUNCTION : del
// DESCRIPTION : To Delete A Record In "candidate.Dat"
//*****************************************************************

void del1()
{
	struct candidate t ;
	FILE *file ;
	FILE *file1 ;
	char ch ;
	int code ;
	clrscr() ;
	gotoxy(72,2) ;
	printf ("<0>=EXIT");
	gotoxy(5,5) ;
	printf ("Enter code of the candidate : ");
	scanf ("%d",&code) ;
	if (code == 0)
		return ;
```

```
clrscr() ;
if (!fcode1(code))
{
        gotoxy(30,24) ;
        printf ("\a Record not found");
        getch() ;
        return ;
}

gotoxy(72,2) ;
printf ("<0>=EXIT");
gotoxy(23,1) ;
printf ("DELETION OF THE CANDIDATE RECORD");
display1(code) ;

do
{
        statusbar("\a Do you wish to remove this record (y/n) ") ;
        ch = getch() ;

        if (ch == 27)
                return ;

        if (ch == 13)
                ch = 'y' ;
        ch = toupper(ch) ;

        if (ch == '0')
                return ;
} while (ch != 'Y' && ch != 'N') ;
if (ch == 'N')
        return ;

file = fopen("candidate.Dat", "rb+") ;
file1 = fopen("Tempdel.Dat", "wb+") ;
while (fread(&t, sizeof(struct candidate),1,file)==1)
{
        if (t.c_code != code)
                fwrite(&t, sizeof(struct candidate),1,file1) ;
}
```

```
        fclose(file) ;
        fclose(file1) ;
        file = fopen("candidate.Dat", "wb+") ;
        file1 = fopen("Tempdel.Dat", "rb+") ;
        while (fread(&t, sizeof(struct candidate),1,file1)==1)
        {
                fwrite(&t, sizeof(struct candidate),1,file) ;
        }
        fclose(file) ;
        fclose(file1) ;

        clrscr() ;
        statusbar("\a Record Deleted") ;
        getch() ;
        statusbar("   Press any key to continue...") ;
        getch() ;
}

//**********************************************************************
// FUNCTION : displaycode1
// DESCRIPTION : To Obtain Code For Displaying A Record
//**********************************************************************

void displaycode1()
{
        int code ;
        clrscr() ;
        gotoxy(72,2) ;
        printf ("<0>=EXIT");
        gotoxy(5,5) ;
        _setcursortype(_SOLIDCURSOR) ;
        printf ("Enter code of the candidate : ");
        scanf ("%d", &code) ;

        if (code == 0)
                return ;

        clrscr() ;

        if (!fcode1(code))
```

```
    {
        _setcursortype(_NOCURSOR) ;
        gotoxy(30,25) ;
        printf ("\a Record not found");
        getch() ;
        return ;
    }

    display1(code) ;
    statusbar("   Press any key to continue...") ;
    getch() ;
}
```

```
DELETION OF THE CANDIDATE RECORD                <0>=EXIT
            CANDIDATE INFORMATION
            CANDIDATE CODE #     2
=====================================================
      Name               : Ms. SUSMA SWARAJ
      Address            : 10TH JANPATH

                           NEW DELHI - 110001

      Contact No.        : 6432001

      Age                : 40

      Total Vote Gain    : 0
Do you wish to remove this record (y/n)
```

Figure 3.15 Removing an existing candidate from list.

```
//**********************************************************************
// FUNCTION : showlist1
// DESCRIPTION : To Display The List Of candidates
//**********************************************************************

void showlist1()
{
        struct candidate t ;
        FILE *file ;
        int row = 6, found=0, flag=0 ;
        int d1, m1, y1 ;
        char ch ;
        struct date d;
        getdate(&d) ;
        d1 = d.da_day ;
        m1 = d.da_mon ;
        y1 = d.da_year ;
        clrscr() ;
        gotoxy(23,2) ;
        printf ("LIST OF CANDIDATES AS ON %d . %d .%d",d1,m1,y1) ;
        lineh(1,80,3,240);
        gotoxy(12,4) ;
        printf ("CODE #           NAME                AGE");
        gotoxy(1,5) ;
        lineh(11,72,5,205) ;
        linev(4,22,10,186) ;
        linev(4,22,19,186) ;
        linev(4,22,51,186) ;
        linev(4,22,72,186) ;
        lineh(1,80,23,240) ;

        file = fopen("candidate.dat", "rb+") ;
        while (fread(&t, sizeof(struct candidate),1,file)==1)
        {
                flag = 0 ;
                found = 1 ;
                gotoxy(12,row) ;
                printf ("%d",t.c_code) ;
                gotoxy(21,row) ;
                printf ("%s",t.c_name) ;
```

```
        gotoxy(53,row) ;
        printf ("%d",t.c_age) ;

        if (row == 18)
        {
                flag = 1 ;
                row = 6 ;
                statusbar(" Press any key to continue or Press <ESC> to exit") ;
                ch = getch() ;

                if (ch == 27)
                        break ;

                clrscr() ;
                gotoxy(31,2) ;
                printf ("LIST OF CANDIDATES");
                lineh(1,90,3,240);
                gotoxy(2,4) ;
                printf ("CODE #          NAME                    AGE");
                gotoxy(1,5) ;
                printf ("~~~~~~~~~~~~~~~~~~~~~~~~~~~~~~~~~~~~~~~~~~~~~~~~~~~~~~~~~~~~~~~~~~~~~~~~~~~~~~~~");
        }
        else
                row++ ;
    }

    if (!found)
    {
        gotoxy(26,14) ;
        printf ("\a Rccords not found");
    }

    if (!flag)
    {
        statusbar("   Press any key to continue...") ;
        getch() ;
    }

    fclose (file) ;
}
```

```
LIST OF CANDIDATES AS ON 4 . 7 . 2000
=====================================================================
 ||  Code #   ||  Name                    ||  Age  ||
 ||=====================================================
 ||           ||                          ||       ||
 ||  1        ||  L.K.ADVANI              ||  45   ||
 ||  2        ||  SUSMA SWARAJ            ||  40   ||
=====================================================================
Press any key to continue....
```

Figure 3.16 Listing all the candidates.

```
//**********************************************************************
// Main Menu
//**********************************************************************

void cmain(void)
{
        main_menu1();
}
```

Source Listing of VOTING3.C

```
#include <conio.h>
#include <string.h>
#include <stdio.h>
#include <dos.h>
#include <dir.h>
#include <stdlib.h>
#include <graphics.h>
//****************************************************************
// All The Fields Related To Voter
//****************************************************************

int fcode (int) ;

//****************************************************************
// All The Functions Related To voter
//****************************************************************

void showlistf(); // Displaying list of candidates and voters
void final();       // Preparing final list for winner
void vote () ;      // Casting vote or checking for vote
void showlist1 () ;
void showlist () ;
void fmain(void);          //To starting voting main menu

// Displaying voting main menu
void vote_menu()
{
        int end=5, present=1, upperlim1=3, currentpos1=1, upperlim2=2, currentpos2=1,
                        upperlim3=3, currentpos3=1;
        char main[] [20] = { " LIST ", " VOTE ", " PRINT ", " HELP ", " EXIT " } ;
        char sub1[] [20] = { "List of Candidate", "Winner ", "Return      " } ;
        char sub2[] [20] = { "Modify voter   ", "Return         " } ;
        char sub3[] [20] = { "After vote ","Winner", "Return       " } ;
        do
        {
                _setcursortype(_NOCURSOR) ;
                present = horizontal_menu(main, present, end, 3, 1) ;
```

```
switch (present)
{
        case 1 :
                currentpos1 = vertical_menu(sub1, currentpos1, upperlim1, 3, 3);

                switch (currentpos1)
                {
                        case 1 :
                                _setcursortype(_SOLIDCURSOR) ;
                                showlistf() ;
                                _setcursortype(_NOCURSOR) ;
                                break ;
                        case 2 :
                                _setcursortype(_SOLIDCURSOR) ;
                                final() ;
                                break ;
                }
                clrscr() ;
                break ;
        case 2 :
                currentpos2 = vertical_menu(sub2, currentpos2, upperlim2, 13, 3);

                switch (currentpos2)
                {
                        case 1 :
                                _setcursortype(_SOLIDCURSOR) ;
                                vote() ;
                                _setcursortype(_NOCURSOR) ;
                                break ;
                }
                clrscr() ;
                break ;
        case 3 :
                currentpos3 = vertical_menu(sub3, currentpos3, upperlim3, 27, 3);

                switch (currentpos3)
                {
                        case 1 :
                                _setcursortype(_SOLIDCURSOR) ;
                                showlistf() ;
```

```
                    print(1,1,80,23);
                    _setcursortype(_NOCURSOR) ;
                    break ;
            case 2 :
                    _setcursortype(_NORMALCURSOR) ;
                    final();
                    print(1,1,80,23);
                    _setcursortype(_NOCURSOR) ;
                    break ;
            }
            clrscr() ;
            break ;
        case 4 : help() ;
            clrscr() ;
            break ;
      }
   } while (present != end);
}
```

FILE	EDIT	PRINT	HELP	EXIT

List of Candidate
Winner
Return

Figure 3.17 Operational menu of VOTING.

```
//****************************************************************
// FUNCTION : vote
// DESCRIPTION : To Check whether or not the voter casted the vote
//          and increment the total votes for the casted candidate
//****************************************************************

void vote()
{
    FILE *file ;
    FILE * file2;
```

```
//
FILE *file3;
struct voter t ;
struct voter te ;
struct candidate c;
struct candidate ce;
FILE *file1 ;
int  code, valid, code1 ;
char  ch, house='N', conv='N', choice='Y' ;
char address[31], city[21], pin[7], phone[10], desig[21] ;
int age;
clrscr() ;
gotoxy(72,2) ;
printf ("Esc=EXIT");
gotoxy(5,5) ;
printf ("Enter code of the voter : ");
scanf ("%d",&code) ;

if (code == 0)
        return ;
clrscr() ;

if (!fcode(code))
{
        gotoxy(30,24) ;
        printf ("\a Record not found");
        getch() ;
        return ;
}

file = fopen("voter.Dat", "rb+") ;
while(fread(&t,sizeof(struct voter),1,file)==1)
{
        if (t.v_code == code)
        {
                if (t.v_done == 'Y')
                {
                        printf (" Already casted the vote");
                        getch();
                        return;
                }
```

```
        }
    }

    fclose(file);

    gotoxy(72,2) ;
    printf ("<0>=EXIT");
    gotoxy(24,2) ;
    printf ("VOTING IS GOING ON");
    gotoxy (5,4);
    printf (" Candidate No     :.......");
    scanf ("%d",&code1);

    if (!fcode1(code1))
    {
        gotoxy(30,24) ;
        printf ("\a Record not found");
        getch() ;
        return ;
    }

    file = fopen("voter.Dat", "rb+") ;
    while (fread(&t, sizeof(struct voter),1,file)==1)
    {
        if (t.v_code == code)
        {
            t.v_done = 'Y';
            strcpy(t.v_name, t.v_name);
            strcpy(t.v_name,t.v_name);
            strcpy(t.v_address,t.v_address);
            strcpy(t.v_city,t.v_city);
            strcpy(t.v_pin,t.v_pin);
            strcpy(t.v_phone,t.v_phone);
            t.v_sex = t.v_sex;
            t.v_age = t.v_age;
            break ;
        }
    }

    file2 = fopen("candidate.Dat", "rb+") ;
```

```
while (fread(&c, sizeof(struct candidate),1,file2)==1)
{
        if (c.c_code == code1)
        {
                c.total++;
                break ;
        }
}

lineh(3,78,17,196);

file = fopen("voter.Dat", "rb+") ;
file1 = fopen("Tempmod.Dat", "wb+") ;
while (fread(&te, sizeof(struct voter),1,file)==1)
{
        if (t.v_code != te.v_code)
                fwrite(&te, sizeof(struct voter),1,file1) ;
        else
                break ;
}

fwrite(&t, sizeof(struct voter),1,file1) ;
while (fread(&te, sizeof(struct voter),1,file)==1)
        fwrite(&te, sizeof(struct voter),1,file1) ;

fclose(file) ;
fclose(file1) ;

file = fopen("voter.Dat", "wb+") ;
file1 = fopen("Tempmod.Dat", "rb+") ;
while (fread(&t, sizeof(struct voter),1,file1)==1)
{
        fwrite(&t, sizeof(struct voter),1,file) ;
}

fclose(file) ;
fclose(file1) ;

file= fopen("Candidate.Dat", "rb+") ;
file1 = fopen("Tempmod1.Dat", "wb+") ;
```

```
while (fread(&ce, sizeof(struct candidate),1,file)==1)
{
        if (c.c_code != ce.c_code)
                fwrite(&ce, sizeof(struct candidate),1,file1);
        else
                break ;
}

fwrite(&c, sizeof(struct candidate),1,file1);
while (fread(&ce, sizeof(struct candidate),1,file)==1)
        fwrite(&ce, sizeof(struct candidate),1,file1);

fclose(file);
fclose(file1);

file = fopen("candidate.Dat", "wb+");
file1 = fopen("Tempmod1.Dat", "rb+");
while (fread(&c, sizeof(struct candidate),1,file1)==1)
{
        fwrite(&c, sizeof(struct candidate),1,file);
}

fclose(file);
fclose(file1);

gotoxy(5,25);
clreol();

do
{
        statusbar("\a Do you wish to save (y/n) ");
        ch = getch();
        ch = toupper(ch);
        if (ch == '0')
                return;
} while (ch != 'Y' && ch != 'N');

if (ch == 'N')
        return;
```

```
        statusbar(" Record Modified.") ;
        getch() ;
}
```

```
                    VOTING IS GOING ON                    <0>=EXIT
--------------------------------------------------------------------

Voter No.            : ...........8

Candidate No         :.........1

Do you wish to save (y/n)
```

Figure 3.18 Voting with voters and candidates.

```
//*******************************************************************
// FUNCTION : showlistf
// DESCRIPTION : To Display The List Of voters together with the total votes
//*******************************************************************

void showlistf()
{
        struct candidate t ;
        FILE *file ;
        int row = 6, found=0, flag=0 ;
        int d1, m1, y1 ;
        char ch ;
        struct date d;
        getdate(&d) ;
        d1 = d.da_day ;
        m1 = d.da_mon ;
        y1 = d.da_year ;
        clrscr() ;
        gotoxy(23,2) ;
        printf ("LIST OF CANDIDATES AS ON %d . %d .%d",d1,m1,y1) ;
```

```
lineh(1,80,3,240) ;
gotoxy(12,4) ;
printf ("CODE #           NAME              TOTAL");
gotoxy(1,5) ;
lineh(11,72,5,205) ;
linev(4,22,10,186) ;
linev(4,22,19,186) ;
linev(4,22,51,186) ;
linev(4,22,72,186) ;
lineh(1,80,23,240) ;

file = fopen("candidate.dat", "rb+") ;
while (fread(&t, sizeof(struct candidate),1,file)==1)
{
        flag = 0 ;
        found = 1 ;
        gotoxy(12,row) ;
        printf ("%d",t.c_code) ;
        gotoxy(21,row) ;
        printf ("%s",t.c_name) ;
        gotoxy(53,row) ;
        printf ("%d",t.total) ;
        if (row == 18)
        {
                flag = 1 ;
                row = 6 ;
                statusbar(" Press any key to continue or Press <ESC> to exit") ;
                ch = getch() ;
                if (ch == 27)
                        break ;
                clrscr() ;
                gotoxy(31,2) ;
                printf ("LIST OF voterS");
                lineh(1,90,3,240);
                gotoxy(2,4) ;
                printf ("CODE #          NAME              TOTAL");
                gotoxy(1,5) ;
                printf ("~~~~~~~~~~~~~~~~~~~~~~~~~~~~~~~~~~~~~~~~~~~~~~~~~~~~~~~~~~~~~~~~~~~~~");
        }
        else
```

```
                row++ ;
        }
        if (!found)
        {
                gotoxy(26,14) ;
                printf ("\a Records not found");
        }

        if (!flag)
        {
                statusbar("   Press any key to continue...") ;
                getch() ;
        }

        fclose (file) ;
}
```

LIST OF CANDIDATES AS ON 4 . 7 . 2000

Code #	Name	Total
1	L. K. ADVANI	3
2	SUSMA SWARAJ	1

Press any key to continue....

Figure 3.19 Listing all the candidates with their status.

```
//*************************************************************
// FUNCTION    : final
// DESCRIPTION : To Display The Winner the election
//*************************************************************
void final()
{
        FILE *file;
        struct candidate t;
        int max = 0;
        int code;
        char name[31];
        clrscr();
        file = fopen("candidate.dat", "rb+");
        fread(&t, sizeof(struct candidate),1,file);
        max = t.total;
        code = t.c_code;
        strcpy(name,t.c_name);
        printf ("%d",max);
        getch();

        while (fread(&t, sizeof(struct candidate),1,file)==1)
        {
                if (t.total > max)
                {
                        max = t.total;
                        code = t.c_code;
                        strcpy(name,t.c_name);
                }
        }

        lineh(1,80,3,240);
        gotoxy(22,5);
        printf ("WINNER    IS ");
        gotoxy(22,7);
        printf (" CODE : %d .....",code);
        gotoxy(22,9);
        printf (" NAME   : %s .....",name);
        gotoxy(22,11);
        printf (" WIN BY:   %d ",max);
        printf ("VOTES");
```

```
        lineh(1,80,12,240) ;
        getch();
        fclose(file);
}
```

```
WINNER IS

CODE :    1......

NAME :    L.K.ADVANI....

W IN BY :   3VOTES
```

Figure 3.20 Winner of the Electronic Voting System.

```
//**********************************************************************
// Main Menu
//**********************************************************************

void fmain(void)
{
        vote_menu() ;
}
```

Banking System

4

The United Bank decides to computerized its facilities in their bank to implement customer records and their daily transaction records. The bank keeps certain information as follow:

INITIAL.dat:

acc_no	: Account number
name	: Name of the Accountee
address	: Address of the accountee
balance	: Initial balance of the account

When any customer will open an account, the bank will keep the above fields in their INITIAL.dat file as master account holder.

BANKING.dat:

acc_no	: Account number
type	: Transaction type by Cash/Cheque
dd,mm,yy	: Date of transaction
tran	: Transaction for Deposit or Withdraw
interest	: Interest rate
amount	: Transaction amount
balance	: Current balance after transaction

While inputting the data record the following validation will be checked:

- the account numbers are generated automatically
- the name, address should not blank
- transaction date is the system date/current date

- initial deposit for any account should not be less than Rs. 500/-
- daily transaction will be entered either in words Cash/Cheque or 'D' for deposit and 'W' for withdrawal

Write a menu driven program for making a daily transaction process for the displaying the following menu options.

1. Open New Account
2. List of Accounts
3. See Individual Account
4. Daily Transaction
5. Monthly Report
6. Edit Account

In the edit account menu the following processing will occur:

1. Modify Account
2. Close Account
0. Quit

The following will be the report format:

Report-1:

Accounts List in Bank

Date:10/10/1998

Accno#	Name	Address	Balance
1	Mr. Sangram	12, E-Block, Rohini	5600
2	Mr. Vikas	234, Vinus Appts. Rohini	12000
_	_____	_____	_____
_	_____	_____	_____

Total Balance in Bank is: _____

Report-2:

Account No. 1 Mr. Sangram Date:11/10/1998
12, E-Block, Rohini

Global Report of Account

Date	Particular	Deposit	Withdraw	Balance
1-10-1998	INITIAL	2000		2000
2-10-1998	CASH	3000		5000
8-10-1998	CHEQUE	4000		9000
9-10-1998	CASH	3400	5600	
Total->:		9000	5600	3400

Report-3:

Account No. 1 Mr. Sangram Date:11/10/1998
12, E-Block, Rohini

Statement Month: 10/01/1999

Date	Particular	Deposit	Withdraw	Balance
1-10-1998	INITIAL	2000		2000
2-10-1998	CASH	3000		5000
8-10-1998	CHEQUE	4000		9000
9-10-1998	CASH	3400	5600	
Total->:		9000	5600	3400

Using C structure concepts and having number of different develop this project user defined function (UDFs) as follows:

line_hor(.....)

This function passes four parameters including three integers and one character to draw different lines to design the screen beautifully. The character parameter draws the ASCII character line-by-line on screen. So, to draw horizontal lines this function is useful.

line_ver(.....)

The DRAW_VER(.....) function is helpful for drawing vertical lines on screen to design either menu or program forms for data entry, modify, display, delete etc..

box(.....)

This function creates different size of boxes on the screen according to the respective parameters. Out of all the parameters they draw boxes till the limit you want.

main_menu(.....)

This is the main screening menu, which will display your six different prompts having different activities. Each prompt is connected with different functions to perform its respective purposes. Out of all the options the last one produces another sub-menu for modifying and deleting existing account information.

While handling the main menu you can press any selective number to perform the operation or press 0 (zero) to exit from the main menu. But it is also helpful in almost all menus that, you can press 0 (zero) to exit from the respective menu.

edit_menu(.....)

This is one of the sub function which is connected from the main_menu() function to perform the modification and deletion operation on banking account data from INITIAL.dat and BANKING.dat data file.

The menus alway perform the operation according to the account number (accno) except the "Open New Account" of main_menu() function because, the "Open New Account" form automatically creates the account number after a brief search to the existing account numbers. Basically, the numbers are generating automatically, like 1, 2, 3 ... respectively.

add_to_file(...)

The function add_to_file is used to append new account details into the INITIAL.dat file. This function receives all the fields as parameter way from the new_account() function and adds it in the data file.

display_list()

This function is used to display all the account data on the screen. Which displays the accountno#, name, address and their respective balance amount in bank. It also shows the total bank balance on the screen. All the records are extracted from INITIAL.dat data file.

delete_account()

This function is used for deleting the account details from INITIAL.dat data file. This is a copy method, which transfers all the records except deleted accno#. And on the same way the records are reversed from the TEMP.dat file to the original data file INITIAL.dat.

update_balance()

When any fresh transactions take place in any existing account either deposit (D) or withdrawal (W), then the respective balance has to be updated in the INITIAL.dat data file. When the transactions are complete the balance amount is overwritten in the data file. This technique occurs by locating the position in the data file only.

modify()

When there is any modification that occurs to the accounts name and address or to the balance amount, then simultaneously it becomes modified in the INITIAL.dat data file through the modify_account() function. This process highly depends on the key field account number.

last_accno()

When a new record has to append into the data file, it has to create an automatic accno#. This process happens when we know the last account number. To know the last account number we use the last_accno() function. After finding the last account number, it returns the last account value into the new_account() function for generating next account number.

found_account()

To do any operation: either for modification, deletion, report(s) or updation, every time the found_account() function first checks the account, which is entered by the user whether it is in the INITIAL.dat data file or not. If it is there then a true value is returned else a false value is returned. Then depending on the value, further processes can occur.

*return_name()

When any reports are occurred, on top of the report the account name is displayed. This function returns the name of the account holder and displays it in appropriate report.

*return_address()

When any reports are occurred, on top of the report the account address is displayed. This function returns the address of the account holder and displays it in appropriate report.

give_balance()

While daily transactions are occurred, the last balance is always required to update the INITIAL.dat data file. So, to know the last balance at the time of daily transactions the give_balance function returns the value to the transaction() function.

recordno()

Either for new_account, update account, or modify account, or modify balance the recordno() function finds the record position of existing account number in the data files, where the transacted record can be overwritten.

display()

The function is used to display the account details from either INITIAL.dat or BANKING.dat data file. While the modify() function activates, the accno parameter searches this account details from the respective file to display on the screen before modifing.

modify_account()

This function is used to modify the existing accounts name and address at the existing location. To modify the account it first searches the accounts location and it is overwritten at the same location using seekg() function.

new_account()

This function is used to create a new account of a customer after entering all the details of the same. In that screen the automatic account number is created and a proper validation are entered into name, address, and initial deposit. After entering all the informations related to the customer, the records are appended in the INITIAL.dat and BANKING.dat data file by using a function add_to_file of both structure initial and account.

close_account()

In the same way like delete_account() function, the close_account() function also closes all the transaction records in BANKING.dat data file. After closing the account there is no transaction record in the data files.

display_account()

This function is used to display all the transactions including the initial deposit in the screen. This is a global report to display all the transaction records in the screen. It shows all the deposits and withdrawal column and datewise balance also.

transaction()

The transaction() function provides a screen for making daily transactions. While transacting it shows the balance amount, and then either a transaction for deposit(D) or withdrawal(W) either by CASH or by CHEQUE.

Then the transacted record is updated in the INITIAL.dat and BANKING.dat data file. Also the same functions use two important functions update_balance() and add_to_file to update balance in INITIAL.dat data file and the transacted record in BANKING.dat data file.

clear()

This function is used to clear the screen from a specified row and column position.

month_report()

Like any other banking transaction, when a customer wants his monthly report statement this function helps to generate the report on the screen. When you enter a date in account number, it searches all the transactions of the previous month of the date entered and extracts a previous balance (B/F...) and then it displays the transactions for the relevant month. And finally it displays the current balance.

add_to_file()

This function is used to append new record into the BANKING.dat data file. While the function activates, it passes all the fields as parameter into the function and appends as a fresh record into the file.

delete_account()

This function is used to delete the account from the BANKING.dat data file. This is a copy method to delete the account from file.

no_of_days()

This function is used to find total number of years, months and days.

box_for_display()

This function is used to display the heading of the report as:

Date Particulars Deposit Withdrawal Balance

Program Source Codes BANK.C

```
// Declaration of header files

#include <stdio.h>
#include <process.h>
#include <string.h>
#include <stdio.h>
#include <ctype.h>
#include <conio.h>
#include <dos.h>
#include <stdlib.h>
#include <graphics.h>

typedef char option[15];
const int ROW = 10, COL = 10;

int scan;        // To hold the special characters for moving the prompt in menu
int ascii;

// To display the main menu options
option a[] = {
                "NewAccount",
                "ListofAccounts",
                "IndAccount",
                "DailyTrans",
                "MonthlyReport",
                "EditAccount",
                "Exit"};

// Displays the modify menu options
option b[] = {
                    "Modify Account",
                    "Closeaccount",
                    "Quit"
             };
```

```
// Function used to do screening
int i, done;

void normalvideo(int x, int y, char *str);
void reversevideo(int x, int y, char *str);
void box1(int x1, int y1, int x2, int y2);

char menu();

// Menu for displaying all the option of the banking system
void control_menu();
char e_menu();
void edit_menu();
void help(void);

/* Member functions for drawing boxes */
void line_hor(int, int, int, char);
void line_ver(int, int, int, char);
void box(int, int, int, int, char);

// Functions contains the initial deposit of customers
void add_to_ini(int, char t_name[30], char t_address[30], float);
void display_ini(void); // Displaying customers account list
void delete_ini(int); // Deleting customers account

// For updating the customer account
void update_ini(int, char t_name[30], char t_address[30], float);
void modify_ini(void);    // To modify the customer account information
int last_accno_ini(void); // To know the last account number

int found_account_ini(int); // To found the account is in "INITIAL.dat" or not
char *return_name_ini(int); // Function for validation entry of customer name
char *return_address_ini(int); // Function for validation entry of customer address
float give_balance_ini(int); // To print the balance amount of a particular customer

// Function to modify the customer account
void modify_account_ini(int, char t_name[30], char t_address[30]);
int recordno_ini(int);
void display_in(int); // To display the customer account
```

```
/* Record Structure for initial account information of customer's when opening a new account */

struct initial
{
        int accno;
        char name[30], address[30];
        float balance;
}ini;

// Fucntions contains the customers daily transaction entry
void new_account(void);  // Function to create a new account
void close_account(void);          // Function to close an account
void display_account(void); // Function to display the accounts
void transaction(void); // To display the transaction process
void clear(int, int); // Function to perform a clear screen function
void month_report(void); // Function to list monthWise transaction report

// Function to add transaction records
void add_to_file(int, int, int, int, char, char t_type[10], float, float, float);
void delete_account(int); // Function to delete a transaction record
int no_of_days(int, int, int, int, int, int); // Function to find the total days
float calculate_interest(int, float); // Function for calculating interest of an account
//void display(int); // Function to display a transaction account
void box_for_display(int); // Function for displaying box

/* Account information of customer's when it was created */

struct account
{
        int accno;
        char type[10];   // Account type as Cheque or Cash
        int dd, mm, yy; // To store the system date/ Enter date
        char tran;                          // As the account type is Deposit or Withdraw
        float interest, amount, balance;
} acc;

// Function to displays all the menu prompt messages from the pointer array of option a[]
void normalvideo(int x, int y, char *str)
{
  gotoxy(x, y);
```

```
    cprintf("%s", str);
}

// Function to move the cursor on the menu prompt with a reverse video color
void reversevideo(int x, int y, char *str)
{
        textcolor(5+143);
        textbackground(WHITE);
        gotoxy(x,y);
        cprintf("%s", str);
        textcolor(GREEN);
        textbackground(BLACK);
}

void box1(int x1, int y1, int x2, int y2)
{
        int col, row;
        for( col = x1; col < x2; col++)
        {
                gotoxy(col, y1);
                cprintf("%c", 196);
                gotoxy(col, y2);
                cprintf("%c", 196);
        }
        for(row = y1; row < y2; row++)
        {
                gotoxy(x1, row);
                cprintf("%c", 179);
                gotoxy(x2, row);
                cprintf("%c", 179);
        }
        gotoxy(x1, y1);
        cprintf("%c", 218);
        gotoxy(x1, y2);
        cprintf("%c", 192);
        gotoxy(x2, y1);
        cprintf("%c", 191);
        gotoxy(x2, y2);
        cprintf("%c", 217);

}
```

```
char menu()
{
        clrscr();
        textcolor(22);
        box1(20, 6, 65, 20);
        box1(18, 4, 67, 22);
        textcolor(5+143);
        gotoxy(36, 5);
        textbackground(BLUE);
        cprintf("B A N K I N G");
        textbackground(BLACK);
        textcolor(22);
        for(i = 1; i < 7; i++)
        normalvideo(32, i+10, a[i]);
        reversevideo(32, 10, a[0]);
        i = done = 0;
        _setcursortype(_NOCURSOR);
        do
        {
                int key = getch();
                switch (key)
                {
                        case 00:
                                key = getch();
                                switch (key)
                                {
                                        case 72:
                                                normalvideo(32, i+10, a[i]);
                                                i--;
                                                if (i == -1)
                                                        i = 6;
                                                reversevideo(32, i+10, a[i]);
                                                break;
                                        case 80:
                                                normalvideo(32, i+10, a[i]);
                                                i++;
                                                if (i == 7)
                                                        i = 0;
                                                reversevideo(32, i+10, a[i]);
                                                break;
```

```
                    }
                    break;
            case 13:
                    done = 1;
        }
    }
    while (!done);

    _setcursortype(_NOCURSOR);
    return(i+49);
}
```

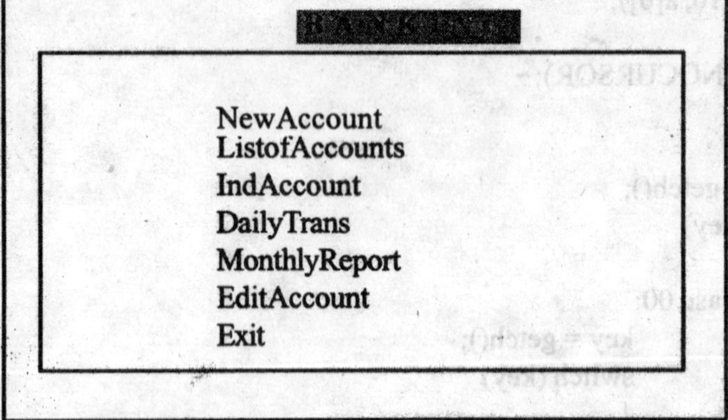

Figure 4.1 Output screen of the function menu().

/* The function control_menu() is used to display the main menu of banking system. This function uses 6 main options and each has its specific purposes for maintaining the account. In this menu, the user can avail the facilities by pressing any number from 1 to 6 and in case he presses any other key the prompt will come back from menu to the source program. Or it is better to press '0' to exit from the menu. Other than 0 and 1..6 if you press any other key the banking system do not response till you press a valid number. */

```
void control_menu()
{
        char choice;
        do
        {
                choice = menu();
                clrscr();
                switch (choice)
                {
                        case '1':
                                _setcursortype(_NORMALCURSOR);
                                box1(3, 1, 75, 24);
                                box1(5, 2, 73, 23);
                                new_account(); // New account member function
                                break;
                        case '2':
                                box1(3, 1, 75, 24);
                                box1(5, 2, 73, 23);
                                display_ini(); // Glogal list of account function
                                break;
                        case '3':
                                box1(3, 1, 75, 24);
                                box1(5, 2, 73, 23);
                                _setcursortype(_NORMALCURSOR);
                                // Displaying individual accounts all transactions
                                display_account();
                                break;
                        case '4':
                                box1(3, 1, 75, 24);
                                box1(5, 2, 73, 23);
                                _setcursortype(_NORMALCURSOR);
                                transaction(); // Daily transaction for individual account
                                break;
```

```
                case '5':
                        box1(3, 1, 75, 24);
                        box1(5, 2, 73, 23);
                        _setcursortype(_NORMALCURSOR);
                        month_report(); // Monthly report for any account
                        break;
                case '6':
                        box1(3, 1, 75, 24);
                        box1(5, 2, 73, 23);
                        gotoxy(10, 10);
                        edit_menu(); // Sub menu for modifying or deleting any account
                        break;
                case '7' :exit(0);
                }
        } while (choice != 6);
}
```

/* This function is used to return the cursor position to the edit menu function where the menu prompt will valid */

```
char e_menu()
{
        clrscr();

        textcolor(22);
        box1(25,6,60,15);
        box1(23,4,62,17);
        textcolor(5+143);

        gotoxy(34,5);
        textbackground(GREEN);
        cprintf("E D I T - M E N U");
        textcolor(22);
        textbackground(BLACK);
        for (i = 1;i < 3; i++)
                normalvideo(32, i+10, b[i]);

        reversevideo(32, 10, b[0]);
        i = done = 0;

        _setcursortype(_NOCURSOR);
```

```
do
{
        int key = getch();
        switch (key)
        {
                case 00:
                        key = getch();
                        switch (key)
                        {
                                case 72:
                                        normalvideo(32, i+10, b[i]);
                                        i--;
                                        if (i == -1)
                                                i = 2;
                                        reversevideo(32, i+10, b[i]);
                                        break;
                                case 80:
                                        normalvideo(32, i+10, b[i]);
                                        i++;
                                        if (i == 3)
                                                i=0;
                                        reversevideo(32, i+10, b[i]);
                                        break;
                        }
                        break;
                case 13:
                        done = 1;
        }
}
while (!done);
_setcursortype(_NOCURSOR);
return(i+49);
}
```

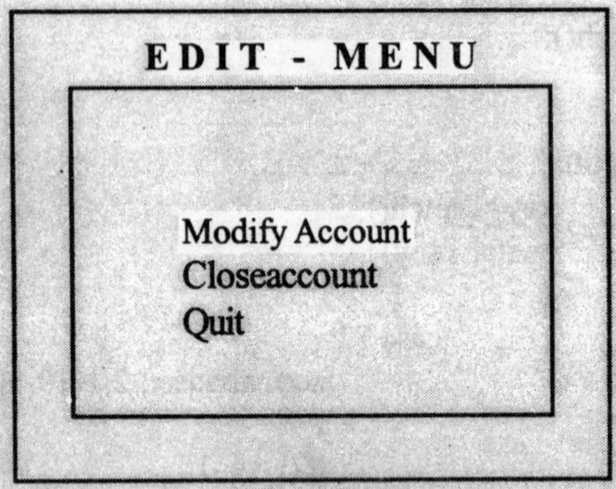

Figure 4.2 Output screen of the function e_menu().

/* Function for edit menu with account modification and close. This is the one of the submenu, which manages two basic operations such as:

- Editing any account
- Deleting any account

While editing any account, you have to enter the account number and it will display the name and address of that particular account and will display a prompt as "Modify this account <y/n> :". If you will press 'y' then the respective information will be modified otherwise it will return to main menu. While deleting any account, you have to enter the account number and will display the name and address of that account holder and will display a prompt as "Close this account? ". If you will press 'y' then all the transactions from "BANKING.dat" file and initial deposit from "INITIAL.dat" file will delete the information of the entered account number. */

```
/* Function for edit menu with account modification and close */
void edit_menu()
{
	char choice;

	do
	{
		choice = e_menu();
		clrscr();
		switch (choice)
```

```
        {
            case '1':
                box1(3, 1, 75, 24);
                box1(5, 2, 73, 23);
                _setcursortype(_NORMALCURSOR);
                modify_ini();
                break;

            case '2':
                box1(3, 1, 75, 24);
                box1(5, 2, 73, 23);
                _setcursortype(_NORMALCURSOR);
                close_account();
                break;

            case '3':
                return;
        }
    } while (choice != 6);
}

/* Function to draw horizontal line */
void line_hor(int column1, int column2, int row, char c)
{
    for (column1; column1 <= column2; column1++)
    {
        gotoxy(column1, row);
        printf("%c", c);
    }
}

/* Function to draw vertical line */
void line_ver(int row1, int row2, int column, char c)
{
    for (row1; row1 <= row2; row1++)
    {
        gotoxy(column, row1);
        printf("%c", c);
    }
}
```

```
/* Function for drawing box */
void box(int column1, int row1, int column2, int row2, char c)
{
        char ch = 218;
        char c1, c2, c3, c4;
        char l1 = 196, l2 = 179;
        if (c == ch)
        {
                c1 = 218;
                c2 = 191;
                c3 = 217;
                c4 = 217;
                l1 = 196;
                l2 = 179;
        }
        else
        {
                c1 = c;
                c2 = c;
                c3 = c;
                c4 = c;
                l1 = c;
                c2 = c;
        }
        gotoxy(column1, row1);
        printf ("%c", c1);
        gotoxy(column2, row1);
        printf ("%c", c2);
        gotoxy(column1, row2);
        printf ("%c", c3);
        gotoxy(column2, row2);
        printf ("%c", c4);
        column1++;
        column2—;
        line_hor(column1, column2, row1, l1); //Horizontal line
        line_hor(column1, column2, row2, l1);
        column1—;
        column2++;
        row1++;
        row2—;
```

```
        line_ver(row1, row2, column1, 12); // Vertical line
        line_ver(row1, row2, column2, 12);
}
/* Function to display help about this project */
void help(void)
{
        clrscr();

        setbkcolor(7);
        settextstyle(7, HORIZ_DIR, 5);
        outtextxy(70, 20, "Welcome to Banking Project");
        settextstyle(2, HORIZ_DIR, 5);
        outtextxy(60, 100, "This project your can keep record of daily banking transaction");
        delay(2);
        outtextxy(60, 130, "This program is capable of holding any no. of account.");
        delay(2);
        outtextxy(60, 160, "-In first option you can open new account");
        delay(2);
        outtextxy(60, 190, "-In second option you can see the list of all the accounts");
        delay(2);
        outtextxy(60, 220,"-In third option you can see all the transaction of individual account");
        delay(2);
        outtextxy(60, 250, "-Through fourth optiion you can do banking transactions");
        delay(2);
        outtextxy(60, 280, "(Deposit/Withdraw)");
        delay(2);
        outtextxy(60, 310, "-In fifth option you can take monthWise individual account report");
        delay(2);
        outtextxy(60, 340,"-In sixth option you can modify or delete any account");
        delay(2);
        outtextxy(60, 370, "Note-: Opening amount should not less that Rs. 500/-");
        delay(2);
        outtextxy(60, 400, "-And last option is Quit (Exit to Window)");
        delay(2);

        settextstyle(7, HORIZ_DIR, 4);
        outtextxy(80, 420, "Press any key to continue...");
        getch();
}
```

```
/* Function for modifying the existing accounts. The modify() function is used to modify an existing
account for its address part only. While modifying, a prompt is always displayed such as "Do you
want to save change <y/n>" means if you will press 'y' then the current memory information will
change with existing information otherwise the previous information remains intact in your data file.
While entering the name and address there is a proper validation and a blank check facility is there,
to prevent mistake and mishandling of data etc.. */

/* Function for modifying the existing accounts */
void modify_ini(void)
{

	int j;
	char t_acc[10];
	int t, t_accno;
	int d1, m1, y1;
	struct date d;		// For extracting system date
	int modified = 0, valid;
	char t_name[30], t_address[30];
	char ch;

	clrscr();
	gotoxy(17, 1);
	printf("<0>=Exit");
	gotoxy(5,5);
	printf("Enter the account no. ");
	gets(t_acc);
	t = atoi(t_acc);
	t_accno = t;
	if (t_accno == 0)
		return;
	clrscr();
	if (!found_account_ini(t_accno))
	{
		gotoxy(5, 5);
		printf("\7Account not found");
		getch();
		return;
	}
	gotoxy(71, 1);
	printf("<0>=Exit");
```

```
 textbackground(WHITE);
 gotoxy(3, 3);
 for (j = 1; j<= 76; j++)
         cprintf(" ");
 textbackground(BLACK);
 textcolor(BLACK+BLINK);
 textbackground(WHITE);
 gotoxy(30, 3);
 cprintf("Modify Account Screen");
 textcolor(LIGHTGRAY);
 textbackground(BLACK);

 getdate(&d);
 d1 = d.da_day;
 m1 = d.da_mon;
 y1 = d.da_year;
 gotoxy(4, 2);
 printf ( "Date: " );
 printf("%d",d1);
 printf ("/");
 printf("%d",m1);
 printf("/");
 printf("%d",y1);

 display_in(t_accno);
 do
 {
         clear(5, 13);
         gotoxy(5, 13);
         printf ("Modify this account <y/n>: ");
         ch = getche();
         if (ch == '0')
                 return;
         ch = toupper(ch);
 }while (ch != 'N' && ch != 'Y');
 if (ch == 'N')
         return;

 gotoxy(5, 15);
 printf ( "Name : ");
```

```
gotoxy(5, 16);
printf ( "Address : ");

do
{
        clear(15, 15);
        clear(5, 23);
        gotoxy(5, 23);
        printf ("Enter Name or Press Enter for No Change");
        valid = 1;
        gotoxy(15, 15);
        gets(t_name);
        strupr(t_name);

        if (t_name[0] == '0')
                return;
        if (strlen(t_name) > 25)
        {
                valid = 0;
                gotoxy(5, 23);
                cprintf("\7Name should not greater than 25");
                getch();
        }
} while (!valid);

do
{
        clear(15, 16);
        clear(5, 23);
        gotoxy(5, 23);
        printf ( "Enter Address or press enter for no Change");
        valid = 1;
        gotoxy(15, 16);
        gets(t_address);
        strupr(t_address);

        if (t_address[0] == '0')
                return;

        if (strlen(t_address) > 25)
```

```
            {
                    valid = 0;
                    gotoxy(5, 23);
                    cprintf("\7Address should not greater than 25");
                    getch();
            }
    }while (!valid);

    if (strlen(t_address) > 0)
            modified = 1;

    if(!modified)
            return;
    // clears the screen at 23rd row and from 5th column
    clear(5,23);

    do
    {
            clear(5, 23);
            gotoxy(5, 18);
            printf ( "Do you want to save Changes <Y/N>: ");
            ch = getche();
            if (ch == '0')
                    return;
            ch = toupper(ch);
    }while (ch != 'N' && ch != 'Y');

    if (ch == 'N')
            return;

    // Passes the parameter to add in data file
    modify_account_ini(t_accno, t_name, t_address);
    gotoxy(5, 21);
    printf ( "\7Record modified");
    gotoxy(5, 23);
    printf ( "Press any key to continue...");
    getch();
}
```

```
Date:    14/10/1999                                          <0>=Exit
                       Modify Account Screen
    Account no.    8

            Name  :  P. SANGRAM
            Address  :  D-12/34, SEC-6, SAKET
            Balance  :  13700.00

    Modify this account <Y/N> : Y

    Name  :P. S. SANGRAM
    Address  :      D-12/34, SEC-6, SAKET-A

    Do you want to save Changes <Y/N> : Y

    Record modified

    Press any key to continue...
```

Figure 4.3 Output screen of the function modify().

```
/* Function for displaying an account when modified */
/* Function for displaying an account when modified. This display() function is used to display all the
account holders account number, name, address, and balance amount at screen. Here the fstream
object is declared to read the data from "INITIAL.dat" data file in input mode only. Whenever there
is record in data file, the read() statement will read the records linearly till end-of-file. */

void display_in(int t_accno)
{
	FILE *file;
	file = fopen("INITIAL.dat", "rb+");
	rewind(file);

	// Displays the record contents matching with t_accno from INITIAL.dat data file
	while (fread(&ini, sizeof(ini), 1, file)==1)
```

```
    {
        if (t_accno == ini.accno)
        {
            gotoxy(8, 5);
            printf ( "Account no. " );
            printf("%d",ini.accno);
            gotoxy(10, 8);
            printf ( "Name : ");
            puts(ini.name);
            gotoxy(10, 9);
            printf ( "Address : ");
            puts(ini.address);
            gotoxy(10, 10);
            printf ("Balance : " );
            printf ("%-10.2f", ini.balance);
            break;
        }
    }
    fclose(file);
}
```

/* Function for updating the modified account into INITIAL.dat file */

/* Function for updating the modified account into INITIAL.dat file. This function modify_account() receives number parameters such as, account number, name, address etc, and will overwrite at the existing place in the "INITIAL.dat" data file. The main logic of the function is that, it uses a function called seekp(location), which means that when a particular record is modified, first we have to know the record position according to data file. Once we find the position (location) then, a single value is decremented from its original location and overwritten by the same ofstream command written into the data file. */

```
void modify_account_ini(int t_accno, char t_name[30], char t_address[30])
{
    int recno;
    int location;
    FILE *file;
    file= fopen("INITIAL.dat", "rb+");

    recno = recordno_ini(t_accno);
    strcpy(ini.name, t_name);
    strcpy(ini.address, t_address);
```

```
        // finds the position in data file

        location = (recno-1) * sizeof(ini);
        fseek(file, location, SEEK_CUR);

        // Overwrites the modified record into INITIAL.dat data file
        fwrite(&ini, sizeof(ini), 1, file);
        fclose(file);
        return;
}
```

/* Function to find the last account number */
/* Function to find the last accounts number. This is an interesting function, which is creating the account numbers automatically. At the first instance when there is no record, the new account number is created as 1. If any account number is there then, the file will search all the records and store the last account number with a variable count. In this situation the function returns the same value by calling the program for automatic code generation. */

```
int last_accno_ini(void)
{
        FILE *file;
        int count = 0;

        file = fopen("INITIAL.dat", "rb+");
        rewind(file);

        // Founds the last account no.
        while (fread(&ini, sizeof(ini), 1, file))
                count = ini.accno;
        fclose(file);
        return count;
}
```

/* This function add_to_file() is used to create new/fresh record in the data file */
/* This function add_to_file() is used to create new/fresh record in the data file, and the parameter is the actual value which will be written into the "INITIAL.dat" file. Each time a transaction is made in an account for either Withdrawal (W) or Deposit (D) the balance amount will be modified in the data file*/

```
void add_to_file_ini(int t_accno, char t_name[30], char t_address[30], float t_balance)
{

        FILE *file;
        ini.accno = t_accno;
        strcpy(ini.name, t_name);
        strcpy(ini.address, t_address);
        ini.balance = t_balance;

        // Appends new account record with the balance into INITIAL.dat data file
        file = fopen("INITIAL.dat", "a+");
        fwrite(&ini, sizeof(ini), 1, file);
        fclose(file);
}


// Function for deleting a account from INITIAL.dat file
/* Function for deleting an account from INITIAL.dat file. This function is used to delete any account
from data file. By this function */

void delete_ini(int t_accno)
{
        FILE *file;
        FILE *temp;

        file = fopen("INITIAL.dat", "rb+");

        temp = fopen("TEMP.dat", "wb");
        rewind(file);

        // Uses a copy method to delete the account from INTITAL.dat data file
        while (fread(&ini, sizeof(ini), 1, file) == 1)
        {
                if (ini.accno != t_accno)
                        fwrite(&ini, sizeof(ini), 1, temp);
        }
        fclose(file);
        fclose(temp);
        remove ("INITIAL.dat");
```

```
        rename("TEMP.dat", "INITIAL.dat");
        file = fopen("INITIAL.dat", "rb+");
}
```

/* Function for add an account details of daily tranaction into BANKING.dat file. */
/* Function to add account details of daily transactions into BANKING.dat file. By using the parameters the information of daily transaction is appended into "BANKING.dat" data file including amount transaction and the current balance value. */

```
void add_to_file(int t_accno, int d1, int m1, int y1, char t_tran, char t_type[10], float t_interest,
float t_amount, float t_balance)
{
        FILE *file;
        file = fopen("BANKING.dat", "a+");
        acc.accno = t_accno;
        getch();
        acc.dd = d1;
        acc.mm = m1;
        acc.yy = y1;
        acc.tran = t_tran;
        strcpy(acc.type, t_type);
        acc.interest = t_interest;
        acc.amount = t_amount;
        acc.balance = t_balance;

        // Appends the transaction record into BANKING.dat data file
        fwrite(&acc, sizeof(acc), 1, file);
        fclose(file);
}
```

/* Function for deleting an account from BANKING.dat file. */
/* Function for deleting an account from BANKING.dat file. This is a copy method, when the user will input any account number, the same account number will be checked in the "BANKING.dat" file, if the account number is matched in to your data file then, it remains in your data file otherwise the remaining records will be transferred into "TEMP.dat" data file. So, your new "TEMP.dat" file holds all the records except inputted account number. In the same way make copy of all the "TEMP.dat" records back into your "BANKING.dat" file for restoring data, the file deletes from the matched account number. */

```
void delete_account(int t_accno)
{
        FILE *file;
        FILE *temp;

        file = fopen("BANKING.dat", "r"); // Open to read records

        temp = fopen("TEMP.dat", "w"); // Open to write records
        rewind(file);                  // Positioned from begining of the file

        // Uses the copy method for deleting the transaction record from BANKING.dat data file
        while (fread(&acc, sizeof(acc), 1, file) == 1)
        {
                if (acc.accno != t_accno)
                        fwrite(&acc, sizeof(acc), 1, temp);
        }
        fclose(file);
        fclose(temp);
        remove("BANKING.dat");
        rename("TEMP.dat", "BANKING.dat");
}

/* Function for displaying an account from "INITIAL.dat". */
/* Function for displaying an account from "INITIAL.dat". This function shows all account holders
data records and their respective current balance amount on the screen. Thus, the bank will be in a
position to know total amount available with it. */

void display_ini(void)
{

        int flag, j;
        float t_bal = 0.0;
        FILE *file;
        int d1, m1, y1;
        struct date d;                 // For extracting system date
        int row = 7;
        clrscr();
        gotoxy(25, 2);
        printf ( "Accounts List in Bank");
        gotoxy(25, 3);
```

```
printf ("==========================");

getdate(&d);
d1 = d.da_day;
m1 = d.da_mon;
y1 = d.da_year;
gotoxy(62, 3);
printf ( "Date: " );
printf("%d", d1);
printf( "/");
printf("%d", m1);
printf( "/");
printf("%d", y1);
gotoxy(1, 4);
for (j = 1; j <= 79; j++)
        printf ( "=");

gotoxy(1, 5);
printf ( "Accno#");
gotoxy(10, 5);
printf ( "Name");
gotoxy(30, 5);
printf ( "Address");
gotoxy(65, 5);
printf ( "Balance");
gotoxy(1, 6);
for (j = 1; j <= 79; j++)
        printf ( "=");
file = fopen("INITIAL.dat", "r");
rewind(file);

// Reads all the records to display on the screen
while (fread(&ini, sizeof(ini), 1, file) == 1)
{
        flag = 0;
        delay(2);
        gotoxy(3, row);
        printf ("%d", ini.accno);
        gotoxy(10, row);
        puts(ini.name);
```

```
        gotoxy(30, row);
        puts(ini.address);
        gotoxy(65, row);

        printf ("%-10.2f", ini.balance);

        t_bal = t_bal + ini.balance;
        row++;
        if (row > 23)
        {
                flag = 1;
                row = 6;
                gotoxy(4, 24);
                printf ( "Press any key to continue.... ");
                getch();
                clrscr();
        }
    }

    gotoxy(1, row);
    for (j = 1; j <= 79; j++)
        printf ("=");
    row++;
    gotoxy(3, row);
    printf ( "Total Balance in Bank is : ");
    gotoxy(65, row);

    printf ( "%-10.2f", t_bal);

    fclose(file);
    if (!flag)
    {
        gotoxy(4, 24);
        printf ( "Press any key to continue...");
        getch();
    }
    getch();
}
```

Accounts List in Bank

Date: 14/10/1999

Accno#	Name	Address	Balance
2	MR. AMAR KUMAR	ROHINI, DELHI	10000.00
3	MR. SANGRAM KESHRI	ROHINI, DELHI	5812.00
4	MR. RAMAN KUMAR	SEC-6, ROHINI, DELHI	5500.00
5	SANATAN SATAPATHY	GURGAON	4500.00
6	MASTER KUMAR	12TH	12639.00
7	P. S. VENKATSH	12TH CROSS MOMBAY EAST	2500.00
8	P. SANGRAM	D-12/34, SEC-6, SAKET	13700.00

Total Balance in Bank is : 54651.20

Press any key to continue...

Figure 4.4 Output screen of the function display_list of accounts.

/* Function for clearing specified row and column. */

/* Function for clearing specified row and column. By using this function you can clear from a specified row and column in your screen. Here the function utilizes two parameters for clearing the row and column. */

```
void clear(int col, int row)
{
    int j;
    for (j = col; j <= 79; j++)
    {
        gotoxy(j, row);
        printf ( " ");
    }
}
```

/* Function to found an account for display account function. */

/* Function to find an account for display account function. This function is used to find any account in the "INITIAL.dat" data file, where the file is searched from the first record position and it searches whether the entered account exist or not. If it exists then the variable found will return a value 1 or

```
0 as the parameter */

int found_account_ini(int t_accno)
{
        FILE *file;
        int found = 0;

        file = fopen("INITIAL.dat", "r");
        rewind(file);

        // Searches the specified record in INITIAL.dat data file
        while (fread(&ini, sizeof(ini), 1, file) == 1)
        {
                if (ini.accno == t_accno)
                {
                        found = 1;
                        break;
                }
        }
        fclose(file);
        return found;
}

/* Function for rcturn name of the account holder from INITIAL.dat. */
/* Function for return name of the account holder from INITIAL.dat. This function is basically used
to return only name of the account holder if the account is in the "INITIAL.dat" data file. When the
name is returned it may simply display / modify other functions */

char *return_name_ini(int t_accno)
{
        FILE *file;
        char t_name[30];
        file = fopen("INITIAL.dat", "r");
        rewind(file);

        // Return the name to display at report screen if found
        while (fread(&ini, sizeof(ini), 1, file) == 1)
        {
```

```
            if (ini.accno == t_accno)
            {
                    strcpy(t_name, ini.name);
                    break;
            }
        }
        fclose(file);
        return t_name;
}
```

/* Function for return address of the account holder from INITIAL.dat. */
/* Function for return address of the account holder from INITIAL.dat. This function is basically used to return only address of the account holder if the account is in the "INITIAL.dat" data file. When the address is returned it may simply display / modify other functions */

```
char *return_address_ini(int t_accno)
{
        FILE *file;
        char t_address[30];
        file = fopen("INITIAL.dat", "r");
        rewind(file);

        // Return the address to display at report screen if found
        while (fread(&ini, sizeof(ini), 1, file) == 1)
        {
            if (ini.accno == t_accno)
            {
                    strcpy(t_address, ini.address);
                    break;
            }
        }
        fclose(file);
        return t_address;
}
```

/* Function for display account details */
/* Function to display account details as: This function displays the heading and the account number, name, address and current date on the screen with other functions like display_account(), month_report() etc.. Also the same function returns the account holders name and address by using two pointer type functions like return_name() and return_address(). */

```
void box_for_display(int t_accno)
{
        int d1, m1, y1, i;
        char t_name[30];
        char t_address[30];
        struct date d;
        getdate(&d);
        d1 = d.da_day;
        m1 = d.da_mon;
        y1 = d.da_year;
        gotoxy(63, 2);
        printf ( "Date: " );
        printf("%d", d1);
        printf( "/" );
        printf("%d", m1);
        printf ( "/" );
        printf ( "%d", y1);
        gotoxy(4, 2);
        printf ( "Account No. " );
        printf("%d", t_accno);

        strcpy(t_name, return_name_ini(t_accno));
        strcpy(t_address, return_address_ini(t_accno));

        gotoxy(25, 2);
        printf ("%s", t_name);
        gotoxy(25, 3);
        printf ("%s", t_address);
        gotoxy(4, 5);
        printf ( "Global Report of Account");
        textbackground(WHITE);
        textcolor(BLACK);
        textbackground(WHITE);
        gotoxy(1, 6);
        for (i = 1; i <=79; i++)
                printf ( "=");
        gotoxy(4, 7);
        cprintf("Date     Particular  Deposit     Withdraw          Balance");
        gotoxy(1, 8);
        for (i = 1; i <=79; i++)
```

```
        printf ( "=");
    textcolor(LIGHTGRAY);
    textbackground(BLACK);
}
```

/* Function for display an account from BANKING.dat file. */
/* Function to display an account from BANKING.dat file. This is a function, which displays all the transactions of any account on screen. And the function shows the account number, name, and address through the function box_for_display(). Also through this function it shows the total deposit, withdrawal and current balance amount globally. */

```
void display_account(void)
{

    char t_acc[10];
    int j;
    float tamt = 0, damt = 0, wamt = 0;
    int t, t_accno;
    int row = 9, flag;

    FILE *file;
    file = fopen("BANKING.dat", "r");

    clrscr();
    gotoxy(71, 1);
    printf ( "<0>=Exit");

    gotoxy(5, 5);
    printf ( "Enter account no. ");
    gets(t_acc);
    t = atoi(t_acc);
    t_accno = t;
    if (t_accno == 0)
        return;
    clrscr();
    if (!found_account_ini(t_accno))
    {
        gotoxy(5, 5);
        printf ( "\7Account not found");
        getch();
```

```
        return;
}

// Display the heading from this function
box_for_display(t_accno);

while (fread(&acc, sizeof(acc), 1, file) == 1)
{
        if (acc.accno == t_accno)
        {
                flag = 0;
                delay(2);
                gotoxy(4, row);
                printf( "%d", acc.dd);
                printf( "-" );
                printf( "%d", acc.mm);
                printf( "-" );
                printf( "%d", acc.yy);
                gotoxy(16, row);
                puts(acc.type);

                if (acc.tran == 'D')
                {
                        damt = damt + acc.amount;
                        tamt = tamt + acc.amount;
                        gotoxy(30, row);
                }
                else
                {
                        wamt = wamt + acc.amount;
                        tamt = tamt - acc.amount;
                        gotoxy(42, row);
                }

                printf ( "%-10.2f", acc.amount);

                gotoxy(66, row);
                printf ( "%-10.2f", acc.balance);

                row++;
```

```
                    if (row > 23)
                    {
                              flag = 1;
                              row = 7;
                              gotoxy(4, 24);
                              printf ( "Press any key to continue");
                              getch();
                              clrscr();
                              box_for_display(t_accno);
                    }
          }
     }

     fclose(file);
     gotoxy(1, row);
     for (j = 1; j <= 79; j++)
               printf ( "=");
     row++;
     gotoxy(4, row);
     printf ( "Total—>:");
     gotoxy(30, row);
     printf ( "%-10.2f", damt);

     gotoxy(42, row);
     printf ( "%-10.2f", wamt);

     gotoxy(66, row);
     printf ( "%-10.2f", tamt);

     if (!flag)
     {
               gotoxy(4, 24);
               printf ( "Press any key to continue...");
               getch();
     }
}
```

Account No. 8	P. SANGRAM D-12/34, SEC-6, SAKET	Date: 14/10/1999

Global Report of Account

Date	Particular	Deposit	Withdraw	Balance
14-10-1999	INITIAL	6000.00		6000.00
Total -->:		6000	0	6000

Press any key to continue...

Figure 4.5 Output screen of the function display accounts.

```
/* Function to list monthWise transaction report. */
/* Function to list monthwise transaction report. This is a monthwise status report for any account, and the user has to feed any date of any month and the account number. When the date and account number is entered the function will check all the transactions of previous month date and will find the previous balance in the variable pre_balance, which will be the "B/F ......" amount for reporting month. Then, from that period all remaining transactions of the relevant month will be displayed on the screen. */

void month_report(void)
{

    int dd1, mm1, yy1;
    char t_acc[10];
    int j;
    float tamt = 0, damt = 0, wamt = 0;
    int t = 0, t_accno = 0;

    int row = 9, flag;
    FILE *file;
    float pre_balance = 0.0; // Previous balance amount
    file = fopen("BANKING.dat", "r");
```

```
clrscr();
gotoxy(10, 5);
printf ( "Enter any date of a month ");
gotoxy(38, 5);
scanf ("%d", &dd1);
gotoxy(40, 5);
printf ( "-");
gotoxy(41, 5);
scanf ("%d", &mm1);
gotoxy(43, 5);
printf ( "-");
gotoxy(44, 5);
scanf ("%d", &yy1);
clrscr();

gotoxy(71, 1);
printf ( "<0>=Exit");
gotoxy(5, 5);
fflush(stdin);     // To flush out the previous memory
printf ( "Enter account no. ");
gets(t_acc);
t = atoi(t_acc);
t_accno = t;
if (t_accno == 0)
        return;                    // If acc_no is 0 then back to main menu

clrscr();
if (!found_account_ini(t_accno))
{
        gotoxy(5, 5);
        printf ( "\7Account not found");
        getch();
        return;
}

box_for_display(t_accno);
gotoxy(4, 5);
printf ( "Statement Month: ");
printf("%d", dd1);
printf ( "/");
```

```
printf ("%d", mm1);
printf( "/" );
printf ("%d", yy1);

// The loop finds the last months balance
while (fread(&acc, sizeof(acc), 1, file) == 1)
{
        // Checks the account no. and till the previous month and till current year
        if ((acc.accno == t_accno) && ((acc.mm < mm1 && acc.yy <= yy1) ||
                (mm1 < acc.mm && acc.yy < yy1)))
        {
                pre_balance = acc.balance;
        }
}

fclose(file);
file = fopen("BANKING.dat", "r");
gotoxy(58, row);
printf ( "B/F ....   " );

printf ( "%-10.2f", pre_balance);
row++;
// The loop displays the current months transaction after previous month
while (fread(&acc, sizeof(acc), 1, file) == 1)
{
        if ((acc.accno == t_accno) && (mm1 == acc.mm && yy1 <= acc.yy))
        {
                flag = 0;
                delay(2);
                gotoxy(4, row);
                printf ( "%d", acc.dd);
                printf ( "-" );
                printf("%d", acc.mm);
                printf ( "-" );
                printf( "%d", acc.yy);
                gotoxy(16, row);
                puts(acc.type);
                if (acc.tran == 'D')
                {
                        damt = damt + acc.amount;
```

```
                    tamt = tamt + acc.amount;
                    gotoxy(30, row);
                }
                else
                {
                    wamt = wamt + acc.amount;
                    tamt = tamt - acc.amount;
                    gotoxy(42, row);
                }
                printf ( "%-10.2f", acc.amount);

                gotoxy(66, row);
                printf ( "%-10.2f", acc.balance);

                row++;

                // If row increases 23 then the next screen continues
                if (row > 23)
                {
                    flag = 1;
                    row = 7;
                    gotoxy(4, 24);
                    printf ( "Press any key to continue");
                    getch();
                    clrscr();
                    box_for_display(t_accno);
                }
            }
    }
    fclose(file);
    gotoxy(1, row);
    for (j = 1; j <= 79; j++)
            printf ( "=");
    row++;
    gotoxy(4, row);
    printf ( "Total—>:");
    gotoxy(30, row);
    // Deposited amount
    printf ( "%-10.2f", damt);
```

```
        gotoxy(42, row);
        //Withdraw amount
        printf ( "%-10.2f", wamt);

        gotoxy(66, row);
        tamt = tamt + pre_balance;
        // Balance amount
        printf ( "%-10.2f", tamt);

        if (!flag)
        {
                gotoxy(4, 24);
                printf ( "Press any key to continue...");
                getch();
        }
        getch();
}
```

```
Account No.   8              P. SANGRAM                    Date: 14/10/1999
                             D-12/34, SEC-6, SAKET

Statement Month:      14/10/1999
===========================================================================
Date          Particular     Deposit       Withdraw          Balance
===========================================================================
                                           B/F .....          0.0
14-10-1999    INITIAL        6000.00                          6000.00
18-10-1999    CASH           3000.00                          9000.00
24-10-1999    CHEQUE                       2000.00            7000.00
28-10-1999    CASH           6700.00                          13700.00
===========================================================================
Total -->:                   15700         2000               13700

Press any key to continue...
```

Figure 4.6 Output screen of the function month_report account.

/* Function for creating new account for new customer. */
/* Function for creating a new account. This is a very important function, which is used to create new account with all the details of the customer. This function uses member function like last_accno(), add_to_file(), delete_account etc. The last_accno() function will create automatically a new account number after checking from the "INITIAL.dat" file. Here the account numbers start from 1 onwards if it is the first record. Also in this function the validation checking occurs to the name, address, verifying person and initial deposit amount. At the time of validation checking the name and address should not blank and should not be more than the specified length. And the initial deposit amount not be less than Rs. 500/-. */

```
void new_account(void)
{
        char ch;
        int i, valid;
        int t_accno;
        int d1, m1, y1;
        struct date d;
        char t_name[30], t[10], t_address[30];
        float t_bal = 0.0, t_balance = 0.0;
        float t_amount, t_interest;
        char t_tran, t_type[10];
        clrscr();

        box(2, 1, 79, 25, 218);
        box(25, 2, 54, 4, 219);

        gotoxy(65, 2);
        printf ("<0>=Exit");
        gotoxy(3,3);
        for (i = 1; i <= 74; i++)
                cprintf(" ");

        textbackground(BLACK);
        textcolor(BLACK+BLINK);
        textbackground(WHITE);
        gotoxy(30, 3);
        cprintf("Open New Account");
        textcolor(LIGHTGRAY);
        textbackground(BLACK);
```

```
getdate(&d);
d1 = d.da_day;
m1 = d.da_mon;
y1 = d.da_year;

t_accno = last_accno_ini();
t_accno++;

// Appends and deletes a false record to create primary position in data files
if (t_accno == 1)
{
        add_to_file_ini(t_accno, "abc", "xyz", 1.1);
        delete_account(t_accno);
        printf ( "Prese xxxxxxx");
        getch();
        add_to_file(t_accno, 1, 1, 1997, 'D', "INITIAL", 1.1, 1.1, 1.1);
        delete_account(t_accno);
}

gotoxy(5, 6);
printf ( "Date: " );
printf("%d", d1);
printf ( "/" );
printf ("%d", m1 );
printf ( "/");
printf ("%d", y1);
gotoxy(5, 8);
printf ( "Account No # " );
printf ("%d", t_accno);
gotoxy(5, 10);
printf ( "Name : ");
gotoxy(5, 11);
printf ( "Address : ");
gotoxy(5, 12);
printf ( "Name of verifying Person : ");
gotoxy(5, 14);
printf ( "Initial Deposit : ");

do
{
```

```
        clear(15, 10);
        clear(5, 23);
        gotoxy(5, 23);
        printf ( "Enter Name of the Person");
        valid = 1;
        gotoxy(15, 10);
        gets(t_name);
        strupr(t_name);

        if (t_name[0] == '0')
                return;

        if (strlen(t_name) == 0 || strlen(t_name) > 25)
        {
                valid = 0;
                gotoxy(5, 23);
                cprintf("\7Name should not greater than 25");
                getch();
        }
}while (!valid);

do
{
        clear(25, 15);
        clear(5, 23);
        gotoxy(5, 23);
        printf ( "Enter Address of the Person ");
        valid = 1;
        gotoxy(15, 11);
        gets(t_address);
        strupr(t_address);

        if (t_address[0] == '0')
                return;

        if (strlen(t_address) == 0 || strlen(t_address) > 25)
        {
                valid = 0;
                gotoxy(5, 23);
                cprintf("\7Address should not greater than 25");
```

```
                getch();
            }
    } while (!valid);

    do
    {
            char vari[30];
            clear(13, 12);
            clear(5, 23);
            gotoxy(5, 23);
            printf ( "Enter name of the varifying Person ");
            valid = 1;
            gotoxy(31, 12);
            gets(vari);
            strupr(vari);
            if (vari[0] == '0')
                return;

            if (strlen(vari) == 0 || strlen(vari) > 25)
            {
                valid = 0;
                gotoxy(5, 23);
                cprintf("Should not blank or greater than 25");
                getch();
            }
    }while (!valid);

    do
    {
            clear(13, 12);
            clear(5, 23);
            gotoxy(5, 23);
            printf ( "Enter initial amount to be deposit ");
            valid = 1;
            gotoxy(23, 14);
            gets(t);
            t_bal = atof(t);
            t_balance = t_bal;

            if (t[0] == '0')
```

```
            {
                    valid = 0;
                    gotoxy(5, 23);
                    cprintf("\7Should not less than 500");
                    getch();
            }

    }while (!valid);
    clear(5, 23);

    do
    {
            clear(5, 17);
            valid = 1;
            gotoxy(5, 17);
            printf ( "Do you want to save the record <Y/N>: ");
            ch = getche();
            if (ch == '0')
                    return;
            ch = toupper(ch);
    }while (ch != 'N' && ch != 'Y');

    if (ch == 'N')
            return;

    t_amount = t_balance;
    t_interest = 0.0;

    t_tran = 'D';
    strcpy(t_type, "INITIAL");

    // Appends the records contents into both INITIAL.dat and BANKING.dat data files
    add_to_file_ini(t_accno, t_name, t_address, t_balance);
    add_to_file(t_accno, d1, m1, y1, t_tran, t_type, t_interest, t_amount, t_balance);
}
```

```
                    Open New Account              <0>=Exit

        Date:     14/10/1999

        Account No       # 8

        Name  :P. SANGRAM
        Address  :        D-12/34, SEC-6, SAKET
        Name of

        Initial Deposit  : 6000

        Do you want to save the record <Y/N> :
```

Figure 4.7 Output screen of the function new_account.

```
/* Function for returning balance amount of an account. This function returns the balance amount of
any account to know the current balance from "INITIAL.dat" data file. */
/* Function for returning balance amount of an account. */

float give_balance_ini(int t_accno)
{
        FILE *file;

        float t_balance;
        file = fopen("INITIAL.dat", "r");

        // Gives the last balance of an individual account
        while (fread(&ini, sizeof(ini), 1, file)==1)
        {
                if (ini.accno == t_accno)
                {
                        t_balance = ini.balance;
                        break;
                }
```

```
    }
    fclose(file);
    return t_balance;
}
```

/* Function for returning the record no. for updating balance */
/* Function for returning the record number for updating the balance. This function checks the position of the account number for updating new balance amount into either "INITIAL.dat" or "BANKING.dat" data files. */

```
int recordno_ini(int t_accno)
{
    FILE *file;
    int count = 0;
    file = fopen("INITIAL.dat", "r");
    rewind(file);

    // Finds the record position in INITIAL.dat data file
    while (fread(&ini, sizeof(ini), 1, file) == 1)
    {
        count++;
        if (t_accno == ini.accno)
            break;
    }
    fclose(file);
    return count;
}
```

/* Function for updating the balance for the given account no. */
/* Function for updating the balance for the given account number. This function is used to update the balance after making any transaction in "INITIAL.dat" data file. While updating balance in "INITIAL.dat" data file, all the fields will transfer into the specified position in the file, because with random file handling when we update any record the size of the record becomes over written at the same place. So, all the fields including balance amount will writte into the same position in "INITIAL.dat" data file. Here this function uses a function seekp(), which searches the location in the data file where the record will be written. */

```
void update_balance_ini(int t_accno, char t_name[30], char t_address[30], float t_balance)
{
    int recno;
    int location;
```

```
    FILE *file;
    file = fopen("INITIAL.dat", "r+");
    recno = recordno_ini(t_accno);
    rewind(file);
    strcpy(ini.name, t_name);
    strcpy(ini.address, t_address);
    ini.balance = t_balance;
    location = (recno-1) * sizeof(ini); // Find the location in file*/
    fseek(file, location,SEEK_CUR);          // Searches the insertion position in data file
    // Updates the balance amount in INITIAL.dat data file*/
    fwrite(&ini, sizeof(ini), 1, file);
    fclose(file);
}

/* Function to return no. days between two dates. */
/* Function to return number of days between two dates. The function calculates total number of
days between two dates. And the function passes parameters as related to date (day, month, year).
*/

int no_of_days(int d1, int m1, int y1, int d2, int m2, int y2)
{
    static int month[] = {31, 28, 31, 30, 31, 30, 31, 30, 31, 30, 31, 30};
    int days = 0;
    while (d1 != d2 || m1 != m2 || y1 != y2)
    {
        days++;
        d1++;
        if (d1 > month[m1-1])
        {
            d1 = 1;
            m1++;
        }
        if (m1 > m2)
        {
            m1 = 1;
            y1++;
        }
    }
    return days;
}
```

/* Function for calculates interest */
/* Function for calculating interest. This function calculates the interest of any account according to the account number and balance from "BANKING.dat" data file. Before calculates the interest, the function also finds total number of days and then finds the interest. */

```
float calculate_interest(int t_accno, float t_balance)
{
    FILE *file;
    int d1, m1, y1, days;
    int d2, m2, y2;
    float t_interest = 0.0;
    int months = 0;
    struct date d;
    file = fopen("BANKING.dat", "r");
    rewind(file);

    while (fread(&acc, sizeof(acc), 1, file) == 1)
    {
        if (acc.accno == t_accno)
        {
            d1 =acc.dd;
            m1 = acc.mm;
            y1 = acc.yy;
            break;
        }
    }

    getdate(&d);
    d2 = d.da_day;
    m2 = d.da_mon;
    y2 = d.da_year;

    if ((y2 < y1) || (y2 == y1 && m2 < m1) || (y2 == y1 && m2 == m1) && (d2 < d1))
        return t_interest;
    days = no_of_days(d1, m1, y1, d2, m2, y2);

    if (days > 30)
    {
        months = days / 30;
        t_interest = ((t_balance * 2) / 100 * months);
```

```
    }
    fclose(file);
    return t_interest;
}
```

/* Function for making daily transaction (Deposit 'D'/Withdraw 'W'. */
/* Function for making daily transaction (Deposit 'D'/Withdrawal 'W'. This is the function used to make daily transaction either for Deposit(D) or for Withdrawal (W). When the screen appears the user has to press the accounts number either for deposit or withdrawal and then either for Cash or Cheque. It also displays the previous balance. After the final entry, it displays "Save Transaction <y/n>?" and if yes, then the transaction data is saved in "BANKING.dat" data file and the current balance is updated in the "INITIAL.dat" data file. */

```
void transaction(void)
{
    char t_acc[10];
    char t_name[30];
    char t_address[30];
    float t_balance;
    int t, t_accno, valid;
    int i;
    char ch;
    float t_interest;
    char t_tran, t_type[10], tm[10];
    float t_amount, t_amt;
    int d1, m1, y1;
    struct date d;

    clrscr();
    gotoxy(71, 1);
    printf ( "<0>=Exit");
    gotoxy(5, 5);
    printf ( "Enter the account no. ");
    gets(t_acc);
    t = atoi(t_acc);
    t_accno = t;
    if (t_accno == 0)
        return;
    clrscr();
    if (!found_account_ini(t_accno))
```

```
{
        gotoxy(5, 5);
        printf ( "\7Account not found");
        getch();
        return;
}
gotoxy(71, 1);
printf ( "<0>=Exit");
gotoxy(3, 3);
for (i = 1; i <= 76; i++)
        cprintf(" ");
textbackground(BLACK);
textcolor(BLACK+BLINK);
textbackground(WHITE);
gotoxy(29, 3);
cprintf ("Transaction in Account");
textcolor(LIGHTGRAY);
textbackground(BLACK);

getdate(&d);
d1 = d.da_day;
m1 = d.da_mon;
y1 = d.da_year;
gotoxy(5, 6);
printf ( "Date: " );
printf ("%d", d1 );
printf ( "/" );
printf ("%d", m1);
printf ( "/" );
printf ("%d", y1);
gotoxy(5, 8);
printf ( "Accnount no. " );
printf ("%d", t_accno);

strcpy(t_name, return_name_ini(t_accno));
strcpy(t_address, return_address_ini(t_accno));
t_balance = give_balance_ini(t_accno);
gotoxy(27, 11);
printf ( "Name : " );
printf ( "%s", t_name);
```

```
gotoxy(27, 12);
printf ( "Address : " );
printf ("%s", t_address);

gotoxy(5, 15);
printf ( "Last balance Rs. " );

printf ("%-10.2f", t_balance);
do
{
        clear(5, 10);
        valid = 1;
        gotoxy(5, 10);
        printf ( "Deposit or Withdraw (D/W) : ");
        t_tran = getch();
        if (t_tran == '0')
                return;
        t_tran = toupper(t_tran);
}while (t_tran != 'D' && t_tran != 'W');

do
{
        clear(5, 19);
        clear(5, 23);
        gotoxy(5, 23);
        printf ( "Enter Transaction by Cash or Cheque ");
        valid = 1;
        gotoxy(5, 19);
        printf ( "Cash/Cheque : ");
        gets(t_type);
        strupr(t_type);
        if (t_type[0] == '0')
                return;
        if (strcmp(t_type. "CASH") && strcmp(t_type, "CHEQUE"))
        {
                valid = 0;
                gotoxy(5, 23);
                cprintf("\7Enter correctly");
                getch();
        }
```

```
}while (!valid);

do
{
        clear(5, 21);
        clear(5, 23);
        gotoxy(5, 23);
        printf ( "Enter Amount for Transaction ");
        valid = 1;
        gotoxy(5, 21);
        printf ( "Amount Rs. ");
        gets(tm);
        t_amt = atof(tm);
        t_amount = t_amt;
        if (tm[0] == '0')
                return;
        if ((t_tran == 'W' && t_amount > t_balance) || (t_amount < 1))
        {
                valid = 0;
                gotoxy(5, 23);
                cprintf("\7Invalid Data entered");
                getch();
        }
}while (!valid);

clear(5, 23);
do
{
        clear(20, 23);
        valid = 1;
        gotoxy(40, 20);
        printf ( "Save Transaction <Y/N> : ");
        ch = getche();
        if (ch == '0')
                return;
        ch = toupper(ch);
}while (ch != 'N' && ch != 'Y');
if (ch == 'N')
        return;
```

```
t_interest = calculate_interest(t_accno, t_balance);
printf( "Interest");
printf(" %f", t_interest);

if (t_tran == 'D')
        t_balance = t_balance + t_amount + t_interest;
else
        t_balance = (t_balance - t_amount) + t_interest;

// Modified records are updated in data bases.
update_balance_ini(t_accno, t_name, t_address, t_balance);
add_to_file(t_accno, d1, m1, y1, t_tran, t_type, t_interest, t_amount, t_balance);
}
```

```
                                                      <0>=Exit
                          Transaction in Account

Date:    14/10/1999

Account no.     8

Deposit or Withdraw (D/W) :
                          Name  :  P. SANGRAM
                          Address  :  D-12/34, SEC-6, SAKET

Last balance Rs.  6000.00

Cash/Cheque    :  CASH

Amount Rs.  3000                        Save Transaction <Y/N>: _
```

Figure 4.8 Output screen of the daily transaction function.

/* Function for closing any account after inputting account number. When any account holder wants to close his/her account then this function is used to close the account completely, it means all the transactions from the "BANKING.dat" and "INITIAL.dat" file deletes the particular record information. The function also uses number of other functions, which fulfill the total close_account procedure as well. */

```
/* Function for closing any account after inputing account number. */
void close_account(void)
{

        char t_acc[10];
        int t, t_accno,i;
        int d1, m1, y1;
        char ch;
        struct date d;
        clrscr();
        gotoxy(71, 1);
        printf ( "<0>=Exit");
        gotoxy(5, 5);
        printf ( "Enter the account no. ");
        gets(t_acc);
        t = atoi(t_acc);
        t_accno = t;

        if (t_accno == 0)
                return;
        clrscr();

        if (!found_account_ini(t_accno))
        {
                gotoxy(5, 5);
                printf ( "\7Account not found ");
                getch();
                return;
        }

        gotoxy(71, 1);
        printf ( "<0>=Exit");
        gotoxy(3, 3);
        textbackground(WHITE);
        for (i = 1; i <= 76; i++)
                cprintf(" ");
        textbackground(BLACK);
        textcolor(BLACK+BLINK);
        textbackground(WHITE);
        gotoxy(30, 3);
```

```
cprintf("Close account screen");
textcolor(LIGHTGRAY);
textbackground(BLACK);
getdate(&d);
d1 = d.da_day;
m1 = d.da_mon;
y1 = d.da_year;
gotoxy(5, 6);
printf ( "Date: " );
printf ("%d", d1 );
printf ( "/" );
printf ("%d", m1 );
printf ( "/" );
printf ("%d", y1);

display_in(t_accno);
do
{
        clear(5, 15);
        gotoxy(5, 15);
        printf ( "Close this account <y/n?? ");
        ch = getche();
        if (ch == '0')
                return;
        ch = toupper(ch);
}while (ch != 'N' && ch != 'Y');

if (ch == 'N')
        return;

// Function calls to delete the existing account no.
delete_ini(t_accno);
delete_account(t_accno);
gotoxy(5, 20);
printf ( "\7Account Deleted");
gotoxy(5, 23);
printf ( "Press any key to continue...");
getch();
}
```

```
                                                    <0>=Exit
                    Close account Screen

        Account no.     8
    Date: 14/10/1999

                Name : P. SANGRAM
                Address : D-12/34, SEC-6, SAKET
                Balance : 13700.00

        Close this account <Y/N> : N
```

Figure 4.9 Output screen of the function close_account.

```
// Main program logic which control the members and member functions.
void main(void)
{
        /* Requesting autodetect of the graphics drivers */
        int gdriver = DETECT, gmode, errorcode;

        /* Set your graphics mode where the graphic files are present */
        initgraph(&gdriver, &gmode, "d:\turboc3");

        help();
        closegraph();
        control_menu();
}
```

Pay Manager

5

This project (Pay Manager) is basically for the users who want to develop C menu driven programs and building real life applications. We assume in this example an organization named XYZ company. The personnel department of the organization interacts with regard to the employee management, the job criteria, and salary behavior of more than 100 employees. Also they have number of terms and conditions for employees (which is given in the programs by comment line either in '//' or ' and */'). It comprises a menu driven program, and includes number of options, procedures for each selective module with a complete structure declaration. The complete project handles one main database such as EMPLOYEE.dat and number of temporary databases at the time program execution.

This project includes number of libraries including different header files and their respective functions, which is noted down after the source code of the project.

According to the requirements, the employer appoints the employees with their proper specification and salary structures. Each employee is given a different salary package, shich may or may not include perks, HRA, DA, PF etc. So, when an employee is appointed, he has to be prompted with different options when required.

These options can be :

1. HRA (House Rent Allowance) - According to the percentage
2. CA (Convenyance Allowance) - According to the percentage
3. DA (Dearness Allwance) - Accoring to the percentage
4. PF (Provident Fund)
6. OT (Over Time) is provided as : (basic/160) * hours

Whereas, at the time of salary slip, the advance amount may deducted and the net salary is payable to employee after proper calculation of the total allowance and total deduction of salary.

This project utilizes the following attributes in the employee structure as :

empcode	- Employee code
dd	- date of join
mm	- month of join
yy	- year of join
empname	- Employee name
empaddress	- employee address
empcity	- employee city
emppin	- employee pincode
empphone	- employee phone number
empdesig	- employee designation
emphouse	- employee accomodation (Y/N)
empconv	- employee convenyance (Y/N)
empsex	- employee sex (M/F)
empbase	- employee basic salary
emppf	- employee provident fund (percentage)
emphra	- employee house rent (percentage)
empca	- employee convenyance (percentage)
empda	- employee dearness allowance (percentage)

This project is developed by using C structure concepts and having number of different user defined functions (UDFs) which are as follows:

statusbar(...) : This is one of the usable function which prints a prompt message on status bar of every screen or an entry item.

getlinedelchar(...) : This function is used to delete a character for getline entry.

getline(...) : To Add Online Editing For Inputing A Line.

lineh (...) : This function passes four parameters including three integers and one character to draw different lines to design the screen beautifully. The character parameter draws the ASCII character line-by-line on screen. So, to draw horizontal line, this function is useful.

linev(...) : The linev(.....) function is helpful for drawing vertical lines on screen to design either menu or program forms for data entry, modify, display, delete etc..

box(...) : This function creates different sizes of the box on the screen according to the respective parameters. Out of all the parameters they draw unlimited boxes.

Design_Screen() : This menu is used to display the first 3 or 4 design screen of pay manager and after flash out the screen the main menu screen will be displayed.

main_menu() : This is the main screening menu, which will display your 5 different prompts and has different activities. Each prompt is connected with different functions to perform their respective purposes.

While handling the main menu you can press any selective number to perform the operation or press 0 (Zero) to exit from the main menu. But it is also helpful in almost all menus so that you can press 0 (zero) to exit from the respective menu.

vertical_menu(...) : The vertical menu is used to display the menu options i.e.; FILE menu options like

New Employee
Display Info
Display List
Salary Slip
Return

horizontal_menu(...) : The horizontal menu is used to display the horizontal bar options like FILE, EDIT, PRINT, HELP and EXIT.

EMP_Add(.....) : The EMP_Add() function declared in the employee structure. This function is used to append new records into Employee.dat data file with all data members of the employee structure.

Emp_Modify() : This function is used to display a modification screen for modifying the employee details by entering the employee number. While modifying the employee number (empcode) will be entered by the user and will search the employee.dat databases, and then the respective records can be modified.

Emp_Del() : This is the sub-function of "EDIT" menu bar. This function is used to delete an existing employee details from employee.dat data file. In this procedure, you have to enter the employee number for delete! and the deleted information will be displayed on the screen through the function and a prompt for delete. If you will press 'Y/y' then the records will be deleted from employee.dat data file.

displaycode() : This function is used to display an existing employee status from employee.dat data file.

Emp_Showlist() : This function is used to display the employee details from employee.dat data file.

Emp_Salslip() : This is an important function, which displays/prints the salary slip of individual employee. The user has to enter the employee code for which the salary slip will be generated. After entering the employee code, again enter the month, year for which the salary has to be paid and then number of days and over time options will be entered. After that, it will display the total salary of the month including all the details of employee. You may print the salary slip with the printer by selecting the menu option PRINT->Salary Slip

Emp_Print(...) : This function is used to activate the printer and sends the buffered output to the printer. It prints all the menus options of PRINT menu bar.

Program Source Codes COMPRO.C

```
//*****************************************************************
/* Program for employee payroll system */
// Required Header files
//*****************************************************************

#include <graphics.h>
#include <string.h>
#include <stdlib.h>
#include <stdio.h>
#include <ctype.h>
#include <conio.h>
#include <dos.h>

//*****************************************************************
// Public Functions Required By Many Different Functions.
//*****************************************************************

void statusbar(char[]) ;
void getlinedelchar(char *, int, int, int *) ;
void getline(char *, int) ;

//*****************************************************************
// The Drawing Functions & The Main Screen.
//*****************************************************************

void lineh (int, int, int, char) ;
void linev (int, int, int, char) ;
void box(int, int, int, int, char) ;
void Design_Screen();

//*****************************************************************
// Functions For Drawing Main Menus
//*****************************************************************

void main_menu () ;
int vertical_menu (char [] [20], int, int, int, int) ;
int horizontal_menu(char [] [20], int, int, int, int);
void Emp_Help () ;
```

```
//**************************************************************
// All The Fields Related To Employee
//**************************************************************

struct employee
{
        int  empcode, dd, mm, yy ;
        char  empname[31], empaddress[31], empcity[21], emppin[7] ;
        char  empphone[10], empdesig[21] ;
        char  emphouse, empconv, empsex ;
        float empbasic, emppf,  emphra, empca,empda;
};

int  Emp_Fcode (int) ;
int  Valid_Date (int, int, int) ;
void Emp_Display (int) ;

//**************************************************************
// All The Functions Related To Employee
//**************************************************************

void Emp_Add() ;
void Emp_Modify() ;
void Emp_Del() ;
void displaycode () ;
void Emp_Showlist () ;
void Emp_Salslip () ;
void Emp_Print (int, int, int, int) ;

//**************************************************************
// FUNCTION : lineh
// DESCRIPTION : To Draw A Horizontal Line   (x1, x2, y)
//**************************************************************

void lineh (int row1, int row2, int column, char c)
{
        for (row1; row1 <= row2; row1++)
        {
                gotoxy (row1, column) ;
                printf ("%c",c) ;
```

```
        }
}

//*****************************************************************
// FUNCTION : linev
// DESCRIPTION : To Draw A Vertical Line (y1, y2, x)
//*****************************************************************

void linev (int column1, int column2, int row, char c)
{
        for (column1; column1 <= column2; column1++ )
        {
                gotoxy (row, column1) ;
                printf ("%c",c) ;
        }
}

//*****************************************************************
// FUNCTION : box
// DESCRIPTION : To Draw A Box  (x1, y1, x2, y2)
//*****************************************************************

void box(int row1, int column1, int row2, int column2, char c)
{
        char ch=218 ;
        char c1, c2, c3, c4 ;
        char l1=196, l2=179 ;

        if (c == ch)
        {
                c1 = 218 ;
                c2 = 191 ;
                c3 = 192 ;
                c4 = 217 ;
                l1 = 196 ;
                l2 = 179 ;
        }
        else
        {
                c1 = c ;
```

```
            c2 = c ;
            c3 = c ;
            c4 = c ;
            l1 = c ;
            l2 = c ;
        }
        gotoxy(row1,column1) ;
        printf ("%c",c1) ;
        gotoxy(row2,column1) ;
        printf ("%c",c2) ;
        gotoxy(row1,column2) ;
        printf ("%c",c3) ;
        gotoxy(row2,column2) ;
        printf ("%c",c4) ;
        row1++ ;
        row2-- ;
        lineh(row1, row2, column1, l1) ;
        lineh(row1, row2, column2, l1) ;
        row1-- ;
        row2++ ;
        column1++ ;
        column2-- ;
        linev(column1,column2,row1,l2) ;
        linev(column1,column2,row2,l2) ;
}

//**********************************************************************
// FUNCTION : Design_Screen
// DESCRIPTION : To Paint The Screen With the The Opening Screen.
//**********************************************************************

void Design_Screen()
{
        int gd=DETECT, gm ;
        int t,i;
        long int k,m,j;
        initgraph(&gd, &gm, "\\turboc3") ;

        setcolor(LIGHTGRAY) ;
        rectangle(0, 0, getmaxx(), getmaxy()) ;
```

```
setfillstyle(SOLID_FILL, LIGHTGRAY) ;
floodfill(getmaxx()/2, getmaxy()/2, LIGHTGRAY) ;

for( t = 1; t < 115; t++)
{
        setcolor(DARKGRAY) ;
        for( m = 0; m < 103000.0; m++) ;
        rectangle(getmaxx()/2-t-150, getmaxy()/2+t, getmaxx()/2+t+150, getmaxy()/2-t) ;
        floodfill(getmaxx()/2, getmaxy()/2, DARKGRAY) ;
}

setcolor(WHITE) ;
settextstyle(GOTHIC_FONT, HORIZ_DIR, 7) ;
settextjustify(CENTER_TEXT, CENTER_TEXT) ;
outtextxy(getmaxx()/2, getmaxy()/2-60, “COMPUTER” ) ;
outtextxy(getmaxx()/2, getmaxy()/2+60, “PROJECT” ) ;

for(j = 0; j < 500; j++)
        for( k = 0; k < 40000.0; k++) ;

setcolor(BLACK) ;
rectangle(0, 0, getmaxx(), getmaxy()) ;
setfillstyle(SOLID_FILL, BLACK) ;
floodfill(getmaxx()/2, getmaxy()/2, BLACK) ;
for( i = 1; i < 150; i++)
{
        setcolor(RED) ;
        settextstyle(GOTHIC_FONT, HORIZ_DIR, 7) ;
        settextjustify(CENTER_TEXT, CENTER_TEXT) ;
        outtextxy(160+i, 40+i, “PAY - MANAGER” ) ;

        for(j = 0 ;j < 100; j++) ;

        setcolor(BLACK) ;
        settextstyle(GOTHIC_FONT, HORIZ_DIR, 7) ;
        settextjustify(CENTER_TEXT, CENTER_TEXT) ;
        outtextxy(160+i, 40+i, “PAY - MANAGER” ) ;
}

setcolor(RED) ;
```

```
settextstyle(GOTHIC_FONT, HORIZ_DIR, 7) ;
settextjustify(CENTER_TEXT, CENTER_TEXT) ;
outtextxy(160+i, 40+i, "PAY - MANAGER" ) ;

for(j = 0; j < 250; j++)
        for(k = 0; k < 40000.0; k++) ;

for(k = i; k > 50; k—)
{
        setcolor(RED) ;
        settextstyle(GOTHIC_FONT, HORIZ_DIR, 7) ;
        settextjustify(CENTER_TEXT, CENTER_TEXT) ;
        outtextxy(160+i, 40.0+k, "PAY - MANAGER" ) ;

        for( j = 0; j < 100; j++) ;

        setcolor(BLACK) ;
        settextstyle(GOTHIC_FONT, HORIZ_DIR, 7) ;
        settextjustify(CENTER_TEXT, CENTER_TEXT) ;
        outtextxy(160+i, 40.0+k, "PAY - MANAGER" ) ;
}
setcolor(RED) ;
settextstyle(GOTHIC_FONT, HORIZ_DIR, 7) ;
settextjustify(CENTER_TEXT, CENTER_TEXT) ;
outtextxy(160+i, 40.0+k, "PAY - MANAGER" ) ;

for(j = 0; j < 250; j++)
        for(k = 0; k < 40000.0; k++) ;

for(i = 1; i < 200; i++)
{
        setcolor(LIGHTRED) ;
        settextstyle(GOTHIC_FONT, HORIZ_DIR, 5) ;
        settextjustify(CENTER_TEXT, CENTER_TEXT) ;
        outtextxy(0+i, getmaxy()/2-10, "Programmed by : " ) ;

        for( j = 0; j < 100; j++) ;

        setcolor(BLACK) ;
        settextstyle(GOTHIC_FONT, HORIZ_DIR, 5) ;
```

```
        settextjustify(CENTER_TEXT, CENTER_TEXT) ;
        outtextxy(0+i, getmaxy()/2-10, "Programmed by : " ) ;
}

setcolor(LIGHTRED) ;
settextstyle(GOTHIC_FONT, HORIZ_DIR, 5) ;
settextjustify(CENTER_TEXT, CENTER_TEXT) ;
outtextxy(0+i, getmaxy()/2-10, "Programmed by : " ) ;

for(j = 0; j < 250; j++)
        for(k = 0; k < 40000.0; k++);

for(i = 1; i < 300; i++)
{
        setcolor(GREEN);
        settextstyle(GOTHIC_FONT, HORIZ_DIR, 5);
        settextjustify(CENTER_TEXT, CENTER_TEXT);
        outtextxy(0+i, getmaxy()/2+50, "Reeta Sahoo" );

        for( j = 0; j < 100; j++);

        setcolor(BLACK);
        settextstyle(GOTHIC_FONT, HORIZ_DIR, 5);
        settextjustify(CENTER_TEXT, CENTER_TEXT);
        outtextxy(0+i, getmaxy()/2+50, "Reeta Sahoo" );
}

setcolor(GREEN);
settextstyle(GOTHIC_FONT, HORIZ_DIR, 5);
settextjustify(CENTER_TEXT, CENTER_TEXT);
outtextxy(0+i, getmaxy()/2+50, "Reeta Sahoo" );

for(j = 0; j < 250; j++)
        for(k = 0; k < 40000.0; k++) ;

for(i = 1; i < 315; i++)
{
        setcolor(LIGHTRED) ;
        settextstyle(GOTHIC_FONT, HORIZ_DIR, 5) ;
        settextjustify(CENTER_TEXT, CENTER_TEXT) ;
```

```
            outtextxy(0+i, getmaxy()/2+95, "&") ;
            for( j = 0; j < 10000; j++) ;

            setcolor(BLACK) ;
            settextstyle(GOTHIC_FONT, HORIZ_DIR, 5) ;
            settextjustify(CENTER_TEXT, CENTER_TEXT) ;
            outtextxy(0+i, getmaxy()/2+95, "&") ;
    }

    setcolor(LIGHTRED) ;
    settextstyle(GOTHIC_FONT, HORIZ_DIR, 5) ;
    settextjustify(CENTER_TEXT, CENTER_TEXT) ;
    outtextxy(0+i, getmaxy()/2+95, "&" ) ;

    for(j = 0; j < 250; j++)
            for(k = 0; k < 40000.0; k++) ;

    for(i = 1; i < 450; i++)
    {
            setcolor(GREEN) ;
            settextstyle(GOTHIC_FONT, HORIZ_DIR, 5) ;
            settextjustify(CENTER_TEXT, CENTER_TEXT) ;
            outtextxy(0+i, getmaxy()/2+140, "Gagan Sahoo" ) ;

            for( j = 0; j < 100; j++) ;

            setcolor(BLACK) ;
            settextstyle(GOTHIC_FONT, HORIZ_DIR, 5) ;
            settextjustify(CENTER_TEXT, CENTER_TEXT) ;
            outtextxy(0+i, getmaxy()/2+140, "Gagan Sahoo" ) ;
    }

    setcolor(GREEN) ;
    settextstyle(GOTHIC_FONT, HORIZ_DIR, 5) ;
    settextjustify(CENTER_TEXT, CENTER_TEXT) ;
    outtextxy(0+i, getmaxy()/2+140, "Gagan Sahoo" ) ;

    for(j = 0; j < 500; j++)
            for(k = 0; k < 40000.0; k++) ;
```

```
        for(i = 0; i < 550; i++)
        {
                for( j = 0; j < 50000.0; j++) ;
                setcolor(BLACK) ;
                rectangle(0+i, 0, 100+i, getmaxy()) ;
        }

        closegraph() ;
}

//**********************************************************************
// FUNCTION : vertical_menu
// DESCRIPTION : To Make Vertical Menu.
//**********************************************************************

int vertical_menu(char menu[] [20], int present, int end, int x, int y)
{
        int ex=0 ;
        int i;
        char ch;
        box(x + 9, y, x + strlen(menu[0]) + 12, y + end + 1, 218) ;

        for ( i=0; i<end; i++)
        {
                gotoxy(x + 10, y + i + 1) ;
                printf ("%s",menu[i]) ;
        }

        do
        {
                int tpresent = present ;
                textcolor(BLACK) ;
                textbackground(WHITE) ;
                gotoxy(x + 10,y + present) ;

                cprintf(menu[present - 1]) ;
                textcolor(WHITE) ;
                textbackground(BLACK) ;
                ch = getch() ;
```

```
switch (ch)
{
        case 75 :
                if (present == 1)
                        present = end ;
                else
                        present— ;
                break ;
        case 77 :
                if (present == end)
                        present = 1 ;
                else
                        present++ ;
                break ;
        case 71 :
                present = 1 ;
                break ;
        case 79 :
                present = end ;
                break ;
        case 72 :
                if (present == 1)
                        present = end ;
                else
                        present— ;
                break ;
        case 80 :
                if (present == end)
                        present = 1 ;
                else
                        present++ ;
                break ;
        case 13 :
                ex = 1 ;
                break ;
        case 27 :
                present = end ;
                ex = 1 ;
}
```

```
            gotoxy(x + 10,y + tpresent) ;
            cprintf(menu[tpresent - 1]) ;

      } while(!ex) ;
      return(present) ;
}

//**********************************************************************
// FUNCTION : horizontal_menu
// DESCRIPTION : To Make Horizontal Menu.
//**********************************************************************

int horizontal_menu(char menu[] [20], int present, int end, int x, int y)
{
      int ex=0, i ;
      char ch;

      for (i = 0; i < end; i++)
      {
            gotoxy(x + (i + 2) * 10 - 5, y) ;
            printf ("%s",menu[i]);
      }

      lineh(1, 80, 2, 205) ;

      do
      {
            int tpresent = present ;
            textcolor(BLACK) ;
            textbackground(WHITE) ;
            gotoxy(x + (present + 1) * 10 - 5, y) ;
            cprintf(menu[present - 1]) ;
            textcolor(WHITE) ;
            textbackground(BLACK) ;
            ch = getch() ;

            switch (ch)
            {
                  case 71 :
                              present = 1 ;
```

```
                    break ;
            case 79 :
                    present = end ;
                    break ;
            case 75 :
                    if (present == 1)
                            present = end ;
                    else
                            present-- ;
                    break ;
            case 77 :
                    if (present == end)
                            present = 1 ;
                    else
                            present++ ;
                    break ;
            case 72 :
                    if (present == 1)
                            present = end ;
                    else
                            present-- ;
                    break ;
            case 80 :
                    if (present == end)
                            present = 1 ;
                    else
                            present++ ;
                    break ;
            case 13 :
                    ex = 1 ;
                    break ;
            case 27 :
                    present = end ;
                    ex = 1 ;
        }

        gotoxy(x + (tpresent + 1) * 10 - 5, y) ;
        cprintf(menu[tpresent - 1]) ;

    } while(!ex) ;
```

```
        return(present) ;
}


//**************************************************************
// FUNCTION : Emp_Help
// DESCRIPTION : To Print The Help Screen For Various Important
//           Operations.
//**************************************************************

void Emp_Help()
{
        clrscr();
        printf ("\n\n\n\t\t\tAbout Pay - Manager ");
        printf ("\n\nPay - Manager is a full fledged human resource management system ");
        printf ("\n\n\n 1) Important instructions are displayed at the status bar at the  ");
        printf ("\n    bottom of the screen.");
        printf ("\n\n 2) Press escape key to exit the immediate screen at any time");
        printf ("\n    during the program.");
        printf ("\n\n\n\n");
        printf ("\t\t\t\t\t\tReeta Sahoo");
        printf ("\n\t\t\t\t\t\tGagan Sahoo");
        getch();
        clrscr() ;
        return ;
}

//**************************************************************
// FUNCTION : main_menu
// DESCRIPTION : To Draw The Main Menu & Call Related Functions
//**************************************************************

void main_menu()
{
        int end=5, present=1, upperlim1=5, currentpos1=1, upperlim2=3, currentpos2=1,
                        upperlim3=4, currentpos3=1;
        char main[] [20] = { " FILE ", " EDIT ", " PRINT ", " HELP ", " EXIT " } ;
        char sub1[] [20] = { "New Employee ", "Display Info ", "Display List ",
                        "Salary Slip  ", "Return      " } ;
        char sub2[] [20] = { "Modify Employee ", "Delete Employee ", "Return        " } ;
```

```
char sub3[] [20] = { "Employee Info ", "Employee List ", "Salary Slip ", "Return        " } ;

Design_Screen() ;

do
{
        _setcursortype(_NOCURSOR) ;
        present = horizontal_menu(main, present, end, 3, 1) ;
        switch (present)
        {
                case 1 :
                        currentpos1 = vertical_menu(sub1, currentpos1, upperlim1, 3, 3) ;
                        switch (currentpos1)
                        {
                                case 1 :
                                        _setcursortype(_SOLIDCURSOR) ;
                                        Emp_Add() ;
                                        _setcursortype(_NOCURSOR) ;
                                        break ;
                                case 2 :
                                        _setcursortype(_SOLIDCURSOR) ;
                                        displaycode() ;
                                        break ;
                                case 3 :
                                        Emp_Showlist() ;
                                        break ;
                                case 4 :
                                        _setcursortype(_SOLIDCURSOR) ;
                                        Emp_Salslip() ;
                                        _setcursortype(_NOCURSOR) ;
                                        break ;
                        }
                        clrscr() ;
                        break ;
                case 2 :
                        currentpos2 = vertical_menu(sub2, currentpos2, upperlim2, 13, 3) ;
                        switch (currentpos2)
                        {
                                case 1 :
                                        _setcursortype(_SOLIDCURSOR) ;
```

```
                        Emp_Modify();
                        _setcursortype(_NOCURSOR) ;
                        break ;
                case 2 :
                        _setcursortype(_NORMALCURSOR) ;
                        Emp_Del() ;
                        _setcursortype(_NOCURSOR) ;
                        break ;
        }
        clrscr() ;
        break ;
case 3 :
        currentpos3 = vertical_menu(sub3, currentpos3, upperlim3, 27, 3) ;
        switch (currentpos3)
        {
                case 1 :
                        _setcursortype(_SOLIDCURSOR) ;
                        displaycode() ;
                        Emp_Print(1,1,80,23) ;
                        _setcursortype(_NOCURSOR) ;
                        break ;
                case 2 :
                        _setcursortype(_NORMALCURSOR) ;
                        Emp_Showlist() ;
                        Emp_Print(1,1,80,23) ;
                        _setcursortype(_NOCURSOR) ;
                        break ;
                case 3 :
                        _setcursortype(_NORMALCURSOR) ;
                        Emp_Salslip() ;
                        Emp_Print(1,1,80,23) ;
                        _setcursortype(_NOCURSOR) ;
                        break ;
        }
        clrscr() ;
        break ;
case 4 :
        Emp_Help() ;
        clrscr() ;
        break ;
```

```
        }
    } while (present != end);
}
```

FILE EDIT PRINT HELP EXIT

New Employee
Display Info
Display List
Salary Slip
Return

Figure 5.1 Output screen of main menu.

```
//**********************************************************************
// FUNCTION : Emp_Fcode
// DESCRIPTION : To Return 0 If The Given Code Is Not Found
//**********************************************************************

int Emp_Fcode(int code)
{
    FILE *file ;
    int found = 0 ;
    struct employee temp;
    file = fopen("Employee.Dat", "rb+") ;
    while (fread(&temp, sizeof(struct employee),1,file))
    {
        if (temp.empcode == code)
        {
            found = 1 ;
            break ;
        }
    }
    fclose(file) ;
    return(found) ;
}
```

```
//**********************************************************************
// FUNCTION : Valid_Date
// DESCRIPTION : To Return '0' If The Date Received Is Invalid
//**********************************************************************

int Valid_Date(int dd, int mm, int yy)
{
        int days=0, valid ;

        if ((yy>1980) && (yy<=1999))
                valid = 1 ;
        else
        {
                valid = 0 ;
                return(0) ;
        }

        switch (mm)
        {
                case 1 :
                        days = 31 ;
                        break ;
                case 2 :
                        if (yy % 4 == 0)
                                days = 29 ;   // leap year
                        else
                                days = 28 ;
                        break ;
                case 3 :
                        days = 31 ;
                        break ;
                case 4 :
                        days = 30 ;
                        break ;
                case 5 :
                        days = 30 ;
                        break ;
                case 6 :
                        days = 31 ;
                        break ;
```

```
        case 7 :
                days = 31 ;
                break ;
        case 8 :
                days = 31 ;
                break ;
        case 9 :
                days = 30 ;
                break ;
        case 10 :
                days = 31 ;
                break ;
        case 11 :
                days = 30 ;
                break ;
        case 12 :
                days = 31 ;
                break ;
        default:
                valid = 0 ;
                break ;
    }
    if ((dd > 0) && (dd <= days))
            valid = 1 ;
    else
            valid = 0 ;
    return (valid) ;
}
```

```
//**********************************************************************
// FUNCTION : Emp_Display
// DESCRIPTION : To Display A Record From "Employee.Dat"
//**********************************************************************
```

/* This function is used to display a particular employee record after searching in the employee.dat data file. This function uses a parameter 'code', which is passes from main procedures and according to that the employee contents will be displayed. This procedure produces a sequential process for employee record on code wise. */

```
void Emp_Display(int code)
{
        FILE *file ;
        struct employee t ;
        char *initial ;

        file = fopen("Employee.Dat", "rb+") ;

        while (fread(&t, sizeof(struct employee),1,file))
        {
                if (t.empcode == code)
                {
                        gotoxy(28,2) ;
                        printf ("EMPLOYEE  INFORMATION");

                        if (t.empsex == 'F')
                                initial = "Ms. ";
                        else
                                initial = "Mr. ";
                        gotoxy(30,3) ;
                        printf ("EMPLOYEE CODE # %d",t.empcode) ;
                        lineh(2,79,4,240) ;
                        gotoxy(20,6) ;
                        printf ("Name               : %s     %s",initial,t.empname) ;
                        gotoxy(20,7) ;
                        printf ("Address            : %s" ,t.empaddress );
                        gotoxy(40,8);
                        printf ("%s - %s",t.empcity,t.emppin );
                        gotoxy(20,9) ;
                        printf ("Contact No.        : %s" ,t.empphone );
                        gotoxy(20,11) ;
                        printf ("Date Of Joining   :%d - %d - %d ",t.dd,t.mm,t.yy );
                        gotoxy(20,13) ;
                        printf ("Designation       : %s",t.empdesig) ;
                        gotoxy(20,15) ;
                        printf ("Accomodation Provided : %c",t.emphouse) ;
                        gotoxy(20,16) ;
                        printf ("Conveyance Provided   : %c",t.empconv) ;
                        gotoxy(20,17) ;
                        printf ("Basic Salary      : Rs. %.2f",t.empbasic) ;
```

```
                gotoxy(20,18);
                printf ("Provident Fund    : Rs. %.2f",(t.emppf/100)*t.empbasic);
                gotoxy(20,19);
                printf ("Daily Allowance   : Rs. %.2f",(t.empda/100)*t.empbasic);
                gotoxy(20,20);
                printf ("Housing Allowance : Rs. %.2f",(t.emphra/100)*t.empbasic);
                gotoxy(20,21);
                printf ("Conveyance Allow  : Rs. %.2f" ,(t.empca/100)*t.empbasic);
                lineh(2,79,22,240);
            }
        }
        fclose(file);
}
```

```
                 EMPLOYEE INFORMATION
                 EMPLOYEE CODE # 1
==========================================================================
        Name                       : Mr.  SANDEEP SHARMA

        Address                    : 10TH CROSS SOUTH EX
                                     DELHI - 110003
        Contact No.                : 654231

        Date Of Joining            : 10 - 5 - 1995

        Designation                : ACCT. MANAGER

        Accomodation Provided : Y
        Convenyance Provided   : Y
        Basic Salary               : Rs. 5600
        Provident Fund             : Rs. 672.00
        Daily Allwance             : Rs. 1960.00
        Housing Allowance          : Rs. 840.00
        Convenyance Allow          : Rs. 728.00
Press any key to continue....
```

Figure 5.2 Individual employee information.

```
//**********************************************************************
// FUNCTION : Emp_Add()
// DESCRIPTION : To Get Data About New Employee
//**********************************************************************
/* This function is used to add new employee in the organisation with the detailed description and the salary package. The user has to enter the basic salary with their HRA and Convence allowance percentage and the provident fund, DA percentages etc. Also this function uses number of sub function to generate an automatic code on serial wise. The employees' name, address details and the designation is entered with proper validation conditions and proper message with the status bar. Also a date validation module is attached for indicating the date of joining the job. *

void Emp_Add()
{
        struct employee t ;
        struct employee te ;

        FILE *file ;
        char ch, choice='Y';
        char d[3], m[3], y[5], basic[10], pf[6], da[6], ca[6], hra[6];
        int code=0, valid ;

        do
        {
                clrscr() ;
                _setcursortype( SOLIDCURSOR) ;
                gotoxy(28,2) ;
                printf ("ADDITION OF NEW EMPLOYEE");
                lineh(20,59,3,240) ;
                gotoxy(31,4) ;
                printf ("Employee Code #");
                gotoxy(29,5) ;
                printf ("~~~~~~~~~~~~~~~~~~~~~~~~");
                gotoxy(5,8) ;
                printf ("Name          : ...........................");
                gotoxy(50,8);
                printf ("Sex (M/F) : .");
                gotoxy(5,9) ;
                printf ("Address       : ...........................");
                gotoxy(50,9) ;
                printf ("City    : ................");
```

```
gotoxy(5,10) ;
printf ("Pin Code     : ......");
gotoxy(50,10) ;
printf ("Phone No. : .........");
lineh(3,78,11,196);
gotoxy(5,12) ;
printf ("JOINING DATE");
gotoxy(5,13) ;
printf ("Day  : ..");
gotoxy(30,13) ;
printf ("Month : ..");
gotoxy(54,13) ;
printf ("Year  : ....");
lineh(3,78,14,196);
gotoxy(5,15) ;
printf ("Designation  : ...................");
lineh(3,78,16,196);
gotoxy(5,17) ;
printf ("Accomodation (y/n) : .");
gotoxy(43,17) ;
printf ("Conveyance (y/n) : .");
lineh(3,78,18,196);
gotoxy(5,19) ;
printf ("Basic Salary       (Rs) :  .........");
gotoxy(5,20);
printf ("Provident Fund     (%) :  .....");
gotoxy(5,21);
printf ("Daily Allowance    (%) :  .....");

file = fopen("Employee.Dat", "rb+") ;
while (fread(&te, sizeof(struct employee),1,file)==1)
        code = te.empcode ;
fclose(file) ;
code++ ;
t.empcode = code ;
gotoxy(47,4) ;
printf ("%d",t.empcode) ;

// Steps to enter the name of the employee
```

```
do
{
        valid = 1 ;
        statusbar(" ENTER THE NAME OF THE EMPLOYEE") ;
        _setcursortype(_SOLIDCURSOR) ;
        gotoxy(20, 8) ;
        printf ("                    ");
        gotoxy(20,8) ;
        gets(t.empname) ;

        if (t.empname[0] == '0')
                return ;
        if (strlen(t.empname) < 1)
        {
                valid = 0 ;
                statusbar("\a ENTER CORRECTLY (LENGTH : 1..30)") ;
                getch() ;
                _setcursortype(_SOLIDCURSOR) ;
        }

} while (!valid) ;

// Steps to enter the sex of the employee
do
{
        statusbar(" ENTER IF EMPLOYEE IS MALE(M) OR FEMALE(F)") ;
        _setcursortype(_SOLIDCURSOR) ;
        gotoxy(62,8) ;
        clreol() ;
        t.empsex = getch() ;

        if (t.empsex == 27)
                return ;
        t.empsex = toupper(t.empsex) ;
        if ((t.empsex == 27) || (t.empsex == '0'))
                return ;

} while ((t.empsex != 'M') && (t.empsex != 'F')) ;
printf ("%c",t.empsex) ;
```

```
// Steps to enter the address of the employee
do
{
        valid = 1 ;
        statusbar(" ENTER ADDRESS OF THE EMPLOYEE") ;
        _setcursortype(_SOLIDCURSOR) ;
        gotoxy(20,9) ;
        printf ("                    ");
        gotoxy(20,9) ;
        gets(t.empaddress);

        if (t.empaddress[0] == '0')
                return ;
        if (strlen(t.empaddress) < 1)
        {
                valid = 0 ;
                statusbar("\a ENTER CORRECTLY (LENGTH : 1..30)") ;
                getch() ;
                _setcursortype(_SOLIDCURSOR) ;
        }

} while (!valid) ;

// Steps to enter the city of the employee
do
{
        valid = 1 ;
        statusbar(" ENTER CITY OF THE EMPLOYEE") ;
        _setcursortype(_SOLIDCURSOR) ;
        gotoxy(62,9) ;
        clreol() ;
        gets(t.empcity) ;
        if (t.empcity[0] == '0')
                return ;

        if (strlen(t.empcity) < 1)
        {
                valid = 0 ;
                statusbar("\a ENTER CORRECLTY (LENGTH : 1..20)") ;
                getch() ;
```

```
                _setcursortype(_SOLIDCURSOR) ;
        }

} while (!valid) ;

// Steps to enter the pin code of the employee
do
{
        valid = 1 ;
        statusbar(" ENTER PIN CODE OF THE EMPLOYEE") ;
        _setcursortype(_SOLIDCURSOR) ;
        gotoxy(20,10) ;
        printf ("                    ");
        gotoxy(20,10) ;
        gets(t.emppin) ;
        if (t.emppin[0] == '0')
                return ;

        if (strlen(t.emppin) != 6)
        {
                valid = 0 ;
                statusbar("\a ENTER CORRECTLY (LENGTH : 6)") ;
                getch() ;
                _setcursortype(_SOLIDCURSOR) ;
        }

} while (!valid) ;

// Steps to enter the phone number of the employee
do
{
        valid = 1 ;
        statusbar(" ENTER PHONE NO. OF THE EMPLOYEE OR
                PRESS <enter> FOR NONE") ;
        _setcursortype(_SOLIDCURSOR) ;
        gotoxy(62,10) ;
        clreol() ;
        gets(t.empphone) ;
        if (t.empphone[0] == '0')
                return ;
```

```
        if ((strlen(t.empphone) < 6 && strlen(t.empphone) > 0) ||
                (strlen(t.empphone) > 7))
        {
            valid = 0 ;
            statusbar("\a ENTER CORRECTLY") ;
            getch() ;
            _setcursortype(_SOLIDCURSOR) ;
        }

    } while (!valid) ;

    if (strlen(t.empphone) == 0)
        strcpy(t.empphone,"—") ;

    // Steps to enter the date of joining of the employee
    do
    {
        valid = 1 ;
        do
        {
            statusbar(" ENTER DAY OF JOINING") ;
            _setcursortype(_SOLIDCURSOR) ;
            gotoxy(13,13) ;
            printf ("    ");
            gotoxy(13,13);
            gets(d) ;
            t.dd = atoi(d) ;
            if (strlen(d) == 0)
            {
                statusbar("\a ENTER CORRECTLY") ;
                getch() ;
                _setcursortype(_SOLIDCURSOR) ;
            }
            if (d[0] == 27)
                return ;
        } while (t.dd == 0) ;

        do
        {
            statusbar(" ENTER MONTH OF JOINING") ;
```

```
        _setcursortype(_SOLIDCURSOR) ;
        gotoxy(38,13) ;
        printf ("     ");
        gotoxy(38,13);
        gets(m) ;
        t.mm = atoi(m) ;
        if (m[0] == 27)
                return ;

        if (strlen(m) == 0)
        {
                statusbar("\a ENTER CORRECTLY") ;
                getch() ;
                _setcursortype(_SOLIDCURSOR) ;
        }

} while (t.mm == 0) ;

do
{
        statusbar(" ENTER YEAR OF JOINING") ;
        _setcursortype(_SOLIDCURSOR) ;
        gotoxy(62,13) ;
        clreol() ;
        gets(y) ;
        t.yy = atoi(y) ;

        if (y[0] == 27)
                return ;

        if (strlen(y) == 0)
        {
                statusbar("\a ENTER CORRECTLY") ;
                getch() ;
                _setcursortype(_SOLIDCURSOR) ;
        }

} while (t.yy == 0) ;

valid = Valid_Date(t.dd, t.mm, t.yy) ;
```

```
            if (valid == 0)
            {
                statusbar("\a ENTER CORRECTLY") ;
                getch() ;
                _setcursortype(_SOLIDCURSOR) ;
                gotoxy(38,13) ;
                printf ("          ");
                gotoxy(62,13) ;
                clreol() ;
            }
        } while (!valid) ;

        // Steps to enter the designation of the employee
        do
        {
            valid = 1 ;
            statusbar(" ENTER DESIGNATION OF THE EMPLOYEE") ;
            _setcursortype(_SOLIDCURSOR) ;
            gotoxy(20,15) ;
            clreol() ;
            gets(t.empdesig) ;

            if (t.empdesig[0] == '0')
                return ;
            if (strlen(t.empdesig) < 1)
            {
                valid = 0 ;
                statusbar("\a ENTER CORRECLTY (LENGTH : 1..20)") ;
                getch() ;
                _setcursortype(_SOLIDCURSOR) ;
            }

        } while (!valid) ;

        // Steps to enter the accomodation facility
        do
        {
            statusbar(" ENTER IF ACCOMODATION IS ALLOTED
                TO EMPLOYEE OR NOT");
            _setcursortype(_SOLIDCURSOR) ;
```

```
        gotoxy(26,17) ;
        printf (" ");
        gotoxy(26,17) ;
        t.emphouse = getch() ;

        if (t.emphouse == 27)
                return ;
        t.emphouse = toupper(t.emphouse) ;
        if (t.emphouse == '0')
                return ;

} while (t.emphouse != 'Y' && t.emphouse != 'N') ;
printf ("%c", t.emphouse) ;

// Steps to enter the conveience facility
do
{
        gotoxy(0,25) ;
        statusbar(" ENTER IF CONVEIENCE ALLOWANCE IS
                ALLOTED TO EMPLOYEE OR NOT") ;
        _setcursortype(_SOLIDCURSOR) ;
        gotoxy(62,17) ;
        clreol() ;
        t.empconv = getch() ;
        t.empconv = toupper(t.empconv) ;
        if (t.empconv == 27)
                return ;

        if (t.empconv == '0')
                return ;
} while (t.empconv != 'Y' && t.empconv != 'N') ;

printf ("%c", t.empconv) ;

// Steps to enter the basic salary of the employee
do
{
        valid = 1 ;
        statusbar(" ENTER BASIC SALARY OF THE EMPLOYEE") ;
        _setcursortype(_SOLIDCURSOR) ;
```

```
            gotoxy(32,19);
            clreol();
            gets(basic) ;
            t.empbasic = atof(basic) ;

            if (basic[0] == 27)
                    return ;

            if ((strlen(basic) == 0) || (t.empbasic>100000.0))
            {
                    valid = 0;
                    statusbar("\a SHOULD NOT BE GREATER THAN 100000") ;
                    getch() ;
                    _setcursortype(_SOLIDCURSOR) ;
            }
    } while (!valid) ;

    // Steps toe enter the PF percentage from basic salary
    do
    {
            valid = 1 ;
            statusbar(" ENTER PERCENTAGE OF BASIC SALARY
                                TAKEN AS PF") ;
            _setcursortype(_SOLIDCURSOR) ;
            gotoxy(32,20);
            clreol();
            gets(pf) ;
            t.emppf = atof(pf) ;

            if (pf[0] == 27)
                    return ;

            if ((strlen(pf) == 0) || (t.emppf>100))
            {
                    valid = 0;
                    statusbar("\a SHOULD NOT BE GREATER THAN 100 %") ;
                    getch() ;
                    _setcursortype(_SOLIDCURSOR) ;
            }
    } while (!valid) ;
```

```
// Steps to enter the DA percentage from basic salary
do
{
        valid = 1 ;
        statusbar(" ENTER PERCENTAGE OF BASIC SALARY
                        TAKEN AS DA") ;
        _setcursortype(_SOLIDCURSOR) ;
        gotoxy(32,21) ;
        clreol() ;
        gets(da) ;
        t.empda = atof(da) ;

        if (da[0] == 27)
                return ;

        if ((strlen(da) == 0) || (t.empda>100))
        {
                valid = 0;
                statusbar("\a SHOULD NOT BE GREATER THAN 100 %") ;
                getch() ;
                _setcursortype(_SOLIDCURSOR) ;
        }

} while (!valid) ;

// Option to choice for house rent allowance
if (t.emphouse == 'Y')
{
        gotoxy(5,22) ;
        printf ("House Rent Allowance (%):  .....");

        // Steps for house rent allowance percentage
        do
        {
                valid = 1 ;
                statusbar(" ENTER PERCENTAGE OF BASIC
                        SALARY TAKEN AS HRA") ;
                _setcursortype(_SOLIDCURSOR) ;
                gotoxy(32,22) ;
                printf ("  ");
```

```
                gotoxy(32,22) ;
                gets(hra) ;
                t.emphra = atof(hra) ;

                if (hra[0] == 27)
                        return ;

                if ((strlen(hra) == 0) || (t.emphra>100))
                {
                        valid = 0;
                        statusbar("\a SHOULD NOT BE GREATER
                                THAN 100 %") ;
                        getch() ;
                        _setcursortype(_SOLIDCURSOR) ;
                }
        } while (!valid) ;
}
else
        t.emphra = 0 ;
// Options for choice of convenyance allowance
if (t.empconv == 'Y')
{
        gotoxy(45,22) ;
        printf ("Conveyance Allowance (%) :  .....");

        do
        {
                valid = 1 ;
                statusbar(" ENTER PERCENTAGE OF BASIC
                                SALARY TAKEN AS CA") ;
                _setcursortype(_SOLIDCURSOR) ;
                gotoxy(72,22) ;
                clreol();
                gets(ca) ;
                t.empca = atof(ca) ;

                if (ca[0] == 27)
                        return ;
                if ((strlen(ca) == 0) || (t.empca>100))
                {
```

```
                        valid = 0;
                        statusbar("\a SHOULD NOT BE GREATER
                                THAN 100 %") ;
                        getch() ;
                        _setcursortype(_SOLIDCURSOR) ;
                    }
            } while (!valid) ;
    }
    else
            t.empca = 0 ;

    do
    {
            statusbar("\a Do you wish to save (y/n) : ") ;
            ch = getch() ;
            ch = toupper(ch) ;

            if (ch == '0'|| ch == 27)
                    return ;
    } while (ch != 'Y' && ch != 'N') ;

    if (ch == 'N')
            return ;

    file = fopen("Employee.Dat", "a+") ;
    fwrite(&t, sizeof(struct employee), 1, file) ;
    fclose(file) ;

    statusbar("\a Add any more (y/n) : ") ;

    do
    {
            choice = getch() ;
            choice = toupper(choice) ;

            if (choice == 13)
                    choice = 'Y' ;

            if (choice == 27)
                    choice = 'N' ;
```

```
        } while((choice != 'Y') && (choice !='N'));

    } while(choice == 'Y');
}
```

```
                 ADDITION OF NEW EMPLOYEE
          ==========================================
                    Employee Code #     1

Name          : SANDEEP SHARMA..........    Sex (F/M)     : M
Address       : 10TH CROSS SOUTH EX......   City          : DELHI
Pin code      : 110003........              Phone No.     : 654231

JOINING DATE
Day    : 10                    Month : 5          Year : 1995

Designation    : ACCT. MANAGER

Accomodation (y/n) : Y                     Convenyance (y/n) : Y

Basic Salary               (Rs)   : 5600
Provident Fund             (%)    : 12
Daily Allwance             (%)    : 35
House Rent Allowance (%)  : 15       Convenyance Allowance (%) : 13

Do you wish to save (y/n) :
```

Figure 5.3 New employee additions screen.

```
//**************************************************************
// FUNCTION : Emp_Modify
// DESCRIPTION : To Provide With Necessary Data Required For
//           Modification Of A Given Record
//**************************************************************
```

/* This function modifies the existing employee contents according the employee code. When you enter the employee code it will search the key in the employee.dat file through Emp_Fcode() function, if it is there, then the details of existing content will be displayed with a prompt message on the status bar for modify (y/n). While modifying the employee details, you may press simply enter on any existing field, the previous data will automatically resume on the same field otherwise you may change with new context. Use same procedure to modify all the data fields and the record contents will be overwritten on the same code in employee.dat data file. */

```
void Emp_Modify()
{
        FILE *file ;
        struct employee t ;
        struct employee te ;
        FILE *file1 ;
        int  code, valid ;
        char  ch, house='N', conv='N', choice='Y' ;
        char  address[31], city[21], pin[7], phone[10], desig[21] ;
        char  tbasic[10], tpf[6], tda[6], tca[6], thra[6] ;
        float basic=0, pf=0, da=0, ca=0, hra=0 ;
        clrscr() ;

        do
        {
                gotoxy(72,2) ;
                printf ("Esc=EXIT");
                gotoxy(5,5) ;
                printf ("Enter code of the Employee : ");
                scanf ("%d",&code) ;

                if (code == 0)
                        return ;
                clrscr() ;

                // Steps to know whether the employee code is there or not
                if (!Emp_Fcode(code))
                {
                        gotoxy(30,24) ;
                        printf ("\a Record not found");
                        getch() ;
                        return ;
                }
```

```
// Sub procedure for displaying the employee contents
Emp_Display(code) ;
gotoxy(72,2) ;
printf ("<0>=EXIT");
gotoxy(24,2) ;
printf ("MODIFICATION OF EMPLOYEE RECORD");

do
{
        statusbar("\a Do you wish to modify this record (y/n) ") ;
        ch = getch() ;
        ch = toupper(ch) ;

        if (ch == '0')
                return ;

        if (ch == 13 )
                ch = 'Y' ;

        if (ch == 27 )
                ch = 'N' ;

} while (ch != 'Y' && ch != 'N') ;

if (ch == 'N')
        return ;
clrscr() ;

// Steps to know whether code is exists or not
file = fopen("Employee.Dat", "rb+") ;

while (fread(&t, sizeof(struct employee),1,file)==1)
{
        if (t.empcode == code)
                break ;
}

gotoxy(72,2) ;
printf ("Esc=EXIT");
gotoxy(26,2) ;
```

```
printf ("MODIFICATION OF NEW EMPLOYEE");
lineh(20,59,3,240) ;
gotoxy(31,4) ;
printf ("Employee Code # %d ",code) ;
gotoxy(29,5) ;
printf ("~~~~~~~~~~~~~~~~~~~~~~~~~~");
gotoxy(5,8) ;
printf ("Name         : ");
gotoxy(50,8);
printf ("Sex (M/F) : ");
gotoxy(5,9) ;
printf ("Address       : ............................");
gotoxy(50,9) ;
printf ("City     : .................");
gotoxy(5,10) ;
printf ("Pin Number   : ......");
gotoxy(50,10) ;
printf ("Phone No. : .........");
lineh(3,78,11,196);
gotoxy(5,12) ;
printf ("JOINING DATE");
gotoxy(5,13) ;
printf ("Day   :  ");
gotoxy(30,13) ;
printf ("Month :  ");
gotoxy(54,13) ;
printf ("Year  :    ");
lineh(3,78,14,196);
gotoxy(5,15) ;
printf ("Designation   : ...................");
lineh(3,78,16,196);
gotoxy(5,17) ;
printf ("Accomodation (y/n) : .");
gotoxy(43,17) ;
printf ("Conveyance (y/n) : .");
lineh(3,78,18,196);
gotoxy(5,19) ;
printf ("Basic Salary        (Rs) :  .........");
gotoxy(5,20) ;
printf ("Provident Fund     (%)  :  .....");
```

```
gotoxy(5,21) ;
printf ("Daily Allowance   (%) : .....");

gotoxy(20,8) ;
printf ("%s",t.empname) ;

gotoxy(62,8) ;
printf ("%c",t.empsex) ;

gotoxy(13,13) ;
printf ("%d",t.dd) ;

gotoxy(38,13) ;
printf ("%d",t.mm) ;

gotoxy(62,13) ;
printf ("%d",t.yy) ;

do
{
        valid = 1 ;
        statusbar(" ENTER ADDRESS OF THE EMPLOYEE OR
                        PRESS <enter> FOR NO CHANGE") ;
        _setcursortype(_SOLIDCURSOR) ;
        gotoxy(20,9) ;
        printf ("                    ");
        gotoxy(20,9) ;
        getline(address, 29) ;

        if (address[0] == '0')
                return ;

        if (strlen(address) > 30)
        {
                valid = 0 ;
                statusbar("\a Enter correctly (Range: 1..30)") ;
                getch() ;
                _setcursortype(_SOLIDCURSOR) ;
        }
```

```
} while (!valid) ;

// Steps if address is not entered, then the previous address will resume
if (strlen(address) == 0)
{
        strcpy(address, t.empaddress) ;
        gotoxy(20,9) ;
        printf ("%s",address) ;
}

do
{
        valid = 1 ;
        statusbar(" ENTER CITY OF THE EMPLOYEE OR
                PRESS <enter> FOR NO CHANGE") ;
        _setcursortype(_SOLIDCURSOR) ;
        gotoxy(62,9) ;
        clreol() ;
        getline(city, 17) ;

        if (city[0] == '0')
                return ;

        if (strlen(city) > 18)
        {
                valid = 0 ;
                statusbar("\a Enter correctly (Length : 1..18)") ;
                getch() ;
                _setcursortype(_SOLIDCURSOR) ;
        }

} while (!valid) ;

// Steps if city is not entered, then the previous city will resume
if (strlen(city) == 0)
{
        strcpy(city, t.empcity) ;
        gotoxy(62,9) ;
        printf ("%s",city) ;
}
```

```
do
{
        valid = 1 ;
        statusbar(" ENTER PIN CODE OR PRESS <enter> FOR NO CHANGE")

        _setcursortype(_SOLIDCURSOR) ;
        gotoxy(20,10) ;
        printf ("              ");
        gotoxy(20,10) ;
        getline(pin, 6) ;

        if (pin[0] == '0')
                return ;

        if (strlen(pin) != 6 && strlen(pin) > 1)
        {
                valid = 0 ;
                statusbar("\a Enter correctly (Length : 6)") ;
                getch() ;
                _setcursortype(_SOLIDCURSOR) ;
        }

} while (!valid) ;

// Steps if pic code is not entered, then the previous pin code will resume
if (strlen(pin) == 0)
{
        strcpy(pin, t.emppin) ;
        gotoxy(20,10) ;
        printf ("%s",pin) ;
}

do
{
        valid = 1 ;
        statusbar(" ENTER PHONE ÑO. OF THE EMPLOYEE OR
                PRESS <enter> FOR NO CHANGE") ;
        _setcursortype(_SOLIDCURSOR) ;
        gotoxy(62,10) ;
        clreol() ;
```

```
        getline(phone, 9) ;

        if (phone[0] == '0')
                return ;

        if ((strlen(phone) < 6 && strlen(phone) > 0) || (strlen(phone) > 7))
        {
                valid = 0 ;
                statusbar("\a Enter correctly") ;
                getch() ;
                _setcursortype(_SOLIDCURSOR) ;
        }
} while (!valid) ;

// Steps if phone no. is not entered, then the previous phone no. will resume
if (strlen(phone) == 0)
{
        strcpy(phone, t.empphone) ;
        gotoxy(62,10) ;
        printf ("%s",phone) ;
}

do
{
        valid = 1 ;
        statusbar(" ENTER DESIGNATION OF THE EMPLOYEE
                OR PRESS <enter> FOR NO CHANGE") ;
        _setcursortype(_SOLIDCURSOR) ;
        gotoxy(20,15) ;
        clreol() ;
        getline(desig, 20) ;

        if (desig[0] == '0')
                return ;

        if (strlen(desig) > 20)
        {
                valid = 0 ;
                statusbar("\a Enter correctly (Range: 1..20)") ;
                getch() ;
```

```
                _setcursortype(_SOLIDCURSOR) ;
        }

    } while (!valid) ;

    // Steps if designation is not entered, then the previous designation will resume
    if (strlen(desig) == 0)
    {
        strcpy(desig, t.empdesig) ;
        gotoxy(20,15) ;
        printf ("%s",desig) ;
    }

    // Steps to modify the accomodation
    do
    {
        statusbar(" ALLOTED ACCOMODATION ?(y/n) OR
                PRESS <enter> FOR NO CHANGE") ;
        _setcursortype(_SOLIDCURSOR) ;
        gotoxy(26,17) ;
        printf ("          ");
        gotoxy(26,17) ;
        house = getch() ;
        house = toupper(house) ;

        if (house == 27)
                return ;

        if (house == 13)
        {
                house = t.emphouse ;
                gotoxy(26,17) ;
        }

    } while (house != 'Y' && house != 'N') ;
    printf ("%c",house) ;

    // Steps to modify the convenyance allowance
    do
    {
```

```
        statusbar(" ALLOTED CONVEYANCE ALLOWANCE ?(y/n)
                OR PRESS <enter> FOR NO CHANGE") ;
        _setcursortype(_SOLIDCURSOR) ;
        gotoxy(62,17) ;
        clreol() ;
        conv = getch() ;
        conv = toupper(conv) ;

        if (conv == 27)
                return ;

        if (conv == 13)
        {
                conv = t.empconv ;
                gotoxy(62,17) ;
        }

} while (conv != 'Y' && conv != 'N') ;
printf ("%c",conv) ;

// Steps to modify the existing basic salary
do
{
        valid = 1 ;
        statusbar(" ENTER BASIC SALARY OF THE EMPLOYEE");
        _setcursortype(_SOLIDCURSOR) ;
        gotoxy(32,19) ;
        clreol() ;
        getline(tbasic,9) ;
        basic = atof(tbasic) ;

        if (basic > 100000.0)
        {
                valid = 0 ;
                statusbar("\a SHOULD NOT BE GREATER THAN 100000") ;
                getch() ;
                _setcursortype(_SOLIDCURSOR) ;
        }

} while (!valid) ;
```

```
// Steps if basic salary is not entered, then the previous basic salary will resume
if (strlen(tbasic) == 0)
{
        basic = t.empbasic ;
        gotoxy(32,19) ;
        printf ("%.2f",basic) ;
}
// Steps to enter the provident fund percentage
do
{
        valid = 1 ;
        statusbar(" ENTER PERCENTAGE OF BASIC SALARY
                TAKEN AS PF") ;
        _setcursortype(_SOLIDCURSOR) ;
        gotoxy(32,20) ;
        clreol() ;
        getline(tpf,5) ;
        pf = atof(tpf) ;
        if (pf > 100)
        {
                valid = 0 ;
                statusbar("\a SHOULD NOT BE GREATER THAN 100 %") ;
                getch() ;
                _setcursortype(_SOLIDCURSOR) ;
        }

} while (!valid) ;

// Steps if pf percentage is not entered, then the previous pf percentage will resume
if (strlen(tpf) == 0)
{
        pf = t.emppf ;
        gotoxy(32,20) ;
        printf ("%.2f",pf) ;
}

// Steps to DA percentage
do
{
        valid = 1 ;
```

```
        statusbar(" ENTER PERCENTAGE OF BASIC SALARY
                TAKEN AS DA") ;
        _setcursortype(_SOLIDCURSOR) ;
        gotoxy(32,21);
        clreol();
        getline(tda,5);
        da = atof(tda);

        if (da > 100)
        {
                valid = 0 ;
                statusbar("\a SHOULD NOT BE GREATER THAN 100 %");
                getch() ;
                _setcursortype(_SOLIDCURSOR) ;
        }
} while (!valid);

// Steps if DA percentage is not entered, then the previous DA
// percentage will resume
if (strlen(tda) == 0)
{
        da = t.empda ;
        gotoxy(32,21);
        printf ("%.2f",da);
}

// Steps to enter the house rent allowance percentage
if (house == 'Y')
{
        gotoxy(5,22);
        printf ("House Rent Allowance (%):  .....");

        do
        {
                valid = 1 ;
                statusbar(" ENTER PERCENTAGE OF BASIC
                        SALARY TAKEN AS HRA");
                _setcursortype(_SOLIDCURSOR) ;
                gotoxy(32,22);
                printf ("  ");
```

```
                gotoxy(32,22);
                getline(thra,5);
                hra = atof(thra) ;
                if (hra > 100)
                {
                        valid = 0 ;
                        statusbar("\a SHOULD NOT BE GREATER
                                THAN 100 %") ;
                        getch() ;
                        _setcursortype(_SOLIDCURSOR) ;
                }
                if (strlen(tda) == 0)
                {
                        hra = t.emphra ;
                        gotoxy(32,22);
                        printf ("%.2f",hra) ;
                }
                else
                        hra = 0 ;

        } while (!valid) ;
}
// Steps to enter the convenyance allowance percentage
if (conv == 'Y')
{
        gotoxy(45,22);
        printf ("Conveyance Allowance (%) : .....");
        do
        {
                valid = 1 ;
                statusbar(" ENTER PERCENTAGE OF BASIC
                        SALARY TAKEN AS CA") ;
                _setcursortype(_SOLIDCURSOR) ;
                gotoxy(72,22);
                clreol();
                getline(tca,5);
                ca = atof(tca) ;
                if (ca > 100)
                {
                        valid = 0 ;
```

```
                statusbar("\a SHOULD NOT BE GREATER
                        THAN 100 %") ;
                getch() ;
                _setcursortype(_SOLIDCURSOR) ;
            }
            if (strlen(tca) == 0)
            {
                ca = t.empca ;
                gotoxy(72,22) ;
                printf ("%.2f",ca) ;
            }
            else
                ca = 0 ;
        } while (!valid) ;
}

// Steps to transfer the temporary field value to structure data members of employee
strcpy(t.empaddress, address) ;
strcpy(t.empcity, city) ;
strcpy(t.emppin, pin) ;
strcpy(t.empphone, phone) ;
strcpy(t.empdesig, desig) ;
t.empcode = code ;
t.emphouse = house ;
t.empconv = conv ;
t.empbasic = basic ;
t.emppf = pf ;
t.empda = da ;
t.emphra = hra ;
t.empca = ca ;

// Steps to update the modifyed record into employee.dat using a temporary
// database tempmod.dat
file = fopen("Employee.Dat", "rb+") ;
file1 = fopen("Tempmod.Dat", "wb+") ;
while (fread(&te, sizeof(struct employee),1,file)==1)
{
        if (t.empcode != te.empcode)
                fwrite(&te, sizeof(struct employee),1,file1) ;
        else
```

```
                    break ;
        }

        fwrite(&t, sizeof(struct employee),1,file1) ;
        while (fread(&te, sizeof(struct employee),1,file)==1)
                fwrite(&te, sizeof(struct employee),1,file1) ;

        fclose(file) ;
        fclose(file1) ;

        // Steps to retransfer the record contents of modified recored from
        // tempmod.dat database to employee.dat database.
        file = fopen("Employee.Dat", "wb+") ;
        file1 = fopen("Tempmod.Dat", "rb+") ;

        while (fread(&t, sizeof(struct employee),1,file1)==1)
        {
                fwrite(&t, sizeof(struct employee),1,file) ;
        }

        fclose(file) ;
        fclose(file1) ;

        gotoxy(5,25) ;
        clreol() ;

        do
        {
                statusbar("\a Do you wish to save (y/n) ") ;
                ch = getch() ;
                ch = toupper(ch) ;
                if (ch == '0')
                        return ;
        } while (ch != 'Y' && ch != 'N') ;

        if (ch == 'N')
                return ;

        statusbar(" Record Modified.") ;
        getch() ;
```

```
        statusbar("\a Modify any more (y/n) : ") ;
        do
        {
                choice = getch() ;
                choice = toupper(choice) ;

                if (choice == 13)
                        choice = 'Y' ;
                if (choice == 27)
                        choice = 'N' ;

        } while((choice != 'Y') && (choice !='N'));

    } while(choice == 'Y');
}
```

MODIFICATION OF NEW EMPLOYEE **Esc = EXIT**

Employee Code # 1

Name	**: SANDEEP SHARMA ....**	**Sex (F/M)**	**: M**
Address	**: 10TH CROSS SOUTH EX......**	**City**	**: DELHI**
Pin code	**: 110003........**	**Phone No.**	**: 6465011**

JOINING DATE

Day : 10 **Month : 5** **Year : 1995**

Designation : MANAGER ACCOUNTS

Accomodation (y/n) : Y **Convenyance (y/n) : Y**

Basic Salary	**(Rs)**	**: 5600**	
Provident Fund	**(%)**	**: 12**	
Daily Allwance	**(%)**	**: 35**	
House Rent Allowance	**(%)**	**: 15**	**Convenyance Allowance (%) : 14**

Do you wish to save (y/n) :

Figure 5.4 Existing employee modification screen.

```
//*********************************************************************
// FUNCTION : Emp_Del
// DESCRIPTION : To Delete A Record In "Employee.Dat"
//*********************************************************************
/* This procedure is used to delete individual record(s) by entering the employee code. When the user will enter the employee code, it will search in the employee.dat and delete it permanently from the database using temporary copy method through the tempdel.dat database. After deleting the record, the tempdel.dat database simultaneously copy the fresh records to employee.dat. */

void Emp_Del()
{
        struct employee t ;
        FILE *file ;
        FILE *file1 ;
        char ch ;
        int code ;
        clrscr() ;
        gotoxy(72,2) ;
        printf ("<0>=EXIT");
        gotoxy(5,5) ;
        printf ("Enter code of the Employee : ");
        scanf ("%d",&code) ;

        if (code == 0)
                return ;
        clrscr() ;

        if (!Emp_Fcode(code))
        {
                gotoxy(30,24) ;
                printf ("\a Record not found");
                getch() ;
                return ;
        }

        gotoxy(72,2) ;
        printf ("<0>=EXIT");
        gotoxy(23,1) ;
        printf ("DELETION OF THE EMPLOYEE RECORD");
        Emp_Display(code) ;
```

```
do
{
        statusbar("\a Do you wish to remove this record (y/n) ") ;
        ch = getch() ;
        if (ch == 27)
                return ;

        if (ch == 13)
                ch = 'y' ;
        ch = toupper(ch) ;

        if (ch == '0')
                return ;

} while (ch != 'Y' && ch != 'N') ;

if (ch == 'N')
        return ;

file = fopen("Employee.Dat", "rb+") ;
file1 = fopen("Tempdel.Dat", "wb+") ;

while (fread(&t, sizeof(struct employee),1,file)==1)
{
        if (t.empcode != code)
                fwrite(&t, sizeof(struct employee),1,file1) ;
}

fclose(file) ;
fclose(file1) ;

file = fopen("Employee.Dat", "wb+") ;
file1 = fopen("Tempdel.Dat", "rb+") ;

while (fread(&t, sizeof(struct employee),1,file1)==1)
{
        fwrite(&t, sizeof(struct employee),1,file) ;
}

fclose(file) ;
```

```
        fclose(file1) ;

        clrscr() ;
        statusbar("\a Record Deleted") ;
        getch() ;
        statusbar("   Press any key to continue...") ;
        getch() ;

}
```

DELETION OF THE EMPLOYEE RECORD
EMPLOYEE INFORMATION
EMPLOYEE CODE # 1

==

Name	**: Mr. SANDEEP SHARMA**
Address	**: 10TH CROSS SOUTH EX DELHI - 110003**
Contact No.	**: 654231**
Date Of Joining	**: 10 - 5 - 1995**
Designation	**: ACCT. MANAGER**
Accomodation Provided	**: Y**
Convenyance Provided	**: Y**
Basic Salary	**: Rs. 5600**
Provident Fund	**: Rs. 672.00**
Daily Allwance	**: Rs. 1960.00**
Housing Allowance	**: Rs. 840.00**
Convenyance Allow	**: Rs. 728.00**

Do you wish to remove this record (y/n)

Figure 5.5 Deletion form of employee record.

```
//*****************************************************************
// FUNCTION : displaycode
// DESCRIPTION : To Obtain Code For Displaying A Record
//*****************************************************************

/* This procedure displays the details of an employee if it exists in employee.dat database. This
function uses the Emp_Display function, which displays the employee contents. */

void displaycode()
{
        int code ;
        clrscr() ;
        gotoxy(72,2) ;

        printf ("<0>=EXIT");
        gotoxy(5,5) ;
        _setcursortype(_SOLIDCURSOR) ;
        printf ("Enter code of the Employee : ");
        scanf ("%d", &code) ;

        if (code == 0)
                return ;
        clrscr() ;

        if (!Emp_Fcode(code))
        {
                _setcursortype(_NOCURSOR) ;
                gotoxy(30,25) ;
                printf ("\a Record not found");
                getch() ;
                return ;
        }

        Emp_Display(code) ;
        statusbar("   Press any key to continue...") ;
        getch() ;
}
```

```
//*******************************************************************
// FUNCTION : Emp_Showlist
// DESCRIPTION : To Display The List Of Employees
//*******************************************************************
/* This function is used to display all the existing employee informations with code, name and
designation from employee.dat database. */

void Emp_Showlist()
{

        struct employee t ;
        FILE *file ;
        int row = 6, found=0, flag=0 ;
        int d1, m1, y1 ;
        char ch ;
        struct date d;
        getdate(&d) ;
        d1 = d.da_day ;
        m1 = d.da_mon ;
        y1 = d.da_year ;
        clrscr() ;

        gotoxy(23,2) ;
        printf ("LIST OF EMPLOYEES AS ON %d . %d .%d",d1,m1,y1) ;
        lineh(1,80,3,240) ;

        gotoxy(12,4) ;
        printf ("CODE #           NAME                DESIGNATION");
        gotoxy(1,5) ;
        lineh(11,72,5,205) ;
        linev(4,22,10,186) ;
        linev(4,22,19,186) ;
        linev(4,22,51,186) ;
        linev(4,22,72,186) ;
        lineh(1,80,23,240) ;

        file = fopen("Employee.dat", "rb+") ;

        while (fread(&t, sizeof(struct employee),1,file)==1)
        {
```

```
        flag = 0 ;
        found = 1 ;
        gotoxy(12,row) ;
        printf ("%d",t.empcode) ;
        gotoxy(21,row) ;
        printf ("%s",t.empname) ;
        gotoxy(53,row) ;
        printf ("%s",t.empdesig) ;

        if (row == 18)
        {
                flag = 1 ;
                row = 6 ;
                statusbar(" Press any key to continue or Press <ESC> to exit") ;
                ch = getch() ;

                if (ch == 27)
                        break ;
                clrscr() ;
                gotoxy(31,2) ;
                printf ("LIST OF EMPLOYEES");
                lineh(1,90,3,240);
                gotoxy(2,4) ;
                printf ("CODE #          NAME                    DESIGNATION");
                gotoxy(1,5) ;
                printf ("~~~~~~~~~~~~~~~~~~~~~~~~~~~~~~~~~~~~~~~~~~~~~~~~~~~~~~~~~~~~~");
        }
        else
                row++ ;
}

if (!found)
{
        gotoxy(26,14) ;
        printf ("\a Records not found");
}

if (!flag)
{
        statusbar("  Press any key to continue...") ;
```

```
        getch() ;
    }

    fclose (file) ;
}
```

LIST OF EMPLOYEES AS ON 4 . 3 . 2000

CODE #	NAME	DESIGNATION
1	SANDEEP SHARMA	ACCT. MANAGER
2	ANITA GOEL	MANAGER
3	SANATAN SATAPATHY	FINANCE MANAGER
4	K. C. SHARMA	DTP OPERATOR
5	GAURAV MITTAL	SR. PROGRAMMER
6	MAMTA VERMA	SYSTEM ANALYST
7	RITU VIZ	DESIGNER

Press any key to continue....

Figure 5.6 Listing all the existing employees in organisation.

```
//**********************************************************************
// FUNCTION : Emp_Salslip
// DESCRIPTION : To Print The Salary Slip Of An Employee On The Screen
//**********************************************************************
```

/* This is an important function, which displays/prints the salary slip of individual employee. The user has to enter the employee code for which the salary slip will be generated. After entering the employee code, again enter the month, year for which the salary will be paid and then number of days and over time options will be entered. After that it will display the total salary of the month including all the details of employee. You may print the salary slip by selecting the menu option PRINT->Salary Slip */

```
void Emp_Salslip()
{
        FILE *file ;
        struct employee t ;
        float hra=0, ca=0, pf=0, ot=0, advance=0;
        float allowance=0, deduction=0, netsalary=0 ;
        long float da = 0;
        int  code, valid=0, days, hours ;
        int  year ;
        char  tdays[3], thours[4], tadvance[6], month[10] ;

        clrscr() ;
        gotoxy(72,2) ;
        printf (“<0>=EXIT”);
        gotoxy(5,5) ;
        printf (“Enter code of the struct employee : “);
        scanf (“%d”,&code) ;

        if (code == 0)
                return ;

        if (!Emp_Fcode(code))
        {
                clrscr() ;
                gotoxy(30,25) ;
                printf (“\a Record not found”);
                getch() ;
                return ;
        }
        clrscr() ;
        gotoxy(5,8) ;
        printf (“Enter month for which SALARY SLIP is to be generated : “);
        scanf (“%s”,&month) ;
        gotoxy(5,11) ;
        printf (“Enter year for which SALARY SLIP is to be generated  : “);
        scanf (“%d”,&year) ;
```

```
clrscr() ;

file = fopen("Employee.Dat", "rb+") ;

while (fread(&t, sizeof(struct employee),1,file)==1)
{
        if (t.empcode == code)
                break ;
}

fclose(file) ;

lineh(1,80,1,223) ;
linev(1,23,1,222) ;
linev(1,23,79,222) ;
lineh(1,80,23,223) ;

gotoxy(32,2) ;
printf ("DEEP MOTORS");
lineh(3,78,3,175) ;
gotoxy(24,4) ;
printf ("SALARY SLIP  -  %s . %d",month,year) ;
lineh(3,78,5,196) ;
gotoxy(4,6) ;
printf ("Employee Name : %s",t.empname) ;
gotoxy(48,6) ;
printf ("Designation : %s",t.empdesig) ;
box(4,7,76,21,218) ;

do
{
        valid = 1 ;
        statusbar(" ENTER NO. OF DAYS WORKED IN THE MONTH ") ;
        _setcursortype(_SOLIDCURSOR) ;
        gotoxy(25,10) ;
        printf ("No. of Days Worked : ");
        getline(tdays,2) ;
        days = atoi(tdays) ;

        if (tdays[0] == 27)
```

```
            return ;

        if (days > 26)
        {
            valid = 0 ;
            statusbar("\a CANNOT BE GREATER THAN 26 ") ;
            getch() ;
            _setcursortype(_SOLIDCURSOR) ;
        }

} while (!valid) ;

do
{
        valid = 1 ;
        statusbar(" ENTER NO. OF HOURS WORKED OVER TIME ") ;
        _setcursortype(_SOLIDCURSOR) ;
        gotoxy(25,12) ;
        printf ("Overtime hours     : ");
        getline(thours,3) ;
        hours = atoi(thours) ;

        if (thours[0] == 27)
            return ;

        if (hours > 41)
        {
            valid = 0 ;
            statusbar("\a MORE THAN 40 Hrs. OVERTIME NOT PERMITTED ");
            getch() ;
            _setcursortype(_SOLIDCURSOR) ;
        }
} while (!valid) ;

do
{
        valid = 1 ;
        statusbar(" ENTER AMOUNT TAKEN AS ADVANCE ") ;
        _setcursortype(_SOLIDCURSOR) ;
        gotoxy(25,14) ;
```

```
            printf ("Advance amount (Rs): ");
            getline(tadvance,6) ;
            advance = atof(tadvance) ;

            if (tadvance[0] == 27)
                return ;

            if (advance > t.empbasic)
            {
                valid = 0 ;
                statusbar("\a  ADVANCE  CANNOT  BE  GREATER  THAN
                                BASIC PAY ") ;
                getch() ;
                _setcursortype(_SOLIDCURSOR) ;
            }
        } while (!valid) ;

        _setcursortype(_NOCURSOR) ;

        gotoxy(25,10) ;
        printf ("                    ");
        gotoxy(25,12) ;
        printf ("                    ");
        gotoxy(25,14) ;
        printf ("                    ");

        gotoxy(7,8) ;
        printf ("BASIC SALARY                         : Rs.");
        gotoxy(7,10) ;
        printf ("ALLOWANCE");
        gotoxy(9,11) ;
        printf ("Daily Allowance       : Rs.");
        gotoxy(9,12) ;
        printf ("Over Time             : Rs.");
        gotoxy(9,13) ;
        printf ("Conveyance Allowance  : Rs.");
        gotoxy(9,14) ;
        printf ("House Rent Allowance  : Rs.");
        gotoxy(7,16) ;
        printf ("DEDUCTIONS");
```

```
gotoxy(9,17) ;
printf ("Provident Fund        : Rs.");
gotoxy(9,18) ;
printf ("Advance Taken         : Rs.");
gotoxy(9,20) ;
printf ("N E T   S A L A R Y                        : Rs.");

hra = (int)((t.emphra  *  t.empbasic)/100) ;
ca  = (int)((t.empca   *  t.empbasic)/100) ;
da  = (int)((t.empda   *  t.empbasic)/100)  ;
pf  = (int)((t.emppf   *  t.empbasic)/100) ;
ot  = (int)((hours) * (t.empbasic/160)) ;
allowance = hra + ca + da + ot + t.empbasic ;
deduction = pf + advance;
netsalary = allowance - deduction ;

gotoxy(54,8) ;
printf ("%.2f",t.empbasic) ;
gotoxy(37,11) ;
printf ("%.2f",da ) ;
gotoxy(37,12) ;
printf ("%.2f",ot) ;
gotoxy(37,13) ;
printf ("%.2f",ca) ;
gotoxy(37,14) ;
printf ("%.2f",hra) ;
gotoxy(47,14) ;
printf (" : Rs. %.2f",allowance) ;
gotoxy(37,17) ;
printf ("%.2f",pf) ;
gotoxy(37,18) ;
printf ("%.2f",advance) ;
gotoxy(47,18) ;
printf (" : Rs. %.2f",deduction) ;
lineh(6,74,19,196) ;
gotoxy(54,20) ;
printf ("%.2f",netsalary) ;
gotoxy(2,1) ;
getch() ;
}
```

Enter code of the struct employee : 1

Enter month for which SALARY SLIP is to be generated : 10

Enter year for which SALARY SLIP is to be generated : 2000

Figure 5.7 First output screen of salary slip.

```
                     DEEP MOTORS
                 SALARY SLIP - 10 . 2000
---------------------------------------------------------------
Employee Name : SANDEEP SHARMA      Designation : ACCT. MANAGER

          No. of Days Worked  : 24

          Overtime hours      : 18

          Advance amount (Rs) : 1000

Press any key to continue....
```

Figure 5.8 Second output screen of salary slip.

```
                         DEEP MOTORS
                    SALARY SLIP - 10 . 2000
-----------------------------------------------------------------------
Employee Name : SANDEEP SHARMA          Designation : ACCT. MANAGER

  Basic Salary                                        : Rs. 5600.00

  ALLOWANCE
   Dearness Allwance              : Rs. 1960.00
   Over Time                      : Rs. 630.00
   Conveyance                     : Rs. 728.00
   House Rent Allwance            : Rs. 840.00        : Rs. 9758.00

  DEDUCTIONS
   Provident Fund                 : Rs. 672.00
   Advance Taken                  : Rs. 1000.00       : Rs. 1672.00

  N E T   S A L A R Y                                 : Rs. 8086.00

Press any key to continue....
```

Figure 5.9 Final output screen of salary slip.

```
//*************************************************************************
// FUNCTION : Emp_Print
// DESCRIPTION : To Read The Characters On The Screen & Save It
//          To A Temp Variable And Then Send It To The Printer.
//*************************************************************************

void Emp_Print(int x1, int y1, int x2, int y2)
{
	const SEGMENT = 0xB800 ;
	unsigned norow = y2 - y1 + 1, nocol = x2 - x1 + 1 ;
	unsigned i = 0, noele = norow * nocol, *ptr ;
	unsigned row,col,offset;
	unsigned char ch;
```

```
        int count = 0 ;
        FILE *prn;
        prn = fopen ("PRN","w");
        ptr = ((unsigned *)malloc(noele) ) ;
        statusbar(" PRINTING PRINTING PRINTING PRINTING PRINTING PRINTING
                    PRINTING PRINTING PRINTING PRINTI") ;

        for ( row=y1; row<=y2; row++)
        {
                for( col=x1; col<=x2; col++)
                {
                        offset = 2*col + 160*row - 162 ;
                        ptr[i++] = peek(SEGMENT,offset) ;
                }
        }

        for(i=0; i<noele; i++, count++)
        {
                ch = ptr[i] % 256 ;
                putc (ch,prn) ;
                if (count == 80)
                {
                        fputs("\n",prn);
                        count = 0 ;
                }
        }
        fclose(prn);
}

//**********************************************************************
// Main Menu of pay manager
//**********************************************************************

void main(void)
{
        main_menu() ;
}

//**********************************************************************
// FUNCTION : statusbar
```

```
// DESCRIPTION : To make the status bar at prefixed coordinates at the bottom of the screen.
//**********************************************************************

void statusbar(char m[])
{
        _setcursortype(_NOCURSOR) ;
        window(1,24,80,25) ;
        textcolor(BLACK) ;
        textbackground(WHITE) ;
        cprintf(m) ;
        clreol() ;
        window(1,1,80,24) ;
        textcolor(WHITE) ;
        textbackground(BLACK) ;
}


//**********************************************************************
// FUNCTION : getlinedelchar
// DESCRIPTION : To Delete A Character For Getline
//**********************************************************************

void getlinedelchar(char *s, int col, int p, int *len)
{
        int i ;
        for (i=p; i<len; i++)
        s[i - 1] = s[i] ;
        gotoxy(col + p - 1,wherey()) ;
        len— ;
        for (i=p - 1; i<len; i++)
                printf ( "%s",s[i]) ;
        printf ( "." );
}

//**********************************************************************
// FUNCTION : getline
// DESCRIPTION : To Add Online Editing For Inputing A Line.
//**********************************************************************
```

```
void getline(char *s , int limit)
{
        int i, curx, done, col ;
        col = wherex() ;
        for (i = 0; i<limit; i++)
                printf (".") ;
        gotoxy(col,wherey()) ;
        done = 0 ;
        curx = 0 ;
        i = 0 ;
        do
        {
                char ch = getch() ;
                ch = toupper(ch) ;
                switch (ch)
                {
                        case 0 : ch = getch();
                                switch(ch)
                                {
                                        case 75 : if (curx>0)
                                                {
                                                        curx— ;
                                                        gotoxy(wherex()-1,wherey()) ;
                                                }
                                                break ;
                                        case 77 : if (curx<i)
                                                {
                                                        curx++ ;
                                                        gotoxy(wherex()+1,wherey()) ;
                                                }
                                                break ;
                                        case 83 : if (i>0)
                                                {
                                                        if (curx<i)
                                                        {
                                                                getlinedelchar(s,col,curx + 1,&i) ;
                                                                gotoxy(col + curx,wherey()) ;
                                                                if (i == 0)
                                                                        s[i] = 0 ;
                                                        }
```

```
                    }
                }
                break ;
            case 8  : if (curx>0)
                {
                        getlinedelchar(s,col,curx,&i) ;
                        gotoxy(col + curx - 1,wherey()) ;
                        curx— ;
                        if (i == 0)
                                s[i] = 0 ;
                }
                break ;
            case 13 : done = 1 ;
                s[i] = 0 ;
                break ;
            case 27 : done = 1 ;
                s[0] = '0' ;
                break ;
            default :
                if (i < limit)
                {
                        if (curx < i)
                        {
                                s[curx] = ch ;
                                printf ("%c",ch) ;
                                curx++ ;
                        }
                        else
                        {
                                s[i] = ch ;
                                printf ("%c",ch) ;
                                i++ ;
                                curx = i ;
                        }
                }
                else
                        s[i] = 0 ;
        }
    } while (!done) ;
    printf ("\n");
}
```

Library Management System

6

READER'S PARADISE is a library, which provides reading services to its members. Any person can become a member of the library by filling a prescribed form and paying appropriate amount of fees. This membership is given for one-year duration, during which members can avail following facilities :

- They can get the books and journals for reading/reference.
- They can get the books issued, so that they can take them home and return them on or before due date.

For providing the reading services, library purchases books from the market. When books arrive in the library, they are physically inspected and if they are found in order, they are taken into account, else they are rejected. Details of the books are noted in the acquisition register. After these formalities, book can be issued to the readers on their request.

When a member requests for a book, librarian searches it in the library according to the acquisition number and the accession number of the book. If it is available (not issued to other member) then it is issued to the member and details of the issue are noted down in a register called issue register.

After reading the book, members return the book to the librarian. At the time of returning of the book, librarian check if the book is being returned within due date. If yes, then he takes the book back else he calculates the amount of fine. Fine amount is collected from the member and issue details are stroked off from the issue register.

Time to time librarian scans through the issue register and finds out list of books, which are overdue.

Followings are the activities of librarian of READER'S PARADISE library:

- Acquisition of books
- Membership maintenance
- Book issue
- Book return
- Renewal of membership
- Answer management queries

Acquisition of Books

Purchase department of the library purchases various books. After purchase, these books are inspected and if found in order a unique number called acquisition number is assigned to each book. Purchase department then sends these books to librarian. Based on the subject, author of the books etc., librarian assigns a code to the book. This code is called as accession number. He also enters various details regarding a book in acquisition register. He changes entries of the acquisition register, if some change in book information takes place. Format of acquisition register is given below:

ACQUISITION REGISTER

Date: ....

Sl. No.	Acq. No.	Acc.No.	Title & Author(s)	Publisher	Price & Pages	Date(p)	Status

Membership Maintenance

A person, who wants to be a member of the library, has to fill an application form and give it to the librarian along with membership fee and caution money. Librarian assigns a unique membership number to him and enters the details of this member in membership register. After some time, if any member wants to reduce or increase his caution money, librarian makes changes accordingly in the membership modification form. If a member want to discontinue in between, librarian strikes off his entry from the membership register and returns the caution money. Format of membership register is given below:

MEMBERSHIP REGISTER

Date: ....

Sl.No	Memb.No	Name & Address	Memb.Date	Expiry Date	Membership Fees	Caution Money

Book Issue

Librarian issues only one book at a time to a member. A member fills a requisition slip and requests the librarian to issue the book to him. Format of the requisition slip is checked by the librarian and the librarian first checks in member register, whether his membership is still continuing. If not, he does not accept the request else he physically checks for the presence of the book in the library. If not present, he rejects the request of the member; otherwise he issues the book to member. Librarian notes down the details in Issue register. Format of issue register is given below:

ISSUE REGISTER

Date: ....

Sl.No.	Memb.No.	Acq.	Acc.No.	Book Issued On	Date Of Return

Book Return

When a member returns a book, librarian first checks whether the member is returning the book in time or not. If it is late return then he charges fine @ Rs. 1.00 per day from the member. He updates the fine register by entering the date of actual return from the schedule return date and fine collected (if charged).

Renewal of Membership

As explained before, library provides membership only for one-year duration. After this, if members wish to continue their membership, they have to give an application to the librarian requesting him to extend their membership for next year duration. This application has to be supported by appropriate amount of renewal fee. On receiving the application librarian makes appropriate entries in the Membership register and renews the membership so that member can avail various facilities of the library, for next year also.

Program Source Codes LIB.C

```
/* Program for library management system */
// Declaration of header files
#include <stdio.h>
#include <process.h>
#include <string.h>
#include <stdio.h>
#include <ctype.h>
#include <conio.h>
#include <dos.h>
#include <stdlib.h>
// Information regarding to library acquisition
struct library
{
        int acq_no;         // Acquisition number
        int acc_no;         // Accession number
        char title[30];
        char author1[30], author2[30];   // Authors
        char publisher[30];        // Name of the publisher
        float price;        // Price of the book
        int dd, mm, yy;  // Date of purchase
        int pages;          // Total pages in book
        char status;        // Present status of book
} lib;

/* Information regarding member */
struct member
{

        int memb_no;    // Membership number
        char name[30]; // Name of the member
        char address[30]; // Address of the employee
        int mdd, mmm, myy; // Membership date
        int edd, emm, eyy; // Expire date
        float memb_fee; // Membership fee
        float caut_fee;  // Caution money
} mem;
```

```
/* Information regarding book issue record(s) */
struct issue
{
	int acq_no;	// Aquisition number
	int acc_no;	// Accession no
	int memb_no;	// Member number
	int idd, imm, iyy;// Issue date
	int rdd, rmm, ryy;		// Return date
} iss;

// Information related to fine register
struct fine
{
	int memb_no; // Member number
	int	acq_no;// fine acquisition no
	int acc_no;	// fine accession no
	int idd, imm, iyy;// Book issue date

	int rdd, rmm, ryy;		// Book purposed return date

	int cdd, cmm, cyy;		// Returned date
	int finfee;
} fin;

// Function to find the expire dates of members
int date_expire(int, int, int);

// Function to find the no of days in between two dates
int no_of_days(int, int, int, int, int, int);

// Function to return the total days in a month
int month_days(int);

// class lib_class
void DRAW_LINE(int, int, int, char);
void DRAW_VER(int, int, int, char);
void DRAW_BOX(int, int, int, int, char);

// Class for main control
void lib_SCREEN(void);
```

```
void MENU_EDIT(void);

void Menu_console(void); // Menu for add, modify and delete of library books
void new_library(void); // Function to enter new library books through the acquisition number
void NEW_lib(int, int, char s_title[30], char s_author1[30], char s_author2[30], char
s_publisher[30], float s_price, int sdd, int smm, int syy, int s_pages, char s_status);
void Lib_delete(int, int); // Deleting library information from data file
// Function to perform a left clear on specified row from a specified column
void Left_clear(int, int);
void Clear_area(int, int, int, int); // Function to clear a specified area in the screen
// Function to perform a right clear on specified row from a specified column
void Right_clear(int, int);
void Change_library(void);        // Function to change the library information

// Function to rewrite the library contents at its original location
void Replace(int, int, char s_title[30], char s_author1[30], char s_author2[30],
        char s_publisher[30], float s_price, int sdd, int smm, int syy, int s_pages, char s_status);
        int recordno(int, int); // Function to find the position in file
void Delete_Accno(void); // Function to delete records from library
void Record_delete(int, int);      // Function to delete the record by copy method
void Book_Issue(void); // Function to issue books to members
void Book_display(int, int); // Function to display the book information at return time

// Report functions on Library of purchase department
// Function to display various option on related to report for answer to management queires
void Report_Menu(void);
void Acqu_Register(void);          // Acquisition register for report


// Class contains information containing the member details
void Memb_console(void); // Menu for add, modify and delete of Membership
void new_member(void); // Function to select addition of members
// Deletes the same record after creating its position
void Memb_delete(int);
void Memb_modify(int); // Library member modification function
void Change_member(void);          // Function to change the members information
void Display_member(int);          // Function to display the existing information for modification

// Function to rewrite the Member contents at its original location
void Replace_mem(int, char s_name[30], char s_address[30], int, int, int, int, int, int, float, float);
```

```
int record_no(int); // Function to find the position in file
void Delete_member(void); // Function to delete member from MEMBER.dat data file
void Member_Renewal(void);    // Function to renewal of membership
void Renewal_member(int);     // Function where the membership date is modified
int Memb_Check(int);    // Membership check
int Expire_Check(int); // Function to check membership date expired or not

// Reporting function for member
void Memb_Register(void); // Function to display the membership register globally
void Expire_Register(void); //Function to display the expired membership register

// Function to simply add records
void NEW_memb(int, char s_name[30], char s_address[30], int, int, int, int, int, int, float, float);

// Information related to issue of books and issue register
// Function to check the book is issued or not while deleting a library book
int Issue_Check(int, int);
void Issue_Add(int, int, int, int, int, int, int, int, int);
void Issue_Delete(int s_acq_no, int s_acc_no, int s_memb_no, int s_idd, int s_imm,
        int s_iyy, int s_rdd, int s_rmm, int s_ryy);
int Issue_memb_check(int); // Function to issue member check
void Book_Return(void); // Function to return books
void Return_Issue(int); // Function for displaying the returned books information

// Function to delete the issued book of member from MASTER.dat data file
void Issue_member_delete(int);
void Issue_Register(void);            // Function to display the issued books in library
void OverDue_Book(void);      // Function for overdue books
void Read_issue(void);

void Fine_add(int, int, int, int, int, int, int, int, int, int, int, int, int);
void Fine_Register(void);         // Function to display the fine collection register

// Function for horizontal line draw
void DRAW_LINE(int column1, int column2, int row, char c)
{

        for (column1; column1 <= column2; column1++)
        {
                gotoxy(column1, row);
```

```
            printf( " %c ",c);
        }
}

// Function for vertical line draw
void DRAW_VER(int row1, int row2, int column, char c)
{
        for (row1; row1 <= row2; row1++)
        {
                gotoxy(column, row1);
                printf ( " %c ", c);
        }
}

// Function for drawing boxes
void DRAW_BOX(int column1, int row1, int column2, int row2, char c)
{
        char ch = 218;
        char c1, c2, c3, c4;
        char l1 = 196, l2 = 179;
        if (c == ch)
        {
                c1 = 218;
                c2 = 191;
                c3 = 192;
                c4 = 217;
                l1 = 196;
                l2 = 179;
        }
        else
        {
                c1 = c;
                c2 = c;
                c3 = c;
                c4 = c;
                l1 = c;
                c2 = c;
        }
        gotoxy(column1+1, row1);
        printf ("%c", c1);
```

```
        gotoxy(column2, row1);
        printf ( " %c ",c2);
        gotoxy(column1+1, row2);
        printf ( "%c", c3);
        gotoxy(column2+1, row2);
        printf ( "%c",c4);
        column1++;
        column2--;
        column1--;
        column2++;
        row1++;
        row2--;
        DRAW_VER(row1, row2, column1, 12); // Vertical line
        DRAW_VER(row1, row2, column2, 12);
}

// Function to clear a row from left of the screen
void Left_clear(int col, int row)
{
        int j;
        for ( j = col; j <= 39; j++)
        {
                gotoxy(j, row);
                printf ( " ");
        }
}

// Function to clear a row from right of the screen
void Right_clear(int col, int row)
{
        int j;
        for (j = col; j <= 79; j++)
        {
                gotoxy(j, row);
                printf ( " ");
        }
}

// Function to clear a specified area in the screen
void Clear_area(int row, int till, int col, int tcol)
```

```
{
        int p , xcol;
        for ( p = row; p <= till; p++)
        {
                xcol = col;
                for ( xcol = xcol; xcol <= tcol; xcol++)
                {
                        gotoxy(xcol, p);
                        printf ( " ");
                }
        }
}

// Function for main menu for library management system
void lib_SCREEN(void)
{
        char ch;
        int xdd, xmm, xyy;
        struct date d;                  // For extracting system date
        while (ch <= '6')
        {
                clrscr();
                getdate(&d);
                xdd = d.da_day;
                xmm = d.da_mon;
                xyy = d.da_year;

                DRAW_BOX(10, 5, 71, 21, 219);
                DRAW_BOX(9, 4, 72, 22, 218);
                textcolor(BLACK);
                textbackground(LIGHTGRAY);
                gotoxy(10, 3);
                printf ( "Date: ");
                printf ("%d", xdd);
                printf (" -");
                printf ( "%d", xmm);
                printf ( "-");
                printf ("%d", xyy);

                gotoxy(65, 3);
```

```
printf ( "<0>=Exit");
gotoxy(27, 25);
printf ( "Developed by Author & Her Team");
gotoxy(15,7);
cprintf(" L I B R A R Y  M A N A G E M E N T  S Y S T E M ");
gotoxy(28,9);
printf ( "1. Acquisition Section");
gotoxy(28, 10);
printf ( "2. Membership Maintenance");
gotoxy(28, 11);
printf ( "3. Book Issue");
gotoxy(28, 12);
printf ( "4. Book Return");
gotoxy(28, 13);
printf ( "5. Renewal of Membership");
gotoxy(28, 14);
printf ( "6. Answer Management Queries");

gotoxy(28, 17);
cprintf("Enter Your Choice ");
ch = getche();
switch (ch)
{
        case '0':
                clrscr();
                exit(0); // Option to exit from main menu
                break;
        case '1':
        {
                Menu_console(); // Library books into LIB.dat
                break;
        }
        case '2':
        {
                Memb_console(); // Members management in MEMFILE.dat
                break;
        }
        case '3':
        {
                Book_Issue();  // Function to issue books
```

```
                    break;
                }
                case '4':
                {
                    Book_Return(); // Function to return books
                    break;
                }
                case '5':
                {
                    Member_Renewal();
                    break;
                }
                case '6':
                {
                    Report_Menu(); // Function for displaying report menu
                    break;
                }
            }
        }
}
```

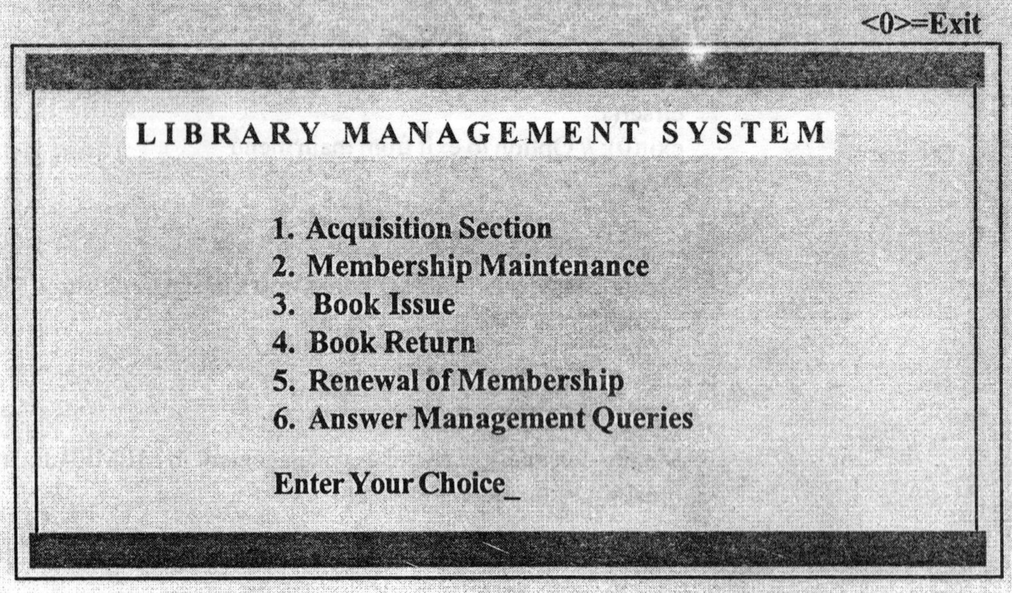

Figure 6.1 Output screen of lib_SCREEN() function

```
// Function for Adding, modifying and deleting from LIB.dat data file
void Menu_console(void)
{
	char ch;
	while (1)
	{
		clrscr();
		gotoxy(65, 3);
		printf ( "<0>=Exit");

		DRAW_BOX(10, 5, 71, 21, 219);
		DRAW_BOX(9, 4, 72, 22, 218);
		textcolor(BLACK);
		textbackground(WHITE);
		gotoxy(22, 8);
		cprintf("L I B R A R Y   C O N S O L E");
		textcolor(LIGHTGRAY);
		textbackground(BLACK);
		gotoxy(25, 12);
		printf ( "1: Keeping New Record");
		gotoxy(25, 13);
		printf ( "2. Changing Existing Record");
		gotoxy(25, 14);
		printf ( "3. Deleting Library Record");

		gotoxy(25, 16);
		printf ( "0. Return");
		gotoxy(25, 18);
		printf ( "Enter your choice : ");
		ch = getche();
		if (ch == 27)
			break;
		else
			if (ch == '1')
			{
				new_library();
			}
			else
				if (ch == '2')
				{
```

```
                    Change_library();
                    break;
            }
            else
                    if (ch == '3')
                    {
                            Delete_Accno();
                            break;
                    }
                    else
                            if (ch == '0')
                                    break;
    }
}
```

```
                                                    <0>=Exit

            LIBRARY CONSOLE

                1. Keeping New Record
                2. Changing Existing Record
                3. Deleting Library Record

                0. Return

                Enter Your Choice : _
```

Figure 6.2 Output screen of Menu_console function for library

```
// Function to append a record into LIB.dat data file
void NEW_lib(int s_acq_no, int s_acc_no, char s_title[30], char s_author1[30], char
s_author2[30], char s_publisher[30], float s_price, int sdd, int smm, int syy, int s_pages, char
s_status)
{
	FILE *sfile;

	lib.acq_no = s_acq_no;
	lib.acc_no = s_acc_no;
	strcpy(lib.title, s_title);
	strcpy(lib.author1, s_author1);
	strcpy(lib.author2, s_author2);
	strcpy(lib.publisher, s_publisher);
	lib.price = s_price;
	lib.dd = sdd;
	lib.mm = smm;
	lib.yy = syy;
	lib.pages = s_pages;
	lib.status = s_status;

	// Append the new record into LIB.dat data file
	sfile = fopen("LIB.dat", "a");
	fwrite(&lib,sizeof(lib),1,sfile);
	fclose(sfile);
}

// Function to delete a selected record from LIB.dat data file
void Lib_delete(int s_acq_no, int s_acc_no)
{
	FILE *file;
	FILE *temp;
	temp = fopen("TEMP.dat", "w");
	file = fopen("LIB.dat", "r");

	// Delete the record using copy method into temporaty file
	while (fread(&lib,sizeof(lib),1,file)==1)
	{
		if ((lib.acq_no != s_acq_no) && (lib.acc_no != s_acc_no))
			fwrite(&lib,sizeof(lib),1,temp);
		else
```

```
            fread(&lib,sizeof(lib),1,file);
        }
        fclose(file);
        fclose(temp);
        remove("LIB.dat");
        rename("TEMP.dat","LIB.dat");
}

// Function for main menu to append new library books LIB.dat
void new_library(void)
{
        char ch;
        int i, valid;
        int s_acq_no;     // Acquisition number
        int s_acc_no;     // Accession number
        char s_title[30];
        char s_author1[30], s_author2[30];        // Authors
        char s_publisher[30];     // Name of the publisher
        float s_price;     // Price of the book
        int sdd, smm, syy;        // Date of purchase
        int s_pages;       // Total pages in book
        char s_status;     // Present status of book
        struct date d;            // For extracting system date

        clrscr();

        gotoxy(3, 3);
        for (i = 1; i<= 76; i++)
                cprintf(" ");

        textbackground(BLACK);
        textcolor(BLACK+BLINK);
        textbackground(WHITE);
        gotoxy(30, 3);
        cprintf("Library Acquisition Entry");
        textcolor(LIGHTGRAY);
        textbackground(BLACK);
        gotoxy(65, 3);
        printf ( "<0>=Exit");
```

```
DRAW_BOX(10, 5, 71, 21, 219);
DRAW_BOX(9, 4, 72, 22, 218);
textcolor(BLACK);
textbackground(LIGHTGRAY);
do
{
        // Function to clear a specified input box from the screen
        Clear_area(6, 18, 11, 70);

        getdate(&d);
        sdd = d.da_day;
        smm = d.da_mon;
        syy = d.da_year;

        gotoxy(50, 7);
        printf ( "Date: " );
        printf ("%d", sdd);
        printf ("-");
        printf (" %d ",smm);
        printf ("-");
        printf (" %d ",syy);
        gotoxy(10, 23);
        printf ( "Enter the Acquisition number");
        gotoxy(13, 7);
        printf ( "Acquisition No. " );
        gotoxy(29, 7);
        scanf (" %d",&s_acq_no);
        Left_clear(10, 23);
        Right_clear(39, 23);

        gotoxy(11, 8);
        for (i = 1; i <= 60; i++)
        printf ("=");

        do
        {
                // Function to clear a specified input box from the screen
                Clear_area(9, 18, 11, 70);

                gotoxy(10, 23);
```

```
printf ( "Enter the Accession number");
gotoxy(13, 9);
printf ( "Accession No. ");
gotoxy(28, 9);
scanf (" %d",&s_acc_no);
Left_clear(10, 23);
Right_clear(39, 23);

if (s_acq_no == 1)
{
        // Creates a temporaty space in LIB.dat data tile
        NEW_lib(s_acq_no, s_acc_no, "aaa", "bbb", "ccc", "ddd", 0,
                        0, 0, 0, 0, 'x');
        // Deletes the same record after creating its position
        Lib_delete(s_acq_no, s_acc_no);
}
if ((s_acq_no == 0) || (s_acc_no == 0))
        return;

gotoxy(13, 10);
printf ( "Title : ");
gotoxy(13, 12);
printf ( "Author(s) : ");
gotoxy(13, 14);
printf ( "Publisher : ");
gotoxy(13, 15);
printf ( "Price : ");
gotoxy(13, 16);
printf ( "Pages : ");
gotoxy(13, 17);
printf ( "Status : ");

do
{
        Left_clear(10, 23);
        gotoxy(10, 23);
        printf ( "Enter Title of the Book");
        valid = 1;
        gotoxy(22, 10);
        gets(s_title);
```

```
        strupr(s_title);
        if (s_title[0] == '0')
            return;
        if (strlen(s_title) == 0 || strlen(s_title) > 30)
        {
            valid = 0;
            gotoxy(10, 23);
            printf ( "\7Title should not greater than 30");
            getch();
        }
    } while (!valid);
    Left_clear(5, 23);
    Right_clear(39, 23);

    do
    {
        gotoxy(10, 23);
        printf ( "Enter Author of the Book ");
        valid = 1;
        gotoxy(26, 12);
        gets(s_author1);
        strupr(s_author1);
        if (s_author1[0] == '0')
            return;
        if (strlen(s_author1) == 0 || strlen(s_author1) > 30)
        {
            valid = 0;
            gotoxy(10, 23);
            printf ( "\7Author should not greater than 30");
            getch();
        }
    } while (!valid);
    Left_clear(10, 23);
    Right_clear(39, 23);

    gotoxy(10, 23);
    printf ( "Enter second author if there");
    // Second author
    gotoxy(26, 13);
    gets(s_author2);
```

```
strupr(s_author2);
Left_clear(5, 23);
Right_clear(39, 23);

do
{
        Left_clear(10, 23);
        Right_clear(39, 23);

        gotoxy(10, 23);
        printf ( "Enter name of the Publisher");
        valid = 1;
        gotoxy(26, 14);
        gets(s_publisher);
        strupr(s_publisher);
        if (s_publisher[0] == '0')
                return;
        if (strlen(s_publisher) == 0 || strlen(s_publisher) > 30)
        {
                valid = 0;
                gotoxy(10, 23);
                printf ( "\7Publisher should not greater than 30");
                getch();
        }
} while (!valid);
Left_clear(10, 23);
Right_clear(39, 23);

gotoxy(10, 23);
printf ( "Enter selling price of the book");
gotoxy(22, 15);
scanf (" %.2f",&s_price);
Left_clear(10, 23);
Right_clear(39, 23);

gotoxy(10, 23);
printf ( "Enter Total pages in the book");
gotoxy(22, 16);
scanf (" %d",s_pages);
Left_clear(10, 23);
```

```
    Right_clear(39, 23);

    // The status is automatically fill as "Y", because the accession is entering
    // fresh books

    gotoxy(22, 17);
    s_status = 'Y';
    printf ( "%c",s_status);

    do
    {
        valid = 1;
        gotoxy(10, 23);
        printf ( "Do you want to save the record <Y/N>: ");
        ch = getche();
        if (ch == '0')
            return;
        ch = toupper(ch);
    }while (ch != 'N' && ch != 'Y');
    if (ch == 'N')
        return;
    NEW_lib(s_acq_no, s_acc_no, s_title, s_author1, s_author2,
        s_publisher, s_price, sdd, smm, syy, s_pages, s_status);
    Left_clear(10, 23);
    Right_clear(39, 23);

    gotoxy(12, 23);
    printf ( "Any Accession <Y/N>: ");
    ch = getche();
    if (ch == '0')
        return;
    Left_clear(12, 23);
    Right_clear(12, 23);

    ch = toupper(ch);
} while (ch == 'Y');

gotoxy(12, 23);
printf ( "Any Acquisition <Y/N>: ");
ch = getche();
```

```
            if (ch == '0')
                    return;
            Left_clear(12, 23);
            Right_clear(12, 23);

            ch = toupper(ch);
    } while (ch == 'Y');

}
```

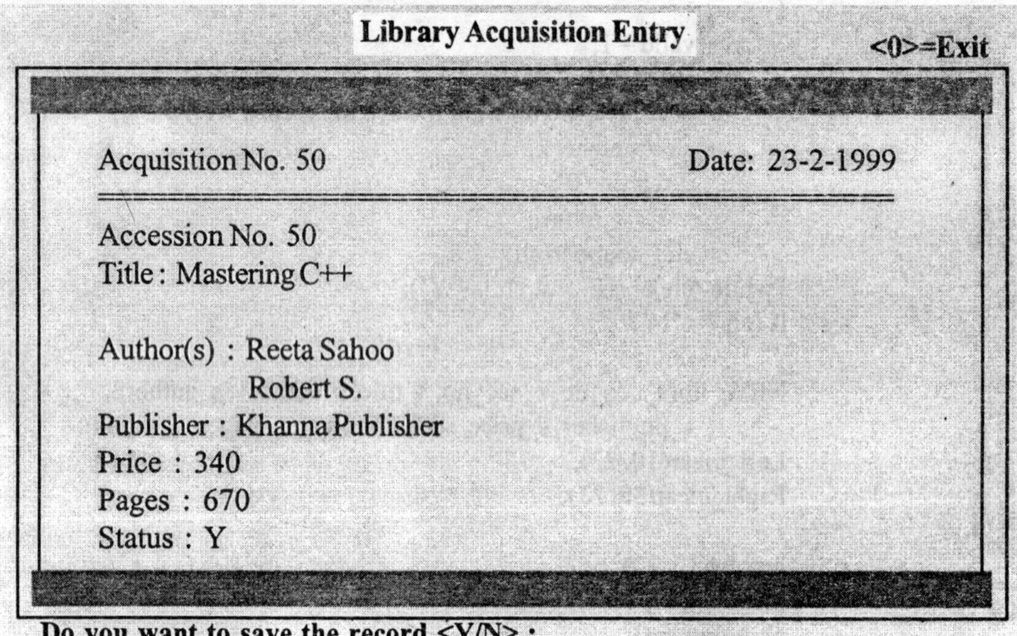
Library Acquisition Entry
<0>=Exit

Acquisition No. 50 Date: 23-2-1999

Accession No. 50
Title : Mastering C++

Author(s) : Reeta Sahoo
Robert S.
Publisher : Khanna Publisher
Price : 340
Pages : 670
Status : Y

Do you want to save the record <Y/N> :

Figure 6.3 Acquisition entry of new_library function of library menu

```
// Function to count the total number of records in LIB.dat data file for
// counting the modification record till found
int recordno(int s_acq_no, int s_acc_no)
{
        FILE *file;
        int count = 0;
        file = fopen("LIB.dat", "r");
```

```
        // Counts the total records in DETAILS.dat data file
        while (fread(&lib, sizeof(lib),1,file)==1)
        {
                count++;
                if ((s_acq_no == lib.acq_no) && (s_acc_no == lib.acc_no))
                        break;
        }
        fclose(file);
        return count;
}

// Modification function for library record
void Replace(int s_acq_no, int s_acc_no, char s_title[30], char s_author1[30], char s_author2[30],
        char s_publisher[30], float s_price, int sdd, int smm, int syy, int s_pages, char s_status)
{
        int recno;
        int location;
        FILE *file;
        file = fopen("LIB.dat", "rb+");
        recno = recordno(s_acq_no, s_acc_no);
        lib.acq_no = s_acq_no;
        lib.acc_no = s_acc_no;
        strcpy(lib.title, s_title);
        strcpy(lib.author1, s_author1);
        strcpy(lib.author2, s_author2);
        strcpy(lib.publisher, s_publisher);
        lib.price = s_price;
        lib.dd = sdd;
        lib.mm = smm;
        lib.yy = syy;
        lib.pages = s_pages;
        lib.status = s_status;

        // Finding the location in file

        location = (recno-1) * sizeof(struct library);

        // Search the position in file
        fseek(file,location,SEEK_CUR);
```

```
        // Re-write the contents in DETAILS.dat data file
        fwrite(&lib, sizeof(lib),1,file);
        fclose(file);
        return;
}

// Function for main menu to change the existing recrod in LIB.dat
void Change_library(void)
{
        char ch;
        int i, valid;
        int s_acq_no = 0;          // Acquisition number

        int s_acc_no = 0;          // Accession number
        char s_title[30];
        char s_author1[30], s_author2[30];         // Authors
        char s_publisher[30];   // Name of the publisher
        float s_price;     // Price of the book
        int sdd, smm, syy;         // Date of purchase
        int s_pages;       // Total pages in book
        char  s_status;  // Present status of book
        struct date d;             // For extracting system date
        FILE *file;
        clrscr();

        gotoxy(3, 3);
        for (i = 1; i<= 76; i++)
                cprintf(" ");

        textbackground(BLACK);
        textcolor(BLACK+BLINK);
        textbackground(WHITE);
        gotoxy(30, 3);
        cprintf("Library Modification");
        textcolor(LIGHTGRAY);
        textbackground(BLACK);
        gotoxy(65, 3);
        printf ( "<0>=Exit");
```

```
DRAW_BOX(10, 5, 71, 21, 219);
DRAW_BOX(9, 4, 72, 22, 218);
textcolor(BLACK);
textbackground(LIGHTGRAY);

do
{
        // Function to clear a specified input box from the screen
        Clear_area(6, 18, 11, 70);
        getdate(&d);
        sdd = d.da_day;
        smm = d.da_mon;
        syy = d.da_year;

        gotoxy(50, 7);
        printf ( "Date: " );
        printf ("%d",sdd);
        printf ("-");
        printf ("%d",smm);
        printf ("-");
        printf ("%d",syy);

        gotoxy(10, 23);
        printf ( "Enter the Acquisition number");
        gotoxy(13, 7);
        printf ( "Acquisition No. " );
        gotoxy(29, 7);
        scanf (" %d",&s_acq_no);
        Left_clear(10, 23);
        Right_clear(39, 23);

        gotoxy(11, 8);
        for (i = 1; i <= 60; i++)
        printf ( "=");

        do
        {
                // Function to clear a specified input box from the screen
                Clear_area(9, 18, 11, 70);
```

```
gotoxy(10, 23);
printf ( "Enter the Accession number");
gotoxy(13, 9);
printf ( "Accession No. ");
gotoxy(28, 9);
scanf (" %d",s_acc_no);
Left_clear(10, 23);
Right_clear(39, 23);
if ((s_acq_no == 0) || (s_acc_no == 0))
        return;


file = fopen("LIB.dat", "r");
rewind(file);
// Search the record for further modification
while (fread(&lib,sizeof(struct library),1,file)==1)
{
        if ((s_acq_no == lib.acq_no) && (s_acc_no == lib.acc_no))
        {
                gotoxy(13, 10);
                printf ( "Existing Information");
                gotoxy(13, 11);
                printf ( "Title : ");
                gotoxy(13, 12);
                printf ( "Author(s) : ");
                gotoxy(13, 14);
                printf ( "Publisher : ");
                gotoxy(13, 15);
                printf ( "Price : ");
                gotoxy(13, 16);
                printf ( "Pages : ");
                gotoxy(13, 17);
                printf ( "Status : ");
                gotoxy(22, 11);
                puts(lib.title);

                gotoxy(26, 12);
                puts(lib.author1);

                gotoxy(26, 13);
```

```
                puts(lib.author2);
                gotoxy(26, 14);
                puts(lib.publisher);
                gotoxy(22, 15);
                printf( "%.2f",lib.price);

                gotoxy(22, 16);
                printf( "%d",lib.pages);
                gotoxy(22, 17);
                printf( "%c",lib.status);
                break;
        }
}
fclose(file);
gotoxy(45, 10);
printf( "New Information");

do
{
        Left_clear(10, 23);
        gotoxy(10, 23);
        printf( "Enter New Title of the Book");
        valid = 1;
        gotoxy(45, 11);
        gets(s_title);
        strupr(s_title);
        if (s_title[0] == '0')
                return;
        if (strlen(s_title) == 0 || strlen(s_title) > 30)
        {
                valid = 0;
                gotoxy(10, 23);
                printf( "\7Title should not greater than 30");
                getch();
        }
} while (!valid);
Left_clear(5, 23);
Right_clear(39, 23);
```

```
do
{
        gotoxy(12, 23);
        printf ( "Enter New Author of the Book ");
        valid = 1;
        gotoxy(45, 12);
        gets(s_author1);
        strupr(s_author1);
        if (s_author1[0] == '0')
                return;
        if (strlen(s_author1) == 0 || strlen(s_author1) > 30)
        {
                valid = 0;
                gotoxy(10, 23);
                printf ( "\7Author should not greater than 30");
                getch();
        }
} while (!valid);
Left_clear(10, 23);
Right_clear(39, 23);

gotoxy(10, 23);
printf ( "Enter second author if there");
// Second author
gotoxy(45, 13);
gets(s_author2);
strupr(s_author2);
Left_clear(5, 23);
Right_clear(39,23);

do
{
        Left_clear(10, 23);
        Right_clear(39, 23);

        gotoxy(10, 23);
        printf ( "Enter name of the Publisher");
        valid = 1;
        gotoxy(45, 14);
        gets(s_publisher);
```

```
        strupr(s_publisher);
        if (s_publisher[0] == '0')
            return;
        if (strlen(s_publisher) == 0 || strlen(s_publisher) > 30)
        {
            valid = 0;
            gotoxy(10, 23);
            printf ( "\7Publisher should not greater than 30");
            getch();
        }
    } while (!valid);
    Left_clear(10, 23);
    Right_clear(39, 23);

    gotoxy(10, 23);
    printf ( "Enter selling price of the book");
    gotoxy(45, 15);
    scanf (" %.2f",&s_price);
    Left_clear(10, 23);
    Right_clear(39, 23);

    gotoxy(10, 23);
    printf ( "Enter Total pages in the book");
    gotoxy(45, 16);
    scanf (" %d",s_pages);
    Left_clear(10, 23);
    Right_clear(39, 23);

    // The status is automatically fill as "Y", because the accession is entering
    // fresh books

    gotoxy(45, 17);
    s_status = 'Y';
    printf ( "%c",s_status);

    do
    {
        valid = 1;
        gotoxy(10, 23);
        printf ( "Do you want to Overwrite the record <Y/N>: ");
```

```
                    ch = getche();
                    if (ch == '0')
                              return;
                    ch = toupper(ch);
          }while (ch != 'N' && ch != 'Y');

          if (ch == 'N')
                    return;
          Replace(s_acq_no, s_acc_no, s_title, s_author1, s_author2, s_publisher,
                    s_price, sdd, smm, syy, s_pages, s_status);
          Left_clear(10, 23);
          Right_clear(39, 23);

          gotoxy(12, 23);
          printf ( "Any Accession <Y/N>: ");
          ch = getche();
          if (ch == '0')
                    return;
          Left_clear(12, 23);
          Right_clear(12, 23);

          ch = toupper(ch);
     } while (ch == 'Y');

     gotoxy(12, 23);
     printf ( "Any Acquisition <Y/N>: ");
     ch = getche();

     if (ch == '0')
          return;
     Left_clear(12, 23);
     Right_clear(12, 23);

     ch = toupper(ch);
} while (ch == 'Y');

}
```

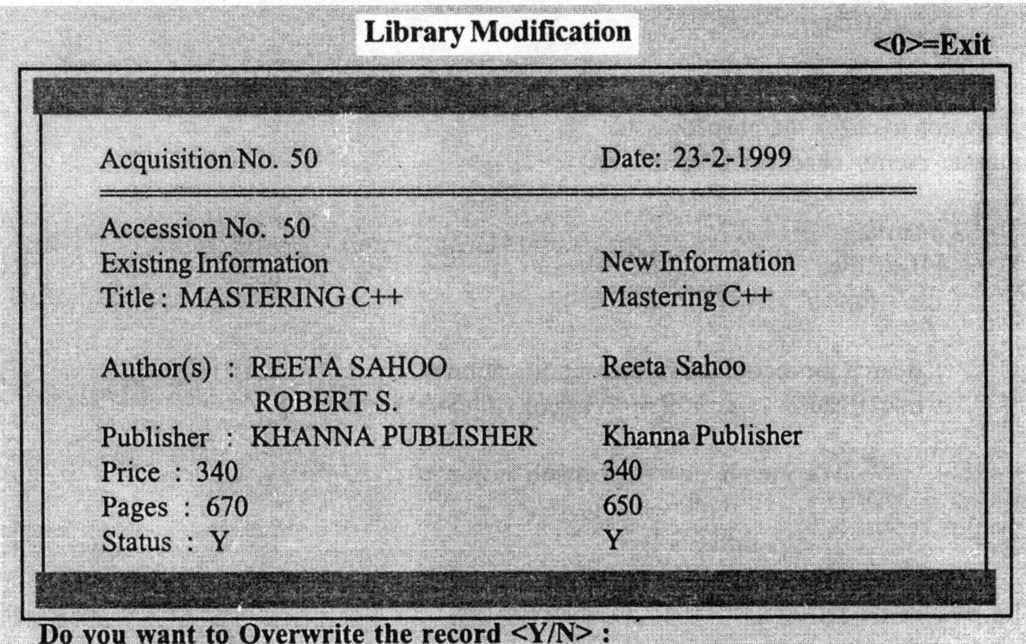

Figure 6.4 Acquisition modification of Change_library function of library menu

```
// Function to find the acquisition number and accession number whether it exists or not
int Issue_Check(int s_acq_no, int s_acc_no)
{
	int tflag = 0;
	FILE *file;
	file = fopen("MASTER.dat", "r");

	// Search the record for further modification
	while (fread(&iss, sizeof(struct issue),1,file)==1)
	{
		if ((s_acq_no == iss.acq_no) && (s_acc_no == iss.acc_no))
		{
			tflag = 1;
			break;
		}
	}
	fclose(file);
```

```
        return (tflag);
}

// Function to check member for issue
int Issue_memb_check(int s_memb_no)
{
        int mflag = 0;
        FILE *file;
        file = fopen("MASTER.dat", "r");

        // Search the record for further modification
        while (fread(&iss, sizeof(struct issue),1,file)==1)
        {
                if (s_memb_no == iss.memb_no)
                {
                        mflag = 1;
                        break;
                }
        }
        fclose(file);
        return (mflag);
}

// Function to find the MEMFILE.dat file, to ascertain whether membership EXISTS or not
int Memb_Check(int s_memb_no)
{
        int mflag = 0;
        FILE *file;
        file = fopen("MEMFILE.dat", "r");

        // Search the record for further modification
        while (fread(&mem, sizeof(struct member),1,file)==1)
        {
                if (s_memb_no == mem.memb_no)
                {
                        mflag = 1;
                        break;
                }
        }
        fclose(file);
```

```
        return (mflag);
}

// Function to delete record from LIB.dat data file by the matching acquition no. and accession no.
void Record_delete(int s_acq_no, int s_acc_no)
{
        FILE *file;
        FILE *temp;
        file = fopen("LIB.dat", "r");
        temp = fopen("TEMP.dat", "w");

        // Delete the record using copy method into temporaty file
        while (fread(&lib, sizeof(struct library),1,file)==1);
        {
                if ((s_acq_no != lib.acc_no) && (s_acc_no != lib.acc_no))
                        fwrite(&lib, sizeof(struct library),1,file);
        }
        fclose(file);
        fclose(temp);
        remove("LIB.dat");
        rename("TEMP.dat","LIB.dat");
}


// Function for main menu to Delete the existing recrod in LIB.dat
void Delete_Accno(void)
{
        char ch;
        int i;
        int s_acq_no = 0;         // Acquisition number
        int flag = 0;
        int tflag = 0;

        int s_acc_no = 0;         // Accession number
        char s_title[30];
        char s_author1[30], s_author2[30];      // Authors
        char s_publisher[30];     // Name of the publisher
        float s_price;     // Price of the book
        int sdd, smm, syy;        // Date of purchase
        int s_pages;       // Total pages in book
```

```
char s_status;   // Present status of book
struct date d;            // For extracting system date
FILE *file;
clrscr();
gotoxy(3, 3);
for (i = 1; i<= 76; i++)
        cprintf(" ");

textbackground(BLACK);
textcolor(BLACK+BLINK);
textbackground(WHITE);
gotoxy(30, 3);
cprintf("Library Deletion");
textcolor(LIGHTGRAY);
textbackground(BLACK);
gotoxy(65, 3);
printf ( "<0>=Exit");

DRAW_BOX(10, 5, 71, 21, 219);
DRAW_BOX(9, 4, 72, 22, 218);
textcolor(BLACK);
textbackground(LIGHTGRAY);

        do
{
        // Function to clear a specified input box from the screen
        Clear_area(6, 18, 11, 70);

        getdate(&d);
        sdd = d.da_day;
        smm = d.da_mon;
        syy = d.da_year;

        gotoxy(50, 7);
        printf ( "Date: " );
        printf ("%d",sdd);
        printf ("-");
        printf ("%d",smm);
        printf ("-");
        printf ("%d",syy);
```

```
gotoxy(10, 23);
printf ( "Enter the Acquisition number");
gotoxy(13, 7);
printf ( "Acquisition No. " );
gotoxy(29, 7);
scanf ("%d", s_acq_no);
Left_clear(10, 23);
Right_clear(39, 23);

gotoxy(11, 8);
for (i = 1; i <= 60; i++)
printf ( "=");

do
{
        // Function to clear a specified input box from the screen
        Clear_area(9, 18, 11, 70);

        gotoxy(10, 23);
        printf ( "Enter the Accession number");
        gotoxy(13, 9);
        printf ( "Accession No. ");
        gotoxy(28, 9);
        scanf ("%d", s_acc_no);
        Left_clear(10, 23);
        Right_clear(39, 23);
        if ((s_acq_no == 0) || (s_acc_no == 0))
                return;


        file = fopen("LIB.dat", "r");

        // Search the record for further modification
        while (fread(&lib, sizeof(struct library), 1, file)==1)
        {
                if ((s_acq_no == lib.acq_no) && (s_acc_no == lib.acc_no))
                {
                        flag = 1;
                        gotoxy(15, 11);
                        printf ( "Title : ");
```

```
                    gotoxy(15, 12);
                    printf ( "Author(s) : ");
                    gotoxy(15, 14);
                    printf ( "Publisher : ");
                    gotoxy(15, 15);
                    printf ( "Price : ");
                    gotoxy(15, 16);
                    printf ( "Pages : ");
                    gotoxy(15, 17);
                    printf ( "Status : ");
                    gotoxy(26, 11);
                    puts(lib.title);

                    gotoxy(26, 12);
                    puts(lib.author1);

                    gotoxy(26, 13);
                    puts(lib.author2);
                    gotoxy(26, 14);
                    puts(lib.publisher);
                    gotoxy(26, 15);
                    printf ( "%.2f",lib.price);

                    gotoxy(26, 16);
                    printf ( "%d",lib.pages);
                    gotoxy(26, 17);
                    printf ( "%c",lib.status);
                    break;
            }
        }
        fclose(file);

        tflag = Issue_Check(s_acq_no, s_acc_no);
        if (tflag == 0)
        {
            do
            {
                    gotoxy(10, 23);
                    printf ( "Are you you sure to Delete this record <Y/N>: ");
                    ch = getche();
```

```
                if (ch == '0')
                        return;
                ch = toupper(ch);
            }while (ch != 'N' && ch != 'Y');
        }
        else
        {
            gotoxy(12, 23);
            printf ( "The is already Issued ...");
        }
        Left_clear(10, 23);
        Right_clear(39, 23);

        if ((ch == 'Y') && (flag == 1))
        {
            Record_delete(s_acq_no, s_acc_no);
        }
        if (flag == 1)
        {
            gotoxy(57, 23);
            printf ( "Record Deleted !");
            getch();
        }
        Left_clear(10, 23);
        Right_clear(39, 23);

        gotoxy(12, 23);
        printf ( "Any Acccssion <Y/N>: ");
        ch = getche();
        if (ch == '0')
            return;
        Left_clear(12, 23);
        Right_clear(12, 23);

        ch = toupper(ch);
    } while (ch == 'Y');

    gotoxy(12, 23);
    printf ( "Any Acquisition <Y/N>: ");
    ch = getche();
```

```
            if (ch == '0')
                return;
            Left_clear(12, 23);
            Right_clear(12, 23);

            ch = toupper(ch);
        } while (ch == 'Y');

}
```

```
                    Library Deletion
                                                    <0>=Exit

    Acquisition No. 10                         Date: 23-2-1999
    ---------------------------------------------------------
    Accession No. 12

       Title : FOXPRO
       Author(s) : GAGAN SAHOO
                      REETA
       Publisher : KHANNA PUBLISHER
       Price : 345
       Pages : 560
       Status : Y

 Are you sure to Delete this record <Y/N> :
```

Figure 6.5 Acquisition deletion of Delete_Accno function of library menu

```
// Function to append a record into MEMFILE.dat data file
void NEW_memb(int s_memb_no, char s_name[30], char s_address[30], int s_mdd, int s_mmm,
        int s_myy, int s_edd, int s_emm, int s_eyy, float s_memb_fee, float s_caut_fee)
{
        FILE *sfile;
        mem.memb_no = s_memb_no;
        strcpy(mem.name, s_name);
        strcpy(mem.address, s_address);
```

```
        mem.mdd = s_mdd;
        mem.mmm = s_mmm;
        mem.myy = s_myy;
        mem.edd = s_edd;
        mem.emm = s_emm;
        mem.eyy = s_eyy;
        mem.memb_fee = s_memb_fee;
        mem.caut_fee = s_caut_fee;

        // Append the new record into MEMFILE.dat data file
        sfile = fopen("MEMFILE.dat", "a");
        fwrite(&mem, sizeof(struct member),1,sfile);
        fclose(sfile);
}

// Function to delete a selected record from MEMFILE.dat data file
void Memb_delete(int s_memb_no)
{
        FILE *file;
        FILE *temp;
        file = fopen("MEMFILE.dat", "r");
        temp = fopen("TEMP.dat", "w");

        // Delete the record using copy method into temporaty file
        while (fread(&mem,sizeof(struct member),1,file)==1)
        {
                if (mem.memb_no != s_memb_no)
                        fwrite(&mem, sizeof(struct member),1,temp);
        }
        fclose(file);
        fclose(temp);
        remove("MEMFILE.dat");
        rename("MEMFILE.dat","TEMP.dat");
}

// Function for main menu to append new members in MEMFILE.dat
void new_member(void)
{
        char ch;
        int i, valid;
```

```
int s_memb_no; // Membership number
char s_name[30];          // Name of the member
char s_address[30]; // Address of the employee
int s_mdd, s_mmm, s_myy; // Membership date
int s_edd, s_emm, s_eyy; // Expire date
float s_memb_fee; // Membership fee
float s_caut_fee;          // Caution money
struct date d;             // For extracting system date

clrscr();
gotoxy(65, 2);
printf ( "<0>=Exit");
DRAW_BOX(10, 5, 71, 21, 219);
DRAW_BOX(9, 4, 72, 22, 218);
textcolor(BLACK);
textbackground(LIGHTGRAY);

gotoxy(3,3);
for (i = 1; i<= 76; i++)
        cprintf(" ");

textbackground(BLACK);
textcolor(BLACK+BLINK);
textbackground(WHITE);
gotoxy(35, 4);
cprintf("Membership Form");
textcolor(LIGHTGRAY);
textbackground(BLACK);

do
{
        Clear_area(6, 18, 12, 70);

        getdate(&d);
        s_mdd = d.da_day;
        s_mmm = d.da_mon;
        s_myy = d.da_year;

        gotoxy(12, 7);
        printf ( "Date: " );
```

```
printf ("%d",s_mdd);
printf ("-");
printf ("%d",s_mmm);
printf ("-");
printf ("%d",s_myy);
gotoxy(12, 23);
printf ( "Enter new membership no.");
gotoxy(12, 9);
printf ( "Membership No. " );
gotoxy(27, 9);
scanf (" %d",s_memb_no);
Left_clear(12, 23);
Right_clear(12, 23);

if (s_memb_no == 1)
{
        // Creates a temporaty space in MEMFILE.dat data tile
        NEW_memb(s_memb_no, "aaa", "bbb", 0, 0, 0, 0, 0, 0, 0.0, 0.0);
        // Deletes the same record after creating its position
        Memb_delete(s_memb_no);
}
if (s_memb_no == 0)
        return;

gotoxy(12, 11);
printf ( "Name : ");
gotoxy(12, 14);
printf ( "Address : ");
gotoxy(12, 15);
printf ( "Memb. Dat : ");
gotoxy(12, 16);
printf ( "Exp. Date : ");
gotoxy(12, 17);
printf ( "Memb. Fees : ");
gotoxy(12, 18);
printf ( "Caution Money : ");

do
{
        Left_clear(12, 23);
```

```
            gotoxy(12, 23);
            printf ( "Enter Name of the Member");
            valid = 1;
            gotoxy(19, 11);
            gets(s_name);
            strupr(s_name);
            if (s_name[0] == '0')
                    return;
            if (strlen(s_name) == 0 || strlen(s_name) > 30)
            {
                    valid = 0;
                    gotoxy(12, 23);
                    cprintf("\7Name should not greater than 30");
                    getch();
            }
    } while (!valid);
    Left_clear(12, 23);
    Right_clear(12, 23);

    do
    {
            Left_clear(12, 23);
            gotoxy(15, 23);
            printf ( "Enter Address of the Member ");
            valid = 1;
            gotoxy(23, 14);
            gets(s_address);
            strupr(s_address);
            if (s_address[0] == '0')
                    return;
            if (strlen(s_address) == 0 || strlen(s_address) > 30)
            {
                    valid = 0;
                    gotoxy(12, 23);
                    cprintf("\7Address should not greater than 30");
                    getch();
            }
    } while (!valid);
    Left_clear(12, 23);
    Right_clear(12, 23);
```

```
gotoxy(12, 23);
printf ( "Enter the membership date");
gotoxy(25, 15);
scanf (" %d",s_mdd);
gotoxy(27, 15);
printf ( "-");
gotoxy(28, 15);
scanf (" %d",s_mmm);
gotoxy(30, 15);
printf ( "-");
gotoxy(31, 15);
scanf (" %d",s_myy);
Left_clear(12, 23);
Right_clear(12, 23);

// Calculation of date of expiring of membership after one year is over
// membership from membership date and will be calculated
// in s_edd, s_emm, s_eyy
s_edd = s_mdd;
s_emm = s_mmm;
// Added 1 with the membership year to know the expire date
s_eyy = s_myy + 1;

gotoxy(25, 16);
printf ( "%d",s_edd);
gotoxy(27, 16);
printf ( "-");
gotoxy(28, 16);
printf ( "%d",s_emm);
gotoxy(30, 16);
printf ( "-");
gotoxy(31, 16);
printf ( "%d",s_eyy);

gotoxy(12, 23);
printf ( "Enter membership fees for a member");
gotoxy(25, 17);
scanf (" %.2f",s_memb_fee);
Left_clear(12, 23);
```

```
            Right_clear(12, 23);

            gotoxy(12, 23);
            printf ( "Enter caution money ");
            gotoxy(28, 18);
            scanf (" %.2f",s_caut_fee);
            Left_clear(12, 23);
            Right_clear(12, 23);

            do
            {
                    valid = 1;
                    gotoxy(12, 23);
                    printf ( "Do you want to save the record <Y/N>: ");
                    ch = getche();
                    if (ch == '0')
                            return;
                    ch = toupper(ch);
            } while (ch != 'Y');
            if (ch == 'N')
                    return;

            NEW_memb(s_memb_no, s_name, s_address, s_mdd, s_mmm,
                    s_myy, s_edd, s_emm, s_eyy, s_memb_fee, s_caut_fee);
            Left_clear(12, 23);
            Right_clear(12, 23);
            gotoxy(12, 23);
            printf ( "Do You Want New Record <Y/N>: ");
            ch = getche();
            if (ch == '0')
                    return;
            Left_clear(12, 23);
            Right_clear(12, 23);

            ch = toupper(ch);
    } while (ch == 'Y');
}
```

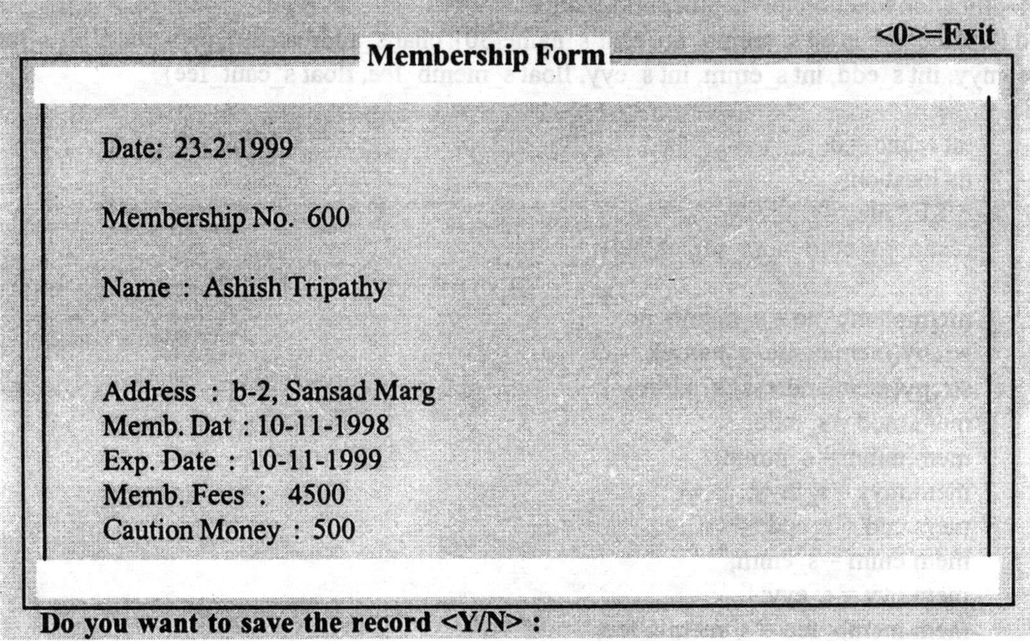
<0>=Exit

Membership Form

Date: 23-2-1999

Membership No. 600

Name : Ashish Tripathy

Address : b-2, Sansad Marg
Memb. Dat : 10-11-1998
Exp. Date : 10-11-1999
Memb. Fees : 4500
Caution Money : 500

Do you want to save the record <Y/N> :

Figure 6.6 Membership entry of new_member function of member menu

```
// Function to count the total number of records in MEMBER.dat data file for
// counting the modification record till found
int record_no(int s_memb_no)
{
        FILE *file;
        int count = 0;
        file = fopen("MEMFILE.dat", "r");

        // Counts the total records in MEMBER.dat data file
        while (fread(&mem, sizeof(struct member),1,file)==1)
        {
                count++;
                if (mem.memb_no == s_memb_no)
                        break;
        }
        fclose(file);
        return (count);
}
```

```
// Modification function for member information
void Replace_mem(int s_memb_no, char s_name[30], char s_address[30], int s_mdd, int s_mmm,
int s_myy, int s_edd, int s_emm, int s_eyy, float s_memb_fee, float s_caut_fee)
{
        int recno = 0;
        int location;
        FILE *file;
        recno = record_no(s_memb_no);

        mem.memb_no = s_memb_no;
        strcpy(mem.name, s_name);
        strcpy(mem.address, s_address);
        mem.mdd = s_mdd;
        mem.mmm = s_mmm;
        mem.myy = s_myy;
        mem.edd = s_edd;
        mem.emm = s_emm;
        mem.eyy = s_eyy;
        mem.memb_fee = s_memb_fee;
        mem.caut_fee = s_caut_fee;
        file = fopen("MEMFILE.dat", "rb+");

        // Finding the location in file
        location = (recno-1) * sizeof(struct member);

        // Search the position in file
        fseek(file,location,SEEK_CUR);

        // Re-write the contents in MEMFILE.dat data file
        fwrite(&mem, sizeof(struct member),1,file);
        fclose(file);
        return;
}

// Function to display the existing member after screen to change the further information
void Display_member(int s_memb_no)
{
                FILE *file;
                file = fopen("MEMFILE.dat", "r");
```

```
while (fread(&mem, sizeof(struct member),1,file)==1)
{
        if (mem.memb_no == s_memb_no)
        {
                gotoxy(12, 11);
                printf ( "Name : ");
                gotoxy(19, 11);
                puts(mem.name);

                gotoxy(12, 14);
                printf ( "Address : ");
                gotoxy(23, 14);
                puts(mem.address);

                gotoxy(12, 15);
                printf ( "Memb. Dat : ");
                gotoxy(25, 15);
                printf ("%d",mem.mdd);
                gotoxy(27,15);
                printf ("-");
                gotoxy(28,15);
                printf ("%d",mem.mmm);
                gotoxy(30,15);
                printf ("-");
                gotoxy(31,15);
                printf ("%d",mem.myy);

                gotoxy(12, 16);
                printf ( "Exp. Date : ");
                gotoxy(25, 16);
                printf ( "%d",mem.edd);
                gotoxy(27, 16);
                printf ( "-");
                gotoxy(28, 16);
                printf ( "%d",mem.emm);
                gotoxy(30, 16);
                printf ( "-");
                gotoxy(31, 16);
                printf ( "%d",mem.eyy);
```

```
                                gotoxy(12, 17);
                                printf ( "Memb. Fees : ");
                                gotoxy(25, 17);
                                printf ( "%.2f",mem.memb_fee);
                                gotoxy(12, 18);
                                printf ( "Caution Money : ");
                                gotoxy(28, 18);
                                printf ( "%.2f",mem.caut_fee );

                                break;
                        }
                }
                fclose(file);
}

// Function for main menu to Change member informations in MEMFILE.dat
void Change_member(void)
{
        char ch;
        int i, valid;
        int s_memb_no; // Membership number
        char s_name[30];         // Name of the member
        char s_address[30]; // Address of the employee
        int s_mdd, s_mmm, s_myy;  // Membership date
        int s_edd, s_emm, s_eyy; // Expire date
        float s_memb_fee; // Membership fee
        float s_caut_fee;        // Caution money
        struct date d;           // For extracting system date

        clrscr();
        gotoxy(65, 2);
        printf ( "<0>=Exit");
        DRAW_BOX(10, 5, 71, 21, 219);
        DRAW_BOX(9, 4, 72, 22, 218);
        textcolor(BLACK);
        textbackground(LIGHTGRAY);

        gotoxy(3,3);
        for (i = 1; i<= 76; i++)
                cprintf(" ");
```

```
textbackground(BLACK);
textcolor(BLACK+BLINK);
textbackground(WHITE);
gotoxy(35, 4);
cprintf("Membership Form");
textcolor(LIGHTGRAY);
textbackground(BLACK);

do
{
        Clear_area(6, 18, 12, 70);

        getdate(&d);
        s_mdd = d.da_day;
        s_mmm = d.da_mon;
        s_myy = d.da_year;

        gotoxy(12, 7);
        printf ( "Date: " );
        printf ("%d",s_mdd);
        printf ("-");
        printf ("%d",s_mmm);
        printf ("-");
        printf ("%d",s_myy);
        gotoxy(12, 23);
        printf ( "Enter new membership no.");
        gotoxy(12, 9);
        printf ( "Membership No. " );
        gotoxy(27, 9);
        scanf (" %d",&s_memb_no);
        Left_clear(12, 23);
        Right_clear(12, 23);

        if (s_memb_no == 0)
                return;

        Display_member(s_memb_no);
        do
        {
                Left_clear(12, 23);
```

```
            gotoxy(12, 23);
            printf ( "Enter New Name of the Member");
            valid = 1;
            gotoxy(45, 11);
            gets(s_name);
            strupr(s_name);
            if (s_name[0] == '0')
                  return;
            if (strlen(s_name) == 0 || strlen(s_name) > 30)
            {
                  valid = 0;
                  gotoxy(12, 23);
                  cprintf("\7Name should not greater than 30");
                  getch();
            }
      } while (!valid);
      Left_clear(12, 23);
      Right_clear(12, 23);
      do
      {
            Left_clear(12, 23);
            gotoxy(15, 23);
            printf ( "Enter New Address of the Member ");
            valid = 1;
            gotoxy(45, 14);
            gets(s_address);
            strupr(s_address);
            if (s_address[0] == '0')
                  return;
            if (strlen(s_address) == 0 || strlen(s_address) > 30)
            {
                  valid = 0;
                  gotoxy(12, 23);
                  cprintf("\7Address should not greater than 30");
                  getch();
            }
      } while (!valid);
      Left_clear(12, 23);
      Right_clear(12, 23);
      gotoxy(12, 23);
```

```
printf ( "Enter New the membership date");
gotoxy(45, 15);
scanf (" %d",s_mdd);
gotoxy(47, 15);
printf ( "-");
gotoxy(48, 15);
scanf (" %d",s_mmm);
gotoxy(50, 15);
printf ( "-");
gotoxy(51, 15);
scanf (" %d",s_myy);
Left_clear(12, 23);
Right_clear(12, 23);

// Calculation of date of expiring of membership
// after one year is over in s_edd, s_emm, s_eyy
s_edd = s_mdd;
s_emm = s_mmm;
s_eyy = s_myy + 1; // Added 1 with the membership year to know the expire date

gotoxy(45, 16);
printf ( "%d",s_edd);
gotoxy(47, 16);
printf ( "-");
gotoxy(48, 16);
printf ( "%d",s_emm);
gotoxy(50, 16);
printf ( "-");
gotoxy(51, 16);
printf ( "%d",s_eyy);

gotoxy(12, 23);
printf ( "Enter membership fees for a member");
gotoxy(45, 17);
scanf (" %.2f",&s_memb_fee);

Left_clear(12, 23);
Right_clear(12, 23);

gotoxy(12, 23);
```

```
            printf ( "Enter caution money ");

            gotoxy(45, 18);
            scanf (" %.2f",&s_caut_fee);
            Left_clear(12, 23);
            Right_clear(12, 23);

            do
            {
                valid = 1;
                gotoxy(12, 23);
                printf ( "Do you want to Modify the record <Y/N>: ");
                ch = getche();
                if (ch == '0')
                    return;
                ch = toupper(ch);
            } while (ch != 'Y');

            if (ch == 'N')
                return;

            Replace_mem(s_memb_no, s_name, s_address, s_mdd, s_mmm,
                s_myy, s_edd, s_emm, s_eyy, s_memb_fee, s_caut_fee);
            Left_clear(12, 23);
            Right_clear(12, 23);
            gotoxy(12, 23);
            printf ( "Do You Want New Record <Y/N>: ");
            ch = getche();
            if (ch == '0')
                return;
            Left_clear(12, 23);
            Right_clear(12, 23);

            ch = toupper(ch);

    } while (ch == 'Y');
}
```

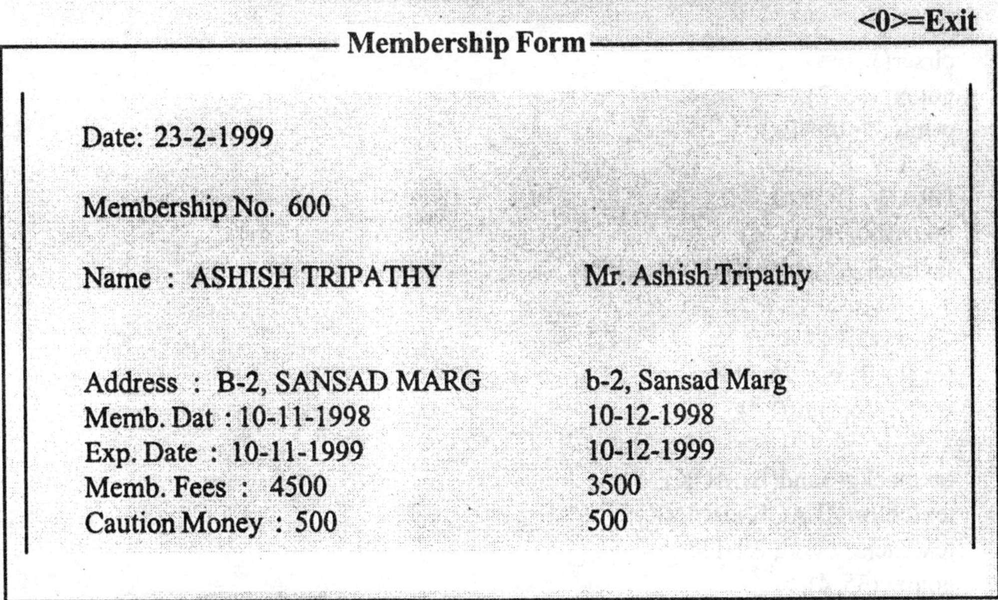
<0>=Exit

Membership Form

Date: 23-2-1999

Membership No. 600

Name : ASHISH TRIPATHY Mr. Ashish Tripathy

Address : B-2, SANSAD MARG b-2, Sansad Marg
Memb. Dat : 10-11-1998 10-12-1998
Exp. Date : 10-11-1999 10-12-1999
Memb. Fees : 4500 3500
Caution Money : 500 500

Do you want to Modify the record <Y/N> :

Figure 6.7 Membership modification of Change_member function of member menu

```
// Function to delete a member from MEMBER.dat data file.
/* While executing the procedure it first displays the member information and
checks in the MASTER.dat data file whether the member has been issued any book or not. If
the member has been issued any book then the record cannot be deleted, otherwise the record will
be deleted from MEMBER.dat data file */
void Delete_member()
{
        char ch;
        int i, flag = 0;

        int s_memb_no; // Membership number
        char s_name[30];          // Name of the member
        char s_address[30]; // Address of the employee
        int s_mdd, s_mmm, s_myy; // Membership date
        int s_edd, s_emm, s_eyy; // Expire date
        float s_memb_fee; // Membership fee
        float s_caut_fee;         // Caution money
```

```
struct date d;              // For extracting system date
clrscr();
gotoxy(65, 2);
printf ( "<0>=Exit");
DRAW_BOX(10, 5, 71, 21, 219);
DRAW_BOX(9, 4, 72, 22, 218);
textcolor(BLACK);
textbackground(LIGHTGRAY);

gotoxy(3,3);
for (i = 1; i<= 76; i++)
        cprintf(" ");

textbackground(BLACK);
textcolor(BLACK+BLINK);
textbackground(WHITE);
gotoxy(35, 4);
cprintf("Membership Deleted Form");
textcolor(LIGHTGRAY);
textbackground(BLACK);

do
{
        Clear_area(6, 18,12, 70);

        getdate(&d);
        s_mdd = d.da_day;
        s_mmm = d.da_mon;
        s_myy = d.da_year;

        gotoxy(12, 7);
        printf ( "Date: " );
        printf ("%d",s_mdd);
        printf ("-");
        printf ("%d",s_mmm);
        printf ("-");
        printf ("%d",s_myy);
        gotoxy(12, 23);
        printf ( "Enter membership no. to delete");
```

```
gotoxy(12, 9);
printf ( "Membership No. " );
gotoxy(27, 9);
scanf (" %d",s_memb_no);
Left_clear(12, 23);
Right_clear(12, 23);

if (s_memb_no == 0)
        return;

Display_member(s_memb_no);
flag = Issue_memb_check(s_memb_no);

if (flag == 1)
{
        gotoxy(12, 23);
        printf ( "Member has already a book. Can't Delete ...!");
        getch();
        Left_clear(12, 23);
        Right_clear(12, 23);
}
else
{
        gotoxy(12, 23);
        printf ( "Are You Sure to delete <Y/N>: ");
        ch = getche();
        ch = toupper(ch);
        if (ch == 'Y')
        {
                Memb_delete(s_memb_no);
                gotoxy(12, 23);
                printf ( "Member Deleted");
                getch();
                Left_clear(12, 23);
                Right_clear(12, 23);
        }
}
gotoxy(12, 23);
printf ( "Do you want to Delete any Record <Y/N>: ");
ch = getche();
```

```
            if (ch == '0')
                return;
            Left_clear(12, 23);
            Right_clear(12, 23);

            ch = toupper(ch);
        } while (ch == 'Y');
}
```

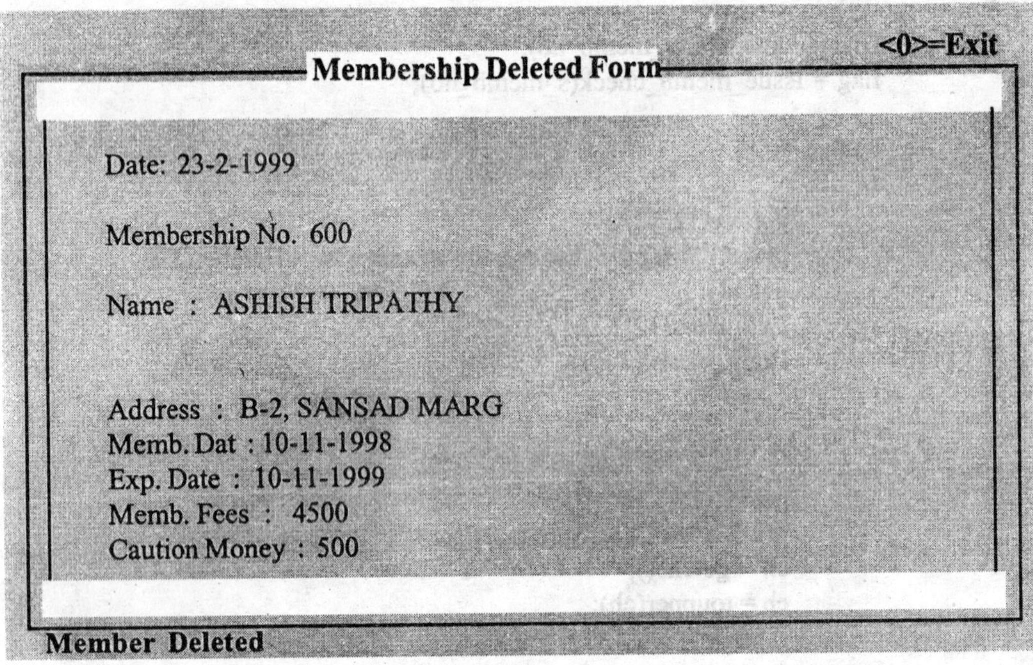
<0>=Exit
Membership Deleted Form
Date: 23-2-1999
Membership No. 600
Name : ASHISH TRIPATHY
Address : B-2, SANSAD MARG
Memb. Dat : 10-11-1998
Exp. Date : 10-11-1999
Memb. Fees : 4500
Caution Money : 500
Member Deleted

Figure 6.8 Membership deletion of Delete_member function of member menu

```
// Function to display the existing member and renewal of the membership date
void Renewal_member(int s_memb_no)
{
            char s_name[30];          // Name of the member
            char s_address[30]; // Address of the employee
            int s_mdd, s_mmm, s_myy;  // Membership date
            int s_edd, s_emm, s_eyy; // Expire date
            float s_memb_fee; // Membership fee
            float s_caut_fee;         // Caution money
```

```
FILE *file;
file = fopen("MEMFILE.dat", "r");
while (fread(&mem, sizeof(struct member),1,file)==1)
{
        if (mem.memb_no == s_memb_no)
        {
                strcpy(s_name, mem.name);
                strcpy(s_address, mem.address);
                s_mdd = mem.mdd;
                s_mmm = mem.mmm;
                s_myy = mem.myy;

                s_edd = mem.edd;
                s_emm = mem.emm;
                s_eyy = mem.eyy;

                s_memb_fee = mem.memb_fee;
                s_caut_fee = mem.caut_fee;

                gotoxy(12, 11);
                printf ( "Name : ");
                gotoxy(19, 11);
                puts(s_name);

                gotoxy(12, 14);
                printf ( "Address : ");
                gotoxy(23, 14);
                puts(s_address);

                gotoxy(12, 15);
                printf ( "Memb. Dat : ");
                gotoxy(25, 15);
                printf ( "%d",s_mdd);
                gotoxy(27, 15);
                printf ( "-");
                gotoxy(28, 15);
                printf ( "%d",s_mmm);
                gotoxy(30, 15);
                printf ( "-");
                gotoxy(31, 15);
```

```
printf ( "%d",s_myy);

gotoxy(12, 16);
printf ( "Exp. Date : ");
gotoxy(25, 16);
printf ( "%d",s_edd);
gotoxy(27, 16);
printf ( "-");
gotoxy(28, 16);
printf ( "%d",s_emm);
gotoxy(30, 16);
printf ( "-");
gotoxy(31, 16);
printf ( "%d",s_eyy);

gotoxy(12, 17);
printf ( "Memb. Fees : ");
gotoxy(25, 17);
printf ( "%.2f",s_memb_fee);

gotoxy(12, 18);
printf ( "Caution Money : ");
gotoxy(28, 18);
printf ( "%.2f",s_caut_fee );

gotoxy(40, 15);
printf ( "Renewal. Dat : ");
gotoxy(55, 15);
scanf (" %d",s_mdd);
gotoxy(58, 15);
printf ( "-");
gotoxy(59, 15);
scanf (" %d",s_mmm);
gotoxy(61, 15);
printf ( "-");
gotoxy(62, 15);
scanf (" %d",s_myy);

// Renewal of membership after one year
s_edd = s_mdd;
```

```
                s_emm = s_mmm;
                s_eyy = s_myy + 1;

                gotoxy(40, 16);
                printf ( "Exp. Date : ");
                gotoxy(55, 16);
                printf ( "%d",s_edd);
                gotoxy(58, 16);
                printf ( "-");
                gotoxy(59, 16);
                printf ( "%d",s_emm);
                gotoxy(61, 16);
                printf ( "-");
                gotoxy(62, 16);
                printf ( "%d",s_eyy);

                break;
            }
        }
        fclose(file);
        if (s_eyy > 0)
            Replace_mem(s_memb_no, s_name, s_address, s_mdd,
            s_mmm, s_myy, s_edd, s_emm, s_eyy, s_memb_fee, s_caut_fee);
}

// Function for main menu for renewal of membership
void Member_Renewal(void)
{
    char ch;
    int i, valid;
    int s_memb_no; // Membership number
    char s_name[30];        // Name of the member
    char s_address[30]; // Address of the employee
    int s_mdd, s_mmm, s_myy; // Membership date
    int s_edd, s_emm, s_eyy; // Expire date
    float s_memb_fee; // Membership fee
    float s_caut_fee;       // Caution money

    struct date d;          // For extracting system date
```

```
clrscr();
gotoxy(65, 2);
printf ( "<0>=Exit");
DRAW_BOX(10, 5, 71, 21, 219);
DRAW_BOX(9, 4, 72, 22, 218);
textcolor(BLACK);
textbackground(LIGHTGRAY);

gotoxy(3,3);
for (i = 1; i<= 76; i++)
        cprintf(" ");

textbackground(BLACK);
textcolor(BLACK+BLINK);
textbackground(WHITE);
gotoxy(35, 4);
cprintf("Membership Renewal Form");
textcolor(LIGHTGRAY);
textbackground(BLACK);

do
{
        Clear_area(6, 18, 12, 70);

        getdate(&d);
        s_mdd = d.da_day;
        s_mmm = d.da_mon;
        s_myy = d.da_year;

        gotoxy(12, 7);
        printf ( "Date: " );
        printf ( "%d",s_mdd);
        printf ("-");
        printf ("%d",s_mmm);
        printf ("-");
        printf ("%d",s_myy);
        gotoxy(12, 23);
        printf ( "Enter new membership no.");
        gotoxy(12, 9);
        printf ( "Membership No. " );
```

```
        gotoxy(27, 9);
        scanf (" %d",s_memb_no);
        Left_clear(12, 23);
        Right_clear(12, 23);

        if (s_memb_no == 0)
                return;

        Renewal_member(s_memb_no);

        ch = toupper(ch);
    } while (ch == 'Y');
}
```

Membership Renewal Form <0>=Exit

Date: 10-10-1999

Membership No. 100

Name : MR. PANKAJ KAPOOR

Address : ROHINI, DELHI
Memb. Dat : 10-10-1998 Renewal. Dat : 10-10-1999_
Exp. Date : 10-10-1999
Memb. Fees : 3400
Caution Money : 400

Figure 6.9 Membership renewal of Member_Renewal function of main menu

```
// Function for Adding, modifying and deleting from MEMFILE.dat data file
void Memb_console(void)
{
    char ch;
```

```
while (1)
{
        clrscr();
        gotoxy(65, 3);
        printf ( "<0>=Exit");

        DRAW_BOX(10, 5, 71, 21, 219);
        DRAW_BOX(9, 4, 72, 22, 218);
        textcolor(BLACK);
        textbackground(WHITE);
        gotoxy(22, 8);
        cprintf("M E M B E R S H I P  C O N S O L E");
        textcolor(LIGHTGRAY);
        textbackground(BLACK);
        gotoxy(25, 12);
        printf ( "1: Recording New Member");
        gotoxy(25, 13);
        printf ( "2. Changing Member Data");
        gotoxy(25, 14);
        printf ( "3. Deleting Member Record");

        gotoxy(25, 17);
        printf ( "0. Return");
        gotoxy(25, 18);
        printf ( "Enter your choice : ");
        ch = getche();
        if (ch == 27)
                break;
        else
                if (ch == '1')
                {
                        new_member();
                }
                else
                        if (ch== '2')
                        {
                                Change_member();
                                break;
                        }
                        else
```

```
                if (ch == '3')
                {
                        Delete_member();
                        break;
                }
                else
                        if (ch == '0')
                                break;
        }
}
```

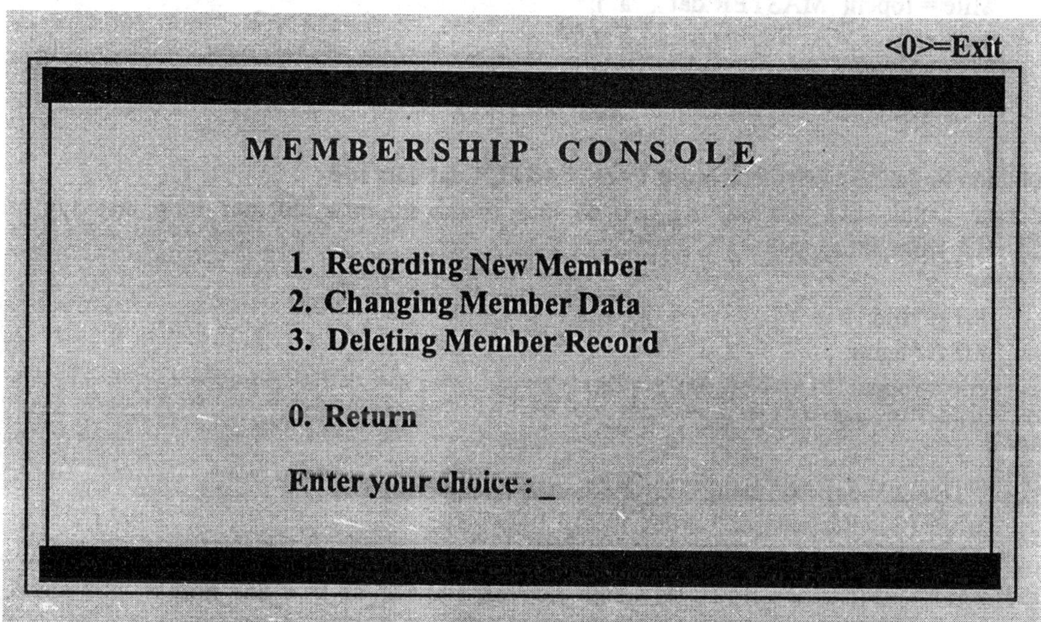

Figure 6.10 Membership options of Memb_console function of member menu

```
// Function to add issued books into MASTER.dat data file
void Issue_Add(int s_acq_no, int s_acc_no, int s_memb_no, int s_idd, int s_imm, int s_iyy, int
s_rdd, int s_rmm, int s_ryy)
{
        FILE *sfile;
        iss.acq_no = s_acq_no;
        iss.acc_no = s_acc_no;
```

```
        iss.memb_no = s_memb_no;
        iss.idd = s_idd;
        iss.imm = s_imm;
        iss.iyy = s_iyy;

        iss.rdd = s_rdd;
        iss.rmm = s_rmm;
        iss.ryy = s_ryy;


        // Append the new record into MASTER.dat data file
        sfile = fopen("MASTER.dat", "a");
        fwrite(&iss, sizeof(struct issue),1,sfile);
        fclose(sfile);
}

// Function to delete a selected record from MASTER.dat data file
void Issue_Delete(int s_acq_no, int s_acc_no, int s_memb_no, int s_idd, int s_imm, int s_iyy, int
s_rdd, int s_rmm, int s_ryy)
{
        FILE *file;
        FILE *temp;
        file = fopen("MASTER.dat", "r");
        temp = fopen("TEMP.dat", "w");

        // Delete the record using copy method into temporary file
        while (fread(&iss,sizeof(struct issue),1,file)==1)
        {
                if ((iss.acq_no != iss.memb_no) && (iss.acc_no != s_acc_no))
                        fwrite(&iss, sizeof(struct issue),1,temp);
        }
        fclose(file);
        fclose(temp);
        remove("MASTER.dat");
        rename("TEMP.dat","MASTER.dat");
}

// Function to find the date of expiring of membership
int date_expire(int s_edd, int s_emm, int s_eyy)
{
```

```
int s_cdd, s_cmm, s_cyy;        // Current date
int pdays = 0;
struct date td;
getdate(&td);
s_cdd = td.da_day;
s_cmm = td.da_mon;
s_cyy = td.da_year;
// when expire day less than current day, expire month equal to current month
// and expire year equal to current year
if ((s_edd < s_cdd) && (s_emm == s_cmm) && (s_eyy == s_cyy))
        pdays = 1;
else

// when expire day less than current day, expire month less than current month
// and expire year equal to current year

if ((s_edd < s_cdd) && (s_emm < s_cmm) && (s_eyy == s_cyy))
        pdays = 1;
else

// when expire day less than current day, expire month less than current month
// and expire year less than current year

if ((s_edd < s_cdd) && (s_emm < s_cmm) && (s_eyy < s_cyy))
        pdays = 1;
else

// when expire day greater than current day, expire month less than current month
// and expire year equal to current year

if ((s_edd > s_cdd) && (s_emm < s_cmm) && (s_eyy == s_cyy))
        pdays = 1;
else

// when expire day greater than current day, expire month less than current month
// and expire year less current year

if ((s_edd > s_cdd) && (s_emm < s_cmm) && (s_eyy < s_cyy))
        pdays = 1;
else
```

```
// when expire day greater than current day, expire month equal to current month
// and expire year less than current year

if ((s_edd > s_cdd) && (s_emm == s_cmm) && (s_eyy < s_cyy))
        pdays = 1;
else

// when expire day greater than current day, expire month greater than current month
// and expire year less than current year

if ((s_edd > s_cdd) && (s_emm > s_cmm) && (s_eyy < s_cyy))
        pdays = 1;
else

// when expire day equal to current day, expire month equal to current month
// and expire year less than current year

if ((s_edd == s_cdd) && (s_emm == s_cmm) && (s_eyy < s_cyy))
        pdays = 1;
else

// when expire day less than current day, expire month equal to current month
// and expire year less than to current year

if ((s_edd < s_cdd) && (s_emm == s_cmm) && (s_eyy < s_cyy))
        pdays = 1;
else

// when expire day equal to current day, expire month less than current month
// and expire year less than current year

if ((s_edd == s_cdd) && (s_emm < s_cmm) && (s_eyy < s_cyy))
        pdays = 1;
else

// when expire day less than current day, expire month greater than current month
// and expire year less than to current year

if ((s_edd < s_cdd) && (s_emm > s_cmm) && (s_eyy < s_cyy))
        pdays = 1;
```

```
        else

        // when expire equal to current day, expire month greater than current month
        // and expire year less than current year

        if ((s_edd == s_cdd) && (s_emm > s_cmm) && (s_eyy < s_cyy))
                pdays = 1;
        return (pdays);
}

// Function to check membership date whether it is expired or not
int Expire_Check(int s_memb_no)
{
        int xflag = 0;

        FILE *file;
        file = fopen("MEMFILE.dat", "r");
        while (fread(&mem, sizeof(struct member),1,file)==1)
        {
                if (s_memb_no == mem.memb_no)
                {
                        xflag = date_expire(mem.edd, mem.emm, mem.eyy);
                        break;
                }
        }
        fclose(file);
        return (xflag);
}

// Function to issue books to members
void Book_Issue()
{
        char ch;
        int i, tflag = 0; //, valid;
        int mday = 0;
        int s_acq_no = 0;          // Acquisition number

        int s_acc_no = 0;          // Accession number
        char s_title[30];
        char s_author1[30], s_author2[30];        // Authors
```

```
char s_publisher[30];     // Name of the publisher
float s_price;    // Price of the book
int s_idd, s_imm, s_iyy; // Date of Issue
int s_rdd, s_rmm, s_ryy;// Date of return
int s_pages;       // Total pages in book
char s_status;  // Present status of book

int s_memb_no; // Member number for issuing books

struct date d;                    // For extracting system date

FILE *file;
clrscr();
gotoxy(65, 3);
printf( "<0>=Exit");
DRAW_BOX(10, 5, 71, 21, 219);
DRAW_BOX(9, 4, 72, 22, 218);
textcolor(BLACK);
textbackground(LIGHTGRAY);

gotoxy(3,3);
for (i = 1; i<= 76; i++)
        cprintf(" ");

textbackground(BLACK);
textcolor(BLACK+BLINK);
textbackground(WHITE);
gotoxy(35, 4);
cprintf("Issue Form");
textcolor(LIGHTGRAY);
textbackground(BLACK);

getdate(&d);

s_idd = d.da_day;
s_imm = d.da_mon;
s_iyy = d.da_year;

// Steps to find the return date of issued book
mday = month_days(s_imm);
```

```
s_rdd = s_idd + 3;
if (s_rdd <= mday)
{
        s_rdd = s_rdd;
        s_rmm = s_imm;
        s_ryy = s_iyy;
}
else
{
        s_rdd = 3 - (mday - s_idd);
        if (s_imm == 12)
        {
                s_rmm = 1;
                s_ryy = s_iyy + 1;
        }
        else
        {
                s_rmm = s_imm + 1;
                s_ryy = s_iyy;
        }
}

gotoxy(48, 7);
printf ( "Issue date: ");
printf ("%d", s_idd);
printf ("-");
printf ("%d",s_imm );
printf ("-");
printf ("%d",s_iyy);
gotoxy(48, 8);
printf ( "Return date: " );
printf ("%d",s_rdd);
printf ("-");
printf ("%d",s_rmm );
printf ("-");
printf ("%d",s_ryy);

gotoxy(10, 23);
printf ( "Enter the Acquisition number");
gotoxy(13, 7);
```

```
printf ( "Acquisition No. " );
gotoxy(29, 7);
scanf (" %d",s_acq_no);
Left_clear(10, 23);
Right_clear(39, 23);

gotoxy(11, 8);
for (i = 1; i <= 60; i++)
        printf ( "=");

gotoxy(10, 23);
printf ( "Enter the Accession number");
gotoxy(13, 9);
printf ( "Accession No. ");
gotoxy(28, 9);
scanf (" %d",s_acc_no);
Left_clear(10, 23);
Right_clear(39, 23);

if ((s_acq_no == 0) || (s_acc_no == 0))
{
        Issue_Add(0, 0, 0, 1, 1, 1, 1, 1, 1);
        Issue_Delete(0, 0, 0, 1, 1, 1, 1, 1, 1);
        return;
}

file = fopen("LIB.dat", "r");

// Search the record to display before issue
while (fread(&lib, sizeof(struct library),1,file)==1)
{
        if ((s_acq_no == lib.acq_no) && (s_acc_no == lib.acc_no))
        {
                gotoxy(15, 11);
                printf ( "Title : ");
                gotoxy(15, 12);
                printf ( "Author(s) : ");
                gotoxy(15, 14);
                printf ( "Publisher : ");
                gotoxy(15, 15);
```

```
printf ( "Price : ");
gotoxy(15, 16);
printf ( "Pages : ");
gotoxy(15,17);
printf ( "Status : ");
gotoxy(26, 11);
puts(lib.title);

gotoxy(26, 12);
puts(lib.author1);

gotoxy(26, 13);
puts(lib.author2);
gotoxy(26, 14);
puts(lib.publisher);
gotoxy(26, 15);
printf ( "%.2f",lib.price);

gotoxy(26, 16);
printf ( "%d",lib.pages);
gotoxy(26, 17);
printf ( "%c",lib.status);

// Function check whether this book is already issued or not to any member
tflag = Issue_Check(s_acq_no, s_acc_no);

if (tflag == 1)
{
        gotoxy(12, 23);
        printf ( "This book is aleardy issued");
        getch();
        Left_clear(10, 23);
        Right_clear(39, 23);
        return;
}
else
{
        tflag = 0;
        gotoxy(45, 9);
        printf ( "Membership No. ");
```

```
gotoxy(64, 9);
scanf (" %d",s_memb_no);

// Function to check such a member exists in
// MEMBER.dat data file or not
tflag = Memb_Check(s_memb_no);

if (tflag == 1)
{
        tflag = 0;
        // Function to check membership expired or not
        tflag = Expire_Check(s_memb_no);

        if (tflag == 0)
        {
                tflag = 0;
                // Function to check whether the member
                // already book issued or not by tflag
                tflag = Issue_memb_check(s_memb_no);

                if (tflag == 0)
                {
                        // Function to append the issued book
                        // into MASTER.dat data file
                        Issue_Add(s_acq_no, s_acc_no,
                                s_memb_no, s_idd, s_imm,
                                s_iyy, s_rdd, s_rmm, s_ryy);
                        gotoxy(12, 23);
                        printf ( "Book Issued");
                        getch();
                        Left_clear(10, 23);
                        Right_clear(39, 23);
                }
                else
                {
                        gotoxy(12, 23);
                        printf ( "The member has already a book");
                        getch();
                }
        }
```

```
                    else
                    {
                            gotoxy(12, 23);
                            printf ( "The membership Expired");
                            getch();
                    }
                }
                else
                {
                    gotoxy(12, 23);
                    printf ( "The member does not exists");
                    getch();
                }
            }
            break;
        }
    }
    fclose(file);
}
```

Issue Form

Acquisition No. 12 Date: 24-2-1999

Accession No. 10

Title : PROGRAMMING IN C++
Author(s) : R. B PATEL
MASTER
Publisher : KHANNA PUBLISHER
Price : 240.00
Pages : 500
Status : Y

Book Issued

Figure 6.11 Issue form for books issue.

```
// Function to add fines if return date is exceeds
void Fine_add(int s_memb_no, int s_acq_no, int s_acc_no, int s_idd, int s_imm, int s_iyy, int
        s_rdd, int s_rmm, int s_ryy, int s_cdd, int s_cmm, int s_cyy, int s_finfee)
{
        FILE *sfile;

        fin.memb_no = s_memb_no;
        fin.acq_no = s_acq_no; // fine acquisition no
        fin.acc_no = s_acc_no; // fine accession no

        fin.idd = s_idd;         // Book issue date
        fin.imm = s_imm;
        fin.iyy = s_iyy;

        fin.rdd = s_rdd; // Book purposed return date
        fin.rmm = s_rmm;
        fin.ryy = s_ryy;

        fin.cdd = s_cdd;         // Returned date
        fin.cmm = s_cmm;
        fin.cyy = s_cyy;

        fin.finfee = s_finfee;

        // Append the fined record into FINE.dat data file if the member returns
        // the book after due date
        sfile = fopen("FINE.dat", "a");
        fwrite(&fin, sizeof(struct fine),1,sfile);
        fclose(sfile);
}

// Function to display the book information at the time of returning the book
void Book_display(int s_acq_no, int s_acc_no)
{
        FILE *file;
        file = fopen("LIB.dat", "r");

        // Search the record for displaying the book information
        while (fread(&lib, sizeof(struct library),1,file)==1)
        {
```

```
        if ((s_acq_no == lib.acq_no) && (s_acc_no == lib.acc_no))
        {
                gotoxy(40, 8);
                printf ( "Title : ");
                gotoxy(40, 9);
                printf ( "Author(s) : ");
                gotoxy(40, 11);
                printf ( "Publisher : ");
                gotoxy(40, 15);
                printf ( "Price : ");
                gotoxy(40, 16);
                printf ( "Pages : ");
                gotoxy(40, 17);
                printf ( "Status : ");
                gotoxy(49, 8);
                puts(lib.title);

                gotoxy(53, 9);
                puts(lib.author1);

                gotoxy(53, 10);
                puts(lib.author2);
                gotoxy(53, 11);
                puts(lib.publisher);
                gotoxy(52, 15);
                printf ( "%d",lib.price);

                gotoxy(52, 16);
                printf ( "%d",lib.pages);
                gotoxy(52, 17);
                printf ( "%c",lib.status);
                break;
        }
    }
    fclose(file);
}

// Function to return the total days in a month
int month_days(int s_cmm)
{
```

```
        int dmon = 0;
        switch (s_cmm)
        {
                case 1: dmon = 31; break;
                case 2: dmon = 28; break;
                case 3: dmon = 31; break;
                case 4: dmon = 30; break;
                case 5: dmon = 31; break;
                case 6: dmon = 30; break;
                case 7: dmon = 31; break;
                case 8: dmon = 31; break;
                case 9: dmon = 30; break;
                case 10: dmon = 31; break;
                case 11: dmon = 30; break;
                case 12: dmon = 31; break;
        }
        return (dmon);
}

// Function to find the days in between two dates
int no_of_days(int s_cdd, int s_cmm, int s_cyy, int s_rdd, int s_rmm, int s_ryy)
{
        int mdays = 0;
        int pdays = 0;
        mdays = month_days(s_rmm);
        if ((s_rdd < s_cdd) && (s_rmm == s_cmm) && (s_ryy == s_cyy))
                pdays = s_cdd - s_rdd;
        else
        if ((s_rdd < s_cdd) && (s_rmm < s_cmm) && (s_ryy == s_cyy))
                pdays = (mdays - s_rdd) + s_cdd + ((s_cmm-1) - s_rmm) * 30;
        else
        if ((s_rdd < s_cdd) && (s_rmm < s_cmm) && (s_ryy < s_cyy))
                pdays = (mdays - s_rdd) + s_cdd + ((s_cmm-1) - s_rmm) * 30 +
                        (s_cyy - s_ryy) * 12 * 30;
        else
        if ((s_rdd > s_cdd) && (s_rmm < s_cmm) && (s_ryy == s_cyy))
                pdays = (mdays - s_rdd) + s_cdd + ((s_cmm-1) - s_rmm) * 30;
        else
        if ((s_rdd > s_cdd) && (s_rmm < s_cmm) && (s_ryy < s_cyy))
```

```
            pdays = (mdays - s_rdd) + s_cdd + ((s_cmm-1) - s_rmm) * 30 +
                    (s_cyy - s_ryy) * 12 * 30;
        else
        if ((s_rdd > s_cdd) && (s_rmm == s_cmm) && (s_ryy < s_cyy))
            pdays = (mdays - s_rdd) + s_cdd + ((s_cmm-1) - s_rmm) * 30 +
                    (s_cyy - s_ryy) * 12 * 30;
        else
        if ((s_rdd > s_cdd) && (s_rmm > s_cmm) && (s_ryy < s_cyy))
            pdays = (mdays - s_rdd) + s_cdd + ((s_cmm-1) - s_rmm) * 30 +
                    (s_cyy - s_ryy) * 12 * 30;
        else
        if ((s_rdd == s_cdd) && (s_rmm == s_cmm) && (s_ryy < s_cyy))
            pdays = (s_cyy - s_ryy) * 12 * 30;
        else
        if ((s_rdd < s_cdd) && (s_rmm == s_cmm) && (s_ryy < s_cyy))
            pdays = (s_cdd - s_rdd) + (s_cyy - s_ryy) * 12 * 30;
        else
        if ((s_rdd == s_cdd) && (s_rmm < s_cmm) && (s_ryy < s_cyy))
            pdays = (s_cmm - s_rmm) * 30 + (s_cyy - s_ryy) * 12 * 30;
        else
        if ((s_rdd < s_cdd) && (s_rmm > s_cmm) && (s_ryy < s_cyy))
            pdays = (mdays - s_rdd) + s_cdd + (12 - s_rmm) * 30 + (s_cmm - 1) * 30 +
                    ((s_cyy - (s_ryy+1)) * 12 * 30) ;
        else
        if ((s_rdd == s_cdd) && (s_rmm > s_cmm) && (s ryy < s_cyy))
            pdays = (12 - s_rmm) * 30 + (s_cmm) * 30 + ((s_cyy - (s_ryy+1)) * 12 * 30) ;
        printf ( "%d",pdays);
        return (pdays);
}

// Function display the books at the time of return
void Return_Issue(int s_memb_no)
{
        FILE *file;
        int s_acq_no, s_acc_no;
        int s_idd, s_imm, s_iyy; // Issue date
        int s_rdd, s_rmm, s_ryy;// Return date
        int s_cdd, s_cmm, s_cyy;          // Current date
        int tdays = 0;    // Variable store the date difference
```

```
int s_finfee;     // Fine amount
struct date d;          // For extracting system date

file = fopen("MASTER.dat", "r");
getdate(&d);
s_cdd = d.da_day;
s_cmm = d.da_mon;
s_cyy = d.da_year;

// Search the record for further displaying the issue and return dates
while (fread(&iss, sizeof(struct issue),1,file)==1)
{
        if (s_memb_no == iss.memb_no)
        {
                s_acq_no = iss.acq_no;
                s_acc_no = iss.acc_no;
                s_idd = iss.idd;
                s_imm = iss.imm;
                s_iyy = iss.iyy;

                s_rdd = iss.rdd;
                s_rmm = iss.rmm;
                s_ryy = iss.ryy;

                // Function to display the book information at the time of return
                Book_display(s_acq_no, s_acc_no);

                gotoxy(12, 19);
                printf ( "Issue Date: " );
                printf ("%d",s_idd);
                printf ("-");
                printf ("%d", s_imm );
                printf ( "-" );
                printf ("%d", s_iyy);
                gotoxy(40, 19);
                printf ( "Return Date: " );
                printf ("%d",s_rdd );
                printf ( "-" );
                printf ("%d", s_rmm );
                printf ( "-" );
```

```
                printf ("%d", s_ryy);
                // The function no_of_days() calculate the difference betwee
                // return date and current date
                tdays = no_of_days(s_cdd, s_cmm, s_cyy, s_rdd, s_rmm, s_ryy);
                if (tdays > 0)
                {
                        s_finfee = tdays;
                        printf ( "%.2f",s_finfee);
                        // Function add a fine record if the member returned the
                        // book after due date
                        Fine_add(s_memb_no, s_acq_no, s_acc_no, s_idd, s_imm, s_iyy,
                                s_rdd, s_rmm, s_ryy, s_cdd, s_cmm, s_cyy, s_finfee);
                }
                break;
            }
        }
        fclose(file);
}

// Function to delete member data from MASTER.dat data file
void Issue_member_delete(int s_memb_no)
{
        FILE *file;
        FILE *temp;
        file = fopen("MASTER.dat", "r");
        temp = fopen("TEMP.dat", "w");

        // Delete the record using copy method into temporaty file
        while (fread(&iss,sizeof(struct issue),1,file)==1)
        {
                if (iss.memb_no != s_memb_no)
                        fwrite(&iss, sizeof(struct issue),1,temp);
        }
        fclose(file);
        fclose(temp);
        remove("MASTER.dat");
        rename("TEMP.dat","MASTER.dat");
}
```

```
// Function to return books in library
// The user has to enter the membership no and the screen will display the details of
// the book which is being returned
void Book_Return(void)
{
	char ch;
	int i, flag = 0;

	int s_memb_no; // Membership number
	char s_name[30];	// Name of the member
	char s_address[30]; // Address of the employee
	int s_mdd, s_mmm, s_myy; // Membership date
	int s_edd, s_emm, s_eyy; // Expire date
	float s_memb_fee; // Membership fee
	float s_caut_fee;	// Caution money

	struct date d;		// For extracting system date

	clrscr();
	gotoxy(65, 3);
	printf( "<0>=Exit");
	DRAW_BOX(10, 5, 71, 21, 219);
	DRAW_BOX(9, 4, 72, 22, 218);
	textcolor(BLACK);
	textbackground(LIGHTGRAY);

	gotoxy(3,3);
	for (i = 1; i<= 76; i++)
		cprintf(" ");

	textbackground(BLACK);
	textcolor(BLACK+BLINK);
	textbackground(WHITE);
	gotoxy(35, 4);
	cprintf("Book Return Form");
	textcolor(LIGHTGRAY);
	textbackground(BLACK);

	do
	{
```

```
Clear_area(6, 18, 12, 70);
getdate(&d);
s_mdd = d.da_day;
s_mmm = d.da_mon;
s_myy = d.da_year;

gotoxy(12, 7);
printf ( "Date: " );
printf ("%d", s_mdd);
printf ("-");
printf ("%d", s_mmm);
printf ("-");
printf ("%d", s_myy);
gotoxy(12, 23);
printf ( "Enter membership no. to Return Book");
gotoxy(12, 9);
printf ( "Membership No. " );
gotoxy(27, 9);
scanf (" %d",s_memb_no);
Left_clear(12, 23);
Right_clear(12, 23);
if (s_memb_no == 0)
        return;

// Function to display member's information at the time of returning the book
Display_member(s_memb_no);
// Function to find the fine and display the issue and return dates
Return_Issue(s_memb_no);

// Function to check whether the member already take a book or not
flag = Issue_memb_check(s_memb_no);
if (flag == 1)
{
        // Member deleted from MASTER.dat data file i.e., book returned
        Issue_member_delete(s_memb_no);
        // Return_function displays the book information and add fine if avail
        Left_clear(12, 23);
        Right_clear(12, 23);
}
else
```

```
            {
                    gotoxy(12, 23);
                    printf ( "Member Does not have any book");
                    getch();
                    Left_clear(12, 23);
                    Right_clear(12, 23);
            }

            gotoxy(12, 23);
            printf ( "Do you want to Return any Record <Y/N>: ");
            ch = getche();
            if (ch == '0')
                    return;

            Left_clear(12, 23);
            Right_clear(12, 23);

            ch = toupper(ch);
        } while (ch == 'Y');
}
```

Book Return Form

```
Date: 24-2-1999
                                    Title  : PROGRAMMING IN C++
Membership No. 300                  Author(s) : R B PATEL
                                                MASTER
Name  :  M. GOVIND RAO              Publisher  :  KHANNA PUB
Accession No.  10

Address  :  F-25/28 SEC-7, ROHINI
Memb. Dat : 5 -5 -1998              Price  :        240.00
Exp. Date  :  5 -5 -1999            Pages  :        500
Memb. Fees  :  4500.00              Status :        Y
Caution Money  :  500.00
Issue Date  :  24-2-1999            Return Date  :  27-2-1999

Do you want to Return any Record <Y/N> :
```

Figure 6.12 Return of book of Book_Return function of main menu

```
// Function for displaying the report menu
void Report_Menu(void)
{

        char ch;
        while (1)
        {
                clrscr();
                gotoxy(65, 3);
                printf( "<0>=Exit");

                DRAW_BOX(10, 5, 71, 21, 219);
                DRAW_BOX(9, 4, 72, 22, 218);
                textcolor(BLACK);
                textbackground(WHITE);
                gotoxy(22, 8);
                cprintf("R E P O R T I N G   C O N S O L E");
                textcolor(LIGHTGRAY);
                textbackground(BLACK);
                gotoxy(25, 12);

                printf( "1: Acquisition Register");
                gotoxy(25, 13);
                printf( "2. Membership Register");
                gotoxy(25, 14);
                printf( "3. Issue Register");
                gotoxy(25, 15);
                printf( "4. List of OverDue Books");
                gotoxy(25, 16);
                printf( "5. Fine Register");
                gotoxy(25, 17);
                printf( "6. List of Expire Members");

                gotoxy(25, 18);
                printf( "0. Return");
                gotoxy(25, 19);
                printf( "Enter your choice : ");
                ch = getche();
```

```
if (ch == 27)
        break;
else
        if (ch == '1')
        {
                Acqu_Register();
        }
        else
                if (ch == '2')
                {
                        Memb_Register();
                }
                else
                        if (ch == '3')
                        {
                                Issue_Register();
                        }
                        else
                                if (ch == '4')
                                {
                                        OverDue_Book();
                                }
                                else
                                        if (ch == '5')
                                        {
                                                Fine_Register();
                                        }
                                        else
                                                if (ch == '6')
                                                {
                                                        Expire_Register();
                                                }
                                                else
                                                        if (ch == '0')
                                                                break;
```

}

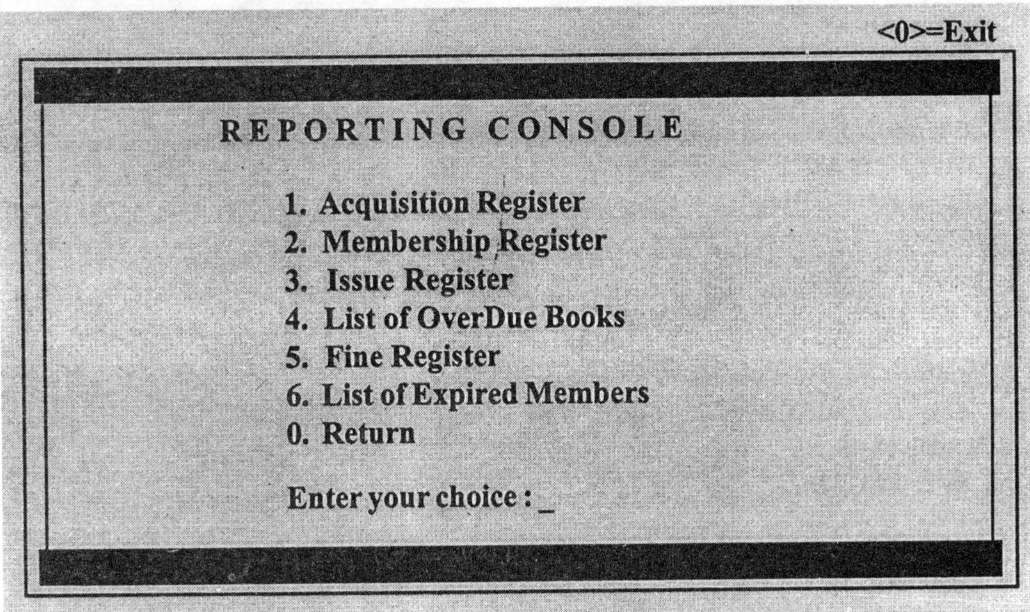

Figure 6.13 Return of book of Report_Menu function of Management queries

```
// The function is used to print the report of acquisition register.
/* The function is used to print the report of acquisition register. The purchase department of the
library purchases various books. After the arrive, these books are inspected and entered into the
library by providing a library number as accession number to each book.*/

void Acqu_Register(void)
{
        FILE *file;

        int s_acq_no;     // Acquisition number
        int s_acc_no;     // Accession number
        char s_title[30];
        char s_author1[30], s_author2[30];          // Authors
        char s_publisher[30];     // Name of the publisher
        float s_price;     // Price of the book
        int s_dd, s_mm, s_yy;     // Date of purchase
        int s_pages;       // Total pages in book
        char s_status;  // Present status of book
        int xdd, xmm, xyy;
```

```
int sln = 0;
int row = 8;
int i;
struct date d;              // For extracting system date

file = fopen("LIB.dat", "r");
clrscr();
gotoxy(30, 2);
printf ( "ACQUISITION REGISTER");
gotoxy(30, 3);
printf ( "———————————————————");

getdate(&d);
xdd = d.da_day;
xmm = d.da_mon;
xyy = d.da_year;
gotoxy(63, 3);
printf ( "Date: ");
printf ("%d",xdd );
printf ( "-" );
printf ("%d", xmm);
printf ("-");
printf ("%d", xyy);

gotoxy(1, 4);
for ( i = 0; i <= 79; i++)
        printf ( "=");
gotoxy(1, 5);
printf ( "Sl.");
gotoxy(6, 5);
printf ( "Acq.");
gotoxy(12, 5);
printf ( "Acc.No.");
// For displaying only 12 characters of each
gotoxy(22, 5);
printf ( "Title &");
gotoxy(40, 5);
printf ( "Publisher");
gotoxy(54, 5);
printf ( "Price &");
```

```
gotoxy(63, 5);
printf ( "Date(p)");
gotoxy(75, 5);
printf ( "Status");

gotoxy(1, 6);
printf ( "No");
gotoxy(6, 6);
printf ( "No.");

// For displaying only 12 characters of each
gotoxy(22, 6);
printf ( "Author(s)");
gotoxy(54, 6);
printf ( "Pages");

gotoxy(1, 7);
for (i = 0; i <= 79; i++)
        printf ( "=");

// Displaying the book information
while (fread(&lib, sizeof(struct library),1,file)==1)
{
        ++sln;
        s_acq_no = lib.acq_no;
        s_acc_no = lib.acc_no;
        strcpy(s_title, lib.title);
        strcpy(s_author1, lib.author1);
        strcpy(s_author2, lib.author2);
        strcpy(s_publisher, lib.publisher);
        s_price = lib.price;
        s_dd = lib.dd;
        s_mm = lib.mm;
        s_yy = lib.yy;
        s_pages = lib.pages;
        s_status = lib.status;

        gotoxy(1, row);
        printf ( "%d",sln);
        gotoxy(6, row);
```

```
printf ( "%d",s_acq_no);
gotoxy(14, row);
printf ( "%d",s_acc_no);
// For displaying only 12 characters of each
gotoxy(21, row);
printf ( "%s",s_title);
gotoxy(40, row);
printf ( "%s",s_publisher);
gotoxy(55, row);
printf ( "%.2f",s_price);

gotoxy(63, row);
printf ( "%d",s_dd);
printf ( "-" );
printf ("%d", s_mm );
printf ( "-");
printf ("%d", s_yy);
gotoxy(78, row);
printf ( "%c",s_status);
row++;
gotoxy(21, row);
printf ( "%s",s_author1);
gotoxy(55, row);
printf ( "%d",s_pages);

row++;
gotoxy(21, row);
printf ( "%s",s_author2);


gotoxy(1, row);
for (i = 0; i <= 79; i++)
        printf ( "-");

row++;
if (row > 23)
{
        row = 8;
        gotoxy(4, 24);
        printf ( "Press any key to continue.... ");
```

```
                getch();
                clrscr();
            }

        }
        gotoxy(1, row);
        for (i = 0; i <= 79; i++)
            printf ( "=");

        getch();
        fclose(file);
}
```

ACQUISITION REGISTER

Date : 24-2-1999

Sl. No.	Acq. No.	Acc.No.	Title & Author(s)	Publisher	Price & Pages	Date(p)	Status
1	10	10	FOXPRO FOR WIN R. K. TAXALI	BPB	250.00 550	23-2-1999	Y
2	10	11	MASTER IN C++ REETA SAHOO	KHANNA	250.00 670	23-2-1999	Y
3	12	10	PROGRAMMING IN C++ ROBERT LOFFER	KHANNA	240.00 500	23-2-1999	Y
4	12	11	UNIX POWERTOOLS STEVEN KERLIN	TMH	230.00 700	23-2-1999	Y

Figure 6.14 Output Screen of Acquisition Register of function Acqu_Register

```
// Function for Membership register
void Memb_Register(void)
{
        int xdd, xmm, xyy,i;
```

```
int s_memb_no; // Membership number
char s_name[30];          // Name of the member
char s_address[30]; // Address of the employee
int s_mdd, s_mmm, s_myy; // Membership date
int s_edd, s_emm, s_eyy; // Expire date
float s_memb_fee; // Membership fee
float s_caut_fee;         // Caution money

struct date d;            // For extracting system date

int sln = 0;
int row = 8;
// Displaying the Members information

FILE *file;

clrscr();
gotoxy(30, 2);
printf ( "MEMBERSHIP REGISTER");
gotoxy(30, 3);
printf ( "___________________");

getdate(&d);
xdd = d.da_day;
xmm = d.da_mon;
xyy = d.da_year;
gotoxy(63, 3);
printf ( "Date: ");
printf ("%d", xdd );
printf ( "-" );
printf ("%d", xmm);
printf ("-" );
printf ("%d",xyy);

gotoxy(1, 4);
for (i = 0; i <= 79; i++)
        printf ("=");
gotoxy(1, 5);
printf ( "Sl.No");
gotoxy(7, 5);
```

```
printf ( "Memb.No.");
gotoxy(17, 5);
printf ( "Name &");
gotoxy(40, 5);
printf ( "Memb.Date");
gotoxy(51, 5);
printf ( "Expir.Date");
gotoxy(63, 5);
printf ( "Membership");
gotoxy(74, 5);
printf ( "Caution");

gotoxy(17, 6);
printf ( "Address");
gotoxy(65, 6);
printf ( "Fees");
gotoxy(75, 6);
printf ( "Money");

gotoxy(1, 7);
for (i = 0; i <= 79; i++)
        printf ( "=");

file = fopen("MEMFILE.dat", "r");
while (fread(&mem, sizeof(struct member),1,file)==1)
{
        ++sln;
        s_memb_no = mem.memb_no;
        strcpy(s_name, mem.name);
        strcpy(s_address, mem.address);
        s_mdd = mem.mdd;
        s_mmm = mem.mmm;
        s_myy = mem.myy;
        s_edd = mem.edd;
        s_emm = mem.emm;
        s_eyy = mem.eyy;
        s_memb_fee = mem.memb_fee;
        s_caut_fee = mem.caut_fee;

        gotoxy(2, row);
```

```
printf ( "%d",sln);
gotoxy(7, row);
printf ( "%d",s_memb_no);
gotoxy(16, row);
printf ( "%s",s_name);
gotoxy(40, row);
printf ( "%d",s_mdd);
printf ("-" );
printf ("%d", s_mmm );
printf ( "-" );
printf ("%d", s_myy);
gotoxy(51, row);
printf ( "%d",s_edd);
printf ( "-");
printf ("%d", s_emm);
printf ( "-" );
printf ("%d", s_eyy);

gotoxy(65, row);
printf ( "%.2f",s_memb_fee);

gotoxy(75, row);
printf ( "%.2f",s_caut_fee);

row++;
gotoxy(16, row);
printf ( "%s",s_address);
row++;
gotoxy(1, row);
for (i = 0; i <= 79; i++)
        printf ( "-");

row++;

if (row > 23)
{
        row = 8;
        gotoxy(4, 24);
        printf ( "Press any key to continue.... ");
        getch();
```

```
                clrscr();
            }
    }
    gotoxy(1, row);
    for (i = 0; i <= 79; i++)
            printf ("=");

    getch();
    fclose(file);
}
```

MEMBERSHIP REGISTER

Date : 24-2-1999

Sl.No.	Memb.No.	Name & Address	Memb.Date	Expir.Date	Membership Fees	Caution Money
1	100	MR. PANKAJ KAPOOR ROHINI, DELHI	10-10-1998	10-10-1999	3400.00	400.00
2	200	STEVENSON F. F-24, SOUTHEXT.	8-8-1999	8-8-1999	3500.00	500.00
3	300	M. GOVIND RAO F-25/28, SEC-7, ROHINI	5-5-1998	5-5-1999	4500.00	500.00

Figure 6.15 Output Screen of Membership Register of function Memb_Register

```
// Function for issue register
void Issue_Register()
{
        int xdd, xmm, xyy,i;
        struct date d;              // For extracting system date

        int s_acq_no;    // Aquisition number
        int s_acc_no;    // Accession no
        int s_memb_no; // Member number
```

```
int s_idd, s_imm, s_iyy;  // Issue date
int s_rdd, s_rmm, s_ryy;// Return date

int sln = 0;
int row = 8;
// Displaying the Issued books information

FILE *file;
clrscr();
gotoxy(35, 2);
printf ( "ISSUE REGISTER");
gotoxy(35, 3);
printf ( "—————————————");

getdate(&d);
xdd = d.da_day;
xmm = d.da_mon;
xyy = d.da_year;
gotoxy(63, 3);
printf ( "Date: ");
printf ("%d", xdd );
printf ( "-" );
printf ("%d", xmm );
printf ( "-");
printf ("%d", xyy);

gotoxy(1, 4);
for ( i = 0; i <= 79; i++)
        printf ( "=");
gotoxy(1, 5);
printf ( "Sl.No");
gotoxy(9, 5);
printf ( "Memb.No.");
gotoxy(18, 5);
printf ( "Acq.no");
gotoxy(28, 5);
printf ( "Acc.No");
gotoxy(49, 5);
printf ( "Books Issued");
gotoxy(63, 5);
```

```
printf ( "Purposed Date");

gotoxy(55, 6);
printf ( "On");
gotoxy(65, 6);
printf ( "Of Return");
gotoxy(1, 7);
for (i = 0; i <= 79; i++)
        printf ( "-");

file = fopen("MASTER.dat", "r");
// Search the record for further modification
while (fread(&iss,sizeof(struct issue),1,file)==1)
{
        ++sln;
        s_acq_no = iss.acq_no;
        s_acc_no = iss.acc_no;
        s_memb_no = iss.memb_no;
        s_idd = iss.idd;
        s_imm = iss.imm;
        s_iyy = iss.iyy;
        s_rdd = iss.rdd;
        s_rmm = iss.rmm;
        s_ryy = iss.ryy;

        gotoxy(1, row);
        printf ( "%d",sln);
        gotoxy(10, row);
        printf ( "%d",s_memb_no);
        gotoxy(20, row);
        printf ( "%d",s_acq_no);
        gotoxy(30, row);
        printf ( "%d",s_acc_no);
        gotoxy(50, row);
        printf ( "%d",s_idd);
        printf ( "-" );
        printf ("%d", s_imm);
        printf ( "-" );
        printf ("%d", s_iyy);
        gotoxy(63, row);
```

```
            printf ( "%d",s_rdd);
            printf ("-");
            printf ("%d", s_rmm);
            printf ( "-" );
            printf ("%d", s_ryy);
            row++;
            if (row > 23)
            {
                    row = 8;
                    gotoxy(4, 24);
                    printf ( "Press any key to continue.... ");
                    getch();
                    clrscr();
            }
        }
        getch();
        fclose(file);
}
```

ISSUE REGISTER					
					Date : 24-2-1999
Sl.No.	Memb.No.	Acq.No.	Acc.No.	Book Issued On	Purposed Date Of Return
1	100	10	10	24-2-1999	27-2-1999
2	200	10	11	24-2-1999	27-2-1999

Figure 6.16 Output Screen of Issue Register of function Issue_Register

```
// Function for overdue books
void OverDue_Book()
{
        int xdd, xmm, xyy,i;
        struct date d;              // For extracting system date
        int sln = 0;
```

```
int row = 8;
// Displaying the Issued books information

FILE *file;

int s_acq_no;     // Aquisition number
int s_acc_no;     // Accession no
int s_memb_no; // Member number
int s_idd, s_imm, s_iyy; // Issue date
int s_rdd, s_rmm, s_ryy;// Return date
int dmonth, ovrdue = 0;
clrscr();
gotoxy(35, 2);
printf ( "OVERDUE BOOK");
gotoxy(35, 3);
printf ( "————————————");

getdate(&d);
xdd = d.da_day;
xmm = d.da_mon;
xyy = d.da_year;
gotoxy(63, 3);
printf ( "Date: ");
printf ("%d", xdd );
printf ( "-" );
printf ("%d", xmm );
printf ( "-" );
printf ("%d", xyy);

gotoxy(1, 4);
for (i = 0; i <= 79; i++)
        printf ("=");
gotoxy(1, 5);
printf ( "Sl.No");
gotoxy(9, 5);
printf ( "Memb.No.");
gotoxy(18, 5);
printf ( "Acq.no");
gotoxy(28, 5);
printf ( "Acc.No");
```

```
gotoxy(40, 5);
printf ( "Issue Date");
gotoxy(53, 5);
printf ( "Return Date");

gotoxy(66, 5);
printf ( "Days Overdue");

gotoxy(66, 6);
printf ( "As on Sys.Date");
        gotoxy(1, 7);
for (i = 0; i <= 79; i++)
        printf ( "-");

file = fopen("MASTER.dat", "r");

// Search the record for further modification
while (fread(&iss, sizeof(struct issue),1,file)==1)
{
        s_acq_no = iss.acq_no;
        s_acc_no = iss.acc_no;
        s_memb_no = iss.memb_no;
        s_idd = iss.idd;
        s_imm = iss.imm;
        s_iyy = iss.iyy;
        s_rdd = iss.rdd;
        s_rmm = iss.rmm;
        s_ryy = iss.ryy;
        ovrdue = no_of_days(xdd, xmm, xyy, s_rdd, s_rmm, s_ryy);

        if (ovrdue > 0)
        {
                ++sln;
                gotoxy(2, row);
                printf ( "%d",sln);
                gotoxy(10, row);
                printf ( "%d",s_memb_no);
                gotoxy(20, row);
                printf ( "%d",s_acq_no);
                gotoxy(30, row);
```

```
                printf ( "%d",s_acc_no);
                gotoxy(40, row);

                printf ( "%d",s_idd );
                printf ( "-" );
                printf ("%d", s_imm);
                printf ( "-");
                printf ("%d", s_iyy);
                gotoxy(53, row);
                printf ( "%d",s_rdd);
                printf ( "-");
                printf ("%d", s_rmm);
                printf ( "-");
                printf ("%d", s_ryy);
                gotoxy(70, row);
                printf ( "%.2f",ovrdue);
                row++;
                gotoxy(1, row);
                for ( i = 0; i <= 79; i++)
                        printf ( "-");
                row++;

                if (row > 23)
                {
                        row = 7;
                        gotoxy(4, 24);
                        printf ( "Press any key to continue... ");
                        getch();
                        clrscr();
                }

            }
    }
    getch();
    fclose(file);

}
```

OVERDUE BOOK						
						Date : 24-2-1999
Sl.No.	Memb.No.	Acq.No.	Acc.No.	Issue Date	Return Date	Days Overdue As on Sys.Date
1	100	10	10	24-2-1999	27-2-1999	1
2	200	10	11	24-2-1999	27-2-1999	1

Figure 6.17 Output Screen of Over Due Books

```
// Function to display the fine register
void Fine_Register()
{
        int xdd, xmm, xyy,i;
        struct date d;              // For extracting system date
        int sln = 0;
        int row = 8;
        // Displaying the Issued books information

        FILE *file;

        int s_memb_no;
        int     s_acq_no;
        int s_acc_no;
        int s_idd, s_imm, s_iyy;  // Book issue date

        int s_rdd, s_rmm, s_ryy;// Book purposed return date

        int s_cdd, s_cmm, s_cyy;        // Returned date
        int s_finfee;

        clrscr();
        gotoxy(35, 2);
        printf ( "FINE REGISTER");
        gotoxy(35, 3);
```

```
printf ( "——————————");
getdate(&d);
xdd = d.da_day;
xmm = d.da_mon;
xyy = d.da_year;
gotoxy(63, 3);
printf ( "Date: ");
printf ("%d", xdd);
printf ( "-");
printf ("%d", xmm);
printf ( "-" );
printf ("%d", xyy);

gotoxy(1, 4);
for ( i = 0; i <= 79; i++)
        printf ( "=");
gotoxy(1, 5);
printf ( "Sl.No");
gotoxy(9, 5);
printf ( "Memb.No.");
gotoxy(18, 5);
printf ( "Acq.no");
gotoxy(28, 5);
printf ( "Acc.No");
gotoxy(39, 5);
printf ( "Issue");
gotoxy(49, 5);
printf ( "Returned");
gotoxy(61, 5);
printf ( "Returned");
gotoxy(74, 5);
printf ( "Fine");

gotoxy(39, 6);
printf ( "Date");
gotoxy(51, 6);
printf ( "Date");
gotoxy(63, 6);
printf ( "On");
gotoxy(1, 7);
```

```
for (i = 0; i <= 79; i++)
        printf ( "-");
file = fopen("Fine.dat", "r");
// Search the record for further modification
while (fread(&fin, sizeof(struct fine),1,file)==1)
{
        ++sln;
        s_memb_no = fin.memb_no;
        s_acq_no = fin.acq_no;
        s_acc_no = fin.acc_no;
        s_idd = fin.idd,
        s_imm = fin.imm,
        s_iyy = fin.iyy;

        s_rdd = fin.rdd,
        s_rmm = fin.rmm,
        s_ryy = fin.ryy;

        s_cdd = fin.cdd,
        s_cmm = fin.cmm,
        s_cyy = fin.cyy;
        s_finfee = fin.finfee;

        gotoxy(1, row);
        printf ( "%d",sln);
        gotoxy(9, row);
        printf ( "%d",s_memb_no);
        gotoxy(18, row);
        printf ( "%d",s_acq_no);
        gotoxy(28, row);
        printf ( "%d",s_acc_no);
        gotoxy(37, row);
        printf ( "%d",s_idd );
        printf ( "-");
        printf ("%d", s_imm);
        printf ( "-" );
        printf ("%d", s_iyy);
        gotoxy(49, row);
        printf ( "%d",s_rdd);
        printf ( "-" );
```

```
                printf ("%d", s_rmm);
                printf ( "-" );
                printf ("%d", s_ryy);
                gotoxy(61, row);
                printf ( "%d",s_cdd);
                printf ( "-");
                printf ("%d", s_cmm);
                printf ( "-");
                printf ("%d", s_cyy);

                gotoxy(75, row);
                printf ( "%.2f",s_finfee);

                row++;
                if (row > 23)
                {
                        row = 8;
                        gotoxy(4, 24);
                        printf ( "Press any key to continue.... ");
                        getch();
                        clrscr();
                }
        }
        getch();
        fclose(file);
}
```

FINE REGISTER

----------------------- Date : 1-3-1999

Sl.No.	Memb.No.	Acq.No.	Acc.No.	Issue Date	Return Date	Returned On	Fine
1	100	10	10	24-2-1999	27-2-1999	28-2-1999	1
2	200	10	11	24-2-1999	27-2-1999	28-2-1999	1

Figure 6.18 Output Screen of Fine Register of function OverDue_Register

```
// Function to list out expiring memberships
void Expire_Register()
{
        int tflag = 0;
        int xdd, xmm, xyy,i;
        int s_memb_no; // Membership number
        char s_name[30];        // Name of the member
        char s_address[30]; // Address of the member
        int s_mdd, s_mmm, s_myy; // Membership date
        int s_edd, s_emm, s_eyy; // Expire date
        float s_memb_fee; // Membership fee
        float s_caut_fee;       // Caution money
        int sln = 0;
        int row = 8;
        FILE *file;
        struct date d;          // For extracting system date

        clrscr();
        gotoxy(20, 2);
        printf ( "List of Expiring Memberships");
        gotoxy(20, 3);
        printf ( "————————————————————————————————");

        getdate(&d);
        xdd = d.da_day;
        xmm = d.da_mon;
        xyy = d.da_year;
        gotoxy(63, 3);
        printf ( "Date: ");
        printf ("%d", xdd);
        printf ( "-");
        printf ("%d", xmm);
        printf ( "-" );
        printf ("%d",xyy);

        gotoxy(1, 4);
        for ( i = 0; i <= 79; i++)
                printf ( "=");
        gotoxy(1, 5);
        printf ( "Sl.No");
```

```
gotoxy(7, 5);
printf ( "Membership ");
gotoxy(20, 5);
printf ( "Name & ");
gotoxy(40, 5);
printf ( "Membership");
gotoxy(58, 5);
printf ( "Membership");

gotoxy(10, 6);
printf ( "No.");
gotoxy(20, 6);
printf ( "Address ");
gotoxy(40, 6);
printf ( "Beginning Date");
gotoxy(58, 6);
printf ( "Expire Date");


gotoxy(1, 7);
for (i = 0; i <= 79; i++)
        printf ( "=");

// Displaying the Members information


file = fopen("MEMFILE.dat", "r");
while (fread(&mem, sizeof(struct member),1,file)==1)
{
        tflag = 0;
        s_memb_no = mem.memb_no;
        strcpy(s_name, mem.name);
        strcpy(s_address, mem.address);
        s_mdd = mem.mdd;
        s_mmm = mem.mmm;
        s_myy = mem.myy;

        s_edd = mem.edd; // Actual expire date
        s_emm = mem.emm;
        s_eyy = mem.eyy;
```

```
// The function returns the value 1 or 0 from date_expire() function
tflag = date_expire(s_edd, s_emm, s_eyy);
if (tflag == 1)
{
        ++sln;
        gotoxy(2, row);
        printf ( "%d",sln);
        gotoxy(9, row);
        printf ( "%d",s_memb_no);
        gotoxy(19, row);
        printf ( "%s",s_name);
        gotoxy(40, row);
        printf ( "%d",s_mdd );
        printf ( "-" );
        printf ("%d", s_mmm);
        printf ( "-");
        printf ("%d", s_myy);
        gotoxy(58, row);
        printf ( "%d",s_edd);
        printf ( "-" );
        printf ("%d", s_emm);
        printf ( "-");
        printf ("%d", s_eyy);

        row++;
        gotoxy(19, row);
        printf ( "%s",s_address);
        row++;
        gotoxy(1, row);
        for (i = 0; i <= 79; i++)
                printf ( "-");

        row++;

        if (row > 23)
        {
                row = 8;
                gotoxy(4, 24);
                printf ( "Press any key to continue.... ");
```

```
                getch();
                clrscr();
            }
        }
    }
    gotoxy(1, row);
    for (i = 0; i <= 79; i++)
        printf ( "=");

    getch();
    fclose(file);
}
```

List of Expiring Memberships				
				Date : 8-8-2002
Sl.No.	Membership No.	Name & Address	Membership Beginning Date	Membership Expiring Date
1	100	MR. PANKAJ KAPOOR ROHINI, DELHI	10-10-1998	10-10-1999
2	200	STEVENSON F. F-24, SOUTH EXT.	8-8-1999	8-8-1999
3	300	M. GOVIND RAO F-25/28, SEC-7, ROHINI	5-5-1998	5-5-1999

Figure 6.19 List of memberships about to expire

```
// Main Program starts here
void main(void)
{
    //control menu;

    lib_SCREEN();
}
```

Music Shop Management

7

We have a music shop. We sale Cassettes & CDs in our shop. We keep all records of Sales, purchases, opeing and closing stocks, expenses of Cassettes & CDs on monghly basis. We divide the Cassettes & CDs in three categories :

(1) Cassettes of films
(2) Non films cassettes
(3) Religious cassettes

Our aim is to make a computer programme such that monthly profit of music shop can be derived and closing stock of three different category of Cassettes & CDs can be ascertained.

Files :

There are separate files for keeping the records of music shop.

(i) One file for recording of numbers of cassettes & CDs of different category purchased during the month.

(ii) We maintain another file for total sales during the month.

(iii) A file for expenses incurred during the year, i.e. Salary to workers, Electricity bills, telephone bills, miscellaneous expenses.

Inputs are :-

- Opeing stock at the beginning of month of 3 different types of Cassettes andCDs.
- Purchase of three different category of Cassettes & CDs during the month.
- Total Sales during the month of three different categories of Cassettes and CDs.
- Total expenses i.e. Salary to workers, Electricity bills, Telephone bills, miscellenious expenses incurred during the month.

Output of the program :

- Profit during the month of all the three different categories of Cassettes and CDs.
- Clsing stock lying of three different categories of Cassettes & CDs with the shop at the end of the month.

Problem Description

A. Requirement analysis :

We have studied the existing system in detail. The finding of our study yield various pieces of information which are described in the following manner:

(a) For the cassettes and with other related modules of MUSIC SHOP, we enter all the details of the cassettes with the following details :

Cassette code - film, nonfilm, religious
Title of the cassette
Cassette company
Total cassette purchased
Date of purchase
Price per cassette

Total number of cassettes in balance
Balance date
Balance date

Cassette Purchased Person Name
Person Address
Number of cassettes purchased
To store the system date/ purchase date

Other expence code
Nature of expense description
Expense date
Expense amount and so on.

B. Required Output of the system :

The computerized system generates the following reports as :

1. The system should be able to generate purchase wise register.
2. Daily/monthly sales report
3. Other expenditure report
4. Closing balance of cassettes
5. Monthly profit in music shop

C. Hardware and software requirements :

Assuming that a typical system offers about 1000's of cassettes & CDs in different companies in all three categories. The volume of the information to be handled is therefore about millions characters. Further the whole information has to be segmented as according to

1. Number of cassettes available in each category.
2. Category to which the cassettes belongs.
3. Preference as indicated by the persons demand.

All this suggest that the choice of a computer 486 or equivalent with about 250 MB Hard Disk and about 8 to 16 MB RAM, a line printer or a dot matrix printer and preferable a laser printer is optimum.

The availability of sophisticated programming tool is imperative and thus a C++ is chosen to program the system.

Having done this next is to carefully analyze the data, identify processing element and design appropriate data base file.

D. Data Design :

Data design is the first of the three design activities that are conducted during system development. The impact of data structure on program structure and procedural complexity causes data design to have a profound influence in systems quality.

All the data objects required by this system are listed below:

1. **cassette.dat**

The cassette.dat database is to be created on the basis of information collected from the cassette. It should contain information related to:

(i) Cassette code - 1- film, 2- nonfilm, 3- religious
(ii) Title of the cassette
(iii) Cassette company
(iv) Total cassette purchased
(v) Date of purchase
(vi) Price per cassette

2. **tbal.dat**

(i) Cassette code - 1- film, 2- nonfilm, 3- religious
(ii) Total number of cassettes in balance
(iii) Balance date
(iv) Balance date

3. **person.dat**

(i) Cassette code - 1- film, 2- nonfilm, 3- religious
(ii) Cassette Purchased Person Name
(iii) Person Address
(iv) Number of cassettes purchased
(v) To store the system date/ purchase date

4. **other.dat**

(i) Other expence code

1	-	Salary to workers,
2	-	Electricity bill
3	-	Telephone bills
4	-	Miscellaneous expenses

(ii) Nature of expense description
(iii) Expense date
(iv) Expense amount and so on.

The above data can be designed in the form of a relational database with course name as the key field.

E. System Design Diagram :

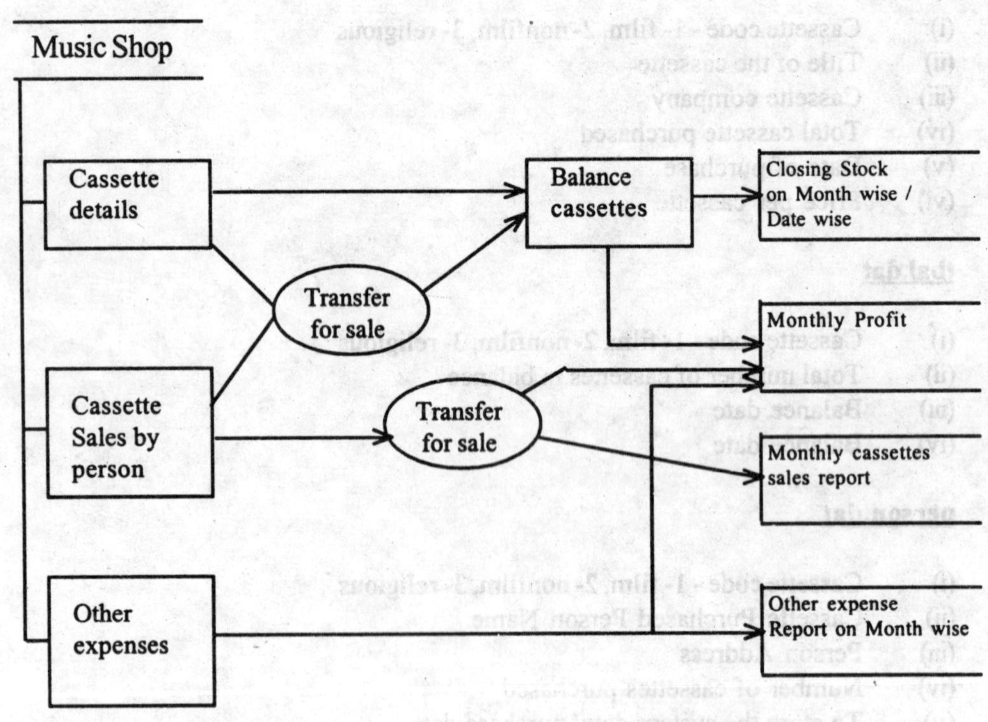

Program Source Codes MUSIC.C

```
/* Declaration of header files       */

#include <process.h>
#include <string.h>
#include <stdio.h>
#include <ctype.h>
#include <conio.h>
#include <dos.h>
#include <stdlib.h>
#include <graphics.h>

typedef char option[15];
const int ROW = 10, COL = 10;

int scan;           // To hold the special characters for moving the prompt in menu
int ascii;

// To display the main menu options
option a[]= {
                        "NewCassPur",
                        "ListOfPurchase",
                        "DailyCassSales",
                        "SalesReport",
                        "AddOtherExp",
                        "OtherExpRep",
                        "ClosingStock",
                        "MonthlyProfit",
                        "Exit"
            };

/* Function to utilize the munus and graphics        */
void Mnormalvideo(int x,int y,char *str);
void Mreversevideo(int x,int y,char *str);
void Mbox(int x1,int y1,int x2,int y2);
char Mmenu();
void Mcontrol_menu();
void Mhelp(void);
```

```
// Variables used to do screening
int i,done;

/* Functions for drawing boxes */
void Sline_hor(int, int, int, char);
void Sline_ver(int, int, int, char);
void Sbox(int, int, int, int, char);


/* Function contains the cassettes information        */
void Cnew_cassettes(void);        // Function to add new cassettes in music shop
// For cassettes entry into the cassettes.dat data file
void Cadd_to_file(int, char t_Cass_name[30], char t_Comp_name[30],
        int, int, int, int, float);
void Cdisplay_list(void); // Displaying the cassettes list
void Cdelete_cassette(int); // Deletes the temporary cassette record
int Clast_cas_code(void); // if the file is exist or not
char *Creturn_name(int); // Function for validation entry of name
char *Creturn_address(int); // Function for validation entry of address
int Crecordno(int);
void Cdisplay(int); // To display the cassette information account

/* Cassette structure to create cassette.dat data file        */
struct cassettes
{
                // Data Members of cassette.dat data file

                int cas_code;    // Cassette code - film, nonfilm, religious
                char Cass_name[30];    // Title of the cassette
                char Comp_name[30];   // Cassette company
                int tot_cassette; // Total cassette purchased
                int dd, mm, yy;  // Date of purchase
                float price;        // Price per cassette
} ini;

/* Function contains the balance cassettes information        */
void Badd_to_file(int, int, int, int, int, float);        // Add record for balance cassette
void Bbalance_cassette(void);    // Function to display the balance cassette
void Bdelete_balance(int);        // Deleting the balance from Tbal.dat
int Bgive_balance(int);  // returns the current balance of a particular cassette code
```

```
void BUpdate_balance(int, int, int , int , int, float); // Function to update balance after cassette sale
float Breturn_price(int); // Return the cassette price

void Bmonthly_profit(void);        // Monthly profit after every transaction

/* Balance structure to create Tbal.dat data file */
struct balance
{
        // Data members of Tbal.dat data file
        int cas_code;    // Cassette code to be balance
        int cas_bal;     // Total number of cassettes in balance
        int dd;  // Balance date
        int mm;
        int yy;
        float price;     // Unit price of cassettes on code wise
} bal;

/* Function contains the cassettes sales information        */
void Anew_account(void); // Function to sale cassettes
void Aclose_account(void);      // Function to close the cassette purchase
void Aclear(int, int); // Function to perform a clear screen function
void ADisplay_sales(void);      // Displaying the sales report of cassettes
int Alast_cas_code(void); // if the file is exist or not
float Asales_status(int m1, int y1, float cod1, float cod2, float cod3);
// Function to add transaction records
void Aadd_to_file(int, char tP_name[30], char tP_address[30],int, int, int, int);
void Adelete_account(int); // Function to delete a transaction record

/* Class contains the customers daily cassette transaction entry  */
struct account
{
        // Data members of person.dat data file
        int cas_code;              // Cassette code - film, nonfilm, religious
        char P_name[30];    // Person Name
        char P_address[30];    // Person Address
        int No_cass;               // Number of cassette
        int dd, mm, yy;  // To store the system date/ purchase date
} acc;
```

```
/* Function to display other expense screen like salary,
 electricity bill, telephone and miscellaneous expences */
void OExpense_other(void);

// Add the data to Other.dat data file
void Oadd_to_file(int, char tNat_Expen[30], int, int, int, float);
void Odisplay_expense(void);     // Display the expenses
float Oother_status(int m1, int y1);

/* Other expenses structure to create other.dat data file */
struct other
{
          // Data members of other.dat data file
          int O_code;              // Other expence code
          /* The other expence code as :
                    1    -    Salary to workers,
                    2    -    Electricity bill
                    3    -    Telephone bills
                    4    -    Miscellaneous expenses */
          char Nat_Expen[30]; // Nature of expense description
          int dd, mm, yy; // Expense date
          float amount; // Expense amount
} oth;

/* Function to displays all the menu prompt messages
 from the pointer array of option a[]      */
void Mnormalvideo(int x,int y,char *str)
{
  gotoxy(x,y);
  cprintf("%s",str);
}

/* Function to move the cursor on the menu prompt
  with a reverse video color      */
void Mreversevideo(int x,int y,char *str)
{
     textcolor(5+143);
     textbackground(WHITE);
     gotoxy(x,y);
     cprintf("%s",str);
```

```
        textcolor(GREEN);
        textbackground(BLACK);
}

/* Functioin to draw box */
void Mbox(int x1,int y1,int x2,int y2)
{
        int col, row;
        for(col=x1;col<x2;col++)
        {
                gotoxy(col,y1);
                cprintf("%c",196);
                gotoxy(col,y2);
                cprintf("%c",196);
        }

        for(row=y1;row<y2;row++)
        {
                gotoxy(x1,row);
                cprintf("%c",179);
                gotoxy(x2,row);
                cprintf("%c",179);
        }
        gotoxy(x1,y1);
        cprintf("%c",218);
        gotoxy(x1,y2);
        cprintf("%c",192);
        gotoxy(x2,y1);
        cprintf("%c",191);
        gotoxy(x2,y2);
        cprintf("%c",217);
}

/* Displaying the main menu of music system     */
char Mmenu()
{
        clrscr();

        textcolor(22);
        Mbox(20, 6, 65, 20);
```

```
Mbox(18, 4, 67, 22);
textcolor(5+143);
gotoxy(36, 5);
textbackground(BLUE);
cprintf("M U S I C");
textbackground(BLACK);
textcolor(22);
for(i = 1; i < 9; i++)
        Mnormalvideo(32, i+10, a[i]);
Mreversevideo(32, 10, a[0]);
i = done = 0;
_setcursortype(_NOCURSOR);
do
{
        int key = getch();

        switch (key)
        {
                case 00:
                        key = getch();

                        switch (key)
                        {
                                case 72:
                                        Mnormalvideo(32, i+10, a[i]);
                                        i—;
                                        if (i == -1)
                                                i = 8;
                                        Mreversevideo(32,i+10, a[i]);
                                        break;
                                case 80:
                                        Mnormalvideo(32, i+10, a[i]);
                                        i++;
                                        if (i == 9)
                                                i = 0;
                                        Mreversevideo(32, i+10, a[i]);
                                        break;

                        }
                        break;
                case 13:
```

```
                    done = 1;
            }
    } while (!done);

    _setcursortype(_NOCURSOR);
    return(i+49);
}

/* The function main_menu() is used to display the main menu system */
void Mcontrol_menu()
{

    char choice;

    do
    {
        choice = Mmenu();
        clrscr();

        switch (choice)
        {
            case '1':
                _setcursortype(_NORMALCURSOR);
                Mbox(3, 1, 75, 24);
                Mbox(5, 2, 73, 23);

                Cnew_cassettes(); // New cassette entry function
                break;
            case '2':
                Mbox(3, 1, 75, 24);
                Mbox(5, 2, 73, 23);
                Cdisplay_list(); // Glogal list of cassettes function
                break;
            case '3':
                Mbox(3, 1, 75, 24);
                Mbox(5, 2, 73, 23);

                _setcursortype(_NORMALCURSOR);

                Anew_account(); // Enter the personwise sale cassette
```

```
                break;
            case '4':
                Mbox(3, 1, 75, 24);
                Mbox(5, 2, 73, 23);

                _setcursortype(_NORMALCURSOR);
                ADisplay_sales(); // Displays the sales cassettes
                break;
            case '5':
                Mbox(3, 1, 75, 24);
                Mbox(5, 2, 73, 23);

                _setcursortype(_NORMALCURSOR);
                OExpense_other(); // Entry of other expenses
                break;
            case '6':
                Mbox(3, 1, 75, 24);
                Mbox(5, 2, 73, 23);
                gotoxy(10,10);
                Odisplay_expense();     // Displays the expenses
                break;
            case '7':
                Mbox(3, 1, 75, 24);
                Mbox(5, 2, 73, 23);
                gotoxy(10,10);
                Bbalance_cassette(); //Function to display the balance cassettes in shop
                break;
            case '8' :
                Mbox(3, 1, 75, 24);
                Mbox(5, 2, 73, 23);
                gotoxy(10,10);
                // Monthly profit after every transaction
                Bmonthly_profit();
                break;
            case '9' :exit(0);
        }
    } while (choice != 8);
}
```

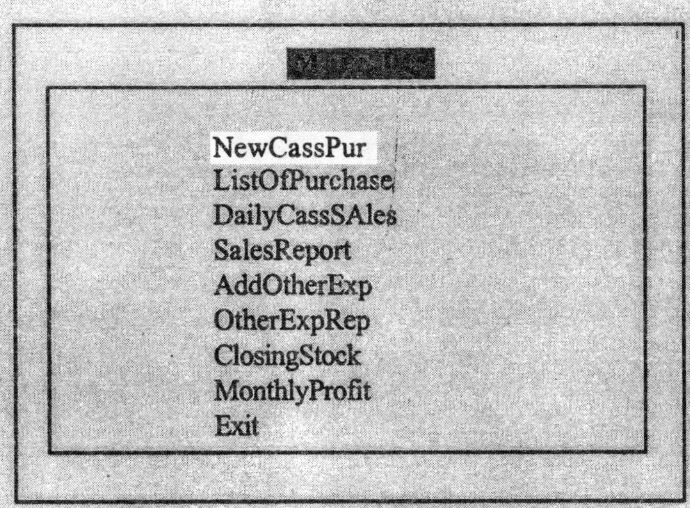

Figure 7.1 Main menu of music shop management

```
/* Function to draw horizontal line for menu*/
void Sline_hor(int column1, int column2, int row, char c)
{
        for (column1; column1 <= column2; column1++)
        {
                gotoxy(column1, row);
                printf("%c", c);
        }
}

/* Function to draw vertical line for menu */
void Sline_ver(int row1, int row2, int column, char c)
{
        for (row1; row1 <= row2; row1++)
        {
                gotoxy(column, row1);
                printf("%c", c);
        }
}
```

```
/* Function for drawing boxes for menu */
void Sbox(int column1, int row1, int column2, int row2, char c)
{
        char ch = 218;
        char c1, c2, c3, c4;
        char l1 = 196, l2 = 179;
        if (c == ch)
        {
                c1 = 218;
                c2 = 191;
                c3 = 217;
                c4 = 217;
                l1 = 196;
                l2 = 179;
        }
        else
        {
                c1 = c;
                c2 = c;
                c3 = c;
                c4 = c;
                l1 = c;
                c2 = c;
        }

        gotoxy(column1, row1);
        printf("%c", c1);
        gotoxy(column2, row1);
        printf("%c", c2);
        gotoxy(column1, row2);
        printf("%c", c3);
        gotoxy(column2, row2);
        printf("%c", c4);
        column1++;
        column2—;
        Sline_hor(column1, column2, row1, l1); //Horizontal line
        Sline_hor(column1, column2, row2, l1);
        column1—;
        column2++;
        row1++;
```

```
        row2—;
        Sline_ver(row1, row2, column1, 12); // Vertical line
        Sline_ver(row1, row2, column2, 12);
}

/* Function to display help about this project */
void Mhelp(void)
{
        clrscr();

        setbkcolor(7);
        settextstyle(7,HORIZ_DIR,5);
        outtextxy(70,10,"Welcome to Music Shop");
        settextstyle(2,HORIZ_DIR,5);
        outtextxy(60,80, "This project your can keep record of daily music cassettes ");
        delay(2);
        outtextxy(60,110, "transaction. This program is capable of holding any no. of cassettes.");
        delay(2);
        outtextxy(60,140, "-In first option you can enter new cassette information");
        delay(2);
        outtextxy(60,170, "-In second option you can see the list of all the cassettes");
        delay(2);
        outtextxy(60,200,"-In third option you can sales the cassettes according to demand");
        delay(2);
        outtextxy(60,230, "-Through fourth optiion you can see the sales status");
        delay(2);
        outtextxy(60,260, "-In the fifth option enter your daily other expenses");
        delay(2);
        outtextxy(60,290, "-In sixth option you can take reports of other expenses");
        delay(2);
        outtextxy(60,320,"-In seventh option you can take monthly closing balance report");
        delay(2);
        outtextxy(60,350,"-In eighth option you can take monthly profit report");
        delay(2);
        outtextxy(60,380, "Note-: Enter only valid data while you maintain this package");
        delay(2);
        outtextxy(60,410, "-And last option is Quit (Exit From Music Window)");
        delay(2);

        settextstyle(7,HORIZ_DIR,3);
```

```
        outtextxy(70,430,"Press any key to continue...");
        getch();
}

/* Function for displaying a cassette information when required */
void Cdisplay(int t_cas_code)
{

        FILE *file; // Declare a file pointer for manipulating record structure
        file = fopen("cassettes.dat", "r");
        rewind(file);      // Position the pointer at the beginning of the file

        // Displays the record contents matching
        // with t_cas_code from cassettes.dat data file

        while (fread(&ini, sizeof(ini), 1, file)==1)
        {
                if (t_cas_code == ini.cas_code)
                {
                        gotoxy(8, 5);
                        printf("Account no. %d", ini.cas_code);
                        gotoxy(10, 8);
                        printf("Name : ");
                        puts(ini.Cass_name);
                        gotoxy(10, 9);
                        printf("Comany Name : ");
                        puts(ini.Comp_name);

                        gotoxy(10, 10);
                        printf("Price : %0.2f ", ini.price);
                        break;
                }
        }

        fclose(file);
}

/* Function to find is their records in cassette.dat file or not */

int Clast_cas_code(void)
```

```
{
        int tcount = 0;
        int count = 0;

        FILE *file; // Declare a file pointer for manipulating record structure
        file = fopen("cassettes.dat", "r");
        rewind(file);       // Position the pointer at the beginning of the file

        /* Founds the last account no. */
        while (fread(&ini, sizeof(ini), 1, file)==1)
        {
                tcount = ini.cas_code;
                count = count + tcount;
        }

        fclose(file);
        return count;
}

/* Function to find is their records in file person.dat or not */

int Alast_cas_code(void)
{
        int tcount = 0;
        int count = 0;

        FILE *file; // Declare a file pointer for manipulating record structure
        file = fopen("Person.dat", "r");
        rewind(file);       // Position the pointer at the beginning of the file

        // Founds the last account no.
        while (fread(&acc, sizeof(acc), 1, file)==1)
        {
                tcount  = acc.cas_code;
                count = count + tcount;
        }
        fclose(file);
        return count;
}
```

```
/* Function for returning balance cassette.
This function returns the balance cassette on code wise
to know the current balance from "Tbal.dat" data file. */

int Bgive_balance(int t_cas_code)
{
        int t_balance = 0;

        FILE *file; // Declare a file pointer for manipulating record structure
        file = fopen("Tbal.dat", "r");
        rewind(file); // Position the pointer at the beginning of the file

        // Gives the last balance of an individual account
        while (fread(&bal, sizeof(bal), 1, file)==1)
        {
                if (bal.cas_code == t_cas_code)
                {
                        t_balance = bal.cas_bal;
                        break;
                }
        }
        fclose(file);
        return t_balance;
}

/* Function to return the cassette price    */
float Breturn_price(int t_cas_code)
{
        float t_price = 0.0;

        FILE *file; // Declare a file pointer for manipulating record structure
        file = fopen("Tbal.dat", "r");
        rewind(file); // Position the pointer at the beginning of the file

        /* Gives the last balance of an individual account */
        while (fread(&bal, sizeof(bal), 1, file)==1)
        {
                if (bal.cas_code == t_cas_code)
                {
                        t_price = bal.price;
```

```
                        break;
                }
        }
        fclose(file);
        return t_price;
}

/* This function add_to_file() is used to create
new/fresh record in the data file */

void Cadd_to_file(int t_cas_code, char t_Cass_name[30],
char t_Comp_name[30], int t_cas, int tdd, int tmm, int tyy, float t_price)
{
        FILE *file; // Declare a file pointer for manipulating record structure

        ini.cas_code = t_cas_code;
        strcpy(ini.Cass_name, t_Cass_name);
        strcpy(ini.Comp_name, t_Comp_name);
        ini.tot_cassette = t_cas;
        ini.dd = tdd;
        ini.mm = tmm;
        ini.yy = tyy;
        ini.price = t_price;

        /* Appends new account record with the price
                into cassettes.dat data file        */
        file = fopen("cassettes.dat", "a+");

        fwrite(&ini, sizeof(ini), 1, file);
        fclose(file);
}

/* This function add_to_file() is used to
create new/fresh record in the data file */

void Badd_to_file(int t_cas_code, int t_cas,
        int tdd, int tmm, int tyy, float t_price)
{
        FILE *file; // Declare a file pointer for manipulating record structure
        FILE *temp;
```

```
int ball = Bgive_balance(t_cas_code);

if (ball > 0)
{

        file = fopen("Tbal.dat", "r");
        temp = fopen("TEMP.dat", "w");
        rewind(file); // Position the pointer at the beginning of the file

        /* Uses a copy method to delete the cassette
          from Tbal.dat data file        */
        while (fread(&bal, sizeof(bal), 1, file) == 1)
        {
                if (bal.cas_code != t_cas_code)
                {
                        fwrite(&bal, sizeof(bal), 1, temp);
                }
                else
                {
                        bal.cas_code = t_cas_code;
                        bal.cas_bal = t_cas + ball;
                        bal.dd = tdd;
                        bal.mm = tmm;
                        bal.yy = tyy;
                        bal.price = t_price;
                        fwrite(&bal, sizeof(bal), 1, temp);
                }
        }

        fclose(file);
        fclose(temp);
        file = fopen("Tbal.dat", "w");
        temp = fopen("TEMP.dat", "r");
        rewind(temp); // Position the pointer at the beginning of the file

        /* Copy the TEMP.dat contents into cassette.dat data file*/
        while (fread(&bal, sizeof(bal), 1, temp))
        {
                fwrite(&bal, sizeof(bal), 1, file);
        }
```

```
            fclose(file);
            fclose(temp);
    }
    else
    {
            bal.cas_code = t_cas_code;
            bal.cas_bal = t_cas;
            bal.dd = tdd;
            bal.mm = tmm;
            bal.yy = tyy;
            bal.price = t_price;

            /* Appends new account record with the
              price into cassettes.dat data file          */
            file = fopen("Tbal.dat", "a+");
            fwrite(&bal, sizeof(bal), 1, file);
            fclose(file);
    }
}

/* Function for deleting a account from cassettes.dat file */
void Cdelete_cassette(int t_cas_code)
{
    FILE *file; // Declare a file pointer for manipulating record structure
    FILE *temp;
    file = fopen("cassettes.dat", "r");

    temp = fopen("TEMP.dat", "w");
    rewind(file); // Position the pointer at the beginning of the file

    /* Uses a copy method to delete the account
      from cassette.dat data file              */
    while (fread(&ini, sizeof(ini), 1, file))
    {

            if (ini.cas_code != t_cas_code)
                    fwrite(&ini, sizeof(ini), 1, file);
    }

    fclose(file);
```

```
        fclose(temp);
        file = fopen("cassettes.dat", "w");
        temp = fopen("TEMP.dat", "r");
        rewind(temp); // Position the pointer at the beginning of the file

        /* Copy the TEMP.dat contents into cassette.dat data file*/
        while (fread(&ini, sizeof(ini), 1, file))
        {

                if (ini.cas_code != t_cas_code)
                        fwrite(&ini, sizeof(ini), 1, file);
        }

        fclose(file);
        fclose(temp);
}

/* Function for deleting a balance from Tbal.dat file          */
void Bdelete_balance(int t_cas_code)
{
        FILE *file; // Declare a file pointer for manipulating record structure
        FILE *temp;
        file = fopen("Tbal.dat", "r");

        temp = fopen("TEMP.dat", "w");
        rewind(file); // Position the pointer at the beginning of the file

        /* Uses a copy method to delete the account from Tbal.dat data file     */
        while (fread(&bal, sizeof(bal), 1, file))
        {
                if (bal.cas_code != t_cas_code)
                        fwrite(&bal, sizeof(bal), 1, file);
        }
        fclose(file);
        fclose(temp);
        file = fopen("Tbal.dat", "w");
        temp = fopen("TEMP.dat", "r");
        rewind(temp); // Position the pointer at the beginning of the file

        /* Copy the TEMP.dat contents into Tbal.dat data file.     */
```

```
    while (fread(&bal, sizeof(bal), 1, file))
    {
        if (bal.cas_code != t_cas_code)
            fwrite(&bal, sizeof(bal), 1, file);
    }

    fclose(file);
    fclose(temp);
}

/* Function for add an account details of
daily tranaction into person.dat file. */

void Aadd_to_file(int t_cas_code, char tP_name[30],
char tP_address[30],int tNo_cass, int d1, int m1, int y1)
{

    FILE *file; // Declare a file pointer for manipulating record structure
    acc.cas_code = t_cas_code;
    strcpy(acc.P_name, tP_name);
    strcpy(acc.P_address, tP_address);
    acc.No_cass = tNo_cass;
    acc.dd = d1;
    acc.mm = m1;
    acc.yy = y1;

    /* Appends the transaction record into person.dat data file        */
    file = fopen("person.dat", "a+");

    fwrite(&acc, sizeof(acc), 1, file);
    fclose(file);
}

/* Function for deleting an account from person.dat file. */
void Adelete_account(int t_cas_code)
{
    FILE *file; // Declare a file pointer for manipulating record structure
    FILE *temp;
    file = fopen("person.dat", "r"); // Open to read records
```

```
temp = fopen("TEMP.dat", "w"); // Open to write records
rewind(file); // Position the pointer at the beginning of the file

/* Uses the copy method for deleting the
 transaction record from person.dat data file      */
while (fread(&acc, sizeof(acc), 1, file))
{
        if (acc.cas_code != t_cas_code)
                fwrite(&acc, sizeof(acc), 1, temp);
}

fclose(file);
fclose(temp);
file = fopen("person.dat", "w");
temp = fopen("TEMP.dat", "r");
rewind(temp); // Position the pointer at the beginning of the file

/* Uses copy method to transfer the record
  from TEMP.dat file to person.dat data file      */
while (fread(&acc, sizeof(acc), 1, temp))
{
        if (acc.cas_code != t_cas_code)
                fwrite(&acc, sizeof(acc), 1, file);
}

fclose(file);
fclose(temp);
}

/* Function for add an other expenses details in other.dat data file */
void Oadd_to_file(int tO_code, char tNat_Expen[30],
int d1, int m1, int y1, float tamount)
{
        FILE *file; // Declare a file pointer for manipulating record structure
        oth.O_code = tO_code;
        strcpy(oth.Nat_Expen, tNat_Expen);
        oth.dd = d1;
        oth.mm = m1;
        oth.yy = y1;
        oth.amount = tamount;
```

```
        /* Appends the transaction record into other.dat data file */
        file = fopen("other.dat", "a+");
        fwrite(&oth, sizeof(oth), 1, file);
        fclose(file);
}

/* Function for displaying an account from "cassettes.dat". */
void Cdisplay_list(void)
{
        int flag,j;
        float tot_price = 0.0, tot_balance = 0.0;
        int row = 7;
        FILE *file; // Declare a file pointer for manipulating record structure
        int d1, m1, y1;
        struct date d;              // For extracting system date
        clrscr();
        gotoxy(25,2);

        printf("List of cassettes in Music Shop");
        gotoxy(25, 3);
        printf("===============================");

        getdate(&d);
        d1 = d.da_day;
        m1 = d.da_mon;
        y1 = d.da_year;
        gotoxy(62, 3);
        printf("Date: %d/%d/%d",d1,m1,y1);
        gotoxy(1, 4);
        for (j = 1; j <= 79; j++)
                printf("=");
        gotoxy(1, 5);
        printf("Code #");
        gotoxy(9, 5);
        printf("Cassette Name");
        gotoxy(34, 5);
        printf("Company Name");
        gotoxy(55, 5);
        printf("Qty");
        gotoxy(61, 5);
        printf("Price");
```

```
gotoxy(72, 5);
printf("Total");
gotoxy(1, 6);
for (j = 1; j <= 79; j++)
        printf("=");

file = fopen("cassettes.dat", "r");
rewind(file); // Position the pointer at the beginning of the file

/* Reads all the records to display on the screen */
while (fread(&ini, sizeof(ini), 1, file) == 1)
{
        tot_price = 0.0;
        flag = 0;
        delay(2);
        gotoxy(3, row);
        printf("%d", ini.cas_code);
        gotoxy(9, row);
        puts(ini.Cass_name);
        gotoxy(34, row);
        puts(ini.Comp_name);
        gotoxy(55, row);
        printf("%d", ini.tot_cassette);
        gotoxy(61, row);
        printf("%0.2f", ini.price);

        tot_price = ini.tot_cassette * ini.price;
        gotoxy(72, row);
        printf("%0.2f", tot_price);

        tot_balance = tot_balance + tot_price;
        row++;
        if (row > 23)
        {
                flag = 1;
                row = 6;
                gotoxy(4, 24);
                printf("Press any key to continue.... ");
                getch();
                clrscr();
        }
}
```

```
    gotoxy(1, row);
    for (j = 1; j <= 79; j++)
            printf("=");
    row++;
    gotoxy(3, row);
    printf("Total price of Cassettes is : ");

    gotoxy(72, row);
    printf("%0.2f", tot_balance);

    fclose(file);
    if (!flag)
    {
            gotoxy(4, 24);
            printf("Press any key to continue...");
            getch();
    }
    getch();
}
```

List of Cassettes in Music Shop

Date : 12/8/2000

Code #	Cassette Name	Company Name	Qty	Price	Total
1	Sift Tumhare	HMV	100	30	3000.00
2	TOP POP	PRIV	200	20	2000.00
3	Best of Ryhmes	INFANTA	150	30	4500.00
1	Moveis	TIPS	100	30	3000.00
2	Queen King	RPG	300	20	6000.00

Total price of cassettes is : **18500.00**

Press any key to continue...

Figure 7.2 List of cassettes in Music shop

```
/* Function for displaying an cassette sales on day wise */
void ADisplay_sales(void)
{

    int flag,j;
    FILE *file; // Declare a file pointer for manipulating record structure
    int d1, m1, y1;
    struct date d;          // For extracting system date
    int tcas_code;
    int xdd, xmm, xyy;
    int row = 8;

    clrscr();
    gotoxy(10, 8);
    printf("Enter the Cassette Code ");
    gotoxy(10, 9);
    printf("As 1 or 2 or 3 ");
    gotoxy(10, 11);
    printf("Enter the date ");
    gotoxy(30, 9);
    scanf (" %d", tcas_code);
    gotoxy(30, 11);
    scanf (" %d", xdd);
    gotoxy(32, 11);
    printf("-");
    gotoxy(33, 11);
    scanf (" %d", xmm);
    gotoxy(35, 11);
    printf("-");
    gotoxy(36, 11);
    scanf (" %d", xyy);
    if (tcas_code < 1)
    {
        gotoxy(5, 23);
        printf("Your entry is not valid");
        getch();
        return;
    }
    else
        if (tcas_code > 3)
```

```
        {
                gotoxy(5, 23);
                printf("Your entry is not valid");
                getch();
                return;
        }

clrscr();
gotoxy(25, 2);
printf("Sales Report in Music Shop");
gotoxy(25, 3);
printf("==========================");

getdate(&d);
d1 = d.da_day;
m1 = d.da_mon;
y1 = d.da_year;
gotoxy(62, 3);
printf("Date: %d/%d/%d ", d1,m1,y1);
gotoxy(1, 5);
for ( j = 1; j <= 79; j++)
        printf("=");

gotoxy(1, 6);
printf("Code #");
gotoxy(9, 6);
printf("Name");
gotoxy(34, 6);
printf("Address");
gotoxy(55, 6);
printf("Qty");
gotoxy(61, 6);
printf("Date");

gotoxy(1, 7);
for (j = 1; j <= 79; j++)
        printf("=");

file = fopen("Person.dat", "r");
rewind(file); // Position the pointer at the beginning of the file
```

```
/* Reads all the records to display on the screen */
while (fread(&acc, sizeof(acc), 1, file) == 1)
{
        if ((tcas_code == acc.cas_code) && (xmm == acc.mm) && (xyy == acc.yy))
        {
                flag = 0;
                delay(2);
                gotoxy(3, row);
                printf("%d", acc.cas_code);
                gotoxy(9, row);
                puts(acc.P_name);
                gotoxy(34, row);
                puts(acc.P_address);
                gotoxy(55, row);
                printf("%d", acc.No_cass);

                gotoxy(61, row);
                printf("%d-%d-%d", acc.dd,acc.mm,acc.yy);
                ++row;
                if (row > 23)
                {
                        flag = 1;
                        row = 6;
                        gotoxy(4, 24);
                        printf("Press any key to continue.... ");
                        getch();
                        clrscr();
                }
        }
}

 ++row;

 gotoxy(1, row);
 for (j = 1; j <= 79; j++)
        printf("=");
 row++;

 fclose(file);
 if (!flag)
```

```
    {
            gotoxy(4, 24);
            printf("Press any key to continue...");
            getch();
    }
    getch();
}
```

Sales Report in Music Shop

Date : 12/8/2000

Code #	Name	Address	Qty	Date
1	M. Sagar	F-23/26, Sec-7, Rohini	2	10-8-2000
2	P.C. Ojha	RZ-123, N.Garh	5	10-8-2000
2	Santosh	D/12, Sec-7, Rohini	7	11-8-2000

Press any key to continue...

Figure 7.3 Sales report in music shop

```
/* Function for displaying other expenses in shop */
void Odisplay_expense(void)
{

        int flag;
        FILE *file; // Declare a file pointer for manipulating record structure
                /* The other expence code as :
                        1       -       Salary to workers,
                        2       -       Electricity bill
                        3       -       Telephone bills
                        4       -       Miscellaneous expenses */
        int tO_code,j;
```

```
int xdd, xmm, xyy;
int d1, m1, y1;
struct date d;              // For extracting system date
int row = 8;

clrscr();
gotoxy(10, 8);
printf("Enter the Expense Code ");
gotoxy(10, 9);
printf("1 Salary to Worker ");
gotoxy(10, 10);
printf("2 Electricity bill ");
gotoxy(10, 11);
printf("3 Telephone bill ");
gotoxy(10, 12);
printf("4 Miscellaneous ");

gotoxy(10, 13);
printf("Enter your Choice");
gotoxy(10, 14);
printf("Enter the date ");
gotoxy(30, 13);
scanf (" %d", tO_code);
gotoxy(30, 14);
scanf (" %d", xdd);
gotoxy(32, 14);
printf("-");
gotoxy(33, 14);
scanf (" %d", xmm);
gotoxy(35, 14);
printf("-");
gotoxy(36, 14);
scanf (" %d", xyy);
if (tO_code < 1)
{
        gotoxy(5, 23);
        printf("Your entry is not valid");
        getch();
        return;
}
```

```
else
        if (tO_code > 4)
        {
                gotoxy(5, 23);
                printf("Your entry is not valid");
                getch();
                return;
        }

clrscr();
gotoxy(25, 2);
printf("Other Expenses in Music Shop");
gotoxy(25, 3);
printf("============================");

getdate(&d);
d1 = d.da_day;
m1 = d.da_mon;
y1 = d.da_year;

gotoxy(62, 3);
printf("Date: %d/%d/%d", d1, m1, y1);

gotoxy(1, 5);
for ( j = 1; j <= 79; j++)
        printf("=");

gotoxy(1, 6);
printf("Code #");
gotoxy(9, 6);
printf("Nature Expense");
gotoxy(34, 6);
printf("Date");
gotoxy(55, 6);
printf("Amount");

gotoxy(1, 7);
for (j = 1; j <= 79; j++)
        printf("=");
```

```
file = fopen("other.dat", "r");
rewind(file); // Position the pointer at the beginning of the file

/* Reads all the records to display on the screen */
while (fread(&oth, sizeof(oth), 1, file) == 1)
{

      if ((tO_code == oth.O_code) && (xmm == oth.mm) && (xyy == oth.yy))
      {
            flag = 0;
            delay(2);
            gotoxy(3, row);

            printf("%d", oth.O_code);
            gotoxy(9, row);
            puts(oth.Nat_Expen);
            gotoxy(34, row);
            printf("%d-%d-%d", oth.dd, oth.mm, oth.yy);
            gotoxy(55, row);
            printf("%0.2f", oth.amount);

            ++row;
            if (row > 23)
            {
                  flag = 1;
                  row = 6;
                  gotoxy(4, 24);
                  printf("Press any key to continue.... ");
                  getch();
                  clrscr();
            }
      }
}

++row;
gotoxy(1, row);
for (j = 1; j <= 79; j++)
      printf("=");
row++;
fclose(file);
```

```
        if(!flag)
        {
                gotoxy(4, 24);
                printf("Press any key to continue...");
                getch();
        }
        getch();
}
```

Other Expenses in Music Shop

Date : 12/8/2000

Code #	Nature of Expense	Date	Amount
1	Salary	10-8-200	2300.00
2	Electricity bill	12-8-200	400.00
3	Telephone bill	12-8-200	550.00

Press any key to continue...

Figure 7.4 Other expenses in music shop

```
/* Function for clearing specified row and column. */
void Aclear(int col, int row)
{
        int j;
        for ( j = col; j <= 79; j++)
        {
                gotoxy(j, row);
                printf(" ");
        }
}
```

```
/* Function for return name of the account
holder from cassettes.dat. */
char *Creturn_name(int t_cas_code)
{
        FILE *file; // Declare a file pointer for manipulating record structure
        char t_Cass_name[30];
        file = fopen("cassettes.dat", "r");
        rewind(file); // Position the pointer at the beginning of the file

        // Return the name to display at report screen if found
        while (fread(&ini, sizeof(ini), 1, file) == 1)
        {
                if (ini.cas_code == t_cas_code)
                {
                        strcpy(t_Cass_name, ini.Cass_name);
                        break;
                }
        }
        fclose(file);
        return t_Cass_name;
}

/* Function for return Comp_name of the account holder from cassettes.dat. */
char *Creturn_address(int t_cas_code)
{
        FILE *file; // Declare a file pointer for manipulating record structure
        char t_Comp_name[30];
        file = fopen("cassettes.dat", "r");
        rewind(file); // Position the pointer at the beginning of the file

        /* Return the Comp_name to display at report screen if found      */
        while (fread(&ini, sizeof(ini), 1, file))
        {
                if (ini.cas_code == t_cas_code)
                {
                        strcpy(t_Comp_name, ini.Comp_name);
                        break;
                }
        }
        fclose(file);
```

```
	return t_Comp_name;
}

/* Function to find the monthly profit using person.dat, cassette.dat and Tbal.dat data files */
void Bmonthly_profit()
{
	int flag,j;
	FILE *file; // Declare a file pointer for manipulating record structure
	int d1, m1, y1;
	struct date d;			// For extracting system date
	float T_bal = 0.0;
	float G_bal = 0.0;
	int row = 7;

	float cod1=0.0;
	float cod2=0.0;
	float cod3=0.0;
	float saltotal = 0.0;
	float gother = 0.0;
	float net_bal = 0.0;
	clrscr();
	gotoxy(25,1);

	printf("Monthly Profit Statement");
	gotoxy(25, 2);
	printf("==========================");

	getdate(&d);
	d1 = d.da_day;
	m1 = d.da_mon;
	y1 = d.da_year;

	gotoxy(55, 3);
	printf("As on Date: %d/%d/%d", d1,m1,y1);

	gotoxy(1, 4);
	for (j = 1; j <= 79; j++)
		printf("=");

	gotoxy(1, 5);
```

```
printf("Code #");
gotoxy(15, 5);
printf("Total Balance");
gotoxy(40, 5);
printf("Date");

gotoxy(50, 5);
printf("Unit Price");

gotoxy(65, 5);
printf("Total Amount");

gotoxy(1, 6);
for (j = 1; j <= 79; j++)
        printf("=");

file = fopen("Tbal.dat", "r");
rewind(file); // Position the pointer at the beginning of the file

/* Reads all the records to display on the screen */
while (fread(&bal, sizeof(bal), 1, file))
{
        flag = 0;
        if (bal.cas_code == 1)
                cod1 = bal.price;
        else
                if (bal.cas_code == 2)
                        cod2 = bal.price;
                else
                        cod3 = bal.price;
        T_bal = bal.cas_bal * bal.price;
        delay(2);
        gotoxy(3, row);
        printf("%d", bal.cas_code);
        gotoxy(20, row);
        printf("%d", bal.cas_bal);
        gotoxy(40, row);
        printf("%d-%d-%d", bal.dd,bal.mm,bal.yy);
        gotoxy(53, row);
        printf("%0.2f", bal.price);
```

```
        G_bal = G_bal + T_bal;

        gotoxy(68, row);
        printf("%0.2f", T_bal);
        T_bal = 0.0;
        row++;
        if (row > 23)
        {
                flag = 1;
                row = 6;
                gotoxy(4, 24);
                printf("Press any key to continue.... ");
                getch();
                clrscr();
        }
}

gotoxy(1, row);
for (j = 1; j <= 79; j++)
        printf("=");
row++;
gotoxy(50, row);
printf("Grand Total");
gotoxy(68, row);
printf("%0.2f", G_bal);

fclose(file);
row++;

/* This function will return total total sales in a particular month  */
saltotal = Asales_status(m1, y1, cod1, cod2, cod3);
row++;

gotoxy(1, row);
for (j = 1; j <= 79; j++)
        printf("=");
row++;
gotoxy(5, row);
printf("This month's Sales Amount");
gotoxy(50, row);
```

```
printf("%0.2f", saltotal);

/* This function will return total other expences in a particular month */
gother =  Oother_status(m1, y1);
row = row + 2;

gotoxy(5, row);
printf("Other expenses ");
gotoxy(50, row);
printf("%0.2f", gother);

row++;
gotoxy(1, row);
for (j = 1; j <= 79; j++)
        printf("=");
row++;
gotoxy(5, row);
printf("Net Profit");

/* Calculate the net balance in a particular month */
net_bal = saltotal - gother;
gotoxy(50, row);
printf("%0.2f", net_bal);

gotoxy(68, row);
printf("%0.2f", G_bal);

if (!flag)
{
        gotoxy(4, 24);
        printf("Press any key to continue...");
        getch();
}
getch();
}
```

Monthly Profit Statement

As on Date : 12/8/2000

Code #	Total Balance	Date	Unit Price	Total Amount
1	50	18-8-200	30	1500.00
2	100	18-8-200	20	2000.00
3	50	18-8-200	30	1500.00
			Grand Total	5000.00

This months sales amount : 15500.00
Other expenses : 5000.00

Net profit : 10500.00 5000.00

Press any key to continue...

Figure 7.5 Monthly profit analysis report in music shop

```
/* Function to find the total sales value in a particular month      */
float Asales_status(int m1, int y1, float cod1, float cod2, float cod3)
{
        FILE *filc; // Declare a file pointer for manipulating record structure
        float ts = 0.0;
        float gts = 0.0;
        file = fopen("Person.dat", "r");
        rewind(file); // Position the pointer at the beginning of the file

        /* Reads all the records to display on the screen  */
        while (fread(&acc, sizeof(acc), 1, file) == 1)
        {
                if ((m1 == acc.mm) && (y1 == acc.yy))
                {
                        if (acc.cas_code == 1)
                                ts = acc.No_cass * cod1;
```

```
                else
                        if (acc.cas_code == 2)
                                ts = acc.No_cass * cod2;
                        else
                                ts = acc.No_cass * cod3;
                gts = gts + ts;
                ts = 0;
            }
        }
        fclose(file);
        return gts;
}

/* Function to find the other expenditure in a particular month         */
float Oother_status(int m1, int y1)
{
        FILE *file; // Declare a file pointer for manipulating record structure
        float goth = 0.0;
        file = fopen("other.dat", "r");
        rewind(file); // Position the pointer at the beginning of the file

        /* Reads all the records to display on the screen */
        while (fread(&oth, sizeof(oth), 1, file) == 1)
        {
            if ((m1 == oth.mm) && (y1 == oth.yy))
            {
                goth = goth + oth.amount;
            }
        }
        fclose(file);
        return goth;
}

/* Function to display the balance cassette in music shop */
void Bbalance_cassette(void)
{
        int flag,j;
        FILE *file; // Declare a file pointer for manipulating record structure
        float T_bal = 0.0;
        float G_bal = 0.0;
```

```
int row = 7;
int d1, m1, y1;
struct date d;               // For extracting system date
clrscr();
gotoxy(25,1);
printf("List of Balance Cassettes");
gotoxy(25, 2);
printf("==============================");

getdate(&d);
d1 = d.da_day;
m1 = d.da_mon;
y1 = d.da_year;

gotoxy(55, 3);
printf("As on Date: %d/%d/%d", d1,m1,y1);

gotoxy(1, 4);
for ( j = 1; j <= 79; j++)
        printf("=");

gotoxy(1, 5);
printf("Code #");
gotoxy(15, 5);
printf("Total Balance");
gotoxy(40, 5);
printf("Date");

gotoxy(50, 5);
printf("Unit Price");

gotoxy(65, 5);
printf("Total Amount");

gotoxy(1, 6);
for (j = 1; j <= 79; j++)
        printf("=");

file = fopen("Tbal.dat", "r");
rewind(file); // Position the pointer at the beginning of the file
```

```
/* Reads all the records to display on the screen */
while (fread(&bal, sizeof(bal), 1, file) == 1)
{
        flag = 0;
        T_bal = bal.cas_bal * bal.price;
        delay(2);
        gotoxy(3, row);
        printf("%d", bal.cas_code);
        gotoxy(20, row);
        printf("%d", bal.cas_bal);
        gotoxy(40, row);
        printf("%d-%d-%d", bal.dd,bal.mm,bal.yy);
        gotoxy(53, row);
        printf("%0.2f", bal.price);
        G_bal = G_bal + T_bal;

        gotoxy(68, row);
        printf("%0.2f", T_bal);
        T_bal = 0.0;
        row++;
        if (row > 23)
        {
                flag = 1;
                row = 6;
                gotoxy(4, 24);
                printf("Press any key to continue.... ");
                getch();
                clrscr();
        }
}

gotoxy(1, row);
for (j = 1; j <= 79; j++)
        printf("=");
row++;
gotoxy(50, row);
printf("Grand Total");
gotoxy(68, row);
printf("%0.2f", G_bal);
```

```
        fclose(file);
        if (!flag)
        {
                gotoxy(4, 24);
                printf("Press any key to continue...");
                getch();
        }
        getch();
}
```

List of Balance Cassettes

Date : 12/8/2000

Code #	Total Balance	Date	Unit Price	Total Amount
1	50	18-8-200	30	1500.00
2	100	18-8-200	20	2000.00
3	50	18-8-200	30	1500.00
			Grand Total	5000.00

Press any key to continue...

Figure 7.6 List of balance cassettes in Music shop

```
/* Function for recording the new cassettes in shop */
void Cnew_cassettes(void)
{
        char ch;
        int i, valid;
        int d1, m1, y1;         // Declare the variable for purchase date of cassette
        struct date d;          // For extracting system date
        char c_code[10];
```

```
/* Declaring the date members for for different operations with
   cassette functions     */

int t_cas_code;
char t_Cass_name[30];
char t_Comp_name[30];
int t_cas;
int tdd, tmm, tyy;
float t_price;

clrscr();

Sbox(2, 1, 79, 25, 218);
Sbox(25, 2, 54, 4, 219);

gotoxy(65, 2);
printf("<0>=Exit");

gotoxy(3,3);
for (i = 1; i<= 76; i++)
        cprintf(" ");
textbackground(BLACK);
textcolor(BLACK+BLINK);
textbackground(WHITE);
gotoxy(30, 3);
cprintf("Add New Cassette");
textcolor(LIGHTGRAY);
textbackground(BLACK);

getdate(&d);        // Extract the system.date
d1 = d.da_day;
m1 = d.da_mon;
y1 = d.da_year;

t_cas_code = Clast_cas_code();

/* Appends and deletes a false record
   to create primary position in data files */
if (t_cas_code == 0)
{
```

```
        Cadd_to_file(t_cas_code, "abc", "xyz", 1, 1, 1, 1, 1.1);
        Cdelete_cassette(t_cas_code);
        Badd_to_file(t_cas_code, 0, 0, 0, 0, 0.0);
        Bdelete_balance(t_cas_code);
}

gotoxy(4, 6);
printf("Date: %d/%d/%d", d1,m1, y1);

gotoxy(5, 8);
printf("Cassette Code # ");
gotoxy(5, 10);
printf("Cassette Name : ");
gotoxy(5, 12);
printf("Company Name : ");
gotoxy(5, 14);
printf("Total Cassettes: ");
gotoxy(5, 16);
printf("Individual Cassette price : ");
gotoxy(5, 18);
printf("Enter the Date ");

/* Steps to enter the cassette code either 1 - 2 - 3.        */
do
{
        Aclear(22, 8);
        Aclear(5, 23);          // Clears the buttom message
        gotoxy(5, 23);
        printf("Enter cassettes Code either 1/2/3 ");
        valid = 1;
        gotoxy(22, 8);
        gets(c_code);
        t_cas_code = atoi(c_code);

        if (t_cas_code <= 0)
        {
                valid = 0;
                Aclear(5, 23);
                gotoxy(5, 23);
                cprintf("\7Should not other than 1, 2, 3");
```

```
                getch();
                gotoxy(5,23);
                printf("Enter cassettes Code either 1/2/3 ");

            }
    } while (!valid);
    Aclear(5,23);

    /* Steps to enter the Cassette name        */
    do
    {
            Aclear(22, 10);
            Aclear(5, 23);
            gotoxy(5, 23);
            printf("Enter Name of the Cassette");
            valid = 1;
            gotoxy(22, 10);
            gets(t_Cass_name);
            strupr(t_Cass_name);
            if (t_Cass_name[0] == '0')
                    return;
            if (strlen(t_Cass_name) == 0 || strlen(t_Cass_name) > 25)
            {
                    valid = 0;
                    gotoxy(5, 23);
                    cprintf("\7Cassette Name should not greater than 25");
                    getch();
            }
    }while (!valid);
    Aclear(5, 23);

    /* Steps to enter company name        */
    do
    {
            Aclear(22, 12);
            Aclear(5, 23);
            gotoxy(5,23);
            printf("Enter Company Name ");
            valid = 1;
            gotoxy(22, 12);
```

```
        gets(t_Comp_name);
        strupr(t_Comp_name);
        if (t_Comp_name[0] == '0')
                return;
        if (strlen(t_Comp_name) == 0 || strlen(t_Comp_name) > 25)
        {
                valid = 0;
                gotoxy(5, 23);
                cprintf("\7Company Name should not greater than 25");
                getch();
        }
}while (!valid);
Aclear(5, 23);

/* Steps to enter the total cassettes purchased          */
do
{
        Aclear(22, 14);
        Aclear(5, 23);
        gotoxy(5, 23);
        printf("Enter Total number of cassettes purchased");
        valid = 1;
        gotoxy(22, 14);
        gets(c_code);
        t_cas = atoi(c_code);
        if (t_cas == 0)
        {
                valid = 0;
                Aclear(5, 23);
                gotoxy(5, 23);
                cprintf("\7Enter valid cassette number");
                getch();
                gotoxy(5, 23);
                printf("Enter Total number of cassettes purchased");

        }
}while (!valid);
Aclear(5, 23);
```

```
/* Steps to enter the cassette/price          */
do
{
        Aclear(35, 16);
        Aclear(5, 23);
        gotoxy(5, 23);
        printf("Enter individual cassette price");
        valid = 1;
        gotoxy(35, 16);
        gets(c_code);
        t_price = atof(c_code);
        if (t_price <= 0)
        {
                valid = 0;
                gotoxy(5, 23);
                cprintf("\7Enter valid price for cassette");
                getch();
        }
}while (!valid);
Aclear(5, 23);

/* Steps to enter the purchase date               */
Aclear(22, 18);
Aclear(5, 23);
gotoxy(5, 23);
printf("Enter date on which the cassette is purchase");
valid = 1;
gotoxy(22, 18);
scanf (" %d", tdd);
gotoxy(25, 18);
printf("-");
gotoxy(26, 18);
scanf (" %d", tmm);
gotoxy(28, 18);
printf("-");
gotoxy(29, 18);
scanf (" %d", tyy);
Aclear(5, 23);
```

```
do
{
        Aclear(5, 20);
        valid = 1;
        gotoxy(5, 20);
        printf("Do you want to save the record <Y/N>: ");
        ch = getche();
        if (ch == '0')
                return;
        ch = toupper(ch);
}while (ch != 'N' && ch != 'Y');
if (ch == 'N')
        return;

/* Appends the records contents into
   both cassettes.dat and person.dat data files          */
Cadd_to_file(t_cas_code, t_Cass_name, t_Comp_name,
        t_cas, tdd, tmm, tyy, t_price);

Badd_to_file(t_cas_code, t_cas, tdd, tmm, tyy, t_price);
}
```

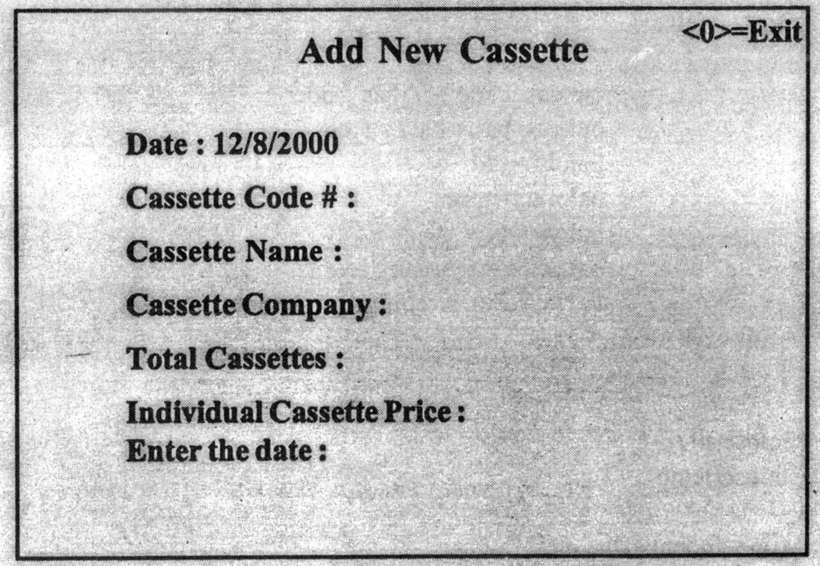

Figure 7.7 Data input screen of new cassettes

```
/* This function update_balance() is used to update the
balance cassette in Tbal.dat data file */

void BUpdate_balance(int t_cas_code,
int t_cas, int tdd, int tmm, int tyy, float t_price)
{

        int bal1 = Bgive_balance(t_cas_code);
        FILE *file; // Declare a file pointer for manipulating record structure
        if (bal1 > 0)
        {
                FILE *temp;
                file = fopen("Tbal.dat", "r");

                temp = fopen("TEMP.dat", "w");
                rewind(file); // Position the pointer at the beginning of the file

                /* Uses a copy method to delete the account from Tbal.dat data file        */
                while (fread(&bal, sizeof(bal), 1, file))
                {
                        if (bal.cas_code != t_cas_code)
                                fwrite(&bal, sizeof(bal), 1, temp);
                        else
                        {
                                bal.cas_code = t_cas_code;
                                bal.cas_bal = bal1 - t_cas;
                                bal.dd = tdd;
                                bal.mm = tmm;
                                bal.yy = tyy;
                                bal.price = t_price;
                                fwrite(&bal, sizeof(bal), 1, temp);
                        }
                }

                fclose(file);
                fclose(temp);

                file = fopen("Tbal.dat", "w");
                temp = fopen("TEMP.dat", "r");
                rewind(temp); // Position the pointer at the beginning of the file
```

```
		/* Copy the TEMP.dat contents into Tbal.dat data file	*/
		while (fread(&bal, sizeof(bal), 1, temp))
		{
			fwrite(&bal, sizeof(bal), 1, file);
		}

		fclose(file);
		fclose(temp);
	}
	else
	{
		bal.cas_code = t_cas_code;
		bal.cas_bal = t_cas;
		bal.dd = tdd;
		bal.mm = tmm;
		bal.yy = tyy;
		bal.price = t_price;

		/* Appends new account record with the price
		   into cassettes.dat data file		*/
		file = fopen("Tbal.dat", "a+");
		fwrite(&bal, sizeof(bal), 1, file);

		fclose(file);
	}
}

/* Function for creating new account for new customer. */
void Anew_account(void)
{
	char ch;
	int i, valid;
	int d1, m1, y1;
	struct date d;			// For extracting system date
	int t_cas_code;

	int C_bal = 0;
	float t_price;
	char c_code[2];
	char tP_name[30];	// Person Name
```

```
char tP_address[30];     // Person Address
int tNo_cass;            // Number of cassette

clrscr();

Sbox(2, 1, 79, 25, 218);
Sbox(25, 2, 54, 4, 219);

gotoxy(65, 2);
printf("<0>=Exit");

gotoxy(3,3);
for (i = 1; i<= 76; i++)
        cprintf(" ");
textbackground(BLACK);
textcolor(BLACK+BLINK);
textbackground(WHITE);
gotoxy(30, 3);
cprintf("Sales of Cassettes");
textcolor(LIGHTGRAY);
textbackground(BLACK);

getdate(&d);
d1 = d.da_day;
m1 = d.da_mon;
y1 = d.da_year;

t_cas_code = Alast_cas_code();

/* Appends and deletes a false record to create
  primary position in data files              */
if (t_cas_code == 0)
{
        Aadd_to_file(t_cas_code, "xxxx", "xxxxx", 1, 1, 1, 1);
        Adelete_account(t_cas_code);
}

gotoxy(5, 6);
printf("Date: %d/%d/%d ", d1,m1,y1);
gotoxy(5, 8);
```

```
printf("Cassette Code ");
gotoxy(5, 10);
printf("Name of Person : ");
gotoxy(5, 12);
printf("Address : ");

gotoxy(5, 14);
printf("Total Cassette : ");

/* Steps to enter the cassette code either 1 - 2 - 3.        */
do
{
        Aclear(22, 8);
        Aclear(5, 23);            // Clears the buttom message
        gotoxy(5, 23);
        printf("Enter cassettes Code either 1/2/3 ");
        valid = 1;
        gotoxy(22, 8);
        gets(c_code);
        t_cas_code = atoi(c_code);

        if (t_cas_code <= 0)
        {
                valid = 0;
                Aclear(5, 23);
                gotoxy(5, 23);
                cprintf("\7Should not other than 1, 2, 3");
                getch();
                gotoxy(5, 23);
                printf("Enter cassettes Code either 1/2/3 ");
        }
        else
        {
                C_bal = Bgive_balance(t_cas_code);
                t_price = Breturn_price(t_cas_code);
                if (C_bal > 0)
                {
                        gotoxy(40, 8);
                        printf("Total cassettes in Shop : %d",C_bal);
                        break;
```

```
            }
            else
            {
                    printf("There is no cassette in shop");
                    return;
            }
        }
    } while (!valid);
    Aclear(5, 23);

    /* Steps to enter the name of the purchase person         */
    do
    {
            Aclear(22, 10);
            Aclear(5, 23);
            gotoxy(5, 23);
            printf("Enter Name of the Person");
            valid = 1;
            gotoxy(22, 10);
            gets(tP_name);
            strupr(tP_name);
            if (tP_name[0] == '0')
                    return;
            if (strlen(tP_name) == 0 || strlen(tP_name) > 25)
            {
                    valid = 0;
                    gotoxy(5, 23);
                    cprintf("\7Name should not greater than 25");
                    getch();
                    Aclear(5, 23);
            }

    }while (!valid);
    Aclear(5, 23);

    /* Steps to enter the address of the purchase person     */
    do
    {
            Aclear(22, 12);
            Aclear(5, 23);
```

```
        gotoxy(5, 23);
        printf("Enter Name of the Person");
        valid = 1;
        gotoxy(22, 12);
        gets(tP_address);
        strupr(tP_address);
        if (tP_address[0] == '0')
                return;
        if (strlen(tP_address) == 0 || strlen(tP_address) > 25)
        {
                valid = 0;
                gotoxy(5, 23);
                cprintf("\7Address should not greater than 25");
                getch();
                Aclear(5, 23);
        }

}while (!valid);
Aclear(5, 23);

do
{
        Aclear(22, 14);
        Aclear(5, 23);
        gotoxy(5, 23);
        printf("No. of cassette ");
        valid = 1;
        gotoxy(22, 14);
        scanf (" %d", tNo_cass);
        if (tNo_cass > C_bal)
        {
                valid = 0;
                gotoxy(5, 23);
                cprintf("\7The availability of cassette is not sufficient");
                getch();
        }
}while (!valid);
Aclear(5, 23);
```

```
do
{
        Aclear(5, 17);
        valid = 1;
        gotoxy(5, 17);
        printf("Do you want to save the record <Y/N>: ");
        ch = getche();
        if (ch == '0')
                return;
        ch = toupper(ch);
}while (ch != 'N' && ch != 'Y');
if (ch == 'N')
        return;

/* Appends the records contents into both person.dat data files      */
Aadd_to_file(t_cas_code, tP_name, tP_address, tNo_cass, d1, m1,  y1);

/* Updates the new balance after deducting the current sales        */

BUpdate_balance(t_cas_code, tNo_cass, d1, m1, y1, t_price);
}
```

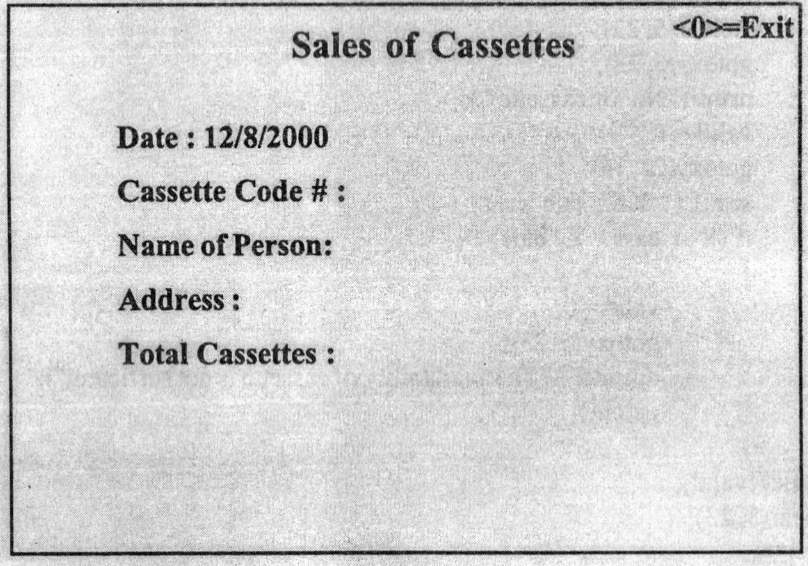

Figure 7.8 Data input screen of sales cassettes

```
/* Function for enter the other expences in other.dat data file. */
void OExpense_other(void)
{
        char ch;
        int i, valid;
        int d1, m1, y1;
        struct date d;              // For extracting system date
        char c_code[2];
        int tO_code;                // Other expence code
        char tNat_Expen[30];    // Nature of expense description
        float tamount;    // Expense amount
        clrscr();
        Sbox(2, 1, 79, 25, 218);
        Sbox(25, 2, 54, 4, 219);
        gotoxy(65, 2);
        printf("<0>=Exit");
        gotoxy(3,3);
        for (i = 1; i<= 76; i++)
                cprintf(" ");
        textbackground(BLACK);
        textcolor(BLACK+BLINK);
        textbackground(WHITE);
        gotoxy(30, 3);
        cprintf("Other Expence in Shop");
        textcolor(LIGHTGRAY);
        textbackground(BLACK);

        getdate(&d);
        d1 = d.da_day;
        m1 = d.da_mon;
        y1 = d.da_year;
        gotoxy(5, 6);
        printf("Date: %d/%d/%d", d1,m1,y1);
        gotoxy(5, 8);
        printf("Expense Code ");
        gotoxy(5, 10);
        printf("Nature of Expense : ");
        gotoxy(5, 12);
        printf("Amount : ");
```

```
/* Steps to enter the other expense code */
do
{
        Aclear(22, 8);
        Aclear(5, 23);              // Clears the buttom message
        gotoxy(5, 23);
        printf("Enter Expense code Code either 1/2/3/4 ");
        valid = 1;
        gotoxy(22, 8);
        gets(c_code);
        tO_code = atoi(c_code);
        if (tO_code <= 0)
        {
                valid = 0;
                Aclear(5, 23);
                gotoxy(5, 23);
                cprintf("\7Expence code should not other than 1/2/3/4");
                getch();
                gotoxy(5, 23);
                printf("Enter other expense Codes either 1/2/3/4 ");
        }
} while (!valid);
Aclear(5, 23);

/* Steps to enter the nature of expense                    */
do
{
        Aclear(22, 10);
        Aclear(5, 23);
        gotoxy(5, 23);
        printf("Enter the Nature of expense");
        valid = 1;
        gotoxy(22, 10);
        gets(tNat_Expen);
        strupr(tNat_Expen);
        if (tNat_Expen[0] == '0')
                return;
        if (strlen(tNat_Expen) == 0 || strlen(tNat_Expen) > 25)
        {
                valid = 0;
```

```
                gotoxy(5, 23);
                cprintf("\7Nature of expense not greater than 25");
                getch();
                Aclear(5, 23);
            }
        }while (!valid);
        Aclear(5, 23);

        gotoxy(22, 12);
        scanf (" %f", tamount);
        do
        {
            Aclear(5, 17);
            valid = 1;
            gotoxy(5, 17);
            printf("Do you want to save the record <Y/N>: ");
            ch = getche();
            if (ch == '0')
                return;
            ch = toupper(ch);
        }while (ch != 'N' && ch != 'Y');
        if (ch == 'N')
            return;
        /* Appends the records contents into both person.dat data files */
        if (tamount > 0)
            Oadd_to_file(tO_code, tNat_Expen, d1, m1, y1, tamount);
}
```

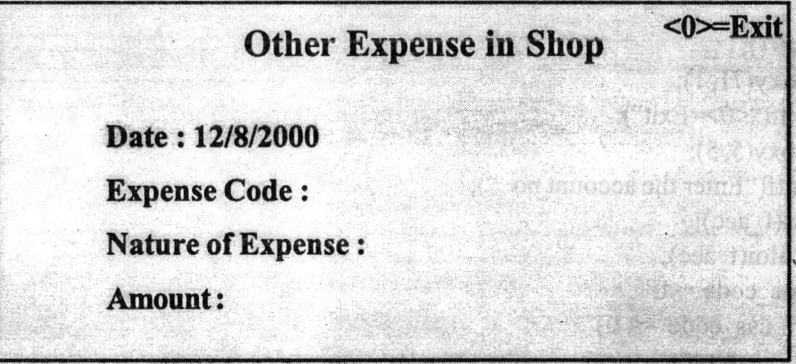

Figure 7.9 Data input screen of Other expenses

```
/* Function for returning the record no. for updating price */
int Crecordno(int t_cas_code)
{
        FILE *file; // Declare a file pointer for manipulating record structure
        int count = 0;
        file = fopen("cassettes.dat", "r");
        rewind(file); // Position the pointer at the beginning of the file

        /* Finds the record position in cassettes.dat data file              */
        while (fread(&ini, sizeof(ini), 1, file) == 1)
        {
                count++;
                if (t_cas_code == ini.cas_code)
                        break;
        }
        fclose(file);
        return count;
}

/* Function for closing any account after inputing account number. */
void Aclose_account(void)
{

        char t_acc[10];
        int t, t_cas_code,i;
        int d1, m1, y1;
        struct date d;
        char ch;

        clrscr();
        gotoxy(71, 1);
        printf("<0>=Exit");
        gotoxy(5, 5);
        printf("Enter the account no. ");
        gets(t_acc);
        t = atoi(t_acc);
        t_cas_code = t;
        if (t_cas_code == 0)
                return;
        clrscr();
```

```
if (!Bgive_balance(t_cas_code))
{
        gotoxy(5, 5);
        printf("\7Account not found ");
        getch();
        return;
}
gotoxy(71, 1);
printf("<0>=Exit");
gotoxy(3, 3);
textbackground(WHITE);
for ( i = 1; i <= 76; i++)
        cprintf(" ");
textbackground(BLACK);
textcolor(BLACK+BLINK);
textbackground(WHITE);
gotoxy(30, 3);
cprintf("Close account screen");
textcolor(LIGHTGRAY);
textbackground(BLACK);

getdate(&d);
d1 = d.da_day;
m1 = d.da_mon;
y1 = d.da_year;
gotoxy(5, 6);
printf("Date: %d/%d/%d", d1,m1,y1);

Cdisplay(t_cas_code);

do
{
        Aclear(5, 15);
        gotoxy(5, 15);
        printf("Close this account <y/n?? ");
        ch = getche();
        if (ch == '0')
                return;
        ch = toupper(ch);
}while (ch != 'N' && ch != 'Y');
```

```
        if (ch == 'N')
                return;

        /* Function calls to delete the existing account no.        */
        Cdelete_cassette(t_cas_code);
        Adelete_account(t_cas_code);
        gotoxy(5, 20);
        printf("\7Account Deleted");
        gotoxy(5, 23);
        printf("Press any key to continue...");
        getch();
}

/* Main program logic which control the functions.              */
void main(void)
{
        int gdriver = DETECT, gmode, errorcode;
        initgraph(&gdriver, &gmode, "");

        Mhelp();
        closegraph();
        Mcontrol_menu();
}
```

Year Calendar

8

This program has been designed to display the calendar of any year monthwise and we can find any date by just typing the month and year.

This program manages two types of options :

1. To see a particular month of year
2. To find out that particular date.

If you will choose the menu option 1 then, you will see the a screen, which will appear for inputting the day, month and year prompt for displaying the calendar. Also, with this option it validates the date, which you entered. Finally you will see the calendar in a tabular form, which you want.

If you choose the menu option 2 then, you will see a screen which will appear for inputting the day, month and year prompt for displaying the character day of inputted date.

Source Codes for CALMENU.C

```
int menu(void)
{
        int z;
        int option;
        clrscr();
        window(1,1,80,25);
        textbackground(WHITE);
        clrscr();
        window(61,7,62,21);
        textbackground(0);
        clrscr();
        window(7,20,62,21);
        textbackground(0);
        clrscr();
        window(5,5,60,20);
        textbackground(4);
        textcolor(10);
        clrscr();

        gotoxy(1,1); //196
        printf ("ÚÄÄÄÄÄÄÄÄÄÄÄÄÄÄÄÄÄÄÄÄÄÄÄÄÄÄÄÄÄÄÄÄÄÄÄÄÄÄÄÄÄxÄÄ¿");
        gotoxy(1,16);
        printf ("ÀÄÄÄÄÄÄÄÄÄÄÄÄÄÄÄÄÄÄÄÄÄÄÄÄÄÄÄÄÄÄÄÄÄÄÄÄÄÄÄÄÄÄÄÄÄÄÄÄÄ¾");

        for( z=2;z<16;z++)
        {
                gotoxy(1,z);
                printf ("³");
                gotoxy(56,z);
                printf ("³");
        }
        gotoxy(14,4);
        printf ("M A I N   M E N U");
        gotoxy(12,5);
        printf ("=========================");
        gotoxy(10,7);
        printf (" 1 :: To see calendar of particular month ");
```

```
    gotoxy(10,9);
    printf (" 2 :: Get day of date");
    gotoxy(10,11);
    gotoxy(10,13);
    printf (" 3 :: Exit");
    gotoxy(20,15);
    printf (" Your option   ");
    option = getch ()-48; // sub to ascii
    printf ("%d",option);
    return (option);
}
```

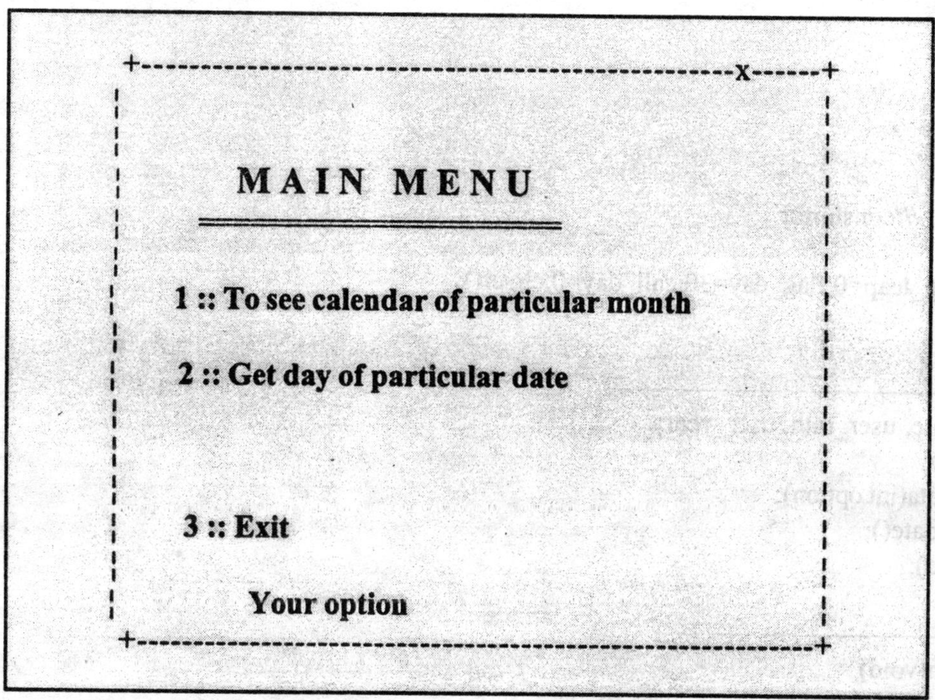

Figure 8.1 Main menu of calendar program.

Source Codes for GIC.C

```
/* Donot compile this file compile gic.c*/

// Program only gives the day of any date from 1 A.D. to __
// Do note down Bugs in this program  NOTE Y2000 will not affect it.

#include<stdlib.h>

int flag_leap;
int flag_day;
int option;

int firstday;
int loop_size;
int call_day;
date(void)  ///consturtor
{
        flag_leap=0;flag_day=30;call_day=0;clrscr();
}

//————————————————————————
int user_date, user_mth, user_year;
int call_day;
int input_data(int option);
int check_date();
int day(void);

 //————————————————————
void screen(void)
{
        clrscr();
        window(4,4,60,10);
        textbackground(2);
        textcolor(4);
        clrscr();
}
```

/*	This function is used to the date, month and year to find the calendar and return month to the main program cal.c */

```
int  input_data(int option)
{

	//clrscr();///in case color remove this line
	screen();

	if (option==2)
	{
		printf ("\n\tEnter Date  :: ");
		scanf ("%d",&user_date);
	}
	else
	{
		user_date=1;
	}

	printf ("\n\tEnter Month  :: ");
	scanf ("%d",&user_mth);
	monthnum=user_mth-1;
	printf ("\n\tEnter Year ::  ");
	scanf ("%d",&user_year);
	return (monthnum);
}	// date::input_data
```

// This function is used to check the date validity, which you entered through the input_data function.

```
int check_date(void)
{
	// for leap year
	int cent; //century year
	int ch;
	//if date 0 or any -ive

	if (user_date<1 || user_date>31||user_mth<1 ||user_mth >12 ||user_year<=0)
	{
		screen();
		printf (" **** ERROR \n\tInvalid date ");
```

```
        if (user_date<1)
                printf ("\n\tDate less than 1");

        if (user_date>31)
                printf ("\n\tDate greater than 31");

        if(user_mth<1)
                printf ("\n\tMonth less than 1");

        if(user_mth>12)
                printf ("\n\tMonth greater than 12");

        if (user_year<=0)
                printf ("\n\tNOT VAILD FOR B.C. dates!!");

        printf ("\n\n\tWana try again \n\t\tPress 1 else any key");

        ch=getch();

        if(ch==49) //ascii 1
        {
                monthnum = input_data( option);//want to enter again so call input function
                check_date();    // clrscr();
        }
        else
                exit(0);
}
if (user_year%4==0)  //leap year
{       /// if(user_year%4==0)

        if (user_year%100==0)       ///century leap year
        {
                cent= user_year/100;
                if (cent%4==0)
                        flag_leap=1;
                else
                        flag_leap=0;
        } //if century year
```

```
        else                //**non-century leap year
                flag_leap=1;
} //if leap year

if (user_mth == 1 || user_mth == 3 || user_mth == 5 || user_mth == 7 || user_mth == 8 ||
                user_mth == 10 || user_mth == 12)  // month day 31's
        flag_day=31;

if (user_mth == 4 || user_mth == 6 || user_mth == 9 || user_mth == 11)  // month day 31's
        flag_day=30;

if (user_mth == 2 && flag_leap == 1)     // month day 29's
        flag_day=29;

if (user_mth == 2 && flag_leap == 0)     // month day 28's
        flag_day=28;

switch (flag_day)
{       //switch
        case 28 :
        {
                if (user_date>28)
                        printf ("Invalid date!!");
                else
                {
                        loop_size=28;
                        call_day=1;
                } //else
                break;
        } //case 28
        case 29 :
        {
                if (user_date>29)
                        printf ("Invalid date!!");
                else
                {
                        loop_size=29;
                        call_day=1;
                } //else
                break;
```

```
            } //case 29
            case 30 :
            {
                    if (user_date>30)
                            printf ("Invalid date!!");
                    else
                    {
                            loop_size=30;
                            call_day=1;
                    } //else
                    break;
            } //case 30
            case 31 :
            {
                    if      (user_date>31)
                            printf ("Invalid date!!");
                    else
                    {
                            loop_size=31;
                            call_day=1;
                    } //else
                    break;
            } //case 31
    }//switch
    return(loop_size);
}

//-----------------------------------------
int day(void)
{
    int odd_day=0;
    int yr_fst=0,yr_lst=0; //year_first, year_last
    int odd_day1=0;
    yr_fst=user_year/100; // quotient  no. of centuries
    yr_lst=user_year%100; //reminder

    odd_day= (yr_fst*100)+ (24 * yr_fst) + (yr_fst/4);
    //century +century contains 24 leap year +leap century year like 400,800..

    odd_day1= (yr_lst-1)+ ((yr_lst-1)/4);
```

```
//total yr-1i.e for 1999 see 98 after century +leap years

if(odd_day1>0) //2000
        odd_day= odd_day+odd_day1;

odd_day=odd_day+user_date;

//last year  +  total leap year +   date
switch (user_mth)
{       // switch
        case 1: odd_day+=0;break;
        case 2: odd_day+=3;break;
        case 3: odd_day+=3;break;
        case 4: odd_day+=6;break;
        case 5: odd_day+=8;break;
        case 6: odd_day+=11;break;
        case 7: odd_day+=13;break;
        case 8: odd_day+=16;break;
        case 9: odd_day=+19;break;
        case 10: odd_day+=21;break;
        case 11: odd_day+=24;break;
        case 12: odd_day+=26;break;
} //switch

///leap yrs & non leap centuries yrs
if (user_mth>2 && yr_lst!=0 && yr_lst%4==0)
        {odd_day++;}

if (user_mth>2 && yr_lst==0 && yr_fst%4==0 )
        {odd_day—;}

if (user_mth<3 && yr_lst==0 && yr_fst%4==0 )
        {odd_day=odd_day-2;}

odd_day = odd_day%7;
firstday=odd_day;
return(odd_day);
} //date::day
```

Source Codes for CAL.C

```
// Uses file anugiv.c   & calmenu.c
// Shows calendar of month on the basis of file anugiv.c

#include <conio.h>
#include <stdio.h>
#include <stdlib.h>
# include <graphics.h>

int monthnum=0;
int firstday; // day num of first day of month
int loop_size;
int option; //option from menu

#include "d:\turboc3\calmenu.c"
#include "d:\turboc3\gic.c"

/* This function shows the calendar of the inputted date */

void show_calendar(void)
{
        char    *month[12] = {"JANUARY", "FEBRUARY", "MARCH", "APRIL", "MAY",
                        "JUNE", "JULY","AUGUST", "SEPTEMBER", "OCTOBER",
                        "NOVEMBER", "DECEMBER"};

        //                  0     1      2      3     4    5     6
        char *day[8]= {"Sun","Mon","Tues","Wed" ,"Thur","Fri","Sat"};
        int i=0;
        clrscr();
        printf ("\n\n\n\t\t\t\t%s %d",month[monthnum],user_year,"\n\n\t");
        printf ("\n\n\n\t");

        // print days mon ......
        for( i=0;i<7;i++)
        {
                printf ("%s",day[i]);
                printf ("\t");

        }
```

```
        // for formatting \n\n
        printf ("\n\n\t");

        // printf blank space till start of day
        for(i=0;i<firstday;i++)
                printf ("\t");

        for( i=1;i<=loop_size;i++)
        {
                printf ("%d",i);
                printf ("\t");
                firstday++;
                if(firstday%7==0)
                {
                        printf ("\n\t");
                        firstday=0;
                } //if ends

        } //for ends
} //fun show_calendar ends

// The function is used to display the main screen of the calendar program

void m_screen(void)
{
        clrscr();
        window(4,4,60,20);
        textbackground(1);
        textcolor(4);
        clrscr();
}

// The exit screen of the calender menu

void screen_scroll(void)
{
        int i,i1;
        clrscr();

        gotoxy(1,8);
```

```
        printf ("                Have  A Nice Day " );//name++;

        for( i=0;i<10000;i++)
                for( i1=0;i1<10000;i1++);
}

// Main menu programming logic started

void main(void)
{
        char ch = 'y';

        while ((ch == 'y') || (ch == 'Y'))
        {
                clrscr();
                option = menu();//calmenu.cpp
                m_screen();

                switch (option)
                {

                        case 1 :
                                {
                                        monthnum = input_data(option);
                                        loop_size = check_date();
                                        firstday = day();
                                        show_calendar();
                                        break;
                                } //case1 show calendar

                        case 2 :
                                {
                                        monthnum = input_data(option);
                                        loop_size = check_date();
                                        firstday = day();
                                        printf ("\n\n\n\t\tRequired Data ");
                                        printf ("\n\n\t DAY    ::");

                                        switch (firstday)
                                        {       //switch
```

```
                                        case 0 : printf (" SUNDAY");break;
                                        case 1 : printf (" MONDAY");break;
                                        case 2 : printf (" TUESDAY");break;
                                        case 3 : printf (" WEDNESDAY");break;
                                        case 4 : printf (" THURSDAY");break;
                                        case 5 : printf (" FRIDAY");break;
                                        case 6 : printf (" SATURDAY");break;

                                } // inner switch over
                                break;
                        }

                case 3 :
                        {
                                screen_scroll();
                                exit(0);
                        }
        } // outer switch over
        getch();
    }
    getch();
} // END of main
```

JUNE 2000

Sun	Mon	Tues	Wed	Thur	Fri	Sat
				1	2	3
4	5	6	7	8	9	10
11	12	13	14	15	16	17
18	19	20	21	22	23	24
25	26	27	28	29	30	

Figure 8.2 Output screen of Calendar month JUNE 2000 of main menu's option 1.

```
Enter Date      :: 10

Enter Month     :: 6

Enter Year      :: 2000

        Required Data

DAY    : WEDNESDAY
```

Figure 8.3 Output screen of character 10-06-2000of main menu's option 2.

Drawing Logo

9

This is a logo package by which you can draw different objects using keyboard. This program uses number of colour patterns and object movement at the time of drawing. This logo manages through a circle by which you can move into different directions. Also, you can increase or decrease the radius of the circle as you wish.

Source Codes of LOGO.C

```
#include <dos.h>
#include <stdio.h>
#include <graphics.h>
#include <stdlib.h>
#include <conio.h>

/* ------------------------------OPENING PAGE------------------------------
                this function is designed to create a
              graphical opening sequence of the program
---------------------------------------------------------------------------*/
```

```
void front()
{
	int x,y,h;

	for( x=0; x<=100; x++)
	{
		settextjustify( CENTER_TEXT, CENTER_TEXT);
		setcolor(1);
		settextstyle(1, 0, 4);
		setusercharsize(x, 6, x, 3);
		setcolor(14);
		moveto(310, 135);
		outtext(". .");
		setcolor(6);
		moveto(310, 130);
		outtext("I I");
		if(x<50)
			delay(30);
		else
		delay(20);
	}

	for( y=0; y<101; y++)
	{
		setcolor(0);
		settextstyle(1, 0, 4);
		setusercharsize(y, 6, y, 3);
		moveto(310, 135);
		outtext(". .");
		moveto(310, 130);
		outtext("I I");

		if(y>20)
		{
			settextstyle(7, 0, 3);
			setusercharsize(y-20, 35, y-20, 20);
			setcolor(9);
			outtext("LOGO II");
			setcolor(2);
			outtext("_________");
```

```
                delay(15);

                if(y<100)
                {
                        settextstyle(7, 0, 3);
                        setusercharsize(y-20, 35, y-20, 20);
                        setcolor(0);
                        outtext("LOGO II");
                } //end if
        }  //end for
    }  //end for

    for( h=400; h>=0; h--)
    {
        setcolor(0);
        line(0, h, 640, h);
        delay(6);
    } //end for

} //end function

/*----------------------------------DECLARATIONS----------------------------------
this program segment declares the various points and variables required
-------------------------------------------------------------------------------*/

const CX=320;
const CY=320;
const R=100;
int col=WHITE;

// Structure to draw points
struct point1
{
    int x;
    int y;
};

// Structure to draw circle
struct circl
{
```

```
        int x;
        int y;
        int r;
};

typedef struct circl circ;
typedef struct point1 point;

/*------------------------------BASIC FUNTIONS------------------------------
this program segment has the basic functions used throughout the program to
------------------------------perform all the functions------------------------------*/

void putcirc(circ c)
{
        circle(c.x,c.y,c.r);
}

void erasecirc(circ c)
{
        setcolor(BLACK);
        putcirc(c);
        setcolor(col);
}

// Place the pixel point at a specified position on the screen
void putp(point p)
{
        putpixel(p.x,p.y,col);
}

circ shiftcu(circ c1)
{
        circ temp;
        temp=c1;
        erasecirc(temp);
        c1.y=c1.y-1;
        putcirc(c1);
        return (c1);
}
```

```
circ shiftcr(circ c1)
{
        circ temp;
        temp=c1;
        erasecirc(temp);
        c1.x=c1.x+1;
        putcirc(c1);
        return (c1);
}

circ shiftcl(circ c1)
{
        circ temp;
        temp=c1;
        erasecirc(temp);
        c1.x=c1.x-1;
        putcirc(c1);
        return(c1);
}

circ shiftcb(circ c1)
{
        circ temp;
        temp=c1;
        erasecirc(temp);
        c1.y=c1.y+1;
        putcirc(c1);
        return (c1);
}

circ increaseradius(circ c1)
{
        circ temp;
        temp=c1;
        erasecirc(temp);
        c1.r=c1.r+1;
        putcirc(c1);
        return (c1);
}
```

```
circ reduceradius(circ c1)
{
        circ temp;
        temp=c1;
        erasecirc(temp);
        c1.r=c1.r-1;
        putcirc(c1);
        return (c1);
}

/*----------------------------ENDING GRAPHICAL SEQUENCE----------------
the following function generates the ending graphical output .
-----------------------------------------------------------------------*/

void end()
{

        int col=0;
        int x1=510;
        int xo,yo,jj;
        char ch;

        for( xo=0; xo<130; xo++)
        {
                cleardevice();
                yo=(xo*xo)/80+6;
                moveto(xo-25, yo);
                setcolor(14);
                settextjustify(LEFT_TEXT, TOP_TEXT);
                settextstyle(8, 0, 6);
                outtext("ARE");
                setcolor(13);
                moveto(260, yo);
                outtext("YOU");
                x1--;
                setcolor(2);
                moveto(x1+7, yo);
                outtext("SURE");
                delay(30);
        }
```

```
        ch=getche();

        if (ch=='y' || ch=='Y')
        {
                int hh=640;

                for( jj=0; jj<=320; jj++)
                {
                        setcolor(0);
                        line(jj, 0, jj, 480);
                        line(hh, 0, hh, 480);
                        hh--;
                        delay(7);
                }
                exit(0);
        }
        else
        {
                cleardevice();
                clrscr();
                cleardevice();
        }
        setcolor(col);
}

/*-----------------------------MAIN----------------------------
this is the command control of the program which generates the user screeen
-------------------------------------------------------------*/

void main()
{
        point center;
        circ circle1;
        char ch;  //used to get user input.
        /* request auto detection */
        int gdriver = DETECT, gmode, errorcode;

        /* initialize graphics and local variables */
        initgraph(&gdriver, &gmode, "\\tclite\\bgi");
```

```
/* read result of initialization */
errorcode = graphresult();
if (errorcode != grOk) /* an error occurred */
{
        printf("Graphics error: %s\n");
        printf ("%d",grapherrormsg(errorcode));
        printf("Press any key to halt:");
        getch();
        exit(1); /* terminate with an error code */
}

front(); //calling the functionn to generate the first screen.

/* the following program code generates the user screen */
start:
setcolor(col);
printf("\n t: UP");
printf("\n g: DOWN");
printf("\n f: LEFT");
printf("\n h: RIGHT");
printf("\n w: CIRCLE UP");
printf("\n s: CIRCLE DOWN");
printf("\n a: CIRCLE LEFT");
printf("\n d: CIRCLE RIGHT");
printf("\n c: CREATE CIRCLE");
printf("\n p: INCREASE RADIUS");
printf("\n o: DECREASE RADIUS");
printf("\n z: ERASER ON");
printf("\n x: ERASER OFF");
printf("\n e: EXIT");
printf("\n l: CLEAR SCREEN");
printf("\n Use number keys ");
printf("\n for colours");

rectangle(0,0,150,295);

//initialising the center point
center.x=CX;
center.y=CY;
putp(center);
```

```
//initialising the primary circle
circle1.x=CX;
circle1.y=CY;
circle1.r=R;

label1:
putp(center);
ch=getche();

switch (ch)
{
        case 't' : center.y--;
                   putp(center);
                   break;
        case 'g' : center.y++;
                   putp(center);
                   break;
        case 'f' : center.x--;
                   putp(center);
                   break;
        case 'h' : center.x++;
                   putp(center);
                   break;
        case 'w' : circle1 = shiftcu(circle1);
                   break;
        case 's' : circle1 =shiftcb(circle1);
                   break;
        case 'a' : circle1 =shiftcl(circle1);
                   break;
        case 'd' : circle1 =shiftcr(circle1);
                   break;
        case 'c' : circle1.x=CX;
                   circle1.y=CY;
                   circle1.r=R;
                   putcirc(circle1);
                   break;
        case 'p' : circle1 =increaseradius(circle1);
                   break;
        case 'o' : circle1 =reduceradius(circle1);
                   break;
```

```
            case 'z' : col=BLACK;
                      break;
            case 'x' : col=WHITE;
                      break;
            case 'e' : end();
                      goto start;
            case 'l' : cleardevice();
                      clrscr();
                      cleardevice();
                      goto start;
            case '1' : col=1;
                      break;
            case '2' : col=2;
                      break;
            case '3' : col=3;
                      break;
            case '4' : col=4;
                      break;
            case '5' : col=5;
                      break;
            case '6' : col=6;
                      break;
            case '7' : col=7;
                      break;
            case '8' : col=8;
                      break;
            case '9' : col=9;
                      break;
            case '0' : col=6;
                      break;
        }
        setcolor(col);
        goto label1;
    }
```

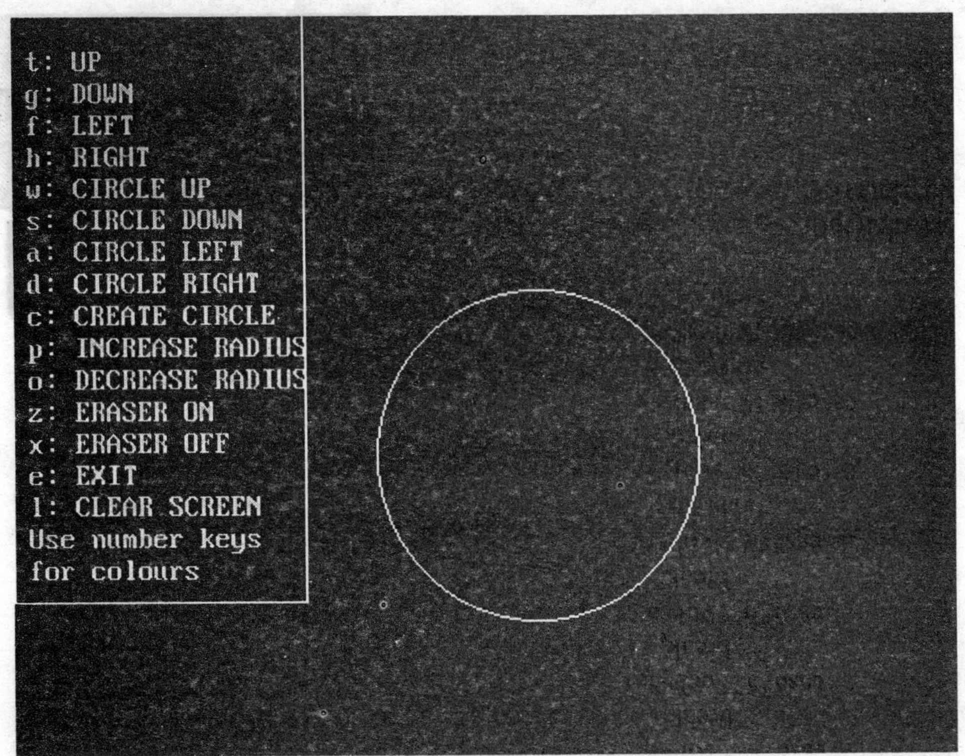

Figure 9.1 Circle output screen of Logo program.

Bricks Game

10

Bricks is a computer game which is played by the single player at a time. In this game four layers of bricks are there and you have to knock out the brick by the ball to get the point. For each knock you get 5 points. You have maximum of four balls and each time you lose the ball 10 marks are deducted from your score. You have to catch the ball on the paddle which is appearing on the bottom on the screen and if you will not able the catch the ball on the paddle you lose the ball. For moving the paddle use left and right arrow key. As the ball and paddle are to be moved throughout the game, we first store their images in the memory using malloc() function which is used to allocate the memory. After this , the image at new coordinates is set erasing the previous location. When the ball reaches to the boundary it will be pushed inside.

This program is made by graphics mode so we have to initialize the graphic mode using initgraph() function before playing this game. When you start the game screen() function is invoked first which displays the instruction related to the game along with the two options - play or exit. If you want to play select play option, then it ask for the level of the player. There are three levels - slow, medium and fast according to which the speed of the ball is assigned. So, you can select any level according to your choice and after that the bricks are displayed on the screen using bricks() function and whenever you hit the ball corresponding ball is deleted using delbrick() function. Whenever you hit more than one brick at a time the message "Good Shot" is displayed on the screen. And when only one ball remains a warning "Last Ball...careful" is displayed on the screen to alert you. Your score is displayed on the left bottom of the screen and balls remaining is displayed on the right bottom of the screen. Different sounds are provided using the bell() function at various places.

Program Source Codes BRICK.C

```
#include <stdio.h>
#include <conio.h>
#include <ctype.h>
# include <process.h>
# include <dos.h>
# include <stdlib.h>
# include <graphics.h>
# include <stdio.h>

# define NULL 0
# define YES 1
# define NO 0
#define ESC     0x1b                    /* Define the escape key          */

int MaxX, MaxY, MidX, MidY ;
int bri[5][20] ;

int  GraphDriver;               /* The Graphics device driver              */
int  GraphMode;                 /* The Graphics mode value                 */
double AspectRatio;             /* Aspect ratio of a pixel on the screen*/
int  MaxXX, MaxYY;              /* The maximum resolution of the screen */
int  MaxColors;                 /* The maximum # of colors available      */
int  ErrorCode;                 /* Reports any graphics errors             */
struct palettetype palette;     /* Used to read palette info*/

// Initialize the graphics mode
void Initialize(void);

// Display the last screen of bricks
void SayGoodbye(void);

// Establish the main window for the demo
void MainWindow(char *header);
```

```
// Display the message Press any key to continue at last screen
void StatusLine(char *msg);

// Draws a boarder line at last screen
void DrawBorder(void);

// Changes the text style
void changetextstyle(int font, int direction, int charsize);

// Welcome screen of bricks game
mainscreen();

// Instruction messages of bricks game
screen();

// To display the bricks (in square box) and paddles in rectangle form and bulbs rounded form
bricks();

// Delete a bricks when bulb hit it
delbrick(int,int);

// Echoes different musics
bell(int);

int graphmode = CGAHI, graphdriver = CGA, level;

main()
{
        union REGS ii, oo ;

        int BallX, BallY, Base1, Base2, dx = 1, dy = -1, OldX, OldY ;
        int totallayer[5] = { 10, 20, 30, 40, 50 }, max = 50, layer = 4 ;
        int i, flag = 0, speed = 25, score = 0, chance = 4, areareq ;

        char *m1, *m2 ;

        /* Function to initialise the graphics mode */
        initgraph ( &graphdriver, &graphmode, "d:\turboc3 " ) ;
        mainscreen();
        initgraph ( &graphdriver, &graphmode, "d:\turboc3 " ) ;
```

```
/* get the maximum value of x and y coordinates of the screen */
MaxX = getmaxx() ;
MaxY = getmaxy() ;
/* finding the center of the screen */
MidX = MaxX / 2 ;
MidY = MaxY / 2 ;


/* create opening  screen and accept the level of the  player's  */
level = screen() ;

/* assign the  speed to ball as per the level chosen */
switch ( level )
{
        case 'M' :
        case 'm' :
                speed = 15 ;
                break ;

        case 'F' :
        case 'f' :
                speed = 10 ;
}

/* draw the four layer of bricks, the paddle and the ball */
rectangle ( 0, 0, MaxX, MaxY - 12 ) ;
bricks() ;
rectangle ( MidX - 25, MaxY - 7 - 12, MidX + 25, MaxY - 12 ) ;
floodfill ( MidX, MaxY - 1 - 12, 12 ) ;
circle ( MidX, MaxY - 13 - 12, 12 ) ;
floodfill ( MidX, MaxY - 10 - 12, 12 ) ;

/* memory allocation for storing the image of the paddle */
areareq = imagesize ( MidX - 12, MaxY - 18, MidX + 12, MaxY - 8 ) ;
m1 =((char*) malloc ( areareq )) ;

/* memory allocation for storing the image of the ball */
areareq = imagesize ( MidX - 25, MaxY - 7, MidX + 25, MaxY - 1 ) ;
m2 =((char *) malloc ( areareq ) );
```

```
/* if unable to alloacte the memory */
if ( m1 == NULL || m2 == NULL )
{
        puts ( "Not Enough memory!!" ) ;
        exit ( 1 ) ;
}

/* image of the paddle and the ball is stored into allocated memory */
getimage ( MidX - 12, MaxY - 7 - 12 - 12 + 1, MidX + 12, MaxY - 8 - 12, m1 ) ;
getimage ( MidX - 25, MaxY - 7 - 12, MidX + 25, MaxY - 1 - 12, m2 ) ;

/* store current position of the paddle and ball */
Base1 = MidX - 25 ;
Base2 = MaxY - 7 - 12 ;
BallX = MidX - 12 ;
BallY = MaxY - 7 - 12 + 1 - 12 ;

/* display balls remaining ( initially 3 ) */
gotoxy ( 45, 25 ) ;
printf( "Balls :" );
for ( i = 0 ; i < 3 ; i++ )
{
        circle ( 515 + i * 35, MaxY - 5, 12 ) ;
        floodfill ( 515 + i * 35, MaxY - 5, 12 ) ;
}

/* display starting score */
gotoxy ( 1, 25 ) ;
printf( "Score:  ");
gotoxy(16,25);
printf("%d",score);

/* select font and alignment for displaying text */
settextjustify ( CENTER_TEXT, CENTER_TEXT ) ;
changetextstyle ( GOTHIC_FONT, HORIZ_DIR, 4 ) ;

while ( 1 )
{
        flag = 0 ;
```

```
/* saving current x and y coordinates of the ball */
OldX = BallX ;
OldY = BallY ;

/* update ballx and bally to move the ball in correct direction */
BallX = BallX + dx ;
BallY = BallY + dy ;

/* according to the position of ball the layer of bricks is determined */
if ( BallY > 40 )
{
        max = 50 ;
        layer = 4 ;
}
else
{
        if ( BallY > 30 )
        {
                max = 40 ;
                layer = 3 ;
        }
        else
        {
                if ( BallY > 20 )
                {
                        max = 30 ;
                        layer = 2 ;
                }
                else
                {
                        if ( BallY > 10 )
                        {
                                max = 20 ;
                                layer = 1 ;
                        }
                        else
                        {
                                max = 10 ;
                                layer = 0 ;
                        }
```

```
                        }
                }
        }

        /* if the ball hits the right boundary, move it to the left */
        if ( BallX > ( MaxX - 24 - 1 ) )
        {
                bell ( 5 ) ;
                BallX = MaxX - 24 - 1 ;
                dx = -dx ;
        }

        /* if the ball hits the left boundary, move it to the right */
        if ( BallX < 1 )
        {
                bell ( 5 ) ;
                BallX = 1 ;
                dx = -dx ;
        }

        /* if the ball hits the top boundary, move it down */
        if ( BallY < 1 )
        {
                bell ( 5 ) ;
                BallY = 1 ;
                dy = -dy ;
        }

        /* if the ball is in the area of the bricks */
        if ( BallY < max )
        {
                /* if there is no brick  at the top of the ball */
                if ( bri[layer][ ( BallX + 10 ) / 32 ] == 1 )
                {
                        /*  if the ball touches a brick */
                        for ( i = 1 ; i <= 6 ; i++ )
                        {
                                /* check whether there is a brick to the right of the ball */
                                if ( bri[layer][ ( BallX + i + 10 ) / 32 ] == 0 )
                                {
```

```
                    /* if there is a brick */
                    BallX = BallX + i ;
                    flag = 1 ;
                    break ;
                }

                /* check whether there is a brick to the left of the ball */
                if ( bri[layer][ ( BallX - i + 10 ) / 32 ] == 0 )
                {
                    BallX = BallX - i ;
                    flag = 1 ;
                    break ;
                }
            }

            /* if the ball does not touch a brick at the top, left or right */
            if ( !flag )
            {
                /* check if the ball has moved above the current layer */
                if ( BallY < totallayer[layer - 1] )
                {
                    /* if so, change current layer appropriately */
                    layer-- ;
                    max = totallayer[layer] ;
                }

                /* restore the image of the ball at the old coordinates */
                putimage ( OldX, OldY, m1, OR_PUT ) ;

                /* erase the image at the old coordinates */
                putimage ( OldX, OldY, m1, XOR_PUT ) ;

                /* place the image of the ball at the new coordinates */
                putimage ( BallX, BallY, m1, XOR_PUT ) ;

                /* delay for fewseconds*/
                delay ( speed ) ;

                /* carry on moving the ball */
                continue ;
```

```
            }
        }

        /* when ball touch the brick control comes to this point */
        bell ( 5 ) ;  /* play music */

        /* erase the touched brick */
        delbrick ( ( BallX + 10 ) / 32, layer ) ;

        /* if the brick hit is on the extreme right */
        if ( ( BallX + 10 ) / 32 == 19 )
                line ( MaxX, 0, MaxX, 50 ) ;  /* redraw right boundary */

        /* if the brick hit is on the extreme left */
        if ( ( BallX + 10 ) / 32 == 0 )
                line ( 0, 0, 0, 50 ) ;  /* redraw left boundary */

        /* if the brick hit is in the topmost layer */
        if ( layer == 0 )
                line ( 0, 0, MaxX, 0 ) ;  /* redraw top boundary */

        /* set appropriate array element to 1 to indicate absence of brick */
        bri[layer][ ( BallX + 10 ) / 32 ] = 1 ;

        BallY = BallY + 1 ;  /* update the y coordinate */
        dy = -dy ;  /* change the current direction of the ball */
        score += 10 ;  /* increment the score by 10 */
        gotoxy ( 16, 25 ) ;
        printf("%d", score);  /* display latest score */

        /* if the first brick is hit during a throw*/
    }

    /* if ball reached the bottom */
    if ( BallY > 180 - 12 )
    {

        /* if paddle missed the ball */
        if ( BallX < Base1 - 20 || BallX > Base1 + 50 )
```

```
{
        /* continue the decrement of the ball */
        while ( BallY < 177 )
        {
                /* erase the image of the ball at the old coordinates */
                putimage ( OldX, OldY, m1, XOR_PUT ) ;

                /* put the image of the ball at the new coordinates */
                putimage ( BallX, BallY, m1, XOR_PUT ) ;

                /* introduce delay for fewseconds */
                delay ( speed ) ;

                /* saveing current x and y coordinates of the ball */
                OldX = BallX ;
                OldY = BallY ;

                /* update ballx and bally to move the ball in
                        correct direction */
                BallX = BallX + dx ;
                BallY = BallY + dy ;
        }

        chance-- ; /* decrement the total number of chances */
        score -= 10 ; /* decrement 10 points for each ball lost */
        gotoxy ( 16, 25 ) ;
        printf("%d",score); /* display latest score */
        bell ( 1 ) ;

        /* erase one of the available balls */
        if ( chance )
                putimage ( 515 + ( chance - 1 ) * 35 - 12 , MaxY - 10,
                        m1, XOR_PUT ) ;

        /* if the last ball is being played */
        if ( chance == 1 )
        {
                gotoxy ( 45, 25 ) ;
                printf( "Last ball... careful!");
        }
```

```
                /* if all the balls are lost */
                if ( !chance )
                {
                        gotoxy ( 45, 25 ) ;
                        printf("Press any key to continue ...              " );
                        outtextxy ( MidX, MidY, "Better luck next time" ) ;
                        bell ( 2 ) ;

                        closegraph() ;
                        restorecrtmode() ;
                        closegraph();   /* Close the graphics mode */
                        Initialize();   /* Intialize the graphics mode */
                        setbkcolor(4);
                        SayGoodbye(); /* Display the That's all Folks message */
                        closegraph(); /* Return the system to text mode */
                        exit ( 0 ) ;
                }
        }

        /* if ball is collected on paddle */
        bell ( 4 ) ;
        BallY = 180 - 12 ; /* restore the y coordinate of ball */
        dy = -dy ; /* move the ball upwards */
}

/* put the image of the ball at the old coordinates */
putimage ( OldX, OldY, m1, OR_PUT ) ;

/* erase the image of the ball at the old coordinates */
putimage ( OldX, OldY, m1, XOR_PUT ) ;

/* put the image of the ball at the upadted coordinates */
putimage ( BallX, BallY, m1, XOR_PUT ) ;

/* if all the bricks have been knockout */
if ( score == 500 - ( ( 4 - chance ) * 20 ) )
{
        outtextxy ( MidX, MidY, "Winner !!" ) ;
```

```
        if ( score < 600 )
                outtextxy ( MidX, MidY + 30, "Try to score 600" ) ;
        else
                outtextxy ( MidX, MidY + 30, " GREAT!" ) ;

        bell ( 2 ) ;

        closegraph() ;
        restorecrtmode() ;
        exit ( 0 ) ;
}

/* introduce delay for few seconds */
delay ( speed ) ;

/* if the key is pressed to move the paddle */
if ( kbhit() )
{
        /* interrupt issue to obtain the ascii and scan codes of key hit */
        ii.h.ah = 0 ;
        int86 ( 22, &ii, &oo ) ;

        /* put the image of the paddle at the old coordinates */
        putimage ( Base1, Base2, m2, OR_PUT ) ;

        /* erase the image of the paddle at the old coordinates */
        putimage ( Base1, Base2, m2, XOR_PUT ) ;

        /* if Esc key has been pressed */
        if ( oo.h.ah == 1 )
                exit ( 0 ) ;

        /* right arrow key */
        if ( oo.h.ah == 75 )
                Base1 = Base1 - 25 ;

        /* left arrow key */
        if ( oo.h.ah == 77 )
                Base1= Base1 + 25 ;
```

```
            /* if paddle goes beyond left boundary */
            if ( Basel < 0 )
                  Basel = 0 ;

            /* if paddle goes beyond right boundary */
            if ( Basel > 589 )
                  Basel = 589 ;

            /* put the image of the paddle at the proper position */
            putimage ( Basel, Base2, m2, XOR_PUT ) ;
      }

   }
   closegraph();
   Initialize();
   SayGoodbye();            /* Give user the closing screen  */
   closegraph();            /* Return the system to text mode      */
   return(0);
}
```


Figure 10.1 Playing screen of bricks game function main()

/* This function creates the opening screen and displys instruction related to the game along with two options play or exit.After selecting the play option it displays three levels of the game and according to your choice you can select any level. This selected level is returned by this function to the main program according to which the speed is assigned to the ball. */

```
screen()
{
	int i, j, lx = 0, ly = 0, ch ;

	rectangle(1,1,600,195);
	setbkcolor(4);
	/* set the textstyle for displaying instruction */
	changetextstyle ( DEFAULT_FONT, HORIZ_DIR, 0 ) ;
	outtextxy ( 150, 55, "        Instructions        " ) ;
	changetextstyle (4, HORIZ_DIR, 5 );
	outtextxy ( 130, 0, " B R I C K S" ) ;
	changetextstyle ( DEFAULT_FONT, HORIZ_DIR, 0 ) ;
	outtextxy ( 30, 68, "Use left and right arrow keys to move paddle." ) ;
	outtextxy ( 30, 88, "If you don't collect the ball on the paddle, you lose the ball." ) ;
	outtextxy ( 30, 108, "On loosing a ball you loose 20 points." ) ;
	outtextxy ( 30, 128, "On taking a brick you gain 5 points." ) ;
	changetextstyle(7, HORIZ_DIR, 3);
	outtextxy ( 100, 148, "Press any key to continue ..." ) ;
	bell ( 3 ) ; /* ring music */
	fflush ( stdin ) ;
	if ( getch() == 0 )
		getch() ;

	closegraph();
	initgraph ( &graphdriver, &graphmode, " d:\turboc3" ) ;
	rectangle(2,2,620,195);
	setbkcolor(4);
	/* display the main menu */
	while ( 1 )
	{

		changetextstyle(4,HORIZ_DIR,5);
		outtextxy ( 60, 8, "Options Available:" ) ;
		outtextxy ( 150, 55, "Play ( P )" ) ;
		outtextxy ( 150, 125, "Exit ( E )" ) ;
```

```
                ch = 0 ;

                /* continue untill you select the correct choice */
                while ( ! ( ch == 'E' ||  ch == 'P' ) )
                {
                        fflush ( stdin ) ;
                        /* if a special key is hit, flush the keyboard buffer */
                        if ( ( ch = getch() ) == 0 )
                                getch() ;
                        else
                                ch = toupper ( ch ) ;   /* store the uppercase of the choice made*/
                }
                if ( ch == 'P' )
                        break ;
                if (ch == 'E')
                        exit ( 0 ) ;
        }

        setviewport ( 1, 125 - 12, MaxX - 1, MaxY - 1, 1 ) ;
        clearviewport() ;
        closegraph();
        initgraph ( &graphdriver, &graphmode, " d:\turboc3" ) ;
        rectangle(2,2,620,195);
        setbkcolor(4);

        /* display menu for the diffrent levels */
        changetextstyle(7,HORIZ_DIR,3);
        outtextxy ( 60, 8, "Select the level for play:" ) ;
        outtextxy ( 150,50, "Slow ( S )" ) ;
        outtextxy ( 150, 100, "Medium ( M )" ) ;
        outtextxy ( 150, 150, "Fast ( F )" ) ;

        /* accept user's choice */
        fflush ( stdin ) ;
        if ( ( ch = getch() ) == 0 )
                getch() ;
        clearviewport() ;
        /* return the choice selected by the user */
        return ( ch ) ;
}
```

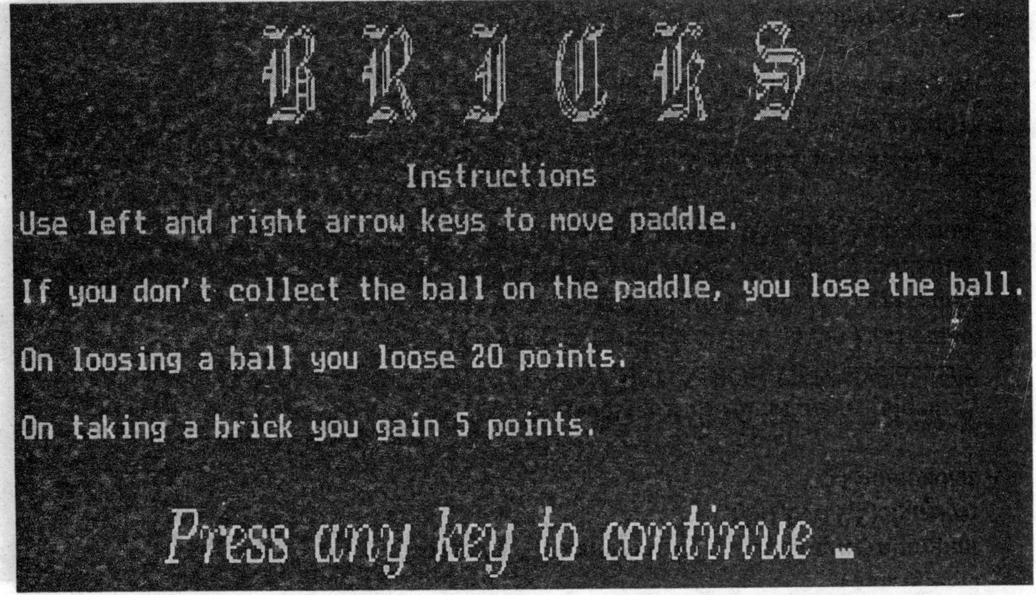

Figure 10.2 Instruction format screen of function screen()

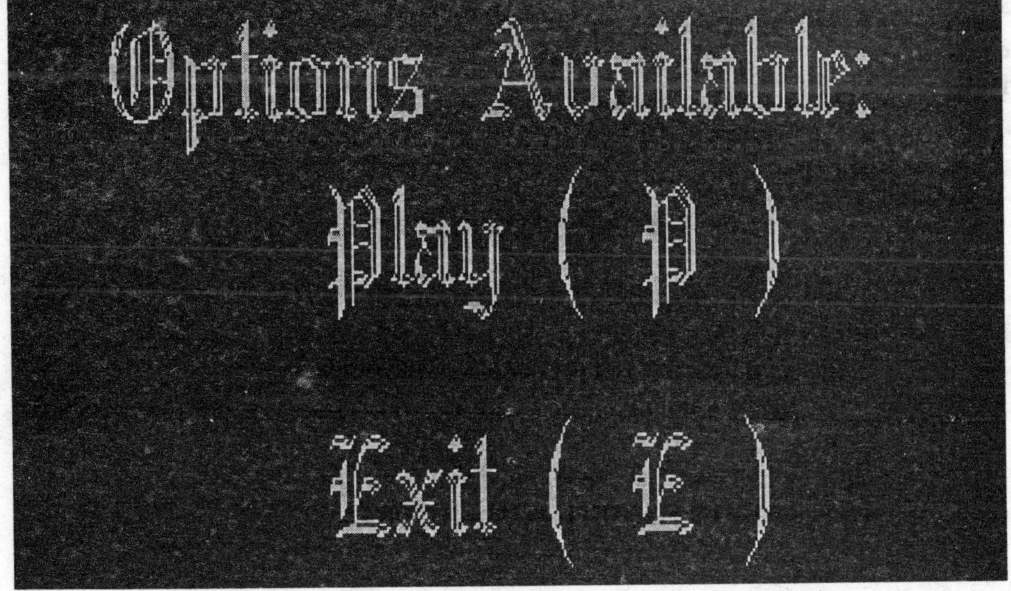

Figure 10.3 Options of bricks game of function screen()

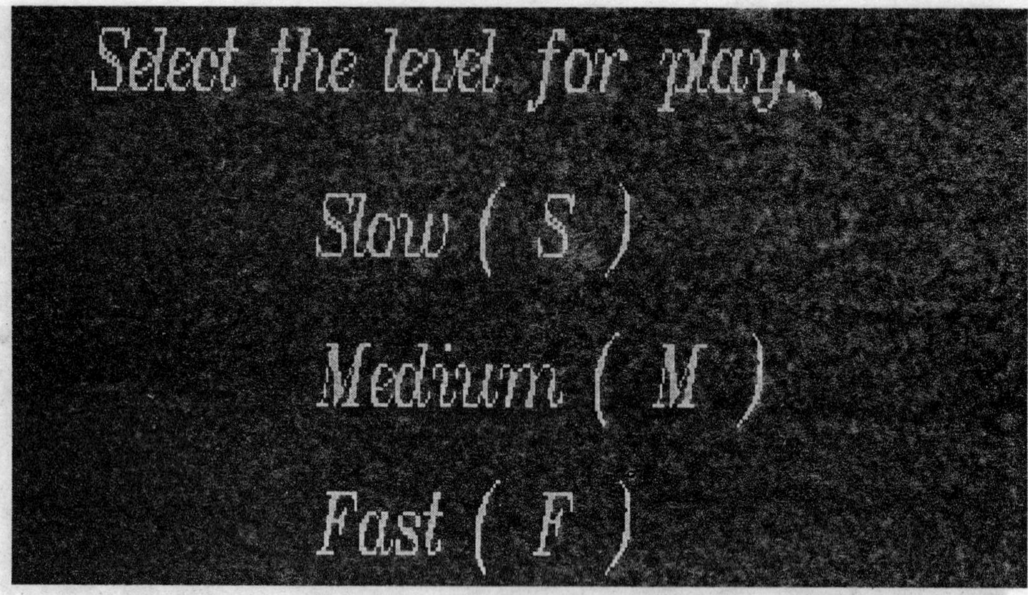

Figure 10.4 Playing level of bricks game of function screen()

```
/* This function draws bricks at the start of the game.There are four layers of
the bricks */
bricks()
{
        int i, j, lx = 0, ly = 0 ;

        for ( i = 0 ; i < 5 ; i++ ) /* 5 rows */
        {
                for ( j = 0 ; j < 30 ; j++ ) /* 20 columns */
                {
                        /* draw a brick at appropriate coordinates */
                        rectangle ( lx, ly, lx + 20, ly + 7 ) ;
                        floodfill ( lx + 1, ly + 1, 2 ) ;

                        lx = lx + 32 ;
                }
                lx = 0 ;
                ly = ly + 10 ;
        }
}
```

```
/* This function erases the  brick which is knocked-off the ball */
delbrick ( int b, int l )
{
        /* b - brick number, l - layer */

        setcolor ( BLACK ) ;
        rectangle ( b * 32, l * 10, ( b * 32 ) + 20 , ( l * 10 ) + 7 ) ;
        rectangle ( b * 32 + 1, l * 10, ( b * 32 ) + 20 - 1, ( l * 10 ) + 7 - 1 ) ;
        rectangle ( b * 32 + 2, l * 10, ( b * 32 ) + 20 - 2, ( l * 10 ) + 7 - 2 ) ;
        rectangle ( b * 32 + 3, l * 10, ( b * 32 ) + 20 - 3, ( l * 10 ) + 7 - 3 ) ;
        rectangle ( b * 32 + 4, l * 10, ( b * 32 ) + 20 - 4, ( l * 10 ) + 7 - 4 ) ;
        rectangle ( b * 32 + 5, l * 10, ( b * 32 ) + 20 - 5, ( l * 10 ) + 7 - 5 ) ;
        rectangle ( b * 32 + 6, l * 10, ( b * 32 ) + 20 - 6, ( l * 10 ) + 7 - 6 ) ;
        setcolor ( CGA_YELLOW ) ;
}

/* plays different types of music */
bell ( int m_no )
{
        /* natural frequencies of 7 notes */
        float wave[6] = { 120.81, 136.83, 144.81, 154.61, 216, 240 } ;
        int n, i ;

        switch ( m_no )
        {
                case 1 :
                        for ( i = 0 ; i < 6 ; i++ )
                        {
                                sound ( wave[i] * 1 ) ;
                                delay ( 30 ) ;
                        }
                        nosound() ;
                        break ;

                case 2 :
                        for ( i = 0 ; i < 15 ; i++ )
                        {
                                n = random ( 6 ) ;
                                sound ( wave[n] * 2 ) ;
                                delay ( 100 ) ;
```

```
                }
                nosound() ;
                break ;

        case 3 :
                while ( !kbhit() )
                {
                        n = random ( 6 ) ;
                        sound ( wave[n] * 2 ) ;
                        delay ( 100 ) ;
                }
                nosound() ;
                /* flush the keyboard buffer */
                if ( getch() == 0 )
                        getch() ;

                break ;

        case 4 :
                for ( i = 5 ; i >= 0 ; i— )
                {
                        sound ( wave[i] * 4 ) ;
                        delay ( 15 ) ;
                }
                nosound() ;
                break ;

        case 5 :
                sound ( wave[2] * 5 ) ;
                delay ( 50 ) ;
                nosound() ;
    }
}

/*      INITIALIZE: Initializes the graphics system and reports  */
/*      any errors which occured.                                 */

void Initialize(void)
{
```

```
        int xasp, yasp;                     /* Used to read the aspect ratio*/

        GraphDriver = DETECT;                       /* Request auto-detection      */
        initgraph( &GraphDriver, &GraphMode, "d:\turboc3" );
        ErrorCode = graphresult();                  /* Read result of initialization*/
        if( ErrorCode != grOk ){                    /* Error occured during init    */
                printf(" Graphics System Error: %s\n", grapherrormsg( ErrorCode ) );
                exit( 1 );
        }

        getpalette( &palette );             /* Read the palette from board   */
        MaxColors = getmaxcolor() + 1; /* Read maximum number of colors*/

        MaxXX = getmaxx();
        MaxYY = getmaxy();                          /* Read size of screen          */

        getaspectratio( &xasp, &yasp ); /* read the hardware aspect      */
        AspectRatio = (double)xasp / (double)yasp; /* Get correction factor     */
}

/*                                                                              */
/*      SAYGOODBYE: Give a closing screen to the user before leaving.           */
/*                                                                              */

void SayGoodbye(void)
{
        struct viewporttype viewinfo;    /* Structure to read viewport   */
        int h, w;

        MainWindow( "== Finale ==" );

        getviewsettings( &viewinfo );    /* Read viewport settings        */
        changetextstyle( TRIPLEX_FONT, HORIZ_DIR, 4 );
        settextjustify( CENTER_TEXT, CENTER_TEXT );

        h = viewinfo.bottom - viewinfo.top;
        w = viewinfo.right  - viewinfo.left;
        outtextxy( w/2, h/2, "That's all, folks!" );

        StatusLine( "Press any key to EXIT" );
```

```
        getch();

        cleardevice();              /* Clear the graphics screen  */

}
```

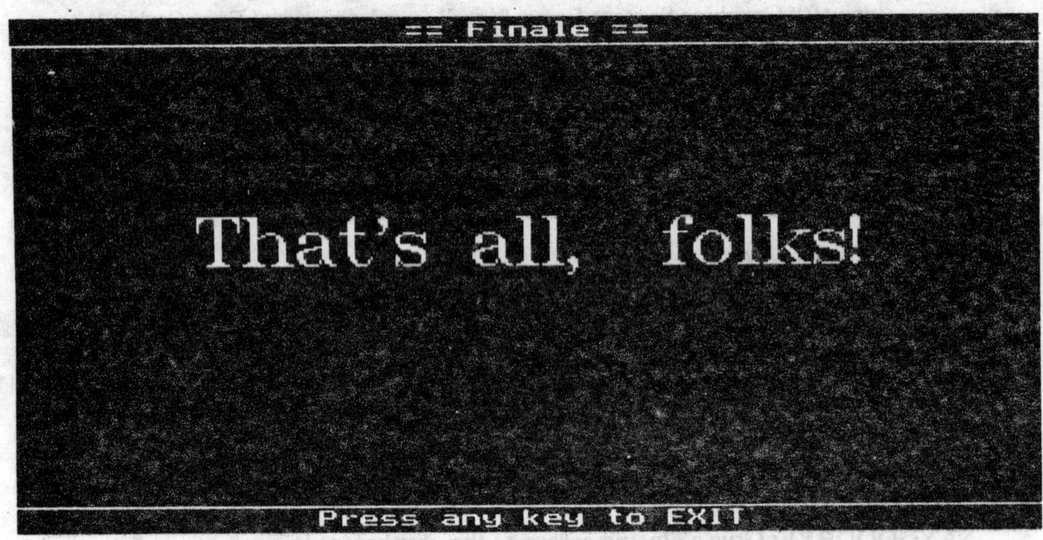

Figure 10.5 Last screen of brick games of function SayGoodBye

```
/*                                                              */
/*      MAINWINDOW: Establish the main window for the demo and set  */
/*      a viewport for the demo code.                           */
/*                                                              */

void MainWindow( char *header )
{
        int height;

        cleardevice();                  /* Clear graphics screen*/
        setcolor( MaxColors - 1 );              /* Set current color to white   */
        setviewport( 0, 0, MaxXX, MaxYY, 1 ); /* Open port to full screen   */

        height = textheight( "H" );     /* Get basic text height      */
```

```
        changetextstyle( DEFAULT_FONT, HORIZ_DIR, 1 );
        settextjustify( CENTER_TEXT, TOP_TEXT );
        outtextxy( MaxXX/2, 2, header );
        setviewport( 0, height+4, MaxXX, MaxYY-(height+4), 1 );
        DrawBorder();
        setviewport( 1, height+5, MaxXX-1, MaxYY-(height+5), 1 );

}

/*                                                                      */
/*      STATUSLINE: Display a status line at the bottom of the screen.  */
/*                                                                      */

void StatusLine( char *msg )
{
        int height;

        setviewport( 0, 0, MaxXX, MaxYY, 1 );  /* Open port to full screen     */
        setcolor( MaxColors - 1 );             /* Set current color to white   */

        changetextstyle( DEFAULT_FONT, HORIZ_DIR, 1 );
        settextjustify( CENTER_TEXT, TOP_TEXT );
        setlinestyle( SOLID_LINE, 0, NORM_WIDTH );
        setfillstyle( EMPTY_FILL, 0 );

        height = textheight( "H" );            /* Detemine current height      */
        bar( 0, MaxYY-(height+4), MaxXX, MaxYY );
        rectangle( 0, MaxYY-(height+4), MaxXX, MaxYY );
        outtextxy( MaxXX/2, MaxYY-(height+2), msg );
        setviewport( 1, height+5, MaxXX-1, MaxYY-(height+5), 1 );

}

/*                                                                      */
/*      DRAWBORDER: Draw a solid single line around the current         */
/*      viewport.                                                       */
/*                                                                      */

void DrawBorder(void)
{
```

```
    struct viewporttype vp;
    setcolor( MaxColors - 1 );              /* Set current color to white    */

    setlinestyle( SOLID_LINE, 0, NORM_WIDTH );
    getviewsettings( &vp );
    rectangle( 0, 0, vp.right-vp.left, vp.bottom-vp.top );

}

/*                                                                        */
/*      CHANGETEXTSTYLE: similar to settextstyle, but checks for         */
/*      errors that might occur while loading the font file.             */
/*                                                                        */

void changetextstyle(int font, int direction, int charsize)
{
    int ErrorCode;

    graphresult();                  /* clear error code     */
    settextstyle(font, direction, charsize);
    ErrorCode = graphresult();      /* check result         */
    if( ErrorCode != grOk ){        /* if error occured     */
        closegraph();
        printf(" Graphics System Error: %s\n", grapherrormsg( ErrorCode ) );
        exit( 1 );
    }
}

/* The main function body of main screen which displays the main screen
creating the opening screen display */
mainscreen()
{
    int maxx, maxy, in, area;

    // get maximum x, y coordinates of the screen
    maxx = getmaxx();
    maxy = getmaxy();

    // setbkcolor sets the current background color using the palette
    setbkcolor(RED);
```

```
    // Draws a rectangle (graphics mode)
    rectangle(0, 0, maxx, maxy);
    // sets the line style and text justification in screen
    changetextstyle(1, HORIZ_DIR, 0);

    // displaying the output text on main screen
    outtextxy(220, 20, "WELCOME");
    outtextxy(240,60,"          TO ");
    outtextxy(220,100," BRICKS");
    changetextstyle(7, HORIZ_DIR, 3);
    bell(3);
    outtextxy(110, 150, "Press any key to continue...");

    // Flushes the standard input device
    fflush(stdin);
    getch();
    closegraph();

}
```

Figure 10.6 Welcome screen of bricks game

Charts & Graphs

11

This program creates an interactive bar, 3D bar and pie charts. Whether you are doing a pie, bar, or line chart, only minor programming differences are required to switch chart styles. In this program we prepare the 3D chart, pie chart and the bar chart on the given temperatures. Also, this program finds the minimum and the maximum temperature.

The description of the different functions are :

grap_screen()...	This function display the opening screen.
mainmenu()...	This function allows the user to create the popup menu.
pop_menu()...	This function allows the user to select the item from the pop up menu.
getkey()...	This function gets the ASCII and scan codes of the key pressed.
showmenu()...	Displays the menu in box drawn by mainmenu().
getoutput()...	This function receives user's response for the menu displayed.
get_temps()...	This function allows the user to enter the temperature from the keyboard and save into the array called temps[].
table_view()...	This function allows the programmer to print the temperature saved in the array called temps[] into the tabular form and also displays the maximum, minimum and average temperature.

min_max()... This function allows the programmer to find the minimum and maximum temperature between the given temperatures

avg_temp()... This function allows the user to find average temperature of the entered temperatures.

initialize()... This function allows the user to initialize the graphics mode.

Bar3DDemo()... This function allows the user to display the 3D graph. The bar chart is used to compare the data values. In this function a 3D effect is given to the bar chart according to the different values of the temperatures, different rectangles are drawn in 3D effect MainWindow: Establish the main window for the demo and set a viewport for the demo code.

DrawBorder()... Draw a solid single line around the current viewport.

StatusLine()... Displays a status line at the bottom of the screen.

changetextstyle()... Similar to settextstyle, but checks for errors that might occur while loading the font file.

graph_view()... This function allows the user to display the bar chart in the screen. The bar chart is normally used to compare the data values. This function shows the 2D graph view of the given temperatures.

save_temps()... This function allows the user to save the temperature into the files for further processing. This file can be utilized by the read_temps() function for reading the temperatures from the file.

read_temps()... This function is used to read the temperature from the file. If user wants to read the temperature values from the desired file instead of keyboard then this function is invoked in the main menu.

Piechart()... This function allows you to draw a pie chart on the screen. The user may enter the temperatures in the get_temps() function and the information from that function is taken and a complete pie chart will automatically be scaled and plotted. The user may plot the chart using this function on the EGA or VGA screen.

This function allows the programmer to enter the values for different temperatures. These values are saved in an array called temps[] and using the readings available in the temps[] the percent for different pie slices are measured and then displays the complete pie chart on the screen.

The intor1.h header file uses different library functions to perform outputs to Charts & Graphs to write string, read characters in the rectangle part, display boxes, display menus in shadow form etc. in the TEST.cpp program file. The following functions are called number of times in the main program.

writech()... This function writes the character into VDU memory.

writeline() ... This function writes an entire string into VDU memory.

Store_video... This function reads the character from the rectangular part of the screen and stores them into the RAM

Restore_video... This reads the character from the RAM and places on the VDU

Display_box()... This function displays the double lined box on the main menu and other menus.

Menu_box()... This function diplays the box with different shadows as the user requires and also without shadows.

Size()... This function is used to change the size of the cursor.

Source code of intro1.h

```
/* writes a character and its attribute in VDU memory*/
writech ( int r, int c, char ch, int attb,char far *memory )
{
        char far *v ;

        /* Calculate address in VDU memory corresponding to row r and column c*/
        v = memory + r * 160 + c * 2 ;

        *v = ch ; /* store ascii value of character*/
        v++ ;
        *v = attb ; /* store attribute of character */
}

/* writes a string into VDU memory in the desired attribute */
writeline ( char *s, int r, int c, int attb,char far *memory )
{
        while ( *s != '\0' )
        {
                /* if next character is hot key, write it in different attribute, otherwise
```

```
                in normal attribute*/

                if ( *s == '^' )
                {
                        s++ ;
                        writech ( r, c, *s, 77,memory ) ;
                }
                else
                        writech ( r, c, *s, attb,memory ) ;

                s++ ;
                c++ ;
        }
}

/* Draws double-lined box */
display_box ( int sr, int sc, int er, int ec, int attribute,char far *memory )
{
        int i ;

        /* draw horizontal lines */
        for ( i = sc + 1 ; i < ec ; i++ )
        {
                writech ( sr, i, 205, attribute,memory ) ;
                writech ( er, i, 205, attribute,memory ) ;
        }

        /* draw vertical lines */
        for ( i = sr + 1 ; i < er ; i++ )
        {
                writech ( i, sc, 186, attribute,memory ) ;
                writech ( i, ec, 186, attribute,memory ) ;
        }

        /* draw four corners */
        writech ( sr, sc, 201, attribute,memory ) ;
        writech ( sr, ec, 187, attribute,memory ) ;
        writech ( er, sc, 200, attribute,memory ) ;
        writech ( er, ec, 188, attribute,memory ) ;
}
```

```
/* Draws filled box with or without shadow */
menubox ( int sr, int sc, int er, int ec, char filler, char shadow,char far *memory )
{
	int i, j ;

	/* draw filled box */
	for ( i = sr ; i < er ; i++ )
	{
		for ( j = sc ; j < ( ec - 1 ) ; j++ )
			writech ( i, j, ' ', filler,memory ) ;
	}

	/* if no shadow is required for the filled box */
	if ( shadow == 0 )
	{
		for ( i = sr ; i <= er ; i++ )
		{
			writech ( i, ec, ' ', filler,memory ) ;
			writech ( i, ( ec - 1 ), ' ', filler,memory ) ;
		}

		for ( j = sc ; j <= ec ; j++ )
			writech ( er, j, ' ', filler,memory ) ;
	}
	else
	{
	/* draw vertical and horizontal shadow */
		for ( i = sr + 1 ; i <= er ; i++ )
		{
			writech ( i, ec, ' ', shadow,memory ) ;
			writech ( i, ( ec - 1 ), ' ', shadow,memory ) ;
		}

		for ( j = sc + 2 ; j <= ec , j++ )
			writech ( er, j, ' ', shadow,memory ) ;
	}
}
```

```
/* Saves screen contents into allocated memory in RAM */
store_video ( int sr, int sc, int er, int ec, char *buffer,char far *memory )
{
        char far *vid ;
        int i, j ;

        for ( i = sr ; i <= er ; i++ )
        {
                for ( j = sc ; j <= ec ; j++ )
                {
                        vid = memory + i * 160 + j * 2 ;  /* calculate address */
                        *buffer = *vid ;  /* store character */
                        vid++ ;
                        buffer++ ;
                        *buffer = *vid ;  /* store attribute */
                        buffer++ ;
                }
        }
}

/* Restores screen contents from allocated memory in RAM */
restore_video ( int sr, int sc, int er, int ec, char *buffer,char far *memory )
{
        char far *vid ;
        int i, j ;

        for ( i = sr ; i <= er ; i++ )
        {
                for ( j = sc ; j <= ec ; j++ )
                {
                        vid = memory + i * 160 + j * 2 ;  /* calculate address */
                        *vid = *buffer ;  /* restore character */
                        vid++ ;
                        buffer++ ;
                        *vid = *buffer ;  /* restore attribute */
                        buffer++ ;
                }
        }
}
```

```
/* Displays or hides the cursor*/
size ( int ssl, int esl )
{
        union REGS iregs, oregs ;

        iregs.h.ah = 1 ;  /* service number*/
        iregs.h.ch = ssl ;  /* starting scan line*/
        iregs.h.cl = esl ;  /* ending scan line*/
        iregs.h.bh = 0 ;  /* video page numbe*/

        /* issue interrupt for changing the size of the cursor*/
        int86 ( 16, &iregs, &oregs ) ;
}
```

Program source code of TEST.C

```
// Declarations of libraries

#include <stdio.h>
#include <conio.h>
#include <math.h>
#include <ctype.h>
#include <stdio.h>
#include <stdlib.h>
#include <graphics.h>
#include <stdarg.h>
#include <dos.h>
#include <dir.h>
#include <fcntl.h>
#include <string.h>
#include <process.h>
#include <alloc.h>
#include "intro1.h"        // User defined library

// Available options in scatter charts

char *main_menu[] = {
                        "^Enter temperatures for scratchpad",
                        "^Store scratchpad to disk",
                        "^Read disk file to scratchpad",
                        "^Table view of current data",
                        "^2D Graph of current data",
                        "^3 D Graph of current data",
                        "^PieChart",
                        "e^Xit"
                    };

/* Prototypes */
void get_temps(void);
void table_view(void);
void min_max(int num_vals, int vals[], int *min_val, int *max_val);
float avg_temp(int num_vals, int vals[]);
void graph_view(void);
void save_temps(void);
```

```
void read_temps(void);
void MainWindow( char *header );
void changetextstyle(int font, int direction, int charsize);
void DrawBorder(void);
void StatusLine( char *msg );
void Bar3DDemo(void);
void Piechart(void);
set_mode(int mode);
void grap_screen();
mainmenu();
pop_menu ( char **main_menu, int count, int sr, int sc, char *hotkeys, int number );
showmenu ( char **main_menu, int counter, int sr, int sc );
getkey();
getoutput ( char **main_menu, char *keys, int sr, int sc, int counter, int number );

/* Global defines */

#define TRUE      1
#define READINGS  8
#define ESC       0x1b              /* Define the escape key      */
#define PI        3.14159           /* Define a value for PI */

/* Global data structures */

int     temps[READINGS];
int     MaxX,MaxY;
int     MaxColors;
int     GraphDriver;                /* The Graphics device driver              */
int     GraphMode;                  /* The Graphics mode value                 */
double  AspectRatio;                /* Aspect ratio of a pixel on the screen   */
int     ErrorCode;                  /* Reports any graphics errors             */
struct  palettetype palette;        /* Used to read palette info               */

char far *memory;
int ascii, scans;

int main(void)
{
        int choice;
```

```
/* store base address of VDU memory and set appropriate video mode */
#ifdef NA
        /* store base address for NA*/
        memory = (char far *)0xb0000000L;
        set_mode(7);
#else
        /* store base address for other type of display adapter */
        memory = (char far *) 0xb8000000L;
        set_mode(3);
#endif

size(32,0);                         /* To hide the cursor displayed on the screen*/
/* display the opening screen */

grap_screen();
/* create screen on which menus are to be popped up */
mainmenu() ;
while ( 1 )
{
        /* pop up main menu and collect choice */
        choice = pop_menu ( main_menu, 8, 7, 24, "ESRT23X", 2 );

        /* test choice received */
        switch ( choice )
        {
                case 1 :
                        get_temps();
                        break;
                case 2 :
                        save_temps();
                        break;
                case 3 :
                        read_temps();
                        break;
                case 4 :
                        table_view();
                        break;
                case 5 :
                        graph_view();
                        break;
```

```
                case 6 :
                                Bar3DDemo();
                                break;
                case 7 :
                                Piechart();
                                break;
                case 8 :
                                exit(0);
                case 27 :
                {
                                size (6,7);
                                clrscr();
                                exit(0);
                }
            }
        }
}
```

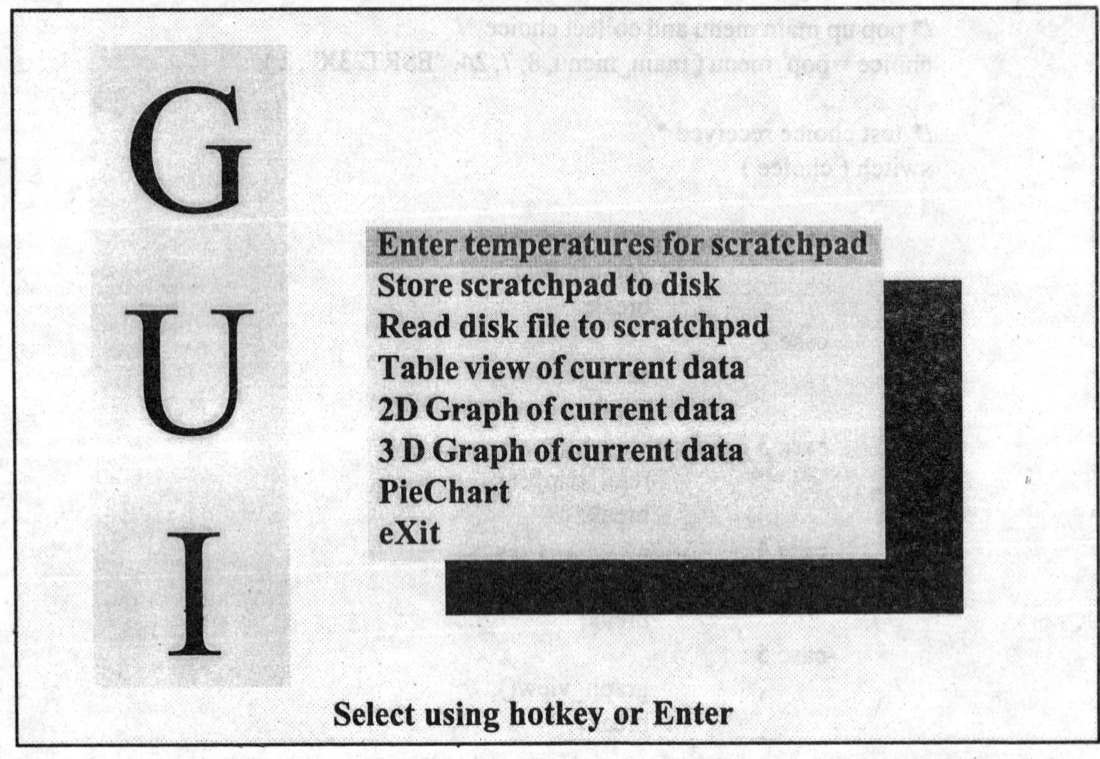

Figure 11.1 Output screen of Charts & Graphs main menu function

```
/*                                                                      */
/* SET_MODE :  This function allows the user to set the desired video mode.  */
/*             Differnt video mode are required for the diffrent            */
/*                             configuration of the system              */

set_mode ( int mode )
{
        union REGS i, o ;

        i.h.ah = 0 ;  /* service no.*/
        i.h.al = mode ;  /* video mode*/
        int86 ( 16, &i, &o ) ;  /* issue interrupt*/
}

/* This fumction display the opening screen */
void grap_screen()
{
        int driver,mode;
        driver = DETECT;

        initgraph(&driver,&mode,"");
        setbkcolor(10);
        setcolor(5);//set the text color

        settextstyle(0, 0, 7);//set default font,horizontal direction,size of text
        outtextxy(10, 100, "GRAPHS   &");
        outtextxy(150, 300, "CHART");

        delay(2000);
        closegraph();

        initgraph(&driver, &mode,"");
        setbkcolor(10);

        setcolor(1); //set background color to blude

        settextstyle(0, 0, 7);
        outtextxy(50, 100, "DEVELOPED");
        outtextxy(50, 300, "   BY ");
```

```
        delay(2000);
        closegraph();

        initgraph(&driver, &mode,"");
        setbkcolor(10);
        setcolor(4); //set background color to green

        settextstyle(0, 0, 5);
        outtextxy(30, 100, "Reeta " );
        outtextxy(120, 200, "Sahoo & ");
        outtextxy(200, 300, "Her Team");

        delay(2000);
        closegraph();

}

/*                                                                              */
/* MAINMENU  : This function allows the user to create the popupmenu menu      */
/*                  and and the GUI message on the side screen of the menu      */
/*                                                                              */

mainmenu()
{
        int i, j ;

        display_box ( 1, 0, 23, 79, 10,memory ) ;

        writech ( 21, 0, 204, 10,memory ) ;
        writech ( 21, 79, 185, 10,memory ) ;

        for ( i = 2 ; i <= 20 ; i++ )
        {
                for ( j = 1 ; j <= 78 ; j += 2 )
                {
                        writech ( i, j, 177, 5,memory ) ;
                        writech ( i, j + 1, 177, 5,memory ) ;
                }
        }
```

```
        writeline ( "ÝÝÝÝÝÝÝÝÝÝ", 3, 4, 143,memory ) ;
        writeline ( "ÝÝÝ       ", 4, 4, 143,memory ) ;
        writeline ( "ÝÝÝ  ÝÝÝÝÝ", 5, 4, 143,memory ) ;
        writeline ( "ÝÝÝ    ÝÝÝ", 6, 4, 143,memory ) ;
        writeline ( "ÝÝÝÝÝÝÝÝÝÝ", 7, 4, 143,memory );

        writeline ( "ÝÝÝ    ÝÝÝ", 9, 4, 143,memory ) ;
        writeline ( "ÝÝÝ    ÝÝÝ", 10, 4, 143,memory ) ;
        writeline ( "ÝÝÝ    ÝÝÝ", 11, 4, 143,memory ) ;
        writeline ( "ÝÝÝ    ÝÝÝ", 12, 4, 143,memory ) ;
        writeline ( "ÝÝÝÝÝÝÝÝÝÝÝÝ", 13, 4, 143,memory ) ;

        writeline ( "ÝÝÝ", 15, 8, 143,memory ) ;
        writeline ( "ÝÝÝ", 16, 8, 143,memory ) ;
        writeline ( "ÝÝÝ", 17, 8, 143,memory ) ;
        writeline ( "ÝÝÝ", 18, 8, 143,memory ) ;
        writeline ( "ÝÝÝ", 19, 8, 143,memory );
        writeline ( "     Select using hotkey or Enter     ", 22, 14, 12,memory ) ;
}

/*                                                                        */
/* POP_MENU        :  This function allows the user to select the item from */
/*                            the pop up menu.                            */
/*                                                                        */

pop_menu ( char **main_menu, int j, int sr, int sc, char *hotkeys, int n )
{
        int er, ec, i, l = 0, area, choice ;
        char *m ;

        /* find the item which is longest in the menu */
        for ( i = 0 ; i < j ; i++ )
        {
                if ( strlen (main_menu[i] ) > l )
                        l = strlen ( main_menu[i] ) ;
        }

        /* calculate the end row for menu */
        er = sr + j + 2 ;
```

```
/* calculate the end column for menu */
ec = sc + l + 3 ;

/* calculate area required to save the current screen contents */
area = ( er - sr + 1 ) * ( ec - sc + 1 ) * 2 ;

m = ((char *)malloc ( area )) ; /* allocate memory */

/* if allocation is not successful then terminate the current process*/
if ( m == NULL )
{
        writeline ( "      Insufficient  memory          ", 22, 14, 9,memory ) ;
        getch() ;
        exit ( 2 ) ;
}

/* save screen contents into allocated memory */
store_video ( sr, sc, er, ec, m,memory ) ;

/* draw a filled box with shadow */
menubox ( sr, sc, er, ec, 277, 1,memory ) ;

/* display the menu in the filled box */
showmenu ( main_menu, j, sr + 1, sc + 1 ) ;

/* receive user's choice */
choice = getoutput (main_menu, hotkeys, sr, sc, j,n ) ;

/* restore original screen contents */
restore_video ( sr, sc, er, ec, m,memory ) ;

/* free allocated memory */
free ( m ) ;
return ( choice ) ;
}
```

```
/*                                                                          */
/*     GETKEY :     This function gets the ascii and scan codes of the key  */
/*                                  pressed                                 */
/*                                                                          */
getkey()
{
        union REGS ii, oo ;

        /* wait till a key is hit */

        while ( !kbhit() )
                ;

        ii.h.ah = 0 ;  /* service number */

        /* issue interrupt */
        int86 ( 22, &ii, &oo ) ;

        scans = oo.h.ah ;
        ascii = oo.h.al ;
}

/*                                                                  */
/* SHOWMENU : displays the menu in box drawn by mainmenu()          */
/*                                                                  */

showmenu ( char **main_menu, int c, int sr, int sc )
{
        int i ;

        for ( i = 0 ; i < c ; i++ )
        {
                /* write menu item in VDU memory */
                writeline ( main_menu[i], sr, sc, 9,memory ) ;
                sr++ ;
        }
}
```

```
/*                                                                  */
/*      GETOUTPUT : This function receives user's response for the  */
/*                  menu displayed                                  */
/*                                                                  */

getoutput ( char **main_menu, char *keys, int sr, int sc, int c, int n )
{
    int ch = 1, len, hotkeyans ;

    /* calculate number of hot keys for the menu */
    len = strlen ( keys ) ;

    /* highlight first menu item */
    writeline ( main_menu[ch - 1], sr + ch, sc + 1, 12,memory ) ;

    while ( 1 )
    {
        getkey() ; /* receive key */

        /* if special key is hit */
        if ( ascii == 0 )
        {
            switch ( scans )
            {
                case 80 : /* down arrow key */

                    /* make highlighted item normal */
                    writeline ( main_menu[ch - 1], sr + ch, sc + 1, 9,
                            memory ) ;

                    ch++ ;
                    n++ ;
                    break ;

                case 72 : /* up arrow key */

                    /* make highlighted item normal */
                    writeline ( main_menu[ch - 1], sr + ch, sc + 1, 9,memory);

                    ch— ;
```

```
                n— ;
                break ;
        }

        /* if highlighted bar is on first item and up arrow key is hit */
        if ( ch == 0 )
        {
            ch = c ;
            n = n + c ;
        }

        /* if highlighted bar is on last item and down arrow key is hit */
        if ( ch > c )
        {
            ch = 1 ;
            n = n - c ;
        }

        /* highlight the appropriate menu item */
        writeline ( main_menu[ch - 1], sr + ch, sc + 1, 12 ,memory) ;
    }
    else
    {
        if ( ascii == 13 )  /* Enter key */
            return ( ch ) ;

        if ( ascii == 27 )  /* Esc key */
            return ( 27 ) ;

        ascii = toupper ( ascii ) ;
        hotkeyans = 1 ;

        /* check whether hot key has been pressed */
        while ( *keys != '\0' )
        {
            if ( *keys == ascii )
                return ( hotkeyans ) ;
            else
            {
                keys++ ;
```

```
                        hotkeyans++ ;
                    }
                }

                /* reset hotkeys to point to the first character in the string */
                keys = keys - len ;
            }
        }
}

/*                                                                          */
/* GET_TEMPS : This function allows the user to enter the temperature      */
/*             from the keyboard and save into the array called temps[]    */
/*                                                                          */

void get_temps(void)
{
        char inbuf[130];
        int reading;
        int area;
        char *m;
        int row = 8;
        int row1=9;

        /* calculate area required to save the current screen contents */
        area = (20 - 5 +1) * (70 - 5 + 1) * 2;

        m = ((char *) malloc (area));  /* allocated memory*/

        /* if allocation is not successful then terminate the current process*/
        if (m == NULL)
        {
                writeline("       Insufficient disk space          ", 22, 14, 12, memory);
                getch();
                writeline("     Press Hot key or Enter to select        ",22, 14, 12, memory);
                return ;
        }
        /* save screen contents into allocated memory */
        store_video(5, 5, 20, 70, m, memory);
```

```
        /* draw a filled box with shadow */
        menubox(5, 20, 17, 60, 12, 66, memory);

        writeline("         Enter temperatures, one at a time ", 6, 22, 12, memory);
        getch();

        for (reading = 0; reading < READINGS; reading++)
        {
                writeline("   Enter reading # ",row, 22, 12, memory);
                row++;

                gotoxy(44,row1);
                scanf("%d", &temps[reading]);
                row1++;
        }
        writeline("         Press HotKey or Enter to select              ", 22, 14, 12, memory);

        /* restore original screen contents */
        restore_video(5,5,20,70,m,memory);

        /* free allocated memory */
        free(m);
        return ;
}

/*                                                                         */
/* TEBLE_VIEW : This function allows the programmer to print the           */
/*              temperature saved in the array called temps[] into         */
/*              the tabular form and also displays the maximum ,           */
/*              minimum and average temperature                            */
/*                                                                         */
void table_view(void)
{
        int reading, min, max;

        int area;
        char *m;
        int row = 9;
        /* calculate area required to save the current screen contents  */
        area = (20 - 5 +1) * (70 - 5 + 1) * 2;
```

```
m = ((char *) malloc (area)); /* allocated memory*/

/* if allocation is not successful then terminate the current process*/
if (m == NULL)
{
        writeline("       Insufficient disk space                  ",22,14,12,memory);
        getch();
        writeline("       Press Hot key or Enter to select              ",22,14,12,memory);
        return ;
}

/* save screen contents into allocated memory */
store_video(5, 5, 20, 70, m, memory);
/* draw a filled box with shadow */
menubox(5, 20, 17, 60, 12, 66, memory);

writeline("Reading", 6, 22, 12, memory);
writeline("Temperature(F)", 6, 42, 12, memory);
writeline("***********************************", 7, 22, 12, memory);
getch();

for (reading = 0; reading < READINGS; reading++)
{
        gotoxy(33, row);
        printf("%d", reading + 1);
        printf("\t\t" );
        printf("%d",temps[reading]);
        row++;
}
getch();
/* restore original screen contents */
restore_video(5, 5, 20, 70, m, memory);

/* save screen contents into allocated memory */
store_video(5, 5, 20, 70, m, memory);

/* draw a filled box with shadow */
menubox(5, 20, 10, 60, 12, 66, memory);

/* finds the minimum and maximum temperature*/
```

```
	min_max(READINGS, temps, &min, &max);

	writeline("Minimum tempeŕature: ", 6, 22, 12, memory);
	gotoxy(44, 7);
	printf("%d", min);
	writeline("Maximum temperature: ", 7, 22, 12, memory);
	gotoxy(44, 8);
	printf("%d", max);
	writeline("Average temperature: ", 8, 22, 12, memory);
	gotoxy(44, 9);

	// Finding average temperature */
	printf("%d", avg_temp(READINGS, temps));
	getch();

	/* restore original screen contents */
	restore_video(5, 5, 20, 70, m, memory);

	/* free allocated memory */
	free(m);
	return;
}

/*                                                                      */
/* MIN_MAX   : This function allows the programmer to find the minimum  */
/*             and maximum temperature between the given temperatures   */
/*                                                                      */

void min_max(int num_vals, int vals[], int *min_val, int *max_val)
{
	int reading;

	*min_val = *max_val = vals[0];

	for (reading = 1; reading < num_vals; reading++)
	{
		if (vals[reading] < *min_val)
			*min_val = vals[reading];
		else
			if (vals[reading] > *max_val)
```

```
                    *max_val = vals[reading];
        }
}

/*                                                                    */
/*      AVG_TEMP : This function allows the user to find average      */
/*                 temperature of the entered temperatures            */
/*                                                                    */

float avg_temp(int num_vals, int vals[])
{
        int reading, total = 0;

        for (reading = 0; reading < num_vals; reading++)
                total += vals[reading];

        return  (float) total/reading;  /* reading equals total vals */
}

/*                                                                    */
/* INITIALIZE  : This function allows the user to intialize the       */
/*               graphics mode                                        */
/*                                                                    */

void Initialize(void)
{
        int xasp, yasp;                 /* Used to read the aspect ratio*/

        GraphDriver = DETECT;           /* Request auto-detection       */
        initgraph( &GraphDriver, &GraphMode, "\\bgi" );
        ErrorCode = graphresult();      /* Read result of initialization*/

        if ( ErrorCode != grOk )
        {                               /* Error occured during init    */
                printf(" Graphics System Error: %s\n", grapherrormsg( ErrorCode ) );
                exit( 1 );
        }

        getpalette( &palette );         /* Read the palette from board  */
        MaxColors = getmaxcolor() + 1; /* Read maximum number of colors*/
```

```
        MaxX = getmaxx();
        MaxY = getmaxy();                       /* Read size of screen          */

        getaspectratio( &xasp, &yasp );         /* read the hardware aspect     */
        AspectRatio = (double)xasp / (double)yasp; /* Get correction factor     */

}

/*                                                                              */
/* BAR3DDEMAO :    This function allows the user to display the 3D              */
/*                 graph. The bar chart is used to compare the data             */
/*                 values. In this function a 3D effect is given to             */
/*                 the bar chart according to the different values of           */
/*                 the temperatures different rectangles are drawn in*/
/*                 3D effect                                                    */
/*                                                                              */

void Bar3DDemo(void)
{
        static int barheight[] = {
                1, 3, 5, 4, 3, 2, 1, 5, 4, 2, 3  };

        struct viewporttype vp;
        int xstep, ystep;
        int i, j, h, color, bheight;
        char buffer[10];

        int area;
        char  *m;
        /* calculate area required to save the current screen contents  */
        area = (20 - 5 +1) * (70 - 5 + 1) * 2;

        m = ((char *) malloc (area));  /* allocated memory */

        /* if allocation is not successful then terminate the current process*/
        if (m == NULL)
        {
                writeline("     Insufficient disk space              ",22,14,12,memory);
                getch();
                writeline("     Press Hot key or Enter to select     ",22,14,12,memory);
```

```
        return ;
}

/* save screen contents into allocated memory */
store_video(5,5,20,70,m,memory);
Initialize();
MainWindow( "Bar 3-D / Rectangle Demonstration" );

h = 3 * textheight( "H" );
getviewsettings( &vp );
settextjustify( CENTER_TEXT, TOP_TEXT );
changetextstyle( TRIPLEX_FONT, HORIZ_DIR, 4 );

outtextxy( MaxX/2, 6, "These are 3-D Bars" );
changetextstyle( DEFAULT_FONT, HORIZ_DIR, 1 );
setviewport( vp.left+50, vp.top+40, vp.right-50, vp.bottom-10, 1 );
getviewsettings( &vp );

line( h, h, h, vp.bottom-vp.top - h );
line( h, (vp.bottom-vp.top)-h, (vp.right-vp.left)-h, (vp.bottom-vp.top)-h );
xstep = ((vp.right-vp.left) - (2 * h)) / 10;
ystep = ((vp.bottom-vp.top) - (2 * h)) / 150;
j = (vp.bottom-vp.top) - h;
settextjustify( CENTER_TEXT, CENTER_TEXT );

for( i=0 ; i<6 ; ++i )
{
        line( h/2, j, h, j );
        itoa( i, buffer, 10 );
        outtextxy( 0, j, buffer );
        j -= ystep;
}

j = h;
settextjustify( CENTER_TEXT, TOP_TEXT );

for( i=0 ; i<9 ; ++i )
{
        color = random( MaxColors );
        setfillstyle( i+1, color );
```

```
            line( j, (vp.bottom-vp.top)-h, j, (vp.bottom-vp.top-3)-(h/2) );
            itoa( i, buffer, 10 );
            outtextxy( j, (vp.bottom-vp.top)-(h/2), buffer );
            if ( i != 8 )
            {
                    bheight = (vp.bottom-vp.top) - h - 1;
                    bar3d( j, (vp.bottom-vp.top-h)-(temps[i]*ystep), j+xstep, bheight, 15, 1 );
            }
            j += xstep;
    }

    getch();
    closegraph();

    /* Display the main pop up menu */
    mainmenu();

    /* restore original screen contents */
    restore_video(5,5,20,70,m,memory);

    /* free allocated memory */
    free(m);
    size(32,0);
    return;

}


/*                                                                              */
/*      MAINWINDOW : Establish the main window for the demo and set            */
/*                          a viewport for the demo code.                       */
/*                                                                              */

void MainWindow( char *header )
{
    int height;

    MaxX = getmaxx();
    MaxY = getmaxy();               /* Read size of screen          */
```

```
cleardevice();                              /* Clear graphics screen*/
setcolor( MaxColors - 1 );                  /* Set current color to white    */
setviewport( 0, 0, MaxX, MaxY, 1 );         /* Open port to full screen      */

height = textheight( "H" );                 /* Get basic text height        */

changetextstyle( DEFAULT_FONT, HORIZ_DIR, 1 );
settextjustify( CENTER_TEXT, TOP_TEXT );
outtextxy( MaxX/2, 2, header );
setviewport( 0, height+4, MaxX, MaxY-(height+4), 1 );
DrawBorder();
setviewport( 1, height+5, MaxX-1, MaxY-(height+5), 1 );


/*                                                                  */
/* DRAWBORDER : Draw a solid single line around the current         */
/*                  viewport                                        */
/*                                                                  */

void DrawBorder(void)
{
    struct viewporttype vp;

    setcolor( MaxColors - 1 );              /* Set current color to white     */

    setlinestyle( SOLID_LINE, 0, NORM_WIDTH );

    getviewsettings( &vp );
    rectangle( 0, 0, vp.right-vp.left, vp.bottom-vp.top );

}

/*                                                                          */
/*    STATUSLINE  :  Display a status line at the bottom of the screen.     */
/*                                                                          */

void StatusLine( char *msg )
{
    int height;
```

```
        setviewport( 0, 0, MaxX, MaxY, 1 );        /* Open port to full screen      */
        setcolor( MaxColors - 1 );                  /* Set current color to white    */

        changetextstyle( DEFAULT_FONT, HORIZ_DIR, 1 );
        settextjustify( CENTER_TEXT, TOP_TEXT );
        setlinestyle( SOLID_LINE, 0, NORM_WIDTH );
        setfillstyle( EMPTY_FILL, 0 );

        height = textheight( "H" );        /* Detemine current height      */
        bar( 0, MaxY-(height+4), MaxX, MaxY );
        rectangle( 0, MaxY-(height+4), MaxX, MaxY );
        outtextxy( MaxX/2, MaxY-(height+2), msg );
        setviewport( 1, height+5, MaxX-1, MaxY-(height+5), 1 );

}

/*                                                                    */
/*      CHANGETEXTSTYLE : similar to settextstyle, but checks for     */
/*                errors that might occur whil loading the font file. */
/*                                                                    */

void changetextstyle(int font, int direction, int charsize)
{
        int ErrorCode;

        graphresult();                  /* clear error code        */
        settextstyle(font, direction, charsize);
        ErrorCode = graphresult();      /* check result            */
        if ( ErrorCode != grOk )
        {               /* if error occured             */
                closegraph();
                printf(" Graphics System Error: %s\n", grapherrormsg( ErrorCode ) );
                exit( 1 );
        }
}

/*                                                                        */
/* GRAPH_VIEW : This function allows the user to display the bar chart    */
/*                in the screen. The bar chart is normally used to        */
/*                compare the data values. This function shows the 2D     */
```

```
/*                    graph view of given the temperatures                    */

void graph_view(void)
{
        int graphdriver = DETECT, graphmode;
        int reading, value;
        int maxx, maxy, left, top, right, bottom, width;
        int  base;              /* zero x-axis for graph              */
        int  vscale = 1.5;      /* value to scale vertical bar size   */
        int  space = 10;        /* spacing between bars               */

        char fprint[20];        /* formatted text for sprintf         */
        int area;
        char  *m;

        /* calculate area required to save the current screen contents  */
        area = (20 - 5 +1) * (70 - 5 + 1) * 2;
        m = ((char *) malloc (area));

        /* if allocation is not successful then terminate the current process*/
        if (m == NULL)
        {
                writeline("       Insufficient disk space              ",22,14,12,memory);
                getch();
                writeline("       Press Hot key or Enter to select        ",22,14,12,memory);
                return ;
        }

        /* save screen contents into allocated memory */
        store_video(5,5,20,70,m,memory);

        initgraph(&graphdriver,&graphmode, "..\\bgi");
        if (graphresult() < 0)          /* make sure initialized OK */
                return;

        maxx  = getmaxx();                      /* farthest right you can go */
        width = maxx /(READINGS + 1);           /* scale and allow for spacing */
        maxy  = getmaxy() - 100;                /* leave room for text */
        left  = 25;
        right = width;
```

```
base  = maxy / 2;            /* allow for neg values below */

for (reading = 0; reading <  READINGS; reading++)
{
        value = temps[reading] * vscale;
        if (value > 0)
        {
                top = base - value;       /* toward top of screen */
                bottom = base;
                setfillstyle(INTERLEAVE_FILL, 1);
        }
        else
        {
                top = base;
                bottom = base - value;      /* toward bottom of screen */
                setfillstyle(INTERLEAVE_FILL, 2);
        }
        bar(left, top, right, bottom);
        left  +=(width + space);           /* space over for next bar */
        right +=(width + space);           /* right edge of next bar */
}

outtextxy(0, base, "0 -");
outtextxy(10, maxy + 20, "Plot of Temperature Readings");

for (reading = 0; reading < READINGS; reading++)
{
        sprintf(fprint, "%d", temps[reading]);
        outtextxy((reading *(width + space)) + 25, maxy + 40, fprint);
}

outtextxy(50, maxy+80, "Press any key to continue");

getch();
closegraph();
mainmenu();
/* restore original screen contents */
restore_video(5,5,20,70,m,memory);

/* free allocated memory */
```

```
        free(m);
        size(32,0);

}

/*                                                                    */
/* SAVE_TEMPS : This function allows the user to save the temperature */
/*              into the files for further processing. This file can  */
/*              be utilize by the read_temps() function for reading   */
/*              the temperatures from the file.                       */
/*                                                                    */

void save_temps(void)
{
        FILE * outfile;
        char file_name[40];
        int area;
        char  *m;
        /* calculate area required to save the current screen contents */
        area = (20 - 5 +1) * (70 - 5 + 1) * 2;
        m = ((char *) malloc (area));

        /* if allocation is not successful then terminate the current process*/
        if (m == NULL)
        {
                writeline("       Insufficient disk space            ",22,14,12,memory);
                getch();
                writeline("       Press Hot key or Enter to select      ",22,14,12,memory);
                return ;
        }

        /* save screen contents into allocated memory */
        store_video(5,5,20,70,m,memory);

        /* draw a filled box with shadow */
        menubox(5,20,10,60,12,66,memory);
        writeline("Save to what filename ? ",6,22,12,memory);

        while (kbhit()); /* "eat" any char already in keyboard buffer */
        {
```

```
        gotoxy(47,7);
        gets(file_name);
    }

    if ((outfile = fopen(file_name,"wb")) == NULL)
    {
        gotoxy(25,7);
        perror("Open failed! ");
        getch();
        return;
    }

    fwrite(temps, sizeof(int), READINGS, outfile);
    fclose(outfile);
    getch();
    /* restore original screen contents */
    restore_video(5,5,20,70,m,memory);

    /* free allocated memory */
    free(m);
}

/*                                                                  */
/* READ_TEMPS : This function is used to read the temperature from the */
/*              file. If user wants to read the temperatures values  */
/*              from the desired file inspite of keyboard then this  */
/*              function is invoked in the main menu.                */
/*                                                                  */
void read_temps(void)
{
    FILE * infile;
    char file_name[40] = "test";

    int area;
    char *m;

    /* calculate area required to save the current screen contents */
    area = (20 - 5 +1) * (70 - 5 + 1) * 2;
    m = ((char *) malloc (area));
```

```
    /* if allocation is not successful then terminate the current process*/
    if (m == NULL)
    {
            writeline("      Insufficient disk space                  ",22,14,12,memory);
            getch();
            writeline("      Press Hot key or Enter to select         ",22,14,12,memory);
            return ;
    }
    /* save screen contents into allocated memory */
    store_video(5,5,20,70,m,memory);

    /* draw a filled box with shadow */
    menubox(5,20,10,65,12,66,memory);
    writeline("Read from which file? ",6,22,12,memory);
    while (kbhit()); /* "eat" any char already in keyboard buffer */
    {
            gotoxy(47,7);
            gets(file_name);
    }

    if ((infile = fopen(file_name,"rb")) == NULL)
    {
            gotoxy(22,8);
            perror("Open failed! ");
            getch();
            restore_video(5,5,20,70,m,memory);
            return;
    }
    fread(temps, sizeof(int), READINGS, infile);
    fclose(infile);
    getch();

    /* restore original screen contents */
    restore_video(5,5,20,70,m,memory);

    /* free allocated memory */
    free(m);
}
```

```
/*                                                                              */
/*      PIECHART    :       This function allows you to draw a pie chart on the  */
/*                          screen. The user may enter the temperatures in the   */
/*                          get_temps() function and the information from that   */
/*                          function is taken and a complete pie chart will      */
/*                          automatically be scaled and plotted.The user may plot */
/*                          the chart using this function on the EGA or VGA screen.*/
/*                          This function allows the programmer to enter the values */
/*                          for different temperatures. These values are saved in */
/*                          an array called temps[] and using the readings       */
/*                          available in the temps[] the percent for different pie */
/*                          slices are measured and then it display the complete pie */
/*                          chart on the screnn.                                 */
/*                                                                              */

void Piechart(void)
{
        int reading, value;
        int area,area1;
        char *m,*graph_ptr;
        double sum=0;
        int start_angle,end_angle;
        double percent[15];
        int x,y;
        char str[12];

        int g_error ;
        int gd,gm;
        /* setup graphics driver and mode */
        gd = CGA ;
        gm = CGAHI ;

        /* calculate area required to save the current screen contents */
        area = (20 - 5 +1) * (70 - 5 + 1) * 2;
        /* calculate area required to display the pie chart */
        area1 = 4+ (640 +7) / 8 *200;
        m = ((char *) malloc (area));
        graph_ptr = ((char *)malloc(area1));

        /* if allocation is not successful then terminate the current process*/
```

```
if ( graph_ptr == NULL)
      exit(0);

/* if allocation is not successful then terminate the current process*/
if (m == NULL)
{
      return;
}

/* save screen contents into allocated memory */
store_video(5,5,20,70,m,memory);

/* initialise the graphics system */
initgraph ( &gd, &gm, "c:\\tc\\bgi" ) ;

/* determine success/failure of initialisation operation */
g_error = graphresult() ;

/* if failure */
if ( g_error != 0 )
{
        /* print error message string */
        printf ( "\ninitgraph error: %s.\n", grapherrormsg ( g_error ) ) ;
        exit ( 1 ) ;
}
for (reading = 0; reading <  READINGS; reading++)
        sum +=fabs(temps[reading]);

start_angle=0;
for (reading = 0; reading <  READINGS; reading++)
{
        end_angle = ceil((fabs(temps[reading]) * 360.0)/sum);
        percent[reading] = 100.0 * end_angle /360;
        end_angle += start_angle;
        if (reading == READINGS-1)
                end_angle = 360;
        if (percent[reading] != 0)
        {

                setfillstyle(1 + reading, RED);
```

```
            sector(319, 99, start_angle, end_angle, 110, 60);
        }
        else
            pieslice(319, 99, start_angle, end_angle, 110);
        start_angle = end_angle;
    }
    x = 10;
    y = 20;

    settextjustify(LEFT_TEXT, TOP_TEXT);
    for (reading = 0; reading < READINGS; reading++)
    {
        setfillstyle(1+reading, RED);
        sector(x, y, 0, 60, 20, 20);
        gcvt(percent[reading], 10, str);
        moveto(x, y+8);
        outtext(str);
        outtext("%");

        y += 50;
        if (reading == 2)
        {
            x = 550;
            y = 20;
        }
    }

    moveto(319, 180);
    gcvt(temps[reading], 10, str);
    outtext(str);

    getimage(0, 0, 639, 199, graph_ptr);
    gotoxy(1, 25);
    printf( "press any key to return");
    getch();
    closegraph();
    /* dispaly the main pop menu */
    mainmenu();
    size(32, 0);
    /* restore original screen contents */
```

```
restore_video(5, 5, 20, 70, m, memory);

/* free allocated memory */
free(m);
/* free allocated memory */
free(graph_ptr);
return;
```

Graphics Demo

12

This project demonstrates the multi-colour graphic display on the screen. In this project the main menu provides the option for different demonstration. The item from the main menu can be selected by using the enter key or by pressing the hotkey which is represented by the bold character. The getoutput() function manages the movement of the cursor and selection of the menu item. This function also uses getkey() function to find which key has been pressed by the user. The Showmenu() function is used to display the menu in box drawn by menubox() available in the "intro1.h". The mainmenu() function prepares the screen for popping up a menu. The pop_menu() pops up a menu on the existing screen contents. The grap_screen function prepares the opening screen, which provides the information about the programmer.

INITIALIZE: Initializes the graphics system and reports any errors that occur.

TEXTDUMP: Displays all the characters in each of the available fonts.

RANDOMBARS: Displays random bars

TEXTDEMO: Shows each font in several sizes to the user.

COLORDEMO: Displays the current color palette on the screen.

ARCDEMO: Displays a random pattern of arcs on the screen until the user says enough.

CIRCLEDEMO:	Displays a random pattern of circles on the screen until the user says enough.
LINERELDEMO:	Displays pattern using moverel and linerel cmds.
PUTPIXELDEMO:	Displays a pattern of random dots on the screen and pick them back up again.
PUTIMAGEDEMO:	Displays the small moving turtle on the screen
LINETODEMO:	Displays a pattern using moveto and lineto commands.
LINESTYLEDEMO:	Displays a pattern using all of the standard line styles that are available.
CRTMODEDEMO:	Demonstrates the effects of the change mode commands on the current screen.
USERLINESTYLEDEMO:	Displays line styles showing the user defined line style functions.
FILLSTYLEDEMO:	Displays the standard fill patterns available.
FILLPATTERNDEMO:	Demonstrates how to use the user definable fill patterns.
POLYDEMO:	Displays a random pattern of polygons on the screen until the user says enough.
POLYDEMO:	Displays a random pattern of polygons on the screen until the user says enough.
SAYGOODBYE:	Gives a closing screen to the user before leaving.
MAINWINDOW:	Establishes the main window for the demo and set a viewport for the demo code.
STATUSLINE:	Displays a status line at the bottom of the screen.
DRAWBORDER:	Draws a solid single line around the current viewport.
CHANGETEXTSTYLE:	Similar to settextstyle, but checks for errors that might occur while loading the font file.

This package provides the demo for "Color", "Palette", "RandomBars", "Arc", "Circle", "Line", "Text", "Poly",. In the main menu the following operations are performed:

ColorDemo
PaletteDemo
RandomBars
ArcDemo
CircleDemo
LineRelDemo
TextDemo

CRTModeDemo
PolyDemo
eXit

Source code of intro1.h

writech()... This function writes the character into VDU memory.

writeline()... This function writes an entire string into VDU memory.

Store_video... This function reads the character from the rectangular part of the screen and stores them into the RAM.

Restore_video... This reads the character from the RAM and places on the VDU.

Display_box()... This function displays the double lined box on the main. menu and others menus.

Menu_box()... This function displays the box with different shadows as the user required and also without shadows.

Size()... This function is used to change the size of the cursor.

```
/* writes a character and its attribute in VDU memory*/
writech ( int r, int c, char ch, int attb,char far *memory )
{
        char far *v ;

        /* calculate address in VDU memory corresponding to row r and column c*/
        v = memory + r * 160 + c * 2 ;

        *v = ch ;  /* store ascii value of character*/
        v++ ;
        *v = attb ;  /* store attribute of character */
}

/* writes a string into VDU memory in the desired attribute */
writeline ( char *s, int r, int c, int attb,char far *memory )
{
        while ( *s != '\0' )
        {
        /* if next character is hot key, write it in different attribute, otherwise in normal attribute*/
```

```
            if ( *s == '^' )
            {
                s++ ;
                writech ( r, c, *s, 77,memory ) ;
            }
            else
                writech ( r, c, *s, attb,memory ) ;

            s++ ;
            c++ ;
    }
}

/* draws double-lined box */
display_box ( int sr, int sc, int er, int ec, int attribute,char far *memory )
{
    int i ;

    /* draw horizontal lines */
    for ( i = sc + 1 ; i < ec ; i++ )
    {
        writech ( sr, i, 205, attribute,memory ) ;
        writech ( er, i, 205, attribute,memory ) ;
    }

    /* draw vertical lines */
    for ( i = sr + 1 ; i < er ; i++ )
    {
        writech ( i, sc, 186, attribute,memory ) ;
        writech ( i, ec, 186, attribute,memory ) ;
    }

    /* draw four corners */
    writech ( sr, sc, 201, attribute,memory ) ;
    writech ( sr, ec, 187, attribute,memory ) ;
    writech ( er, sc, 200, attribute,memory ) ;
    writech ( er, ec, 188, attribute,memory ) ;
}
```

```
/* draws filled box with or without shadow */
menubox ( int sr, int sc, int er, int ec, char filler, char shadow,char far *memory )
{
	int i, j ;

	/* draw filled box */
	for ( i = sr ; i < er ; i++ )
	{
		for ( j = sc ; j < ( ec - 1 ) ; j++ )
			writech ( i, j, ' ', filler,memory ) ;
	}

	/* if no shadow is required for the filled box */
	if ( shadow == 0 )
	{
		for ( i = sr ; i <= er ; i++ )
		{
			writech ( i, ec, ' ', filler,memory ) ;
			writech ( i, ( ec - 1 ), ' ', filler,memory ) ;
		}

		for ( j = sc ; j <= ec ; j++ )
			writech ( er, j, ' ', filler,memory ) ;
	}
	else
	{
	/* draw vertical and horizontal shadow */
		for ( i = sr + 1 ; i <= er ; i++ )
		{
			writech ( i, ec, ' ', shadow,memory ) ;
			writech ( i, ( ec - 1 ), ' ', shadow,memory ) ;
		}

		for ( j = sc + 2 ; j <= ec ; j++ )
			writech ( er, j, ' ', shadow,memory ) ;
	}
}
```

```
/* saves screen contents into allocated memory in RAM */
store_video ( int sr, int sc, int er, int ec, char *buffer,char far *memory )
{
	char far *vid ;
	int i, j ;

	for ( i = sr ; i <= er ; i++ )
	{
		for ( j = sc ; j <= ec ; j++ )
		{
			vid = memory + i * 160 + j * 2 ; /* calculate address */
			*buffer = *vid ; /* store character */
			vid++ ;
			buffer++ ;
			*buffer = *vid ; /* store attribute */
			buffer++ ;
		}
	}
}

/* restores screen contents from allocated memory in RAM */
restore_video ( int sr, int sc, int er, int ec, char *buffer,char far *memory )
{
	char far *vid ;
	int i, j ;

	for ( i = sr ; i <= er ; i++ )
	{
		for ( j = sc ; j <= ec ; j++ )
		{
			vid = memory + i * 160 + j * 2 ; /* calculate address */
			*vid = *buffer ; /* restore character */
			vid++ ;
			buffer++ ;
			*vid = *buffer ; /* restore attribute */
			buffer++ ;
		}
	}
}
```

```
/*displays or hides the cursor*/
size ( int ssl, int esl )
{
        union REGS iregs, oregs ;

        iregs.h.ah = 1 ;            /* service number*/
        iregs.h.ch = ssl ;          /* starting scan line*/
        iregs.h.cl = esl ;          /* ending scan line*/
        iregs.h.bh = 0 ;            /* video page numbe*/

        /* issue interrupt for changing the size of the cursor*/
        int86 ( 16, &iregs, &oregs ) ;
}
```

Source Listing of BAR1.C

```
#ifdef __TINY__
#error BGIDEMO will not run in the tiny model.
#endif

#include<stdio.h>
#include <dos.h>
#include <math.h>
#include <conio.h>
#include <stdio.h>
#include <stdlib.h>
#include <stdarg.h>
#include <graphics.h>
#include <string.h>
#include <ctype.h>
#include <d:\turboc3\projectc\intro1.h>

#define TRUE  1                 /* Define some handy constants */
#define FALSE 0                 /* Define some handy constants */
#define PI      3.14159         /* Define a value for PI */
#define ON      1               /* Define some handy constants */
#define OFF     0               /* Define some handy constants */

#define NFONTS 11
```

```
// Declaration of fonts at for demo display
char *Fonts[NFONTS] = {
                        "DefaultFont",
                        "TriplexFont",
                        "SmallFont",
                        "SansSerifFont",
                        "GothicFont",
                        "ScriptFont",
                        "SimplexFont",
                        "TriplexScriptFont",
                        "ComplexFont",
                        "EuropeanFont",
                        "BoldFont"
                  };

// Declaration of lining style
char *LineStyles[] = {
                        "SolidLn",
                        "DottedLn",
                        "CenterLn",
                        "DashedLn",
                        "UserBitLn"
                  };

// The area fill style in demo
char *FillStyles[] = {
                        "EmptyFill",
                        "SolidFill",
                        "LineFill",
                        "LtSlashFill",
                        "SlashFill",
                        "BkSlashFill",
                        "LtBkSlashFill",
                        "HatchFill",
                        "XHatchFill",
                        "InterleaveFill",
                        "WideDotFill",
                        "CloseDotFill"
};
```

```
// Text display direction
char *TextDirect[] = {
                                    "HorizDir", "VertDir"
                              };

// Text adjustment
char *HorizJust[] = {
                                    "LeftText",  "CenterText", "RightText"
                              };

// Text justification
char *VertJust[] = {
                                    "BottomText", "CenterText", "TopText"
                              };

// Main menu options
char *main_menu[] = {
                                    "^ColorDemo",          /* Begin actual
demonstration              */
                                    "^PaletteDemo",
                                    "^RandomBars",
                                    "^ArcDemo",
                                    "C^ircleDemo",
                                    "^LineRelDemo",
                                    "^TextDemo",
                                    "CRT^ModeDemo",
                                    "Pol^yDemo",
                                    "e^Xit"
                              };

struct PTS
{
        int x, y;
};      /* Structure to hold vertex points*/

int   GraphDriver;              /* The Graphics device driver           */
int   GraphMode;                /* The Graphics mode value              */
double AspectRatio;             /* Aspect ratio of a pixel on the screen*/
int   MaxX, MaxY;               /* The maximum resolution of the screen */
int   MaxColors;                /* The maximum # of colors available    */
int   ErrorCode;                /* Reports any graphics errors          */
struct palettetype palette;     /* Used to read palette info       */
```

```
/*                                                              */
/*          Function prototypes                                 */
/*                                                              */

void Initialize(void);
void ReportStatus(void);
void TextDump(void);
void RandomBars(void);
void TextDemo(void);
void ColorDemo(void);
void ArcDemo(void);
void CircleDemo(void);
void LineRelDemo(void);
void PutPixelDemo(void);
void PutImageDemo(void);
void LineToDemo(void);
void LineStyleDemo(void);
void CRTModeDemo(void);
void UserLineStyleDemo(void);

void FillStyleDemo(void);
void FillPatternDemo(void);
void PaletteDemo(void);
void PolyDemo(void);
void SayGoodbye(void);
void MainWindow(char *header);
void StatusLine(char *msg);
void DrawBorder(void);
void changetextstyle(int font, int direction, int charsize);
void  grap_screen();
set_mode(int mode);
mainmenu();

pop_menu ( char **main_menu, int count, int sr, int sc, char *hotkeys, int number );
showmenu ( char **main_menu, int counter, int sr, int sc );
getkey();

getoutput ( char **main_menu, char *keys, int sr, int sc, int counter, int number );
```

```
/*                                                              */
/*      Begin main function                                     */
/*                                                              */

char far *memory;
int ascii,scans;
int main(void)
{
  int choice;
  /* store base address of VDU memory and set appropriate video mode */
      #ifdef  NA
      /* store base address for NA*/
      memory = (char far *)0xb0000000L;
      set_mode(7);
  #else
      /* store base address for other type of display adapter */
      memory = (char far *) 0xb8000000L;
      set_mode(3);
  #endif

      size(32,0);                    /* To hide the cursor displayed on the screen*/

       grap_screen();

      /* create screen on which menus are to be popped up */
      mainmenu() ;

      while ( 1 )
      {
          /* pop up main menu and collect choice */
          choice = pop_menu ( main_menu, 10, 4, 24, "CPRAILTMYX", 2 );

          /* test choice received */
          switch ( choice )
          {
              case 1 :
                      /* Set system into Graphics mode          */
                      Initialize();
                      /* Begin actual demonstration             */
                      ColorDemo();
```

```
                        break;
        case 2 :
                        Initialize();
                        if( GraphDriver==EGA || GraphDriver==EGALO ||
                                    GraphDriver==VGA )
                              PaletteDemo();
                        PutPixelDemo();
                        PutImageDemo();
                        break;
        case 3 :
                        Initialize();
                        RandomBars();
                        break;
        case 4 :
                        Initialize();
                        ArcDemo();
                        break;
        case 5 :
                        Initialize();
                        CircleDemo();
                        break;
        case 6 :
                        Initialize();
                        LineRelDemo();
                        LineToDemo();
                        LineStyleDemo();
                        UserLineStyleDemo();
                        break;
        case 7 :
                        Initialize();
                        TextDump();
                        TextDemo();
                        break;
        case 8 :
                        Initialize();
                        CRTModeDemo();
                        FillStyleDemo();
                        FillPatternDemo();
                        break;
        case 9 :
```

```
                                    Initialize();
                                    PolyDemo();
                                    break;
                        case 10 :
                        case 27 :
                                    size (6,7);
                                    clrscr();
                                    exit(0);
                  }
        }
        getch();
        SayGoodbye();               /* Give user the closing screen   */
        getch();
        closegraph();               /* Return the system to text mode      */
        return(0);
}

/* sets video mode*/
set_mode ( int mode )
{
        union REGS i, o ;

        i.h.ah = 0 ;        /* service no.*/
        i.h.al = mode ;  /* video mode*/
        int86 ( 16, &i, &o ) ; /* issue interrupt*/
}

/* Display the opening screen */
void grap_screen()
{
        int driver,mode;
        driver=DETECT;
        initgraph(&driver,&mode,"");
        setbkcolor(10);
        setcolor(5);        //set the text color
        //set default font,horizontal direction,size of text
        settextstyle(0,0,6);
        outtextxy(10,100,"GRAPHICS-DEMO");
        outtextxy(150,300,"PACKAGE");
        delay(2000);
```

```
        closegraph();

        initgraph(&driver,&mode,"");
        setbkcolor(10);
        setcolor(1); //set background color to blude
        settextstyle(0,0,7);
        outtextxy(50,100,"DEVELOPED");
        outtextxy(50,300,"  BY ");
        delay(2000);
        closegraph();

        initgraph(&driver,&mode,"");
        setbkcolor(10);
        setcolor(4); //set background color to green
        settextstyle(0,0,5);
        outtextxy(30,100,"Author" );
        outtextxy(120,200," & ");
        outtextxy(200,300,"Her Team");
        delay(2000);
        closegraph();

}
```

GRAPHICS-DEMO

PACKAGE

Figure 12.1 First Output Screen of Graphics Demo function grap_screen

Figure 12.2 Second Output Screen of Graphics Demo function grap_screen

Figure 12.3 Third Output Screen of Graphics Demo function grap_screen

```
/* prepares the screen for popping up a menu*/
mainmenu()
{
        int i, j ;

        display_box ( 1, 0, 23, 79, 10,memory ) ;

        writech ( 21, 0, 204, 10,memory ) ;
        writech ( 21, 79, 185, 10,memory ) ;

        for ( i = 2 ; i <= 20 ; i++ )
        {
                for ( j = 1 ; j <= 78 ; j += 2 )
                {
                        writech ( i, j, 177, 5,memory ) ;
                        writech ( i, j + 1, 177, 5,memory ) ;
                }
        }

        // The ascii character is" "

        writeline ( "ÝÝÝÝÝÝÝÝÝÝ", 3, 4, 143, memory ) ;
        writeline ( "ÝÝÝ       ", 4, 4, 143, memory ) ;
        writeline ( "ÝÝÝ  ÝÝÝÝÝ", 5, 4, 143, memory ) ;
        writeline ( "ÝÝÝ    ÝÝÝ", 6, 4, 143, memory ) ;
        writeline ( "ÝÝÝÝÝÝÝÝÝÝ", 7, 4, 143, memory );

        writeline ( "ÝÝÝ     ÝÝÝ", 9, 4, 143, memory ) ;
        writeline ( "ÝÝÝ     ÝÝÝ", 10, 4, 143, memory ) ;
        writeline ( "ÝÝÝ     ÝÝÝ", 11, 4, 143, memory ) ;
        writeline ( "ÝÝÝ     ÝÝÝ", 12, 4, 143, memory ) ;
        writeline ( "ÝÝÝÝÝÝÝÝÝÝÝ", 13, 4, 143, memory ) ;

        writeline ( "ÝÝÝ", 15, 8, 143,memory ) ;
        writeline ( "ÝÝÝ", 16, 8, 143,memory ) ;
        writeline ( "ÝÝÝ", 17, 8, 143,memory ) ;
        writeline ( "ÝÝÝ", 18, 8, 143,memory ) ;
        writeline ( "ÝÝÝ", 19, 8, 143,memory );
        writeline ( "     Select using hotkey or Enter        ", 22, 14, 12,memory ) ;
```

```
/* pops up a menu on the existing screen contents */
pop_menu ( char **main_menu, int count, int sr, int sc, char *hotkeys, int number )
{
        int er, ec, i, l = 0, area, choice ;
        char *m ;

        /* calculate ending row for menu */
        er = sr + count + 2 ;

        /* find longest menu item */
        for ( i = 0 ; i < count ; i++ )
        {
                if ( strlen (main_menu[i] ) > l )
                        l = strlen ( main_menu[i] ) ;
        }

        /* calculate ending column for menu */
        ec = sc + l + 3 ;

        /* calculate area required to save screen contents where menu is to be popped up */
        area = ( er - sr + 1 ) * ( ec - sc + 1 ) * 2 ;

        m = ((char *)malloc ( area )) ; /* allocate memory */

        /* check if allocation is successful */
        if ( m == NULL )
        {
                writeline ( "        Insufficient  memory          ", 22, 14, 9,memory ) ;
                getch() ;
                exit ( 2 ) ;
        }

        /* save screen contents into allocated memory */
        store_video ( sr, sc, er, ec, m,memory ) ;

        /* draw filled box with shadow */
        menubox ( sr, sc, er, ec, 277, 1,memory ) ;

        /* display the menu in the filled box */
        showmenu ( main_menu, count, sr + 1, sc + 1 ) ;
```

```
    /* receive user's choice */
    choice = getoutput (main_menu, hotkeys, sr, sc, count,number ) ;

    /* restore original screen contents */
    restore_video ( sr, sc, er, ec, m,memory ) ;

    /* free allocated memory */
    free ( m ) ;
    return ( choice ) ;
}
```

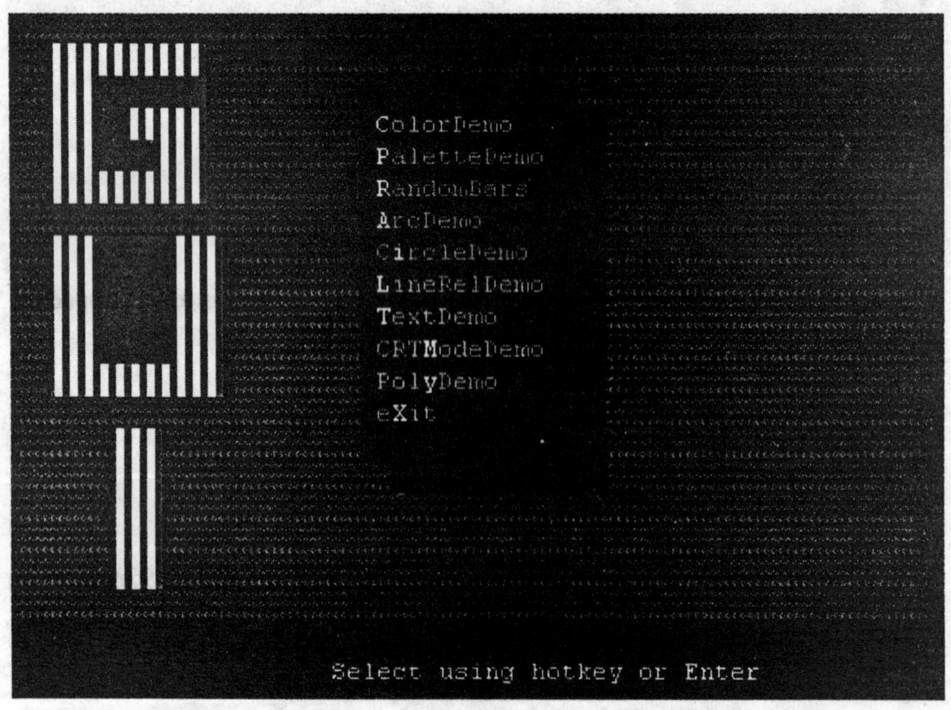

12.4 Output Screen of Graphics Demo function pop_menu

```
/* gets the ascii and scan codes of the key pressed */
getkey()
{
    union REGS ii, oo ;

    /* wait till a key is hit */
```

```
        while ( ! kbhit() )
            ;

        ii.h.ah = 0 ;  /* service number */

        /* issue interrupt */
        int86 ( 22, &ii, &oo ) ;

        scans = oo.h.ah ;
        ascii = oo.h.al ;
}

/* displays the menu in box drawn by menubox() */
showmenu ( char **main_menu, int counter, int sr, int sc )
{
        int i ;

        for ( i = 0 ; i < counter ; i++ )
        {
            /* write menu item in VDU memory */
            writeline ( main_menu[i], sr, sc, 9,memory ) ;
            sr++ ;
        }
}

/* receives user's response for the menu displayed */
getoutput ( char **main_menu, char *keys, int sr, int sc, int counter, int number )
{
        int ch = 1, len, hotkeyans ;

        /* calculate number of hot keys for the menu */
        len = strlen ( keys ) ;

        /* highlight first menu item */
        writeline ( main_menu[ch - 1], sr + ch, sc + 1, 12,memory ) ;

        while ( 1 )
        {
            getkey() ; /* reccive key */
```

```
/* if special key is hit */
if ( ascii == 0 )
{
        switch ( scans )
        {
                case 80 :  /* down arrow key */

                        /* make highlighted item normal */
                        writeline ( main_menu[ch - 1], sr + ch, sc + 1, 9,memory) ;

                        ch++ ;
                        number++ ;
                        break ;

                case 72 :  /* up arrow key */

                        /* make highlighted item normal */
                        writeline ( main_menu[ch - 1], sr + ch, sc + 1, 9,memory);

                        ch— ;
                        number— ;
                        break ;
        }

        /* if highlighted bar is on first item and up arrow key is hit */
        if ( ch == 0 )
        {
                ch = counter ;
                number = number + counter ;
        }

        /* if highlighted bar is on last item and down arrow key is hit */
        if ( ch > counter )
        {
                ch = 1 ;
                number = number - counter ;
        }

        /* highlight the appropriate menu item */
        writeline ( main_menu[ch - 1], sr + ch, sc + 1, 12 ,memory) ;
```

```
        }
        else
        {
                if ( ascii == 13 ) /* Enter key */
                        return ( ch ) ;

                if ( ascii == 27 ) /* Esc key */
                        return ( 27 ) ;

                ascii = toupper ( ascii ) ;
                hotkeyans = 1 ;

                /* check whether hot key has been pressed */
                while ( *keys != '\0' )
                {
                        if ( *keys == ascii )
                                return ( hotkeyans ) ;
                        else
                        {
                                keys++ ;
                                hotkeyans++ ;
                        }
                }

                /* reset hotkeys to point to the first character in the string */
                keys = keys - len ;
        }
    }
}

/*                                                                      */
/*      INITIALIZE: Initializes the graphics system and reports        */
/*      any errors which occured.                                       */
/*                                                                      */

void Initialize(void)
{
        int xasp, yasp;                 /* Used to read the aspect ratio*/

        GraphDriver = DETECT;           /* Request auto-detection       */
```

```
        initgraph( &GraphDriver, &GraphMode, "" );
        ErrorCode = graphresult();          /* Read result of initialization*/
        if( ErrorCode != grOk )
        {                                   /* Error occured during init     */
                printf(" Graphics System Error: %s\n", grapherrormsg( ErrorCode ) );
                exit( 1 );
        }

        getpalette( &palette );             /* Read the palette from board   */
        MaxColors = getmaxcolor() + 1; /* Read maximum number of colors*/

        MaxX = getmaxx();
        MaxY = getmaxy();                   /* Read size of screen           */

        getaspectratio( &xasp, &yasp ); /* read the hardware aspect         */
        AspectRatio = (double)xasp / (double)yasp;     /* Get correction factor */
}

/*                                                                     */
/*      TEXTDUMP: Displays all the characters in each of the           */
/*      available fonts.                                               */
/*                                                                     */

void TextDump()
{
        static int CGASizes[] = {
                                        1, 3, 7, 3, 3, 2, 2, 2, 2, 2, 2 };
        static int NormSizes[] = {
                                        1, 4, 7, 4, 4, 2, 2, 2, 2, 2, 2 };

        char buffer[80];
        int font, ch, wwidth, lwidth, size;
        int area;
        struct viewporttype vp;
        int maxx,maxy;
        char *m;
        int row = 8;
        int row1 = 9;
        maxx = getmaxx();
        maxy = getmaxy();
```

```
area = (20 - 5 +1) * (70 - 5 + 1) * 2;
m = ((char *) malloc (area));
if (m == NULL)
{
        writeline("          Insufficient disk space            ",22,14,12,memory);
        getch();
        writeline("          Press Hot key or Enter to select   ",22,14,12,memory);
        return ;
}

store_video(5,5,20,70,m,memory);
menubox(5,20,17,60,12,66,memory);
setviewport(0,0,maxx,maxy,1);
clearviewport();

for( font=0 ; font<NFONTS ; ++font )
{       /* For each available font         */
        sprintf( buffer, "%s Character Set", Fonts[font] );
        MainWindow( buffer );           /* Display fontname as banner   */
        getviewsettings( &vp );         /* read current viewport */

        settextjustify( LEFT_TEXT, TOP_TEXT );
        moveto( 2, 3 );

        buffer[1] = '\0';               /* Terminate string        */
        wwidth = vp.right - vp.left;    /* Determine the window width */
        lwidth = textwidth( "H" );      /* Get average letter width   */

        if( font == DEFAULT_FONT )
        {
                changetextstyle( font, HORIZ_DIR, 1 );
                ch = 0;
                while( ch < 256 )
                {                               /* For each possible character  */
                        buffer[0] = ch;         /* Put character into a string  */
                        outtext( buffer );      /* send string to screen */
                        if ((getx() + lwidth) > wwidth )
                                moveto( 2, gety() + textheight("H") + 3 );
                        ++ch;                   /* Goto the next character      */
                }
```

```
        }
        else
        {
                size = (MaxY < 200) ? CGASizes[font] : NormSizes[font];
                changetextstyle( font, HORIZ_DIR, size );

                ch = '!';                    /* Begin at 1st printable */
                while( ch < 256 )
                {                            /* For each printable character */
                        buffer[0] = ch;  /* Put character into a string      */
                        outtext( buffer );           /* send string to screen */
                        if( (lwidth+getx()) > wwidth )  /* Are we still in window? */
                                moveto( 2, gety()+textheight("H")+3 );
                        ++ch;                        /* Goto the next character */
                }

        }

        getch();
    }           /* End of FONT loop        */
}


/*                                                              */
/*      RANDOMBARS: Display random bars                        */
/*                                                              */

void RandomBars(void)
{
    int color;

    MainWindow( "Random Bars" );
    StatusLine( "Esc aborts or press a key..." ); /* Put msg at bottom of screen   */
    while( !kbhit() )
    {               /* Until user enters a key... */
        color = random( MaxColors-1 )+1;
        setcolor( color );
        setfillstyle( random(11)+1, color );
        bar3d( random( getmaxx() ), random( getmaxy() ),
        random( getmaxx() ), random( getmaxy() ), 0, OFF);
```

```
    }

    getch();
    closegraph();
    size(32,0);
    menubox ( 0, 0, 24, 79, 7, 10,memory ) ;
    display_box ( 1, 0, 21, 79, 10 ,memory) ;
    mainmenu();
    return ;
}
```

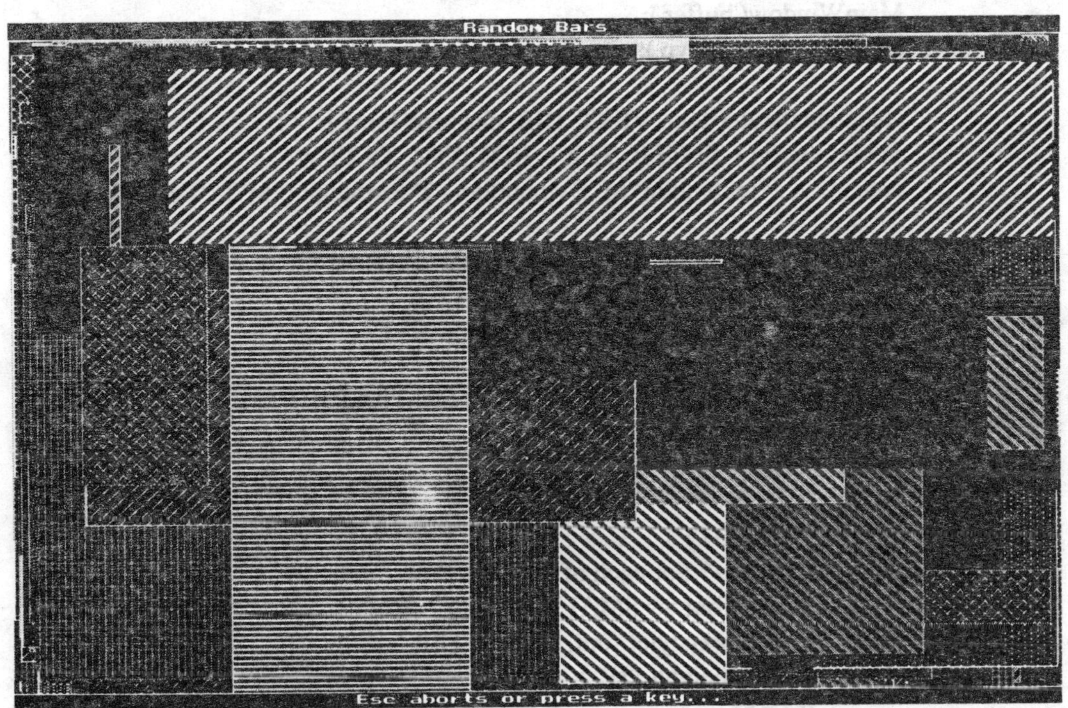

12.5 Output Screen of Graphics Demo function RandomBars

```
/*                                                              */
/*      TEXTDEMO: Shows each font in several sizes to the user. */
/*                                                              */

void TextDemo(void)
{
    int charsize[] = {
```

```
                                    1, 3, 7, 3, 4, 2, 2, 2, 2, 2, 2  };
int font, size;
int h, x, y, i;
struct viewporttype vp;
char buffer[80];

for( font=0 ; font<NFONTS ; ++font )
{       /* For each of the avail. fonts     */

        sprintf( buffer, "%s Demonstration", Fonts[font] );
        MainWindow( buffer );
        getviewsettings( &vp );

        changetextstyle( font, VERT_DIR, charsize[font] );
        settextjustify( CENTER_TEXT, BOTTOM_TEXT );
        outtextxy( 2*textwidth("M"), vp.bottom - 2*textheight("M"), "Vertical" );

        changetextstyle( font, HORIZ_DIR, charsize[font] );
        settextjustify( LEFT_TEXT, TOP_TEXT );
        outtextxy( 2*textwidth("M"), 2, "Horizontal" );

        settextjustify( CENTER_TEXT, CENTER_TEXT );
        x = (vp.right - vp.left) / 2;
        y = textheight( "H" );

        for( i=1 ; i<5 ; ++i )
        {               /* For each of the sizes */
                size = (font == SMALL_FONT) ? i+3 : i;
                changetextstyle( font, HORIZ_DIR, size );
                h = textheight( "H" );
                y += h;
                sprintf( buffer, "C  Project %d", size );
                outtextxy( x, y, buffer );

        }

        if( font != DEFAULT_FONT )
        {                       /* Show user declared font size */
                y += h / 2;     /* Move down the screen         */
                settextjustify( CENTER_TEXT, TOP_TEXT );
```

```
                setusercharsize( 5, 6, 3, 2 );
                changetextstyle( font, HORIZ_DIR, USER_CHAR_SIZE );
                outtextxy( (vp.right-vp.left)/2, y, "User Defined Size" );
            }

            getch();
        }                                   /* End of FONT loop          */
        closegraph();
        menubox ( 0, 0, 24, 79, 7, 10,memory ) ;
        display_box ( 1, 0, 21, 79, 10 ,memory) ;
        mainmenu();
        return ;
}
```


12.6 Output Screen of Graphics Demo function TextDemo

```
/*                                                              */
/*      COLORDEMO: Displays the current color palette on the screen.*/
/*                                                              */

void ColorDemo(void)
{
        struct viewporttype vp;
        int color, height, width;
        int x, y, i, j;
        char cnum[5];
```

```
MainWindow( "Color Demonstration" ); /* Show demonstration name     */

color = 1;
getviewsettings( &vp );                  /* Get the current window size  */
width  = 2 * ( (vp.right+1) / 16 );      /* Get box dimensions           */
height = 2 * ( (vp.bottom-10) / 10 );

x = width / 2;
y = height / 2;   /* Leave 1/2 box border */

for( j=0 ; j<3 ; ++j )
{                    /* Row loop                     */
        for( i=0 ; i<5 ; ++i )
        {                /* Column loop                      */
                setfillstyle(SOLID_FILL, color);/* Set to solid fill in color     */
                setcolor( color );               /* Set the same border color     */
                bar( x, y, x+width, y+height );  /* Draw the rectangle            */
                rectangle( x, y, x+width, y+height ); /* outline the rectangle    */

                if ( color == BLACK )
                {               /* If box was black...         */
                        setcolor( WHITE );          /* Set drawing color to white */
                        rectangle( x, y, x+width, y+height ); /* Outline black in white*/
                }

                itoa( color, cnum, 10 );            /* Convert # to ASCII          */
                outtextxy( x+(width/2), y+height+4, cnum ); /* Show color #       */

                color = ++color % MaxColors;  /* Advance to the next color       */
                x += (width / 2) * 3;         /* move the column base            */
        }                                     /* End of Column loop          */

        y += (height / 2) * 3;                /* move the row base           */
        x = width / 2;                        /* reset column base           */
}                                             /* End of Row loop             */
getch();
closegraph();
size(32,0);
menubox ( 0, 0, 24, 79, 7, 10,memory );
display_box ( 1, 0, 21, 79, 10 ,memory);
```

```
        mainmenu();
        return ;
}
```

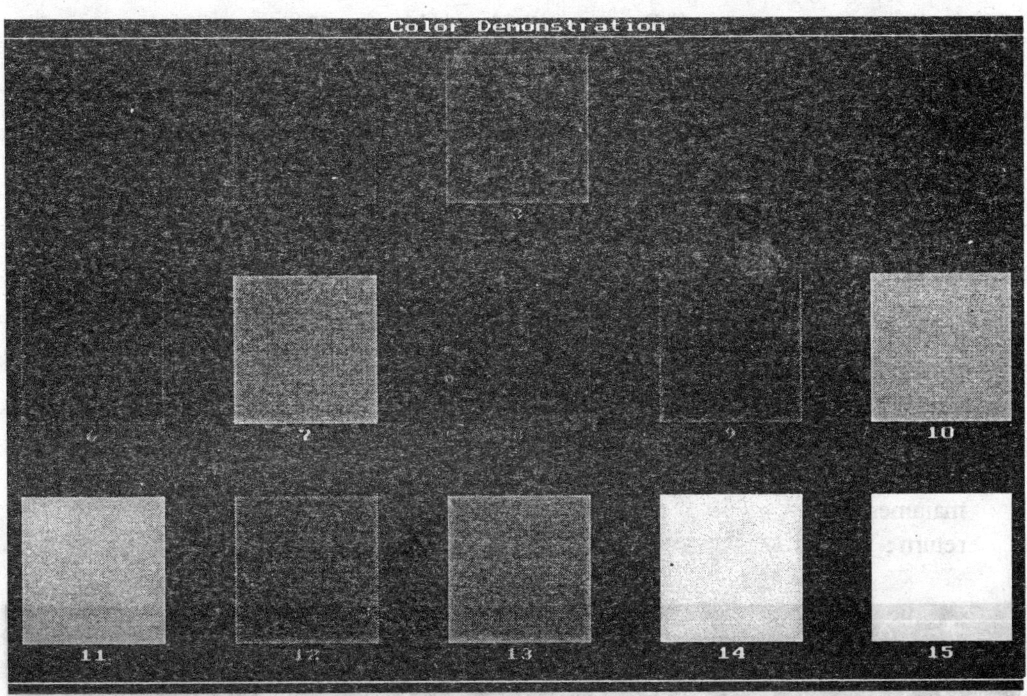

12.7 Output Screen of Graphics Demo function ColorDemo

```
/*                                                                    */
/*      ARCDEMO: Displays a random pattern of arcs on the screen      */
/*      until the user says enough.                                   */
/*                                                                    */

void ArcDemo(void)
{
        int mradius;                    /* Maximum radius allowed       */
        int eangle;                     /* Random end angle of Arc      */
        struct arccoordstype ai;        /* Used to read Arc Cord info   */

        MainWindow( "Arc Demonstration" );
        StatusLine( "ESC Aborts - Press a Key to stop" );
```

```
    mradius = MaxY / 10;                          /* Determine the maximum radius */

    while( !kbhit() )
    {                   /* Repeat until a key is hit          */
        setcolor( random( MaxColors - 1 ) + 1 ); /* Randomly select a color      */
        eangle = random( 358 ) + 1;              /* Select an end angle          */
        arc( random(MaxX), random(MaxY), random(eangle), eangle, mradius );
        getarccoords( &ai );                     /* Read Cord data               */
        line( ai.x, ai.y, ai.xstart, ai.ystart );  /* line from start to center */
        line( ai.x, ai.y,   ai.xend,   ai.yend );  /* line from end to center   */
    }                                            /* End of WHILE not KBHIT       */

    getch();
    closegraph();
    size(32,0);
    menubox ( 0, 0, 24, 79, 7, 10,memory ) ;
    display_box ( 1, 0, 21, 79, 10 ,memory) ;
    mainmenu();
    return ;
}
```

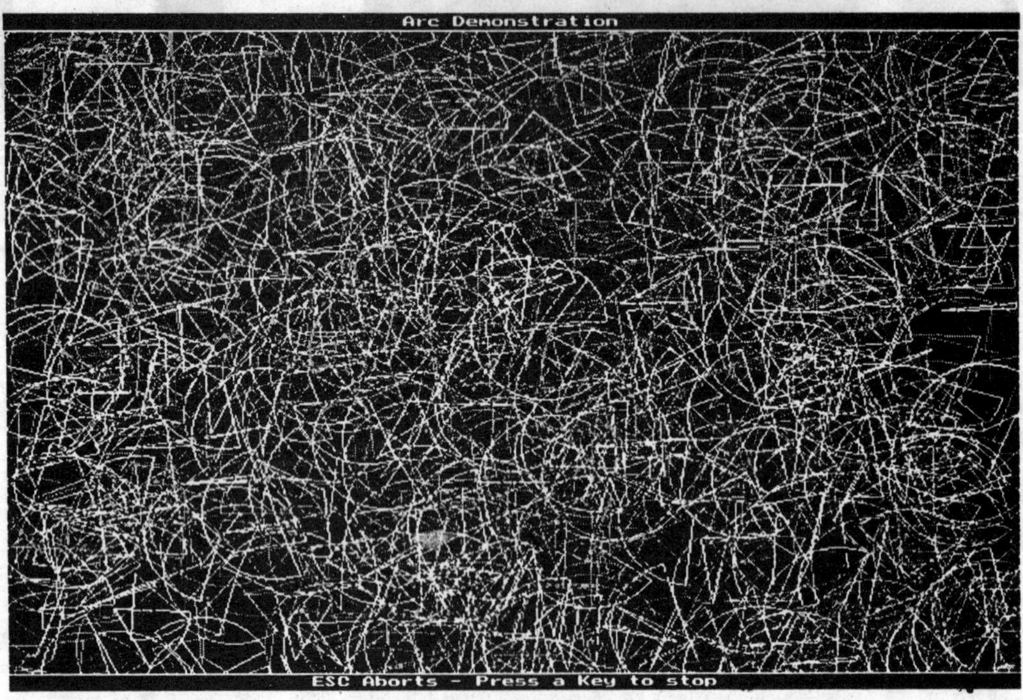

12.8 Output Screen of Graphics Demo function ArcDemo

```
/*                                                                    */
/*   CIRCLEDEMO: Displays a random pattern of circles on the screen  */
/*   until the user says enough.                                     */
/*                                                                    */

void CircleDemo(void)
{
    int mradius;                          /* Maximum radius allowed       */

    MainWindow( "Circle Demonstration" );
    StatusLine( "ESC Aborts - Press a Key to stop" );

    mradius = MaxY / 10;                  /* Determine the maximum radius */

    while( !kbhit() )
    {                          /* Repeat until a key is hit        */
        setcolor( random( MaxColors - 1 ) + 1 ); /* Randomly select a color     */
        circle( random(MaxX), random(MaxY), random(mradius) );
    }                                     /* End of WHILE not KBHIT     */

    getch();
    closegraph();
    size(32,0);
    menubox ( 0, 0, 24, 79, 7, 10,memory ) ;
    display_box ( 1, 0, 21, 79, 10 ,memory) ;
    mainmenu();
    return ;
}
```

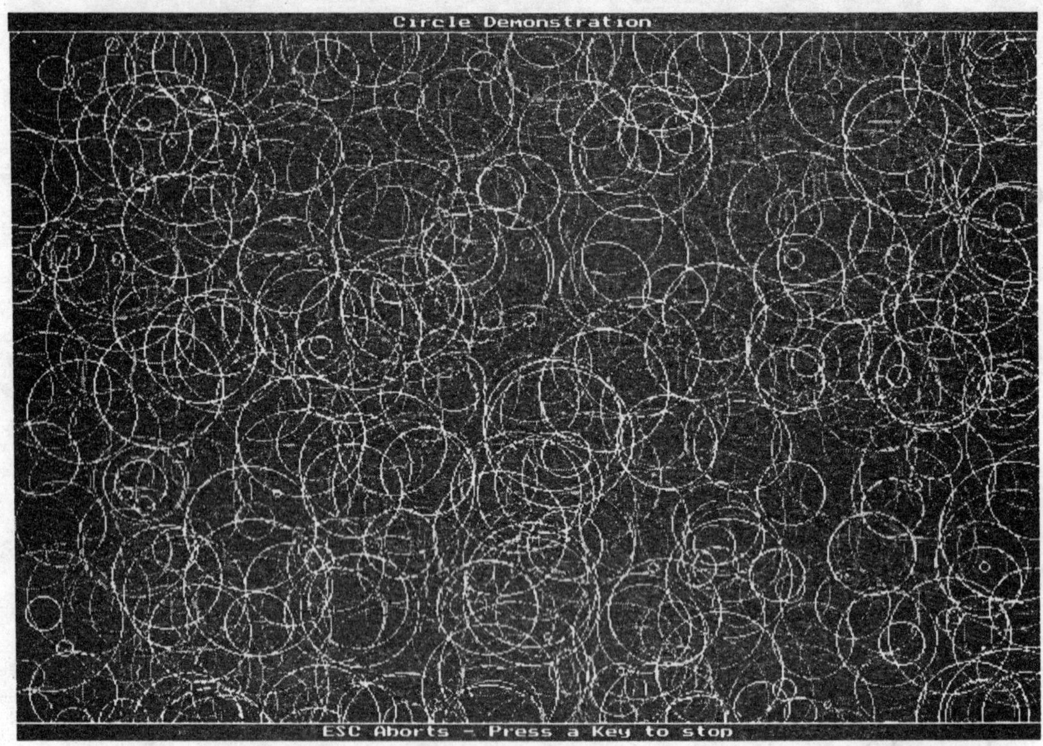

12.9 Output Screen of Graphics Demo function CircleDemo

```
/*                                                                    */
/*      LINERELDEMO: Displays pattern using moverel and linerel cmds.  */
/*                                                                    */

void LineRelDemo(void)
{
        struct viewporttype vp;
        int h, w, dx, dy, cx, cy;
        struct PTS outs[7];

        MainWindow( "MoveRel / LineRel Demonstration" );
        StatusLine( "Press any key to continue, ESC to Abort" );

        getviewsettings( &vp );
        cx = (vp.right  - vp.left) / 2;        /* Center of the screen coords   */
        cy = (vp.bottom - vp.top ) / 2;
```

```
h  = (vp.bottom - vp.top ) / 8;
w  = (vp.right  - vp.left) / 9;

dx = 2 * w;
dy = 2 * h;

setcolor( BLACK );

setfillstyle( SOLID_FILL, BLUE );
bar( 0, 0, vp.right-vp.left, vp.bottom-vp.top );        /* Draw backgnd */

outs[0].x = cx -  dx;
outs[0].y = cy -  dy;
outs[1].x = cx - (dx-w);
outs[1].y = cy - (dy+h);
outs[2].x = cx +  dx;
outs[2].y = cy - (dy+h);
outs[3].x = cx +  dx;
outs[3].y = cy +  dy;
outs[4].x = cx + (dx-w);
outs[4].y = cy + (dy+h);
outs[5].x = cx -  dx;
outs[5].y = cy + (dy+h);
outs[6].x = cx -  dx;
outs[6].y = cy -  dy;

setfillstyle( SOLID_FILL, WHITE );
fillpoly( 7, (int far *)outs );

outs[0].x = cx - (w/2);
outs[0].y = cy + h;
outs[1].x = cx + (w/2);
outs[1].y = cy + h;
outs[2].x = cx + (w/2);
outs[2].y = cy - h;
outs[3].x = cx - (w/2);
outs[3].y = cy - h;
outs[4].x = cx - (w/2);
outs[4].y = cy + h;
```

```
    setfillstyle( SOLID_FILL, BLUE );
    fillpoly( 5, (int far *)outs );

    /*      Draw a Tesseract object on the screen using the LineRel and      */
    /*      MoveRel drawing commands.                                        */

    moveto( cx-dx, cy-dy );
    linerel(  w, -h );
    linerel(  3*w,    0 );
    linerel(  0,  5*h );
    linerel( -w,      h );
    linerel( -3*w,    0 );
    linerel(  0, -5*h );

    moverel( w, -h );
    linerel(  0,  5*h );
    linerel( w+(w/2), 0 );
    linerel(  0, -3*h );
    linerel( w/2,  -h );
    linerel( 0, 5*h );

    moverel(  0, -5*h );
    linerel( -(w+(w/2)), 0 );
    linerel( 0, 3*h );
    linerel( -w/2, h );

    moverel( w/2, -h );
    linerel( w, 0 );

    moverel( 0, -2*h );
    linerel( -w, 0 );

    getch();
}
```

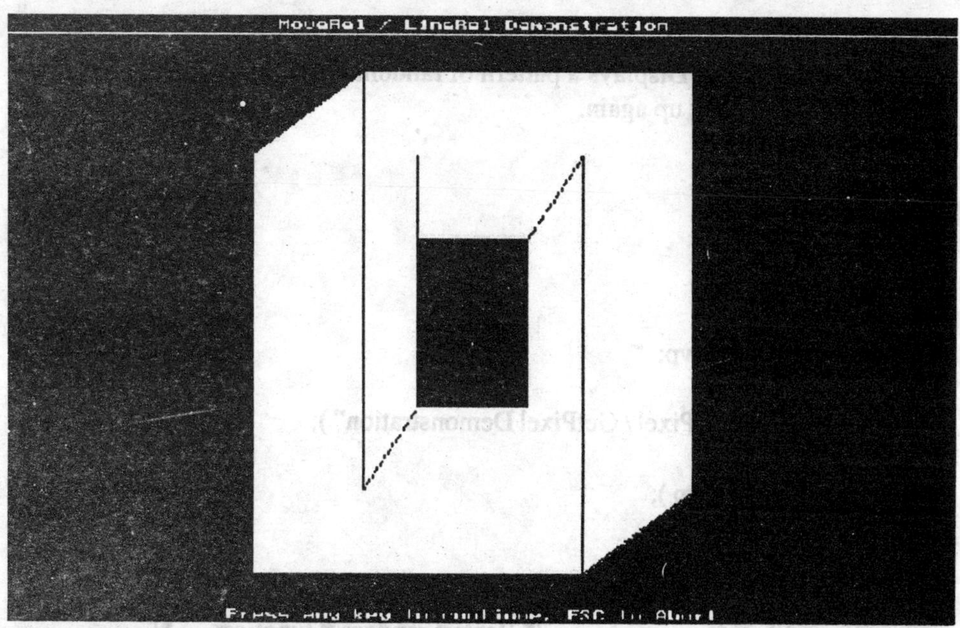

12.10 First Output Screen of Graphics Demo function LineRelDemo

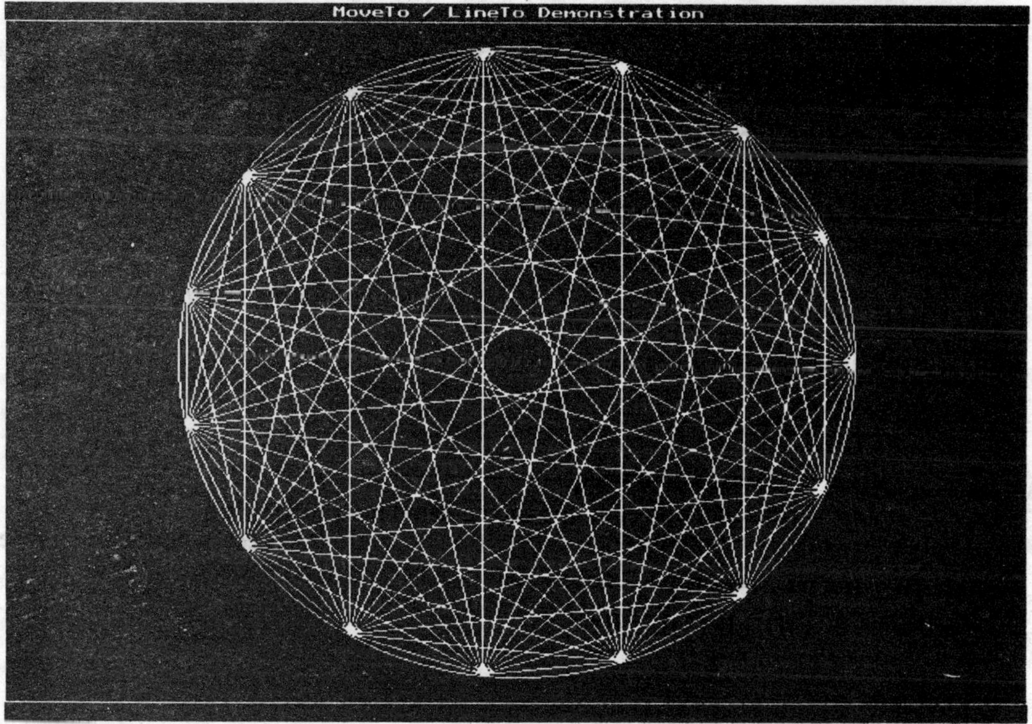

12.11 Second Output Screen of Graphics Demo function LineRelDemo

```
/*                                                                    */
/*   PUTPIXELDEMO: Displays a pattern of random dots on the screen    */
/*   and picks them back up again.                                    */
/*                                                                    */

void PutPixelDemo(void)
{
    int seed = 1958;
    int i, x, y, h, w, color;
    struct viewporttype vp;

    MainWindow( "PutPixel / GetPixel Demonstration" );

    getviewsettings( &vp );
    h = vp.bottom - vp.top;
    w = vp.right     - vp.left;

    srand( seed );                      /* Restart random # function    */

    for( i=0 ; i<5000 ; ++i )
    {                                   /* Put 5000 pixels on screen    */
        x = 1 + random( w - 1 );        /* Generate a random location   */
        y = 1 + random( h - 1 );
        color = random( MaxColors );
        putpixel( x, y, color );
    }

    srand( seed );                      /* Restart Random # at same #  */

    for( i=0 ; i<5000 ; ++i )
    {                                   /* Take the 5000 pixels off     */
        x = 1 + random( w - 1 );        /* Generate a random location   */
        y = 1 + random( h - 1 );
        color = getpixel( x, y );       /* Read the color pixel   */
        if( color == random( MaxColors ) )   /* Used to keep RANDOM in sync */
            putpixel( x, y, 0 );             /* Write pixel to BLACK         */
    }

    getch();
}
```

```
/*                                                          */
/*   PUTIMAGEDEMO                                           */
/*                                                          */
void PutImageDemo(void)
{
        static int r          = 20;
        static int StartX = 100;
        static int StartY = 50;

        struct viewporttype vp;
        int PauseTime, x, y, ulx, uly, lrx, lry, size, i, width, height, step;
        void *Saucer;

        MainWindow("GetImage / PutImage Demonstration");
        getviewsettings( &vp );

        /* Draw Saucer */
        setfillstyle( SOLID_FILL, getmaxcolor() );
        fillellipse(StartX, StartY, r, (r/3)+2);
        ellipse(StartX, StartY-4, 190, 357, r, r/3);

        line(StartX+7, StartY-6, StartX+10, StartY-12);
        circle(StartX+10, StartY-12, 2);
        line(StartX-7, StartY-6, StartX-10, StartY-12);
        circle(StartX-10, StartY-12, 2);

        /* Read saucer image */
        ulx = StartX-(r+1);
        uly = StartY-14;
        lrx = StartX+(r+1);
        lry = StartY+(r/3)+3;
        width = lrx - ulx + 1;
        height = lry - uly + 1;
        size = imagesize(ulx, uly, lrx, lry);

        Saucer = malloc( size );
        getimage(ulx, uly, lrx, lry, Saucer);
        putimage(ulx, uly, Saucer, XOR_PUT);

        /* Plot some "stars" */
```

```
for ( i=0 ; i<1000; ++i )
        putpixel(random(MaxX), random(MaxY), random( MaxColors-1 )+1);
x = MaxX / 2;
y = MaxY / 2;
PauseTime = 70;

/* until a key is hit */
while ( !kbhit() )
{

        /* Draw the Saucer */
        putimage(x, y, Saucer, XOR_PUT);                /*  draw image  */
        delay(PauseTime);
        putimage(x, y, Saucer, XOR_PUT);                /* erase image  */

        /* Move Saucer */

        step = random( 2*r );
        if ((step/2) % 2 != 0 )
                step = -1 * step;
        x = x + step;
        step = random( r );
        if ((step/2) % 2 != 0 )
                step = -1 * step;
        y = y + step;

        if (vp.left + x + width - 1 > vp.right)
                x = vp.right-vp.left-width + 1;
        else
                if (x < 0)
                        x = 0;
        if (vp.top + y + height - 1 > vp.bottom)
                y = vp.bottom-vp.top-height + 1;
        else
                if (y < 0)
                        y = 0;
}
free( Saucer );
getch();
closegraph();
```

```
        menubox ( 0, 0, 24, 79, 7, 10,memory ) ;
        display_box ( 1, 0, 21, 79, 10 ,memory) ;
        mainmenu();
        return ;
}

/*                                                                    */
/*      LINETODEMO: Displays a pattern using moveto and lineto commands.  */
/*                                                                    */

#define MAXPTS          15

void LineToDemo(void)
{
        struct viewporttype vp;
        struct PTS points[MAXPTS];
        int i, j, h, w, xcenter, ycenter;
        int radius, angle, step;
        double  rads;

        MainWindow( "MoveTo / LineTo Demonstration" );

        getviewsettings( &vp );
        h = vp.bottom - vp.top;
        w = vp.right     - vp.left;

        xcenter = w / 2;                    /* Determine the center of circle */
        ycenter = h / 2;
        radius  = (h - 30) / (AspectRatio * 2);
        step    = 360 / MAXPTS;                  /* Determine # of increments   */

        angle = 0;                               /* Begin at zero degrees*/
        for( i=0 ; i<MAXPTS ; ++i )
        {                                        /* Determine circle intercepts  */
                rads = (double)angle * PI / 180.0;          /* Convert angle to radians      */
                points[i].x = xcenter + (int)( cos(rads) * radius );
                points[i].y = ycenter - (int)( sin(rads) * radius * AspectRatio );
                angle += step;                              /* Move to next increment        */
        }
```

```
        circle( xcenter, ycenter, radius ); /* Draw bounding circle */

        for( i=0 ; i<MAXPTS ; ++i )
        {                                   /* Draw the cords to the circle */
                for( j=i ; j<MAXPTS ; ++j )
                {       /* For each remaining intersect */
                        moveto(points[i].x, points[i].y);   /* Move to beginning of cord    */
                        lineto(points[j].x, points[j].y);   /* Draw the cord                */
                }
        }

        getch();
}

/*                                                                      */
/*      LINESTYLEDEMO: Displays a pattern using all of the standard     */
/*      line styles that are available.                                 */
/*                                                                      */

void LineStyleDemo(void)
{
        int style, step;
        int x, y, w;
        struct viewporttype vp;
        char buffer[40];

        MainWindow( "Pre-defined line styles" );

        getviewsettings( &vp );
        w = vp.right    - vp.left;

        x = 35;
        y = 10;
        step = w / 11;

        settextjustify( LEFT_TEXT, TOP_TEXT );
        outtextxy( x, y, "Normal Width" );

        settextjustify( CENTER_TEXT, TOP_TEXT );
```

```
    for( style=0 ; style<4 ; ++style )
    {
            setlinestyle( style, 0, NORM_WIDTH );
            line( x, y+20, x, vp.bottom-40 );
            itoa( style, buffer, 10 );
            outtextxy( x, vp.bottom-30, buffer );
            x += step;
    }

    x += 2 * step;

    settextjustify( LEFT_TEXT, TOP_TEXT );
    outtextxy( x, y, "Thick Width" );
    settextjustify( CENTER_TEXT, TOP_TEXT );

    for( style=0 ; style<4 ; ++style )
    {
            setlinestyle( style, 0, THICK_WIDTH );
            line( x, y+20, x, vp.bottom-40 );
            itoa( style, buffer, 10 );
            outtextxy( x, vp.bottom-30, buffer );
            x += step;
    }

    settextjustify( LEFT_TEXT, TOP_TEXT );

    getch();
}
```

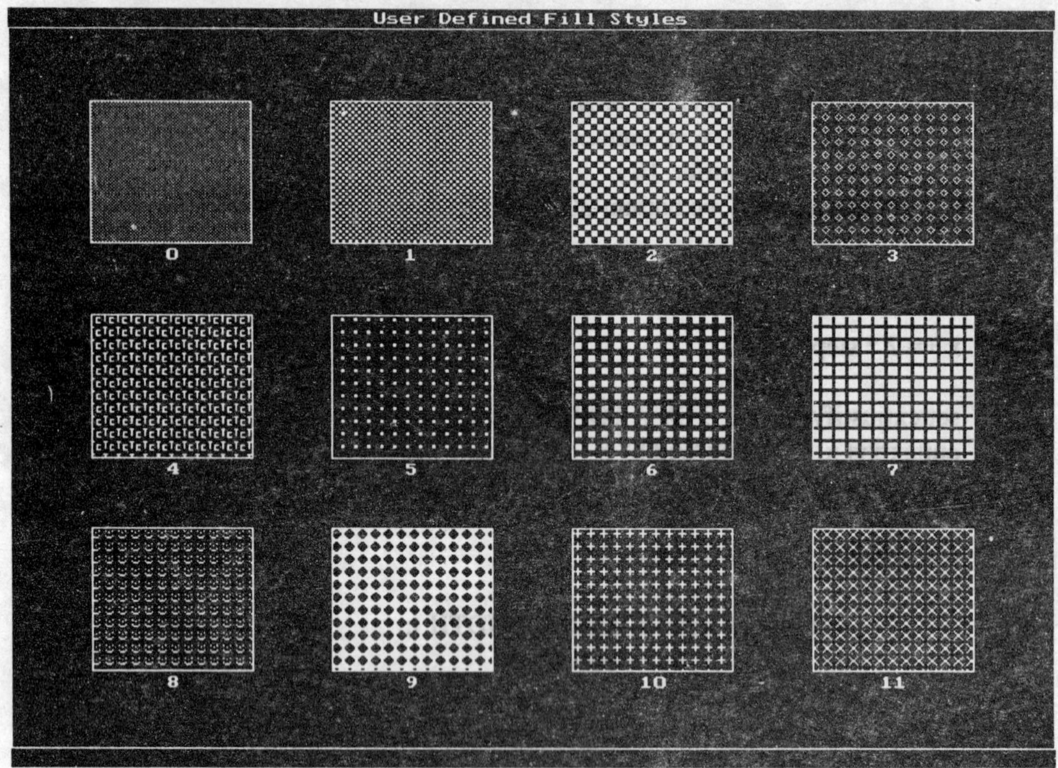

12.12 Second Output Screen of Graphics Demo function LineStyleDemo

```
/*                                                                    */
/*      CRTMODEDEMO: Demonstrates the effects of the change mode      */
/*      commands on the current screen.                               */
/*                                                                    */

void CRTModeDemo(void)
{
        struct viewporttype vp;
        int mode;

        MainWindow( "SetGraphMode / RestoreCRTMode demo" );
        getviewsettings( &vp );
        mode = getgraphmode();
        settextjustify( CENTER_TEXT, CENTER_TEXT );

        outtextxy( (vp.right-vp.left)/2, (vp.bottom-vp.top)/2,
```

```
                        "Now you are in graphics mode..." );
    StatusLine( "Press any key for text mode..." );
    getch();

    restorecrtmode();
    printf( "Now you are in text mode.\n\n" );
    printf( "Press any key to go back to graphics..." );
    getch();

    setgraphmode( mode );
    MainWindow( "SetGraphMode / RestoreCRTMode demo" );
    settextjustify( CENTER_TEXT, CENTER_TEXT );
    outtextxy( (vp.right-vp.left)/2, (vp.bottom-vp.top)/2,
                        "Back in Graphics Mode..." );

    getch();
}

/*                                                                */
/*    USERLINESTYLEDEMO: Displays line styles showing the user*/
/*    defined line style functions.                               */
/*                                                                */

void UserLineStyleDemo(void)
{
    int x, y, i, h, flag;
    unsigned int style;
    struct viewporttype vp;

    MainWindow( "User defined line styles" );

    getviewsettings( &vp );
    h = vp.bottom - vp.top;

    x = 4;
    y = 10;
    style = 0;
    i = 0;

    settextjustify( CENTER_TEXT, TOP_TEXT );
```

```
    flag = TRUE;                          /* Set the bits in this pass        */

    while( x < vp.right-2 )
    {           /* Draw lines across the screen */

        if( flag )                        /* If flag, set bits...             */
            style = style | (1 << i);     /*   Set the Ith bit in word        */
        else                              /* If no flag, clear bits           */
            style = style & !(0x8000 >> i);   /*   Clear the Ith bit in word */

        setlinestyle( USERBIT_LINE, style, NORM_WIDTH );
        line( x, y, x, h-y );             /* Draw the new line pattern        */

        x += 5;                           /* Move the X location of line      */
        i = ++i % 16;                     /* Advance to next bit pattern      */

        if ( style == 0xffff )
        {                            /* Are all bits set?                */
            flag = FALSE;   /*  begin removing bits                 */
            i = 0;                   /* Start with whole pattern         */
        }
        else
        {                                 /* Bits not all set...              */
            if( style == 0 )              /* Are all bits clear?              */
                flag = TRUE;      /*  begin setting bits              */
        }
    }

    settextjustify( LEFT_TEXT, TOP_TEXT );
    getch();
    closegraph();
    size(32,0);
    menubox ( 0, 0, 24, 79, 7, 10,memory ) ;
    display_box ( 1, 0, 21, 79, 10 ,memory) ;
    mainmenu();
    return ;
}
```

```
/*                                                                  */
/*      FILLSTYLEDEMO: Display the standard fill patterns available. */
/*                                                                  */

void FillStyleDemo(void)
{
        int h, w, style;
        int i, j, x, y;
        struct viewporttype vp;
        char buffer[40];

        MainWindow( "Pre-defined Fill Styles" );

        getviewsettings( &vp );
        w = 2 * ((vp.right  + 1) / 13);
        h = 2 * ((vp.bottom - 10) / 10);

        x = w / 2;
        y = h / 2;              /* Leave 1/2 blk margin */
        style = 0;

        for( j=0 ; j<3 ; ++j )
        {                       /* Three rows of boxes          */
                for( i=0 ; i<4 ; ++i )
                {               /* Four column of boxes */
                        setfillstyle(style, MaxColors-1); /* Set the fill style and WHITE  */
                        bar( x, y, x+w, y+h );            /* Draw the actual box           */
                        rectangle( x, y, x+w, y+h );      /* Outline the box               */
                        itoa( style, buffer, 10 );        /* Convert style 3 to ASCII      */
                        outtextxy( x+(w / 2), y+h+4, buffer );
                        ++style;                          /* Go on to next style #         */
                        x += (w / 2) * 3;                 /* Go to next column             */
                }                                         /* End of coulmn loop            */
                x = w / 2;                                /* Put base back to 1st column   */
                y += (h / 2) * 3;                         /* Advance to next row           */
        }                                                 /* End of Row loop               */

        settextjustify( LEFT_TEXT, TOP_TEXT );
        getch();
}
```

```
/*                                                              */
/*      FILLPATTERNDEMO: Demonstrate how to use the user definable */
/*      fill patterns.                                          */
/*                                                              */

void FillPatternDemo(void)
{
        int style;
        int h, w;
        int x, y, i, j;
        char buffer[40];
        struct viewporttype vp;
        static char patterns[][8] = {
                { 0xAA, 0x55, 0xAA, 0x55, 0xAA, 0x55, 0xAA, 0x55 },
                { 0x33, 0x33, 0xCC, 0xCC, 0x33, 0x33, 0xCC, 0xCC },
                { 0xF0, 0xF0, 0xF0, 0xF0, 0x0F, 0x0F, 0x0F, 0x0F },
                { 0x00, 0x10, 0x28, 0x44, 0x28, 0x10, 0x00, 0x00 },
                { 0x00, 0x70, 0x20, 0x27, 0x24, 0x24, 0x07, 0x00 },
                { 0x00, 0x00, 0x00, 0x18, 0x18, 0x00, 0x00, 0x00 },
                { 0x00, 0x00, 0x3C, 0x3C, 0x3C, 0x3C, 0x00, 0x00 },
                { 0x00, 0x7E, 0x7E, 0x7E, 0x7E, 0x7E, 0x7E, 0x00 },
                { 0x00, 0x00, 0x22, 0x08, 0x00, 0x22, 0x1C, 0x00 },
                { 0xFF, 0x7E, 0x3C, 0x18, 0x18, 0x3C, 0x7E, 0xFF },
                { 0x00, 0x10, 0x10, 0x7C, 0x10, 0x10, 0x00, 0x00 },
                { 0x00, 0x42, 0x24, 0x18, 0x18, 0x24, 0x42, 0x00 }
        };

        MainWindow( "User Defined Fill Styles" );

        getviewsettings( &vp );
        w = 2 * ((vp.right  + 1) / 13);
        h = 2 * ((vp.bottom - 10) / 10);

        x = w / 2;
        y = h / 2;      /* Leave 1/2 blk margin */
        style = 0;

        for( j=0 ; j<3 ; ++j )
        {               /* Three rows of boxes          */
                for( i=0 ; i<4 ; ++i )
```

```
        {           /* Four column of boxes */
            setfillpattern( &patterns[style][0], MaxColors-1 );
            bar( x, y, x+w, y+h );          /* Draw the actual box      */
            rectangle( x, y, x+w, y+h );    /* Outline the box          */
            itoa( style, buffer, 10 );      /* Convert style 3 to ASCII */
            outtextxy( x+(w / 2), y+h+4, buffer );
            ++style;                        /* Go on to next style # */
            x += (w / 2) * 3;               /* Go to next column        */
        }                                   /* End of coulmn loop       */
        x = w / 2;                          /* Put base back to 1st column */
        y += (h / 2) * 3;                   /* Advance to next row      */
    }                                       /* End of Row loop          */

    settextjustify( LEFT_TEXT, TOP_TEXT );

    getch();
    closegraph();
    size(32,0);
    menubox ( 0, 0, 24, 79, 7, 10,memory ) ;
    display_box ( 1, 0, 21, 79, 10 ,memory) ;
    mainmenu();
    return ;
}

/*                                                              */
/*  POLYDEMO: Displays a random pattern of polygons on the screen */
/*  until the user says enough.                                 */
/*                                                              */

void PaletteDemo(void)
{
    int i, j, x, y, color;
    struct viewporttype vp;
    int height, width;

    MainWindow( "Palette Demonstration" );
    StatusLine( "Press any key to continue, ESC to Abort" );

    getviewsettings( &vp );
    width = (vp.right - vp.left) / 15; /* get width of the box  */
```

```
    height = (vp.bottom - vp.top) / 10;        /* Get the height of the box      */

    x = y = 0;                                  /* Start in upper corner  */
    color = 1;                                  /* Begin at 1st color            */

    for ( j=0 ; j<10 ; ++j )
    {              /* For 10 rows of boxes */
        for( i=0 ; i<15 ; ++i )
        {             /* For 15 columns of boxes      */
            setfillstyle( SOLID_FILL, color++ );     /* Set the color of box */
            bar( x, y, x+width, y+height );          /* Draw the box           */
            x += width + 1;                          /* Advance to next col  */
            color = 1 + (color % (MaxColors - 2));   /* Set new color          */
        }                                       /* End of COLUMN loop     */
        x = 0;                                  /* Goto 1st column        */
        y += height + 1;                        /* Goto next row          */
    }                                           /* End of ROW loop        */

    while( !kbhit() )
    {                      /* Until user enters a key...  */
        setpalette( 1+random(MaxColors - 2), random( 65 ) );
    }

    setallpalette( &palette );

    getch();
}
```

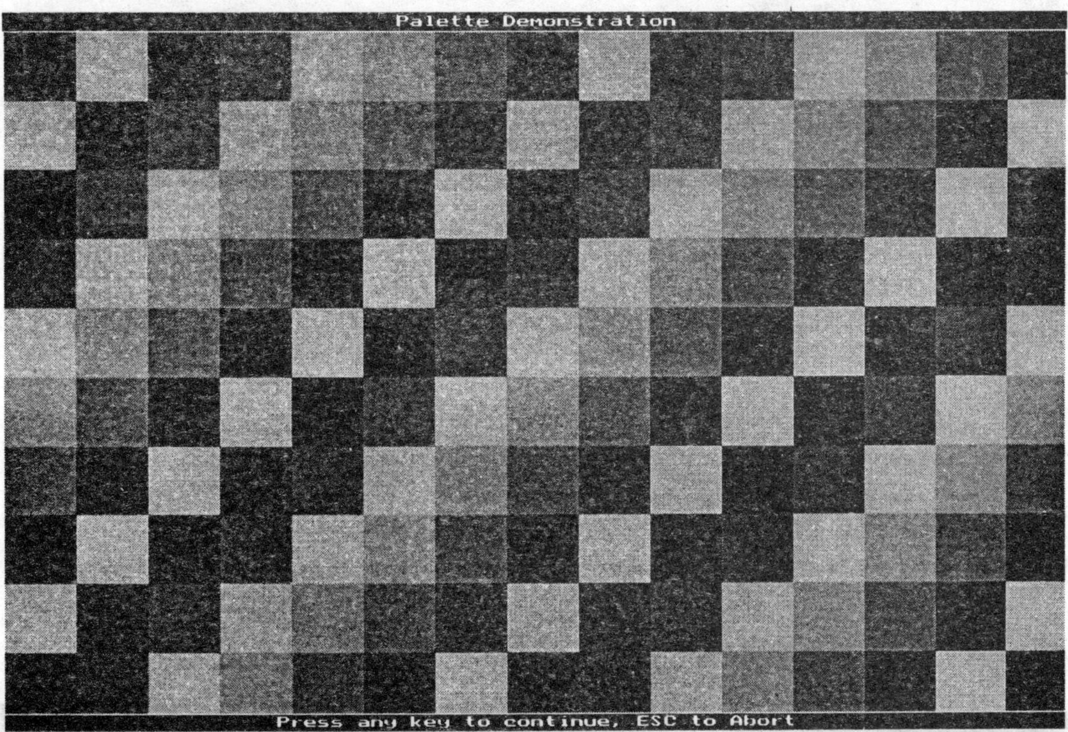

12.13 Output Screen of Graphics Demo function PaletteDemo

```
/*                                                                   */
/*      POLYDEMO: Displays a random pattern of polygons on the screen */
/*      until the user says enough.                                   */
/*                                                                   */
#define MaxPts        6              /* Maximum # of pts in polygon  */

void PolyDemo(void)
{
        struct PTS poly[ MaxPts ];           /* Space to hold datapoints   */
        int color;                           /* Current drawing color      */
        int i;
        MainWindow( "DrawPoly / FillPoly Demonstration" );
        StatusLine( "ESC Aborts - Press a Key to stop" );
        while( !kbhit() )
        {                      /* Repeat until a key is hit      */

                color = 1 + random( MaxColors-1 );    /* Get a random color # (no blk)*/
```

```
        setfillstyle( random(10), color );          /* Set a random line style          */
        setcolor( color );                          /* Set the desired color  */
        for( i=0 ; i<(MaxPts-1) ; i++ )
        {       /* Determine a random polygon  */
                poly[i].x = random( MaxX );         /* Set the x coord of point         */
                poly[i].y = random( MaxY );         /* Set the y coord of point         */
        }
        poly[i].x = poly[0].x;                      /* last point = first point  */
        poly[i].y = poly[1].y;
        fillpoly( MaxPts, (int far *)poly );        /* Draw the actual polygon          */
    }                                               /* End of WHILE not KBHIT   */
    getch();
    closegraph();
    size(32,0);
    menubox ( 0, 0, 24, 79, 7, 10,memory ) ;
    display_box ( 1, 0, 21, 79, 10 ,memory) ;
    mainmenu();
    return ;
}
```

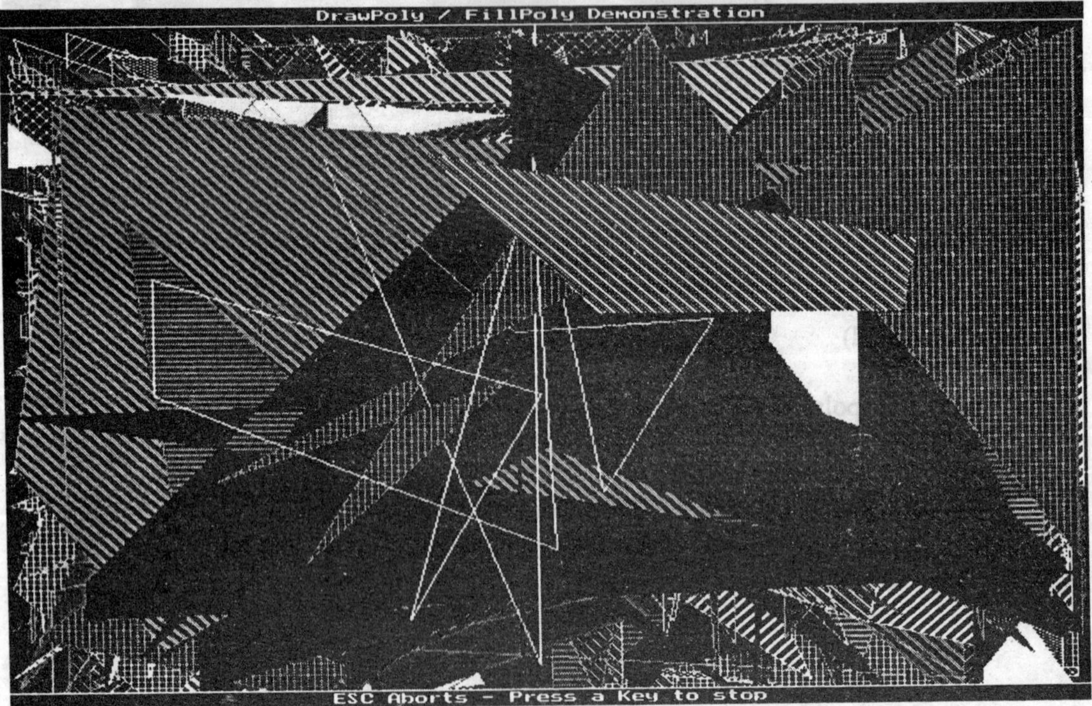

12.14 Output Screen of Graphics Demo function PaletteDemo

```
/*                                                                    */
/*      SAYGOODBYE: Gives a closing screen to the user before leaving. */
/*                                                                    */

void SayGoodbye(void)
{
        struct viewporttype viewinfo;    /* Structure to read viewport   */
        int h, w;

        MainWindow( "== Finale ==" );

        getviewsettings( &viewinfo );    /* Read viewport settings       */
        changetextstyle( TRIPLEX_FONT, HORIZ_DIR, 4 );
        settextjustify( CENTER_TEXT, CENTER_TEXT );

        h = viewinfo.bottom - viewinfo.top;
        w = viewinfo.right  - viewinfo.left;
        outtextxy( w/2, h/2, "That's all, folks!" );

        StatusLine( "Press any key to EXIT" );
        getch();

        cleardevice();                   /* Clear the graphics screen    */

}

/*                                                                    */
/*      MAINWINDOW: Establishes the main window for the demo and set  */
/*      a viewport for the demo code.                                 */
/*                                                                    */

void MainWindow( char *header )
{
        int height;

        cleardevice();                          /* Clear graphics screen*/
        setcolor( MaxColors - 1 );              /* Set current color to white   */
        setviewport( 0, 0, MaxX, MaxY, 1 );     /* Open port to full screen     */

        height = textheight( "H" );      /* Get basic text height        */
```

```
        changetextstyle( DEFAULT_FONT, HORIZ_DIR, 1 );
        settextjustify( CENTER_TEXT, TOP_TEXT );
        outtextxy( MaxX/2, 2, header );
        setviewport( 0, height+4, MaxX, MaxY-(height+4), 1 );
        DrawBorder();
        setviewport( 1, height+5, MaxX-1, MaxY-(height+5), 1 );
}

/*                                                                  */
/*      STATUSLINE: Displays a status line at the bottom of the screen.*/
/*                                                                  */
void StatusLine( char *msg )
{
        int height;

        setviewport( 0, 0, MaxX, MaxY, 1 );        /* Open port to full screen    */
        setcolor( MaxColors - 1 );                 /* Set current color to white  */

        changetextstyle( DEFAULT_FONT, HORIZ_DIR, 1 );
        settextjustify( CENTER_TEXT, TOP_TEXT );
        setlinestyle( SOLID_LINE, 0, NORM_WIDTH );
        setfillstyle( EMPTY_FILL, 0 );

        height = textheight( "H" );          /* Detemine current height      */
        bar( 0, MaxY-(height+4), MaxX, MaxY );
        rectangle( 0, MaxY-(height+4), MaxX, MaxY );
        outtextxy( MaxX/2, MaxY-(height+2), msg );
        setviewport( 1, height+5, MaxX-1, MaxY-(height+5), 1 );

}

/*                                                              */
/*      DRAWBORDER: Draws a solid single line around the current */
/*      viewport.                                               */
/*                                                              */

void DrawBorder(void)
{
        struct viewporttype vp;
```

```
        setcolor( MaxColors - 1 );                  /* Set current color to white      */

        setlinestyle( SOLID_LINE, 0, NORM_WIDTH );

        getviewsettings( &vp );
        rectangle( 0, 0, vp.right-vp.left, vp.bottom-vp.top );

}

/*                                                                          */
/*      CHANGETEXTSTYLE: similar to settextstyle, but checks for           */
/*      errors that might occur while loading the font file.                */
/*                                                                          */

void changetextstyle(int font, int direction, int charsize)
{
        int ErrorCode;

        graphresult();                              /* clear error code              */
        settextstyle(font, direction, charsize);
        ErrorCode = graphresult();                  /* check result          */
        if( ErrorCode != grOk )
        {               /* if error occured            */
            closegraph();
            printf(" Graphics System Error: %s\n", grapherrormsg( ErrorCode ) );
            exit( 1 );
        }
}
```

Utility Services

13

In this project the main menu is divided into two main services: first one is the directory services and the second one is the file services. The item from the main menu can be selected by using the enter key or by pressing the hotkey which is represented by the bold character. The getoutput() function manages the movement of the cursor and selection of the menu item. This function also uses getkey() function to find which key has been pressed by the user. The Showmenu() function is used to display the menu in box drawn by menubox() available in the "intro.h".

The mainmenu() function prepares the screen for popping up a menu.

The pop_menu() pops up a menu on the existing screen contents.

The dserver() and fserver() functions manage the directory services and file services menu respectively

In this project we use the library <dos.h> which defines various constants and gives declarations needed for DOS and 8086-specific calls. All the DOS utility is provided with the help of <dos.h> header file. The union REFGS available in the <dos.h> is used to pass information to and from the functions int86(). The declaration for the REGS is :

```
union REGS {
```

```
    struct  WORDREGS  x;
    struct  BYTEREGS  h;
};
```

The BYTEREGS and WORDREGS are Structures for storing byte and word registers.

```
struct BYTEREGS  {
    unsigned char  al, ah, bl, bh;
    unsigned char  cl, ch, dl, dh;
};

struct WORDREGS  {
    unsigned int  ax, bx, cx, dx;
    unsigned int  si, di, cflag, flags;
};
```

In the above declaration the variable ah stores the DOS utility number and the dx stores the base address of the file or directory. The cflag is used to check the error and if the value of oregs.x.cflag = 0 then the desired operation is done successfully . The variables ax,bx, cx etc.. denote the different types of errors which may occur during the different functions. The user just pass the file or directory name along with the DOS utility number and the int86() function process that utility according the DOS utility number.

This utility provides the maintenance of files and directories. In the directory services the following operations are performed as :

Make directory
Change directory
Delete directory
List directory
Return to main menu

and in the file management as:

Compress file
Decompress file
Get file attributes
Set file attributes
Encrypt file
Decrypt file
Type file
Delete file
Return to main menu.

While managing the menus, all the menu prompts displays appropriate messages for the menu operations and descriptions at the time of operations.

The menu as:

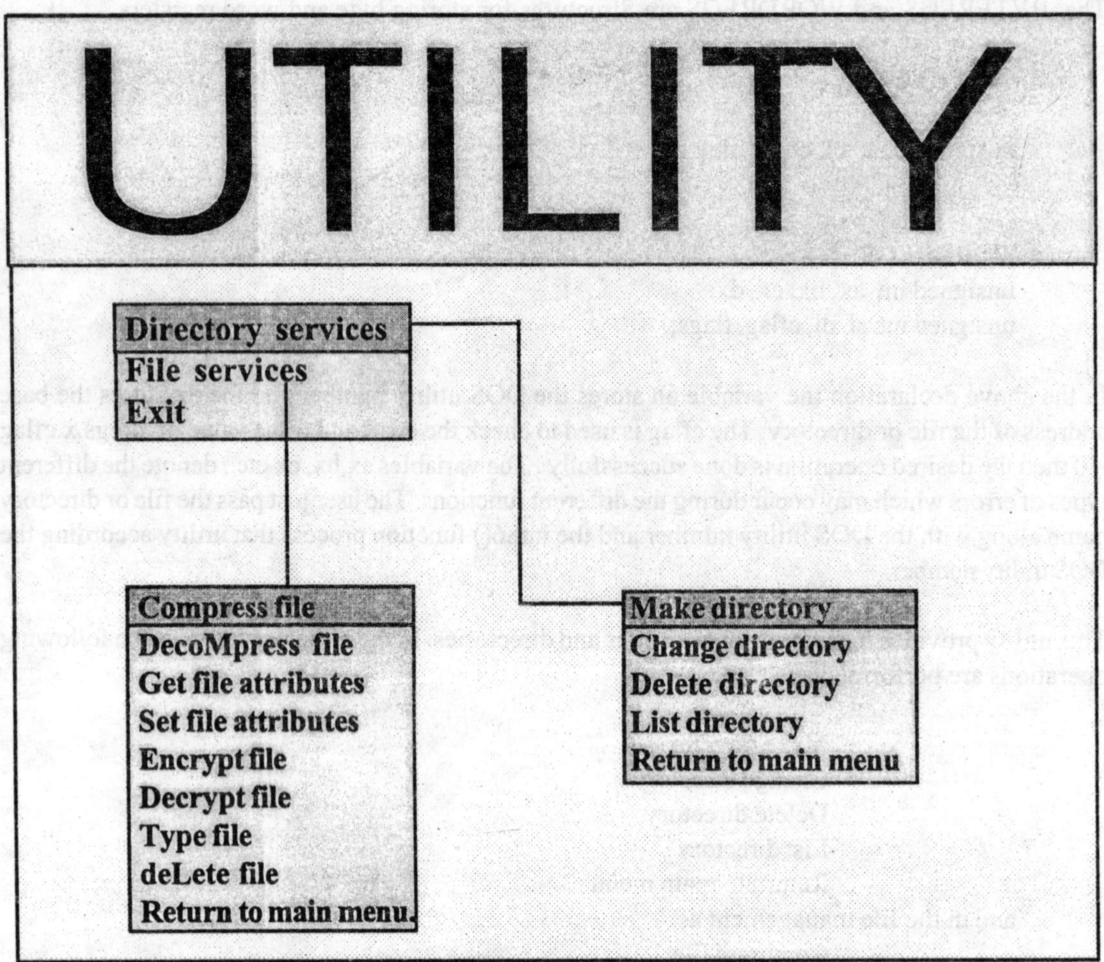

Figure 13.1 Menu description of utility program

Also in this utility, it includes the header file (library) intro.h having the following functions as:

writech().... This function writes the character into VDU memory.

writeline().... This function writes an entire string into VDU memory.

Store_video....	This function reads the character from the rectangular part of the screen and stores them into the RAM
Restore_video....	This reads the character from the RAM and places on the VDU
Display_box()....	This function displays the double lined box on the main menu and others menus.
Menu_box()....	This function displays the box with different shadows as the user required and also without shadows.
Size()....	This function is used to change the size of the cursor.

Source code of intro.h

```
/* writes a character and its attribute in VDU memory*/
writech ( int r, int c, char ch, int attb,char far *memory )
{
        char far *v ;

        /* calculate address in VDU memory corresponding to row r and column c*/
        v = memory + r * 160 + c * 2 ;  x

        *v = ch ;           /* store ascii value of character*/
        v++ ;
        *v = attb ;         /* store attribute of character */
}

/* writes a string into VDU memory in the desired attribute */
writeline ( char *s, int r, int c, int attb,char far *memory )
{
        while ( *s != '\0' )
        {
        /* if next character is hot key, write it in different attribute, otherwise in normal attribute*/

                if ( *s == '^' )
                {
                        s++ ;
                        writech ( r, c, *s, 77,memory ) ;
                }
                else
                        writech ( r, c, *s, attb,memory ) ;

                s++ ;
                c++ ;
        }
}
/* draws double-lined box */
display_box ( int sr, int sc, int er, int ec, int attribute,char far *memory )
{
        int i ;

        /* draw horizontal lines */
```

```
        for ( i = sc + 1 ; i < ec ; i++ )
        {
                writech ( sr, i, 205, attribute,memory ) ;
                writech ( er, i, 205, attribute,memory ) ;
        }

        /* draw vertical lines */
        for ( i = sr + 1 ; i < er ; i++ )
        {
                writech ( i, sc, 186, attribute,memory ) ;
                writech ( i, ec, 186, attribute,memory ) ;
        }

        /* draw four corners */
        writech ( sr, sc, 201, attribute,memory ) ;
        writech ( sr, ec, 187, attribute,memory ) ;
        writech ( er, sc, 200, attribute,memory ) ;
        writech ( er, ec, 188, attribute,memory ) ;
}

/* draws filled box with or without shadow */
menubox ( int sr, int sc, int er, int ec, char filler, char shadow,char far *memory )
{
        int i, j ;

        /* draw filled box */
        for ( i = sr ; i < er ; i++ )
        {
                for ( j = sc ; j < ( ec - 1 ) ; j++ )
                        writech ( i, j, ' ', filler,memory ) ;
        }

        /* if no shadow is required for the filled box */
        if ( shadow == 0 )
        {
                for ( i = sr ; i <= er ; i++ )
                {
                        writech ( i, ec, ' ', filler,memory ) ;
                        writech ( i, ( ec - 1 ), ' ', filler,memory ) ;
                }
```

```
            for ( j = sc ; j <= ec ; j++ )
                writech ( er, j, ' ', filler,memory ) ;
        }
        else
        {
            /* draw vertical and horizontal shadow */

            for ( i = sr + 1 ; i <= er ; i++ )
            {
                writech ( i, ec, ' ', shadow,memory ) ;
                writech ( i, ( ec - 1 ), ' ', shadow,memory ) ;
            }

            for ( j = sc + 2 ; j <= ec ; j++ )
                writech ( er, j, ' ', shadow,memory ) ;
        }
}

/* saves screen contents into allocated memory in RAM */
store_video ( int sr, int sc, int er, int ec, char *buffer,char far *memory )
{
        char far *vid ;
        int i, j ;

        for ( i = sr ; i <= er ; i++ )
        {
            for ( j = sc ; j <= ec ; j++ )
            {
                vid = memory + i * 160 + j * 2 ; /* calculate address */
                *buffer = *vid ; /* store character */
                vid++ ;
                buffer++ ;
                *buffer = *vid ; /* store attribute */
                buffer++ ;
            }
        }
}
```

```
/* restores screen contents from allocated memory in RAM */
restore_video ( int sr, int sc, int er, int ec, char *buffer,char far *memory )
{
	char far *vid ;
	int i, j ;

	for ( i = sr ; i <= er ; i++ )
	{
		for ( j = sc ; j <= ec ; j++ )
		{
			vid = memory + i * 160 + j * 2 ; /* calculate address */
			*vid = *buffer ; /* restore character */
			vid++ ;
			buffer++ ;
			*vid = *buffer ; /* restore attribute */
			buffer++ ;
		}
	}
}

/*displays or hides the cursor*/
size ( int ssl, int esl )
{
	union REGS i, o ;

	i.h.ah = 1 ; /* service number*/
	i.h.ch = ssl ; /* starting scan line*/
	i.h.cl = esl ; /* ending scan line*/
	i.h.bh = 0 ; /* video page numbe*/

	/* issue interrupt for changing the size of the cursor*/
	int86 ( 16, &i, &o ) ;
}

/* displays the logo on the screen */
logo(char far *memory)
{
	int i, j ;
	setbkcolor(10);
	setcolor(5);
```

```
settextstyle(7,HORIZ_DIR,10);
outtextxy(60,100,"UTILITY");
settextstyle(7,HORIZ_DIR,5);
outtextxy(250,300,"By : ");
outtextxy(300,400,"Reeta Sahoo");
getch() ;
}
```

Source code of UTIL.C

```
#include<stdio.h>
# include "stdio.h"
# include "process.h"
# include "string.h"
# include "stdlib.h"
# include "ctype.h"
# include "conio.h"
# include "fcntl.h"
# include "types.h"
# include "stat.h"
# include "dir.h"
# include "dos.h"
# include "graphics.h"
# include "d:\turboc3\cproject\intro.h"

// Function to delete a file
delete_file(char far *memory);

// Function to display the current attribute of files
get_attb(char far *memory) ;

// Sets new attributes to a file
set_attb(char far *memory);

file_attb(char far *memory) ;
encrypt_file(char far *memory) ;
decrypt_file(char far *memory) ;
compress_file(char far *memory) ;
decompress_file(char far *memory) ;
type_file(char far *memory) ;
writeattr ( int attb, int col ,char far *memory);

// Delete the desired file
delete_file(char far *memory)
{
        union REGS iregs, oregs ;
        int area ;
```

```
char fname[20], *m ;

area = ( 20 - 5 + 1 ) * ( 70 - 5 + 1 ) * 2 ;
m = ((char *) malloc ( area )) ;
if ( m == NULL )
{
        writeline ( "        Press any key to continue...            ", 22, 14, 12,memory ) ;
        getch() ;

        writeline ("        Select using hotkey or Enter            ", 22, 14, 12,memory ) ;
        return 0;
}

store_video ( 5, 5, 20, 70, m ,memory) ;
menubox ( 8, 5, 13, 60, 277, 1,memory ) ;

writeline ( "           File delete service              ", 22, 14, 112,memory ) ;

writeline ( "Enter name of file to be deleted:", 9, 8, 12,memory ) ;
size ( 6, 7 ) ;
gotoxy ( 43, 10 ) ;
gets ( fname ) ;
size ( 32, 0 ) ;

/* issue interrupt for deleting file */
iregs.h.ah = 65 ;                          /* dos service number */
iregs.x.dx = ( unsigned int ) fname ;      /* store base address */
intdos ( &iregs, &oregs ) ;

/* check if successful in deleting file */
if ( oregs.x.cflag == 0 )
        writeline ( "File was successfully deleted!", 11, 8, 12,memory ) ;
else
{
        switch ( oregs.x.ax )
        {
                        case 2 :
                        writeline ( "File not found!", 11, 8, 12,memory ) ;
                        break ;
```

```
                case 3 :
                        writeline ( "Invalid path!", 11, 8, 12,memory ) ;
                        break ;

                case 5 :
                        writeline ( "Access denied!", 11, 8, 12,memory ) ;
                        break ;

                case 0x11 :
                        writeline ( "Invalid drive name!",11, 8,12 ,memory) ;
                        break ;

                default :
                        writeline ( "Improper request!", 11, 8, 12 ,memory) ;
        }
    }

    writeline ( "          Press Enter to return              ", 22, 14, 12,memory ) ;
    getch() ;
    writeline ( "       Select using hotkey or Enter           ", 22, 14, 12 ,memory) ;
    restore_video ( 5, 5, 20. 70, m,memory ) ;
    free ( m ) ;
}

/* displays the current attributes of a file */
get_attb(char far *memory)
{
    union REGS iregs, oregs ;
    int a, area ;
    char fname[20], *m ;

    area = ( 20 - 5 + 1 ) * ( 70 - 5 + 1 ) * 2 ;
    m =((char *) malloc ( area ) );
    if ( m == NULL )
    {
        writeline ("     Press any key to continue...             ", 22, 14, 12,memory ) ;
        getch() ;

        writeline ("       Select using hotkey or Enter        ", 22, 14, 12,memory ) ;
        return( 0);
```

```
	}

	store_video ( 5, 5, 20, 70, m,memory ) ;
	menubox ( 8, 5, 18, 60, 227, 1,memory ) ;

	writeline ( "        Get file attribute service        ", 22, 14, 12 ,memory) ;

	writeline ( "Enter name of file:", 9, 8, 12 ,memory) ;
	size ( 6, 7 ) ;
	gotoxy ( 29, 10 ) ;
	gets ( fname ) ;
	size ( 32, 0 ) ;

	iregs.h.ah = 67 ;	/* dos service number */
	iregs.h.al = 0 ;	/* 0 - get attributes, 1 - set attributes */
	iregs.x.dx = ( unsigned int ) fname ;	/* store base address */
	intdos ( &iregs, &oregs ) ;	/* issue interrupt */

	/* if successful display attributes, else display error message */
	if ( oregs.x.cflag == 0 )
	{
		writeline ( "ATTRIBUTES", 11, 27, 12 ,memory) ;
		writeline ( "ÄÄÄÄÄÄÄÄÄÄ", 12, 27, 12 ,memory) ;
		a = oregs.x.cx ;
		writeattr ( a, 24,memory ) ;
	}
	else
	{
		switch ( oregs.x.ax )
		{
			case 2 :
				writeline ( "File not found!", 11, 8, 12 ,memory) ;
				break ;

			case 3 :
				writeline ( "Invalid path!", 11, 8, 12,memory ) ;
				break ;

			case 5 :
				writeline ( "Access denied!", 11, 8, 12,memory ) ;
```

```
                break ;

            case 0x11 :
                writeline ( "Invalid drive name!", 11, 8, 12,memory ) ;
                break ;

            default :
                writeline ( "Improper request!", 11, 8, 12,memory ) ;
        }
    }

    writeline ( "        Press Enter to return               ", 22, 14, 12,memory ) ;
    getch() ;

    writeline ("      Select using hotkey or Enter            ", 22, 14, 12,memory ) ;
    restore_video ( 5, 5, 20, 70, m,memory ) ;
    free ( m ) ;
}

/* displays attributes of the file */
writeattr ( int attb, int col,char far *memory )
{
    writeline ( "Read only :", 13, col, 12 ,memory) ;
    if ( ( attb & 1 ) == 0 )
        writeline ( "OFF", 13, ( col + 12 ), 12,memory ) ;
    else
        writeline ( "ON", 13, ( col + 12 ), 12 ,memory) ;

    writeline ( "Hidden    :", 14, col, 12,memory ) ;
    if ( ( attb & 2 ) == 0 )
        writeline ( "OFF", 14, ( col + 12 ), 12,memory ) ;
    else
        writeline ( "ON", 14, ( col + 12 ), 12 ,memory) ;

    writeline ( "System    :", 15, col, 12 ,memory) ;
    if ( ( attb & 4 ) == 0 )
        writeline ( "OFF", 15, ( col + 12 ), 12,memory ) ;
    else
        writeline ( "ON", 15, ( col + 12 ), 12,memory ) ;
```

```
        writeline ( "Archive  :", 16, col, 12,memory ) ;
        if ( ( attb & 32 ) == 0 )
                writeline ( "OFF", 16, ( col + 12 ),12,memory ) ;
        else
                writeline ( "ON", 16, ( col + 12 ), 12 ,memory) ;
}

/* sets new attributes for a file */
set_attb(char far *memory)
{
        union REGS iregs, oregs ;
        int old, new1, area ;
        char fname[20], *m, ch ;

        area = ( 20 - 5 + 1 ) * ( 70 - 5 + 1 ) * 2 ;
        m = ((char *) malloc ( area )) ;
        if ( m == NULL )
        {
                writeline ("      press any key to continue    ", 22, 14, 12,memory ) ;
                getch() ;

                writeline ( "         Select using hotkey or Enter           ", 22, 14, 12,memory ) ;
                return 0;
        }

        store_video ( 5, 5, 20, 70, m ,memory) ;
        menubox ( 8, 5, 18, 60, 277, 1,memory ) ;

        writeline ( "          Set file attribute service          ", 22, 14, 12 ,memory) ;

        writeline ( "Enter name of file:", 9, 8, 12,memory ) ;
        size ( 6, 7 ) ;
        gotoxy ( 29, 10 ) ;
        gets ( fname ) ;
        size ( 32, 0 ) ;

        iregs.h.ah = 67 ;              /* dos service number */
        iregs.h.al = 0 ;               /* 0 - get attributes, 1 - set attributes */
        iregs.x.dx = ( unsigned int ) fname ;      /* base address of filename */
        intdos ( &iregs, &oregs ) ;                /* issue interrupt */
```

```
/* if successful display attributes, else display error message */
if ( oregs.x.cflag == 0 )
{
        old = new1 = oregs.x.cx ;
        writeline ( "Existing Attributes",11, 8, 12,memory ) ;
        writeline ( "——————————————", 12, 8, 12,memory ) ;
         writeattr ( old, 8 ,memory) ; /* display existing attributes */
}
else
{
        switch ( oregs.x.ax )
        {
                case 2 :
                        writeline ( "File not found!", 11, 8,12 ,memory) ;
                        break ;

                case 3 :
                        writeline ( "Invalid path!", 11, 8, 12,memory ) ;
                        break ;

                case 5 :
                        writeline ( "Access denied!", 11, 8, 12,memory ) ;
                        break ;

                case 0x11 :
                        writeline ( "Invalid drive name!",11, 8, 12 ,memory) ;
                        break ;

                default :
                        writeline ( "Improper request!", 11, 8, 12,memory ) ;
        }

        writeline ( "          Press Enter to return          ", 22, 14, 12,memory ) ;
        getch() ;

        restore_video ( 5, 5, 20, 70, m,memory) ;
        free ( m ) ;
        rcturn 0;
}
```

```
/* collect new attributes or keep old attributes */
writeline ( "Change (Y/N):", 13, 30, 12,memory ) ;
size ( 6, 7 ) ;
gotoxy ( 45, 14 ) ;
fflush ( stdin ) ;              /* flush keyboard buffer */
ch = getch() ;
ch = toupper ( ch ) ;
writech ( 13, 44, ch, 112,memory ) ;

if ( ch == 'Y' )
        new1 = ( new1 ^ 1 ) ;

writeline ( "Change (Y/N):", 14, 30, 12,memory ) ;
gotoxy ( 45, 15 ) ;
fflush ( stdin ) ;
ch = toupper ( getch() ) ;
writech ( 14, 44, ch, 112 ,memory) ;

if ( ch == 'Y' )
        new1 = ( new1 ^ 2 ) ;

writeline ( "Change (Y/N):", 15, 30, 12,memory ) ;
gotoxy ( 45, 16 ) ;
fflush ( stdin ) ;
ch = toupper ( getch() ) ;
writech ( 15, 44, ch, 112,memory ) ;

if ( ch == 'Y' )
        new1 = ( new1 ^ 4 ) ;

writeline ( "Change (Y/N):", 16, 30, 12,memory ) ;
gotoxy ( 45, 17 ) ;
fflush ( stdin ) ;
ch = toupper ( getch() ) ;
writech ( 16, 44, ch, 112,memory ) ;

size ( 32, 0 ) ;

if ( ch == 'Y' )
        new1 = ( new1 ^ 32 ) ;
```

```
    /* issue interrupt to set new file attributes */
    iregs.h.ah = 67 ;
    iregs.h.al = 1 ;
    iregs.x.cx = new1 ;
    iregs.x.dx = ( unsigned int ) fname ;
    intdos ( &iregs, &oregs ) ;

    menubox ( 8, 5, 18, 60, 12, 66,memory ) ;
    writeline ( "File name:", 9, 8, 12,memory ) ;
    writeline ( fname, 10, 19, 12 ,memory) ;

    /* if successful display old and new attributes, else display error message */
    if ( oregs.x.cflag == 0 )
    {
        writeline ( "Old Attributes", 11, 8, 12,memory ) ;
        writeline ( "————————", 12, 8, 12,memory ) ;
        writeattr ( old, 8 ,memory) ;
        writeline ( "New Attributes", 11, 40, 12,memory ) ;
        writeline ( "————————", 12, 40, 12 ,memory) ;
        writeattr ( new1, 40 ,memory) ;
    }
    else
        writeline ( "Error - New attributes not set!", 13, 8, 12,memory ) ;

    writeline ( "         Press Enter to return            ", 22, 14, 12 ,memory) ;
    getch() ;

    writeline (" Select using hotkey or Enter         ", 22, 14, 12,memory ) ;
    restore_video ( 5, 5, 20, 70, m,memory ) ;
    free ( m ) ;
}

// Encrypt the desired file
encrypt_file(char far *memory)
{
    char s_file[20], t_file[20], *m, ch ;
    FILE *fp1 , *fp2 ;
    int area, flag ;

    area = ( 20 - 5 + 1 ) * ( 70 - 5 + 1 ) * 2 ;
```

```
m =((char *) malloc ( area )) ;
if ( m == NULL )
{
        writeline ( "   Press any key to continue            ", 22, 14, 12,memory ) ;
        getch() ;

        writeline ( "       Select using hotkey or Enter           ", 22, 14, 12,memory ) ;
        return 0;
}

store_video ( 5, 5, 20, 70, m ,memory) ;
menubox ( 6, 5, 13, 60, 227, 1,memory ) ;

writeline ( "           File coding service              ", 22, 14, 12 ,memory) ;

writeline ( "Enter source file name:", 7, 8, 12,memory ) ;
size ( 6, 7 ) ;
gotoxy ( 33, 8 ) ;
fflush ( stdin ) ;
gets ( s_file ) ;
size ( 32, 0 ) ;

/* open source file */
fp1 = fopen ( s_file, "r" ) ;
if ( fp1 == NULL )
{
        writeline ( "Unable to open source file!", 9, 8, 12,memory ) ;
        writeline ( "       Press Enter to return", 22, 14, 12,memory ) ;
        getch() ;

        writeline ( "       Select using hotkey or Enter           ", 22, 14, 12,memory ) ;
        restore_video ( 5, 5, 20, 70, m .memory) ;
        free ( m ) ;
        return 0;
}

writeline ( "Enter target file name:", 9, 8, 12,memory ) ;
size ( 6, 7 ) ;
gotoxy ( 33, 10 ) ;
gets ( t_file ) ;
```

```
size ( 32, 0 ) ;

/* open target file */
fp2 = fopen ( t_file, "w" ) ;
if ( fp2 == NULL )
{
        writeline ( "Unable to open target file!", 11, 8, 12,memory ) ;
        writeline ( "        Press Enter to return            ", 22, 14, 12,memory ) ;
        getch() ;

        fclose ( fp1 ) ;
        writeline ( "      Select using hotkey or Enter         ", 22, 14, 12,memory ) ;
        restore_video ( 5, 5, 20, 70, m ,memory) ;
        free ( m ) ;
        return 0;
}

/* read each character, offset it by 127, write to target file */
while ( ( ch = getc ( fp1 ) ) != EOF )
{
        if ( ch == '\n' )
                flag = putc ( '\n', fp2 ) ;
        else
                flag = putc ( ( ch + 127 ), fp2 ) ;

        /* if error in writing */
        if ( flag == EOF )
                break ;
}

if ( flag == EOF )
        writeline ( "Unable to encrypt file!", 11, 8, 12,memory ) ;
else
        writeline ( "File is successfully encrypted!", 11, 8, 12,memory ) ;

writeline( "        Press Enter to return            ", 22, 14, 12,memory ) ;
getch() ;

fclose ( fp1 ) ;
fclose ( fp2 ) ;
```

```
        writeline ("          Select using hotkey or Enter              ", 22, 14, 12,memory ) ;
        restore_video ( 5, 5, 20, 70, m ,memory) ;
        free ( m ) ;
}

// Decrypt the desired file
decrypt_file(char far *memory)
{
        char s_file[20], t_file[20], *m, ch ;
        FILE *fp1, *fp2 ;
        int area, flag ;

        area = ( 20 - 5 + 1 ) * ( 70 - 5 + 1 ) * 2 ;
        m =((char *) malloc ( area ) );
        if ( m == NULL )
        {
                writeline ( "          Press any key to continue        ", 22, 14, 12,memory ) ;
                getch() ;

                writeline ( "         Select using hotkey or Enter            ", 22, 14, 12,memory ) ;
                return 0;
        }

        store_video ( 5, 5, 20, 70, m,memory ) ;
        menubox ( 6, 5, 13, 60, 227, 1 ,memory) ;

        writeline ( "           File decode service              ", 22, 14, 112,memory ) ;

        writeline ( "Enter source file name:", 7, 8, 12,memory ) ;
        size ( 6, 7 ) ;
        gotoxy ( 33, 8 ) ;
        gets ( s_file ) ;
        size ( 32, 0 ) ;

        /* open source file */
        fp1 = fopen ( s_file, "r" ) ;
        if ( fp1 == NULL )
        {
                writeline ( "Unable to open source file!", 9, 8, 12,memory ) ;
                writeline ( "          Press Enter to return               ", 22, 14, 12 ,memory) ;
```

```
        getch() ;
        writeline ( "      Select using hotkey or Enter        ", 22, 14, 12 ,memory) ;
        restore_video ( 5, 5, 20, 70, m ,memory) ;
        free ( m ) ;
        return 0;
}

writeline ( "Enter target file name:", 9, 8, 12,memory ) ;
size ( 6, 7 ) ;
gotoxy ( 33, 10 ) ;
gets ( t_file ) ;
size ( 32, 0 ) ;

/* open target file */
fp2 = fopen ( t_file, "w" ) ;
if ( fp2 == NULL )
{
        writeline ( "Unable to open target file!", 11, 8, 12,memory ) ;
        writeline ( "           Press Enter to return          ", 22, 14, 12,memory ) ;
        getch() ;

        fclose ( fp1 ) ;
        writeline ( "      Select using hotkey or Enter        ", 22, 14, 12 ,memory) ;
        restore_video ( 5, 5, 20, 70, m ,memory) ;
        free ( m ) ;
        return 0;
}

/* read each character, reduce by offset, write to target file */
while ( ( ch = getc ( fp1 ) ) != EOF )
{
        if ( ch == '\n' )
                flag = putc ( '\n', fp2 ) ;
        else
                flag = putc ( ( ch - 127 ), fp2 ) ;

        /* if error in writing */
        if ( flag == EOF )
                break ;
}
```

```
        if ( flag == EOF )
                writeline ( "Unable to decrypt file!", 11, 8, 12,memory ) ;
        else
                writeline ( "File successfully decrypted!", 11, 8, 12,memory ) ;

        writeline ( "          Press Enter to return          ", 22, 14, 12 ,memory) ;
        getch() ;

        fclose ( fp1 ) ;
        fclose ( fp2 ) ;
        writeline ( "        Select using hotkey or Enter          ", 22, 14, 12 ,memory) ;
        restore_video ( 5, 5, 20, 70, m ,memory) ;
        free ( m ) ;
}

// Compress the desired file
compress_file(char far *memory)
{
        char *m, s_file[20], t_file[20] ;
        FILE *fp1, *fp2 ;
        int area, count, ch, flag ;

        area = ( 12 - 5 + 1 ) * ( 60 - 5 + 1 ) * 2 ;
        m =((char *) malloc ( area )) ;
        if ( m == NULL )
        {
                writeline ( "     press any key to continue       ", 22, 14, 12,memory ) ;
                getch() ;

                writeline ("          Select using hotkey or Enter    ", 22, 14, 12 ,memory) ;
                return 0;
        }

        store_video ( 5, 5, 12, 60, m,memory ) ;
        menubox ( 5, 5, 12, 60, 227, 1 ,memory) ;

        writeline ( "          File compress service          ", 22, 14, 112 ,memory) ;

        writeline ( "Enter source file name:", 6, 8, 12 ,memory) ;
        size ( 6, 7 ) ;
```

```
gotoxy ( 33, 7 ) ;
gets ( s_file ) ;
size ( 32, 0 ) ;

/* open source file */
fp1 = fopen ( s_file, "r" ) ;
if ( fp1 == NULL )
{
        writeline ( "Unable to open source file!", 8, 8, 12 ,memory) ;
        writeline ( "            Press Enter to return              ", 22, 14, 12,memory ) ;
        getch() ;

        writeline ("          Select using hotkey or Enter          ", 22, 14, 12 ,memory) ;
        restore_video ( 5, 5, 12, 60, m ,memory) ;
        free ( m ) ;
        return 0;
}

writeline ( "Enter target file name:", 8, 8, 12,memory ) ;
size ( 6, 7 ) ;
gotoxy ( 33, 9 ) ;
gets ( t_file ) ;
size ( 32, 0 ) ;

/* open target file */
fp2 = fopen ( t_filc, "w") ;
if ( fp2 == NULL )
{
        writeline ( "Unable to open target file!", 10, 8, 12,memory ) ;
        writeline ( "            Press Enter to return              ", 22, 14, 12 ,memory) ;
        getch() ;

        fclose ( fp1 ) ;
        writeline ("          Select using hotkey or Enter          ", 22, 14, 12 ,memory) ;
        restore_video ( 5, 5, 12, 60, m ,memory) ;
        free ( m ) ;
        return 0;
}
```

```
        /* read each character till end of file is reached */
        while ( ( ch = getc ( fp1 ) ) != EOF )
        {
                /* check for space */
                if ( ch == ' ' )
                {
                        count = 1 ;

                        /* count number of consecutive spaces */
                        while ( ( ch = getc ( fp1 ) ) == ' ' )
                                count++ ;

                        flag = putc ( count + 127, fp2 ) ;
                        flag = putc ( ch, fp2 ) ;
                }
                else
                        flag = putc ( ch, fp2 ) ;

                if ( flag == EOF )
                        break ;
        }

        if ( flag == EOF )
                writeline ( "Unable to compress file!", 10, 8,12,memory ) ;
        else
                writeline ( "File successfully compressed!", 10, 8, 12 ,memory) ;

        writeline ( "          Press Enter to return              ", 22, 14, 12,memory ) ;
        getch() ;

        fclose ( fp1 ) ;
        fclose ( fp2 ) ;
        writeline ( "        Select using hotkey or Enter          ", 22, 14, 12 ,memory) ;
        restore_video ( 5, 5, 12, 60, m ,memory) ;
        free ( m ) ;
}

//Decompress the desired file
decompress_file(char far *memory)
{
```

```
char *m, s_file[20], t_file[20] ;
FILE *fp1, *fp2 ;
int ch, count, area, flag ;

area = ( 12 - 5 + 1 ) * ( 60 - 5 + 1 ) * 2 ;
m =((char *) malloc ( area )) ;
if ( m == NULL )
{
        writeline ( "          Press any key to continue ", 22, 14, 12,memory ) ;
        getch() ;

        writeline ("        Select using hotkey or Enter           ", 22, 14, 12 ,memory) ;
        return 0;
}

store_video ( 5, 5, 12, 60, m,memory ) ;
menubox ( 5, 5, 12, 60, 227, 1 ,memory) ;

writeline ( "          File decompress service           ", 22, 14, 112 ,memory) ;
writeline ( "Enter source file name:", 6, 8, 12 ,memory) ;
size ( 6, 7 ) ;
gotoxy ( 33, 7 ) ;
gets ( s_file ) ;
size ( 32, 0 ) ;

/* open source file */
fp1 = fopen ( s_file, "r" ) ;
if ( fp1 == NULL )
{
        writeline ( "Unable to open source file!", 8 , 8, 12 ,memory) ;
        writeline ( "          Press Enter to return          ", 22, 14, 12 ,memory) ;
        getch() ;

        writeline ("        Select using hotkey or Enter        ", 22, 14, 12 ,memory) ;
        restore_video ( 5, 5, 12, 60, m ,memory) ;
        free ( m ) ;
        return 0;
}

writeline ( "Enter target file name:", 8, 8, 12,memory ) ;
```

```
size ( 6, 7 );
gotoxy ( 33, 9 );
gets ( t_file );
size ( 32, 0 );

/* open target file */
fp2 = fopen ( t_file, "w" );
if ( fp2 == NULL )
{
        writeline ( "Unable to open target file!", 10, 8, 12 ,memory) ;
        writeline ( "           Press Enter to return              ", 22, 14, 12 ,memory) ;
        getch() ;

        fclose ( fp1 ) ;
        writeline ("         Select using hotkey or Enter          ", 22, 14, 12 ,memory) ;
        restore_video ( 5, 5, 12, 60, m ,memory) ;
        free ( m ) ;
        return 0;
}

/* read each character till end of file is reached */
while ( ( ch = getc ( fp1 ) ) != EOF )
{
        /* if ascii value of character read exceeds 127 */
        if ( ch > 127 )
        {
                ch = ch - 127 ;

                /* write back original spaces */
                for ( count = 1 ; count <= ch ; count++ )
                        flag = putc ( ' ', fp2 ) ;
        }
        else
                flag = putc ( ch, fp2 ) ;

        /* if error in writing */
        if ( flag == EOF )
                break ;
}
```

```
        if ( flag == EOF )
                writeline ( "Unable to decompress file!", 10, 8, 12 ,memory) ;
        else
                writeline ( "File successfully decompressed!", 10, 8, 12,memory ) ;

        writeline ( "           Press Enter to return              ", 22, 14, 12 ,memory) ;
        getch() ;

        fclose ( fp1 ) ;
        fclose ( fp2 ) ;
        writeline ( "      Select using hotkey or Enter          ", 22, 14, 12 ,memory) ;
        restore_video ( 5, 5, 12, 60, m ,memory) ;
        free ( m ) ;
}

// Type the content of the file
type_file(char far *memory)
{
        char *m, fname[20], ch, string[5] ;
        int pg = 1, row = 2, col = 1, area ;
        FILE *fp ;

        area = ( 25 - 0 + 1 ) * ( 80 - 0 + 1 ) * 2 ;
        m =((char *) malloc ( area )) ;
        if ( m == NULL )
        {
                writeline ( "        Press any key to continue ", 22, 14, 12,memory ) ;
                getch() ;

                writeline ( "        Select using hotkey or Enter        ", 22, 14, 12 ,memory) ;
                return 0;
        }

        store_video ( 0, 0, 24, 79, m ,memory) ;
        menubox ( 5, 5, 10, 60, 227, 1 ,memory) ;

        writeline ( "           File display service          ", 22, 14, 112 ,memory) ;

        writeline ( "Enter name of file:", 6, 8, 12,memory ) ;
        size ( 6, 7 ) ;
```

```
gotoxy ( 29, 7 ) ;
gets ( fname ) ;
size ( 32, 0 ) ;

/* open file to be displayed */
fp = fopen ( fname, "r" ) ;
if ( fp == NULL )
{
        writeline ( "Unable to open source file!", 8, 8,12 ,memory) ;
        writeline ( "          Press Enter to return                ", 22, 14,12 ,memory) ;
        getch() ;

        writeline ( "       Select using hotkey or Enter            ", 22, 14, 12 ,memory) ;
        restore_video ( 0, 0, 24, 79, m ,memory) ;
        free ( m) ;
        return 0;
}

menubox ( 0, 0, 1, 79, 27, 27 ,memory) ;
menubox ( 1, 0, 24, 79, 127, 32 ,memory) ;
display_box ( 1, 0, 23, 78, 112,memory ) ;
display_box ( 1, 0, 21, 78, 112,memory ) ;
writech ( 21, 0, 204, 112 ,memory) ;
writech ( 21, 78, 185, 112,memory ) ;

/* display file name and current page number */
writeline ( "File :-", 0, 0, 7,memory ) ;
writeline ( fname, 0, 8, 7 ,memory) ;
writeline ( "Page No :- ", 0, 54, 7,memory ) ;
itoa ( pg, string, 10 ) ;
writeline ( string, 0, 65, 7 ,memory) ;

/* read each character till end of file is reached */
while ( ( ch = getc ( fp ) ) != EOF )
{
        /* if character read is not a newline, carriage return or tab */
        if ( ( ch != '\n' ) && ( ch != '\r' ) && ( ch != '\t' ) )
                writech ( row, col, ch, 112 ,memory) ;

        /* if tab, increment column by 4 otherwise by 1 */
```

```
        if ( ch == '\t' )
                col += 4 ;
        else
                coi++ ;

        /* if column exceeds 77 or end of line is met */
        if ( col > 77 || ch == '\n' )
        {
                col = 1 ;
                row++ ;

                /* if screen is full */
                if ( row > 20 )
                {
                        writeline ( "    Press Enter to return         ", 22, 17, 12 memory);
                        getch() ;

                        row = 2 ;
                        pg++ ;

                        menubox ( 2, 1, 20, 77, 1, 0,memory ) ;

                        writeline ( "File :-", 0, 0, 7 ,memory) ;
                        writeline ( fname, 0, 8, 7,memory ) ;
                        writeline ( "Page No :- ", 0, 54, 7,memory ) ;
                        itoa ( pg, string, 10 ) ;
                        writeline ( string, 0, 65, 7 ,memory) ;
                }
        }
}

writeline ( "        Press any key to return...        ", 22, 14, 12 ,memory) ;
getch() ;

fclose ( fp ) ;
writeline ("        Select using hotkey or Enter            ", 22, 14, 12 ,memory) ;
restore_video ( 0, 0, 24, 79, m ,memory) ;
free ( m ) ;
}
```

```
create_dir(char far *memory);
list_dir(char far *memory);
change_dir(char far *memory);
delete_dir(char far *memory);

// Function to create the directory
create_dir(char far *memory)
{
        union REGS iregs, oregs ;
        int area ;
        char dname[20], *m ;

        area = ( 20 - 5 + 1 ) * ( 70 - 5 + 1 ) * 2 ;
        m =((char *) malloc ( area) );
        if ( m == NULL )
        {
                writeline ("     Insufficient memory                 ", 22, 15, 112,memory ) ;
                getch();
                writeline("   Select using hotkey or Enter     ",22,14,12,memory);
                return 0;
        }
        store_video(5,5,20,70,m,memory);
        menubox(6,5,11,60,12,66,memory);
        writeline("          Create directory service          ",22,15,12,memory);
        writeline ( "Enter name of directory:", 7, 8, 112,memory ) ;
        size ( 6, 7 ) ;
        gotoxy ( 34, 8 ) ;
        gets ( dname ) ;
        size ( 32, 0 ) ;

        iregs.h.ah = 57 ;                   /*dos service number*/
        iregs.x.dx = (unsigned int) dname;          /* base address of directory name*/
        intdos(&iregs,&oregs);          /* issue interrupt*/

        /* if successful in creation of directory*/
        if (oregs.x.cflag == 0)
        writeline(" Directory created ",9,8,12,memory);
        else
        {
                if (oregs.x.ax == 5);
```

```
            writeline("Improper acces",9,8,12,memory);
            if ( oregs.x.ax == 3 )
                writeline ( "Invalid path!", 9, 8, 112,memory );
        }

        writeline ("                Press  any  key to continue                ", 22, 14, 112 ,memory) ;
        getch() ;

        writeline( "  Select using hotkey or Enter          ",22,14,112,memory);
        restore_video(5,5,20,70,m,memory);
        free(m);
}

// Function to change the directory
change_dir(char far *memory)
{
        union REGS  iregs,oregs;
        int area ;
        char dname[20], *m ;

        area = ( 20 - 5 + 1 ) * ( 76 - 5 + 1 ) * 2 ;
        m =((char *) malloc ( area )) ;
        if ( m == NULL )
        {
            writeline ( "          Insufficient  memory              ", 22, 14, 12 ,memory) ;
            getch() ;

            writeline (  "          Select using hotkey or Enter          ", 22, 14,12 ,memory) ;
            return 0;
        }

        store_video ( 5, 5, 20, 70, m ,memory) ;
        menubox ( 6, 5, 11, 60 ,12, 66 ,memory) ;

        writeline("        Change Directory Service        ",22,14,12,memory);
        writeline("Enter name of directory :",7,8,12,memory);
        size ( 6, 7 ) ;
        gotoxy ( 34, 8 ) ;
        gets ( dname ) ;
        size ( 32, 0 ) ;
```

```
    /* issue interrupt for removing directory*/
    iregs.h.ah = 59 ;
    iregs.x.dx = ( unsigned int ) dname ;
    intdos ( &iregs, &oregs ) ;

    /* check if successful in changing directory*/
    if ( oregs.x.cflag == 0 )
            writeline ( "Directory was changed!", 9, 8, 12 ,memory) ;
    else

    {
            if (oregs.x.ax == 5);
            writeline("Improper acces",9,8,12,memory);
            if ( oregs.x.ax == 3 )
                    writeline ( "Invalid path!", 9, 8, 12,memory ) ;
    }
    writeline("          Press any key to continue              ",22,14,12,memory);
    getch();
    writeline("      Select using hotkey or Enter              ",22,14,12,memory);
    restore_video(5,5,20,70,m,memory);
    free(m);
}

// Function to delete the directory
delete_dir(char far *memory)
{
    union REGS iregs,oregs;
    int area ;
    char dname[20], *m ;

    area = ( 20 - 5 + 1 ) * ( 76 - 5 + 1 ) * 2 ;
    m =((char *) malloc ( area )) ;
    if ( m == NULL )
    {
            writeline ("   Insufficient memory       ", 22, 14, 12 ,memory) ;
            getch() ;

            writeline ("     Select using hotkey or Enter          ", 22, 14,12 ,memory) ;
            return 0;
    }
```

```
store_video ( 5, 5, 20, 76, m ,memory) ;
menubox ( 6, 5, 12, 75 ,112, 66 ,memory) ;

writeline("     Delete Directory Service          ",22,14,12,memory);
writeline("Enter name of directory :",7,8,12,memory);
writeline(" Enter path ",8,8,12,memory);
size ( 6, 7 ) ;
gotoxy ( 35, 8 ) ;
gets ( dname ) ;
size ( 32, 0 ) ;

/* issue interrupt for changing directory*/
iregs.h.ah = 58 ;
iregs.x.dx = ( unsigned int ) dname ;
intdos ( &iregs, &oregs ) ;

/* check if successful in changing directory*/
if ( oregs.x.cflag == 0 )
        writeline ( "Directory was removed!", 9, 8, 12 ,memory) ;
else
{
        switch ( oregs.x.ax )
        {
                case 3 :
                        writeline ( "Invalid path!", 10, 8, 112 ,memory) ;
                        break ;

                case 5 :
                        writeline ( "Improper access!",10, 8, 112,memory ) ;
                        break ;

                case 2 :
                        writeline ( "Directory does not exist!", 10, 8, 112 ,memory) ;
                        break ;

                case 0x10 :
                        writeline ( "Cannot remove current directory!", 10, 8, 112 ,memory);
        }
}
```

```
        writeline ("          Press any key to continue              ", 22, 14, 112 ,memory) ;
        getch() ;

        writeline ( "         Select using hotkey or Enter           ",22, 14, 112 ,memory) ;
        restore_video ( 5, 5, 20, 76, m,memory ) ;
        free ( m ) ;
}

// Function to list the directory
list_dir(char far *memory)
{
        int area ;
        char *m, fname[20] ;
        char sz[10], d[10], mm[10], y[10], hr[10], minute[10], temp[3] = "0" ;
        struct ffblk file ;
        unsigned int find, row, col, a, year, month, day, hour, min ;

        area = ( 20 - 3 + 1 ) * (70 - 3 + 1 ) * 2 ;
        m =((char *) malloc ( area )) ;
        if ( m == NULL )
        {
                writeline ( "      Press any key to continue           ", 22, 14, 12,memory ) ;
                getch() ;

                writeline ( "      Select using hotkey or Enter          ", 22, 14, 12 ,memory) ;
                return 0;
        }
        store_video ( 5, 5, 20, 70, m ,memory) ;
        menubox ( 6, 5, 11, 60, 12, 66 ,memory) ;

        writeline ( "       List directory service         ", 22, 15, 12 ,memory) ;

        writeline ( "Enter skeleton for searching:", 7, 8, 12 ,memory) ;
        size ( 6, 7 ) ;
        gotoxy ( 39, 8 ) ;
        gets ( fname ) ;
        size ( 32, 0 ) ;
```

```
/* find first file which matches the skeleton */
find = findfirst ( fname, &file, FA_DIREC ) ;

/* if successful in finding the first file */
if ( find == 0 )
{
        menubox ( 5, 5, 20, 70, 12, 66,memory);
        row = 8;
        col =8;
        writeline("Directory ",6,28,12,memory);
        writeline("**********",7,28,12,memory);

        /* carry out search for rest of the files matching the skeleton */
        while ( find == 0 )
        {
                row++ ;
                writeline ( file.ff_name, row, col, 12,memory ) ;

                /* if not a sub-directory entry */
                if ( ( file.ff_attrib & 16 ) == 0 )
                {
                        ltoa ( file.ff_fsize, sz, 10 ) ;
                        writeline ( sz, row, col + 19, 12 ,memory) ;

                        /* calculate and print date and time */
                        a = file.ff_fdate ;

                        year = 80 + ( a >> 9);
                        month = ( a << 7) >> 12;
                        day = ( a << 11 ) >>1;

                        itoa(day,d,10);

                        /* if a single digit day, concatenate it to 0 */
                        if ( strlen ( d ) == 1 )
                                strcat ( temp, d ) ;
                        else
                                strcpy ( temp, d ) ;

                        writeline ( temp, row, col + 30, 12,memory ) ;
```

```
writech ( row, col + 32, '/', 12 ,memory) ;

/* reinitialise temp */
strcpy ( temp, "0" ) ;

itoa ( month, mm, 10 ) ;

/* if a single digit month, concatenate it to 0 */
if ( strlen ( mm ) == 1 )
        strcat ( temp, mm ) ;
else
        strcpy ( temp, mm ) ;

writeline ( temp, row, col + 33, 12 ,memory) ;
writech ( row, col + 35, '/', 12 ,memory) ;

strcpy ( temp, "0" ) ;

itoa ( year, y, 10 ) ;
if ( strlen ( y ) == 1 )
        strcat ( temp, y ) ;
else
        strcpy ( temp, y ) ;

writeline ( temp, row, col + 36, 12,memory ) ;

strcpy ( temp, "0" ) ;

a = file.ff_ftime ;
hour = ( a >> 11 ) ;
min = ( a << 5 ) >> 10 ;

if ( hour == 0 )
        hour = 12 ;

strcpy ( temp, "0" ) ;

itoa ( hour, hr, 10 ) ;
if ( strlen ( hr ) == 1 )
        strcat ( temp, hr ) ;
```

```
                    else
                            strcpy ( temp, hr ) ;

                    writeline ( temp, row, col + 45, 12,memory ) ;
                    writech ( row, col + 47, ':', 12,memory ) ;

                    strcpy ( temp, "0" ) ;

                    itoa ( min, minute, 10 ) ;
                    if ( strlen ( minute ) == 1 )
                            strcat ( temp, minute ) ;
                    else
                            strcpy ( temp, minute ) ;

                    writeline ( temp, row, col + 48, 12,memory ) ;

                    strcpy ( temp, "0" ) ;
            }
            else
                    writeline ( "<DIR>", row, col + 15, 12,memory ) ;

            /* find the next file matching the skeleton */
            find = findnext ( &file ) ;

            /* if screen is full */
            if ( row == 18 )
            {
                    row = 8 ;
                    writeline ( "    Press any key to continue    ", 22, 14, 12,memory);
                    getch() ;

                    menubox ( 5, 5, 20, 70, 12, 66 ,memory) ;
                    writeline ( "Directory listing", 6, 28, 12,memory ) ;
                    writeline ( "ÄÄÄÄÄÄÄÄÄÄÄÄÄÄÄÄÄ", 7, 28, 12,memory);
            }
        }
}
else
        writeline ( "File not found!", 9, 8, 12 ,memory) ;
```

```
        writeline ("        Press any key to continue          ", 22, 14, 12 ,memory) ;
        getch() ;

        writeline ( "      Select using hotkey or Enter        ", 22, 14, 12 ,memory) ;
        restore_video ( 5, 5, 20, 70, m,memory ) ;
        free ( m ) ;
}

/* various menu definitions */
/* character following ^ symbol is the hot key */
char *main_menu[] =     {
                                "^Directory services",
                                "^File services",
                                "^Exit"
                        } ;

char *f_services[] = {
                                        "^Compress file",
                                        "Deco^Mpress file",
                                        "^Get file attributes",
                                        "^Set file attributes",
                                        "^Encrypt file",
                                        "^Decrypt file",
                                        "^Type file",
                                        "de^Lete file",
                                        "^Return to main menu",
                        } ;

char *d_services[] = {
                                        "^Make directory",
                                        "^Change directory",
                                        "^Delete directory",
                                        "^List directory",
                                        "^Return to main menu"

                        } ;

/* help messages for different menu items */
char *comment[] =       {
                                        " Utility ",
```

```
                                        "        Select using hotkey or Enter ",
                                        "Handle various file services",
                                        "Handle various directory services",
                                        "Return to DOS",
                                        "Compress text file",
                                        "Decompress a compressed file",
                                        "Display  file attributes",
                                        "Change  file attributes",
                                        "Code a file ",
                                        "Decode a coded file",
                                        "Display contents of file",
                                        "Delete a file",
                                        "Return to main menu",
                                        "Create a new directory ",
                                        "Change default directory",
                                        "Delete an existing directory",
                                        "List existing directory contents",
                                        "Return to main menu",
                                        "        Press any key to continue...        ",
                                        "     Insufficient space! Press any key...        "
                                } ;

char far *memory ;
int ascii, scans ;
set_mode(int);
pop_menu ( char **main_menu, int count, int sr, int sc, char *hotkeys, int helpnumber );
showmenu ( char **main_menu, int count, int sr, int sc );
fserver();
dserver();
delete_file();

getoutput ( char **menu, char *hotkeys, int sr, int sc, int count, int helpnumber );
intro();
mainmenu();
presskey();

display_dir() ;
memsize() ;

listdir();
```

```
/* request auto detection */
int gdriver = DETECT, gmode, errorcode;
/* initialize graphics mode */

main()
{
        int choice ;

        /* store base address of VDU memory and set appropriate video mode */
        #ifdef MA

                /* store base address for MA */
                memory = ( char far * ) 0xb0000000L ;
                set_mode ( 7 ) ;
        #else
                /* store base address for other display adapters */
                memory = ( char far * ) 0xb8000000L ;
                set_mode ( 3 ) ;
        #endif

        size ( 32, 0 ) ; /* hide cursor */
        /* create opening screen display */
        menubox ( 0, 0, 24, 79, 7, 7,memory ) ;
        display_box ( 1, 0, 21, 79, 7 ,memory) ;

        initgraph(&gdriver, &gmode, "");
        logo(memory) ;
        // Shuts down the graphics system
        closegraph();
        /* create screen on which menus are to be popped up */
        mainmenu() ;
        while ( 1 )
        {
                /* pop up main menu and collect choice */
                choice = pop_menu ( main_menu, 3, 7, 3, "DFE", 2 );

                /* test choice received */
                switch ( choice )
                {
                        case 1 :
```

```
                dserver() ;
                break ;

            case 2 :
                fserver() ;
                break ;

            case 3 :
            case 27 :
                size ( 6, 7 ) ;
                clrscr() ;
                exit ( 1 ) ;
        }
    }
}
```

Figure 13.2 Output screen of main utility program

```
/* sets video mode*/
set_mode ( int mode )
{
        union REGS i, o ;

        i.h.ah = 0 ;  /* service no.*/
        i.h.al = mode ;  /* video mode*/
        int86 ( 16, &i, &o ) ;  /* issue interrupt*/
}

/* prepares the screen for popping up a menu*/
mainmenu()
{
        int i, j ;

        display_box ( 1, 0, 23, 79, 7,memory ) ;
        display_box ( 5, 0, 21, 79, 7,memory ) ;

        writech ( 5, 0, 204, 7,memory ) ;
        writech ( 5, 79, 185, 7,memory ) ;
        writech ( 21, 0, 204, 7,memory ) ;
        writech ( 21, 79, 185, 7,memory ) ;

        for ( i = 6 ; i <= 20 ; i++ )
        {
                for ( j = 1 ; j <= 78 ; j += 2 )
                {
                        writech ( i, j, 177, 12,memory ) ;
                        writech ( i, j + 1, 177, 12,memory ) ;
                }
        }

        writeline("ÝÝ",2,4,1,memory);
        writeline("ÝÝ",2,7,1,memory);
        writeline("ÝÝ",3,4,1,memory);
        writeline("ÝÝ",3,7,1,memory);
        writeline("ÝÝÝÝÝ",4,4,1,memory);

        writeline("ÝÝÝÝÝÝ",2,16,1,memory);
        writeline("ÝÝ",3,18,1,memory);
```

```
        writeline("ÝÝ",4,18,1,memory);

        writeline("ÝÝ",2,29,1,memory);
        writeline("ÝÝ",3,29,1,memory);
        writeline("ÝÝ",4,29,1,memory);

        writeline("ÝÝ",2,38,1,memory);
        writeline("ÝÝ",2,38,1,memory);
        writeline("ÝÝ",3,38,1,memory);
        writeline("ÝÝÝÝ",4,38,1,memory);


        writeline("ÝÝ",2,49,1,memory);
        writeline("ÝÝ",3,49,1,memory);
        writeline("ÝÝ",4,49,1,memory);
        writeline("ÝÝÝÝÝÝ",2,57,1,memory);
        writeline("ÝÝ",3,59,1,memory);
        writeline("ÝÝ",4,59,1,memory);

        writeline("ÝÝ",2,70,1,memory);
        writeline("ÝÝ",2,74,1,memory);
        writeline("ÝÝÝÝ",3,71,1,memory);
        writeline("ÝÝ",4,72,1,memory);

        writeline ( comment[1], 22, 14, 12,memory ) ;
}

/* pops up a menu on the existing screen contents */
pop_menu ( char **main_menu, int count, int sr, int sc, char *hotkeys, int number )
{
        int er, ec, i, l = 0, area, areaforhelp, choice ;
        char *m, *n ;

        /* calculate ending row for menu */
        er = sr + count + 2 ;

        /* find longest menu item */
        for ( i = 0 ; i < count ; i++ )
        {
                if ( strlen (main_menu[i] ) > l )
```

```
        l = strlen ( main_menu[i] ) ;
}

/* calculate ending column for menu */
ec = sc + l + 3 ;

/* calculate area required to save screen contents where menu is to be popped up */
area = ( er - sr + 1 ) * ( ec - sc + 1 ) * 2 ;

m = ((char *)malloc ( area )) ;  /* allocate memory */

/* check if allocation is successful */
if ( m == NULL )
{
        writeline ( comment[20], 22, 14, 9,memory ) ;
        getch() ;
        exit ( 2 ) ;
}

/* save screen contents into allocated memory */
store_video ( sr, sc, er, ec, m,memory ) ;

/* draw filled box with shadow */
menubox ( sr, sc, er, ec, 277, 1,memory ) ;

/* display the menu in the filled box */
showmenu ( main_menu, count, sr + 1, sc + 1 ) ;

/* calculate area required for help box */
areaforhelp = ( 9 - 6 + 1 ) * ( 78 - 35 + 1 ) * 2 ;

n =((char *) malloc ( areaforhelp )) ;
if ( n == NULL )
{
        writeline ( comment[20], 22, 14, 12 ,memory) ;
        getch() ;
        exit ( 3 ) ;
}
store_video ( 8, 35,11, 74, n ,memory) ;
menubox ( 8, 35, 11, 74, 277, 1,memory ) ;
```

```
        /* display help message */
        writeline ( comment[number], 9, 36, 143,memory ) ;

        /* receive user's choice */
        choice = getoutput (main_menu, hotkeys, sr, sc, count,number ) ;

        /* restore original screen contents */
        restore_video ( sr, sc, er, ec, m,memory ) ;
        restore_video ( 8, 35, 11, 74, n ,memory) ;

        /* free allocated memory */
        free ( m ) ;
        free ( n ) ;

        return ( choice ) ;
}

/* gets the ascii and scan codes of the key pressed */
getkey()
{
        // A union is similar to a struct, except it allows
        //  you to define variables that share storage space.

        union REGS iregs, oregs ;

        /* wait till a key is hit */
        while ( ! kbhit() )
                ;

        iregs.h.ah = 0 ;  /* service number */

        /* issue interrupt */
        int86 ( 22, &iregs, &oregs ) ;

        scans = oregs.h.ah ;
        ascii = oregs.h.al ;
}
```

```
/* displays the menu in box drawn by menubox() */
showmenu ( char **main_menu, int counter, int sr, int sc )
{
	int i ;

	for ( i = 0 ; i < counter ; i++ )
	{
		/* write menu item in VDU memory */
		writeline ( main_menu[i], sr, sc, 9,memory ) ;
		sr++ ;
	}
}

/* receives user's response for the menu displayed */
getoutput ( char **main_menu, char *keys, int sr, int sc, int counter, int number )
{
	int ch = 1, len, hotkeyans ;

	/* calculate number of hot keys for the menu */
	len = strlen ( keys ) ;

	/* highlight first menu item */
	writeline ( main_menu[ch - 1], sr + ch, sc + 1, 12,memory ) ;

	while ( 1 )
	{
		getkey() ; /* receive key */

		/* if special key is hit */
		if ( ascii == 0 )
		{
			switch ( scans )
			{
				case 80 : /* down arrow key */

					/* make highlighted item normal */
					writeline ( main_menu[ch - 1], sr + ch, sc + 1, 9,memory) ;

					ch++ ;
					number++ ;
```

```
                    break ;

                case 72 :  /* up arrow key */

                    /* make highlighted item normal */
                    writeline ( main_menu[ch - 1], sr + ch, sc + 1, 9,memory);

                    ch— ;
                    number— ;
                    break ;
            }

            /* if highlighted bar is on first item and up arrow key is hit */
            if ( ch == 0 )
            {
                ch = counter ;
                number = number + counter ;
            }

            /* if highlighted bar is on last item and down arrow key is hit */
            if ( ch > counter )
            {
                ch = 1 ;
                number = number - counter ;
            }

            /* highlight the appropriate menu item */
            writeline ( main_menu[ch - 1], sr + ch, sc + 1, 12 ,memory) ;
            menubox ( 8, 35, 11, 74, 277, 1 ,memory) ;

            /* write the corresponding help message */
            writeline ( comment[number], 9, 36, 143,memory ) ;
        }
        else
        {
            if ( ascii == 13 )  /* Enter key */
                return ( ch ) ;

            if ( ascii == 27 )  /* Esc key */
                return ( 27 ) ;
```

```
                ascii = toupper ( ascii ) ;
                hotkeyans = 1 ;

                /* check whether hot key has been pressed */
                while ( *keys != '\0' )
                {
                        if ( *keys == ascii )
                                return ( hotkeyans ) ;
                        else
                        {
                                keys++ ;
                                hotkeyans++ ;
                        }
                }

                /* reset hotkeys to point to the first character in the string */
                keys = keys - len ;
            }
        }
}

/* pops up File Services menu, receives choice and branches to appropriate function */
fserver()
{
        int f_choice ;

        while ( 2 )
        {
            f_choice = pop_menu ( f_services, 9, 8, 11, "CMGSEDTLR", 5 ) ;

            switch ( f_choice )
            {
                case 1 :
                        compress_file(memory) ;
                        break ;
                case 2 :
                        decompress_file(memory) ;
                        break ;
                case 3:
                        get_attb(memory) ;
```

```
                        break ;
                case 4:
                        set_attb(memory) ;
                        break ;
                case 5 :
                        encrypt_file(memory) ;
                        break ;
                case 6:
                        decrypt_file(memory) ;
                        break ;
                case 7 :
                        type_file(memory) ;
                        break ;
                case 8 :
                        delete_file(memory) ;
                        break ;
                case 9 :
                        return 0;
        }
    }
}

/* pops up Directory Services menu, receives choice and branches to appropriate function */
dserver()
{
    int d_choice ;

    while ( 2 )
    {
        d_choice = pop_menu ( d_services, 5, 8, 11, "MCDLR", 14 ) ;

        switch ( d_choice )
        {
                case 1 :
                        create_dir(memory) ;
                        break ;
                case 2 :
                        change_dir(memory) ;
                        break ;
                case 3 :
```

```
                delete_dir(memory) ;
                break ;
            case 4 :
                list_dir(memory) ;
                break ;
            case 5 :
                return 0;
        }
    }
}
```

Inbuild Functions

A

_setcursortype()	Selects cursor appearance.
abc()	abs (a macro) gets the absolute value of an integer.
arc	arc (x, y, single, endangle, radius) draws an arc with centre point x, y at a start angle stangle, and end angle endangle and the radius is radius.
atof()	atof converts a string to a floating point
atoi()	atoi converts a string pointed to by s to int.
circle()	arc draws a circular arc in the current drawing color. circle draws a circle in the current drawing color.
cleardevice()	cleardevice erases the entire graphics screen and moves the CP (current position) to home (0,0).
clearviewport()	clearviewport erases the viewport and moves the CP (current position) to home (0,0), relative to the viewport.
close()	Each of these functions closes the file associated with handle.
clrscr()	clrscr clears the current text window and places the cursor in the upper left-hand corner (at position 1,1).
delay()	With a call to delay, the current program is suspended from execution

	for the time specified by the argument milliseconds.
cprintf()	cprintf sends formatted output to the text window on the screen
clreol()	Clears to end of line in text window
closegraph()	Shuts down the graphics system
DETECT	Enum: BGI graphics drivers

Constant	Value
DETECT	0 (requests autodetection)
CGA	1
MCGA	2
EGA	3
EGA64	4
EGAMONO	5
IBM8514	6
HERCMONO	7
ATT400	8
VGA	9
PC3270	10

detectgraph()	detectgraph detects your system's graphics adapter and chooses the mode that provides the highest resolution for that adapter. If no graphics hardware is detected, detectgraph sets *graphdriver to grNotDetected, and graphresult returns grNotDetected. The main reason to call detectgraph directly is to override the graphics mode that detectgraph recommends to initgraph.
delay()	With a call to delay, the current program is suspended from execution for the time specified by the argument milliseconds.
ellipse()	ellipse draws an elliptical arc in the current drawing color.
eof()	eof determines whether the file associated with handle has reached end-of-file.

exit()	exit terminates the calling process. Before termination, exit does the following: closes all files writes buffered output (waiting to be output) calls any registered "exit functions" (posted with atexit)
fclose()	fclose closes the named stream. All buffers associated with the stream are flushed before closing. System-allocated buffers are freed upon closing. Buffers assigned with setbuf or setvbuf are not automatically freed. (But if setvbuf is passed null for the buffer pointer, it will free it upon close.)
fflush()	If the given stream has buffered output, fflush writes the output for stream to the associated file. The stream remains open after fflush has executed. fflush has no effect on an unbuffered stream.
fgetc()	fgetc returns the next character on the named input stream. It is a function version of the getc macro.
fclose()	fclose closes the named stream. All buffers associated with the stream are flushed before closing. System-allocated buffers are freed upon closing.
fillellipse()	fillellipse draws an ellipse, then fills the ellipse with the current fill color and fill pattern.
floodfill()	floodfill fills an enclosed area on bitmap devices. The area bounded by the color border is flooded with the current fill pattern and fill color. (x,y) is a "seed point". If the seed is within an enclosed area, the inside will be filled. If the seed is outside the enclosed area, the exterior will be filled.
fopen()	fopen opens a file and associate a stream with it. Both functions return a pointer that identifies the stream in subsequent operations.
fread()	fread reads a specified number of equal-sized data items from an input stream into a block.

free()	free deallocates a memory block allocated by a previous call to calloc, malloc, or realloc.
fwrite()	fwrite appends a specified number of equal-sized data items to an output file.
FILE	File control structure for streams.
getaspectratio()	getaspectratio gets the current graphics mode's aspect ratio
getch()	getch reads a single character directly from the keyboard, without echoing to the screen.
getche()	getche reads a single character from the keyboard and echoes it to the current text window, using direct video or BIOS.
getdate()	Gets or sets DOS system date
getimage()	getimage copies an image from the screen to memory.
getmaxx()	getmaxx returns the maximum x value (screen-relative) for the current graphics driver and mode.
getmaxy()	getmaxy returns the maximum y value (screen-relative) for the current graphics driver and mode.
getmaxcolor()	getmaxcolor returns the highest valid color value that can be passed to setcolor for the current graphics driver and mode.
getpalette()	getpalette fills the palettetype structure *palette with information about the current palette's size and colors.
gets()	gets returns when it encounters a newline; everything up to the newline is copied into s.
getviewsettings()	getviewsettings fills a structure with information about the current viewport.
gotoxy()	gotoxy moves the cursor to the given position in the current text window.

If the coordinates are invalid, the call to gotoxy is ignored.

graphresult()	graphresult returns the error code for the last graphics operation that reported an error, then resets the error level to grOk.
grapherrormsg()	grapherrormsg returns a pointer to the error message string associated with errorcode, the value returned by graphresult.
highvideo()	highvideo selects high-intensity characters by setting the high-intensity bit of the currently selected foreground color.
imagesize()	imagesize determines the size of the memory area required to store a bit image.
initgraph()	To start the graphics system, you must first call initgraph. initgraph initializes the graphics system by loading a graphics driver from disk (or validating a registered driver) then putting the system into graphics mode. initgraph also resets all graphics settings (color, palette, current position, viewport, etc.) to their defaults, then resets graphresult to 0.
int86()	int86 and int86x execute an 8086 software interrupt specified by the argument intno. With int86x, you can invoke an 8086 software interrupt that takes a value of DS different from the default data segment, and/or takes an argument in ES.
kbhit()	kbhit checks to see if a keystroke is currently available.
itoa()	itoa value to a null-terminated string and store the result in string.
line()	line draws a line from (x1, y1) to (x2, y2) using the current color, line style, and thickness. It does not update the current position (CP).
malloc()	malloc allocates a block of size bytes from the memory heap. It allows a program to allocate memory explicitly as it's needed, and in the exact amounts needed.
nosound()	nosound turns the speaker off after it has been turned on by a call

	to sound.
outtext()	outtext displays a text string, using the current justification settings and the current font, direction, and size. outtext outputs textstring at the current position (CP)
outtextxy()	outtextxy displays a string at the specified location (graphics mode)
printf()	printf sends formatted output to stdin
putc()	putc outputs the character given by c to the stream given by stream.
putchar()	putchar is a macro defined as putc(c, stdout) putchar puts the character given by c on the output stream stdout.
putimage()	putimage puts the bit image previously saved with getimage back onto the screen, with the upper left corner of the image placed at (left,top).
open()	Opens a file for an fstream.
outtext	outtext displays a string in the viewport (graphics mode)
outtextxy	outtextxy displays a string at the specified location (graphics mode)
write()	write writes a buffer of data to a file or device.
putpixel()	putpixel plots a pixel at a specified point putpixel plots a point in the color defined by color at (x,y).
puts()	puts copies the null-terminated string s to the standard output stream stdout and appends a newline character.
random()	random returns a random number between 0 and (num-1). random(num) is a macro defined in STDLIB.H.
randomize()	randomize initializes the random number generator with a random value.
read()	read attempts to read bytes from a file into a buffer.

rectangle() — rectangle draws a rectangle in the current line style, thickness, and drawing color.

restorecrtmode() — restorecrtmode restores the original video mode detected by initgraph.
This function can be used in conjunction with setgraphmode to switch back and forth between text and graphics modes.

seekg() — Moves to a position relative to the current position, following this definition: enum seek_dir { beg, cur, end }

seekp() — Moves to a position relative to the current position, following this definition: enum seek_dir { beg, cur, end };

setbkcolor() — setbkcolor sets the current background color using the palette

COLORS (text mode)

Constant	Value	Background	Foreground
BLACK	0	Yes	Yes
BLUE	1	Yes	Yes
GREEN	2	Yes	Yes
CYAN	3	Yes	Yes
RED	4	Yes	Yes
MAGENTA	5	Yes	Yes
BROWN	6	Yes	Yes
LIGHTGRAY	7	Yes	Yes
DARKGRAY	8	No	Yes
LIGHTBLUE	9	No	Yes
LIGHTGREEN	10	No	Yes
LIGHTCYAN	11	No	Yes
LIGHTRED	12	No	Yes
LIGHTMAGENTA	13	No	Yes
YELLOW	14	No	Yes
WHITE	15	No	Yes
BLINK	128	No	***

setcolor() — setcolor sets the current drawing color to color, which can range

	from 0 to getmaxcolor.
setfillstyle()	setfillstyle sets the current fill pattern and fill color.
setlinestyle()	setlinestyle sets the style for all lines drawn by line, lineto, rectangle, drawpoly, etc.
settextstyle()	settextstyle sets the text font, the direction in which text is displayed, and the size of the characters.
settextjustify()	Sets text justification for graphics mode settextjustify affects text written with outtext and can't be used with text-mode and stream functions.
setviewport()	Sets the current viewport for graphics output The viewport's corners are given in absolute screen coordinates by (left,top) and (right,bottom). The current position (CP) is moved to (0,0) in the new window. The clip argument determines whether drawings are clipped (truncated) at the current viewport boundaries. If clip is non-zero, all drawings will be clipped to the current viewport.
setwritemode()	Sets the writing mode for line drawing in graphics mode
sizeof()	Returns the size, in bytes, of the given expression or type (as type size_t).
sound()	sound turns the PC speaker on at the specified frequency. frequency specifies the frequency of the sound in hertz (cycles pe second).
strcat()	strcat appends a copy of src to the end of dest. The length of the resulting string is strlen(dest) + strlen(src).
strcpy()	Copies string src to dest, stopping after the terminating null character has been moved.
strlen()	Calculates length of a string. Returns the number of characters in s, not counting the terminating null character.

strncpy()	Copies at most maxlen characters of src to dest. The target string, dest, might not be null-terminated if the length of src is maxlen or more.
strupr()	Converts s to all lowercase
tolower()	Translate characters to lowercase. tolower is a function that converts an integer ch (in the range EOF to 255) to its lowercase value (a to z; if it was uppercase, A to Z). All others are left unchanged.
toupper()	Translate characters to uppercase.
textbackground()	textbackground selects a new text background color
textheight()	textheight takes the current font size and multiplication factor, and determines the height of textstring in pixels.
textwidth	textwidth takes the string length, current font size, and multiplication factor, and determines the width of textstring in pixels. These functions are useful for adjusting the spacing between lines, computing viewport heights, sizing a title to make it fit on a graph or in a box, etc..
textmode()	Changes screen mode (in text mode). When textmode is called, the current window is reset to the entire screen, and the current text attributes are reset to normal, corresponding to a call to normvideo. Specifying LASTMODE to textmode causes the most recently selected text mode to be reselected. textmode should be used only when the screen is in text mode (presumably to change to a different text mode). When the screen is in graphics mode, use restorecrtmode to escape temporarily to text mode
void	Empty data type When used as a function return type, void means that the function does not return a value.
window	Defines active text-mode window window defines a text window onscreen. If the coordinates are in any way invalid, the call to window is ignored.

ASCII Character Set

B

	0	1	2	3	4	5	6	7	8	9
0	nul	soh	stx	etx	eot	enq	ack	bel	bs	ht
1	nl	vt	ff	cr	so	si	dle	dc1	dc2	dc3
2	dc4	nak	syn	etb	can	em	sub	esc	fs	gs
3	rs	us	sp	!	“	#	$	%	&	`
4	(	)	*	+	,	-	.	/	0	1
5	2	3	4	5	6	7	8	9	:	;
6	<	=	>	?	@	A	B	C	D	E
7	F	G	H	I	J	K	L	M	N	O
8	P	Q	R	S	T	U	V	W	X	Y
9	Z	[	\	]	^	_	‘	a	b	c
10	d	e	f	g	h	i	j	k	l	m
11	n	o	p	q	r	s	t	u	v	w
12	x	y	z	{	|	}	~	del		

The digits at the left of the table are the decimal equivalent (0-127) of the character code, and the digits at the top of the table are the right digits of the character code. For example, the character code for ‘F’ is 70, and the character code for ‘&’ is 38.